Learning
Microsoft®
Publisher 2013

Catherine Skintik

PEARSON

Prentice Hall

Boston • Columbus • Indianapolis • New York • San Francisco • Upper Saddle River
Amsterdam • Cape Town • Dubai • London • Madrid • Milan • Munich • Paris • Montreal • Toronto
Delhi • Mexico City • Sao Paulo • Sydney • Hong Kong • Seoul • Singapore • Taipei • Tokyo

10/14

Editor in Chief: Michael Payne
Product Development Manager: Laura Burgess
Director of Business & Technology Marketing:
  Maggie Moylan Leen
Marketing Manager: Brad Forrester
Marketing Coordinator: Susan Osterlitz
Marketing Assistant: Darshika Vyas
Production Project Manager: Kayla Smith-Tarbox
Operations Director: Alexis Heydt

Senior Operations Specialist: Maura Zaldivar-Garcia
Text and Cover Designer: Vanessa Moore
Media Project Manager, Production: Renata Butera
Editorial and Product Development: Emergent Learning, LLC
Composition: Vanessa Moore
Printer/Binder: Webcrafters, Inc.
Cover Printer: Lehigh-Pheonix Color
Text: 10/12 Helvetica

74.00

Credits and acknowledgements borrowed from other sources and reproduced, with permission, in this textbook are as follows: All photos courtesy of Shutterstock.com.

Microsoft® and Windows® are registered trademarks of the Microsoft Corporation in the U.S.A. and other countries. Screen shots and icons reprinted with permission from the Microsoft Corporation. This book is not sponsored or endorsed by or affiliated with the Microsoft Corporation.

PEARSON

ISBN 10: 0-13-314860-2

ISBN 13: 978-0-13-314860-2

1 2 3 4 5 6 7 8 9 10   V064   16 15 14 13

Table of Contents

Chapter 5
Exploring Publication
Types. 280

Introduction

Microsoft Publisher 2013 is Microsoft's tool for creating professional-looking print publications and basic Web pages. Use Publisher to create publications that today's information-driven world demands, from businesses, governments, schools, and virtually every organization that needs to communicate.

How the Book Is Organized

Learning Microsoft Publisher 2013 is made up of five chapters. Chapters are comprised of short lessons designed for using Microsoft Publisher 2013 in real-life business settings. Each lesson is made up of six key elements:

- **What You Will Learn.** Each lesson starts with an overview of the learning objectives covered in the lesson.
- **Words to Know.** Key terms are included and defined at the start of each lesson, so you can quickly refer back to them. The terms are then highlighted in the text.
- **What You Can Do.** Concise notes for learning the computer concepts.
- **Try It.** Hands-on practice activities provide brief procedures to teach all necessary skills.

- **Practice.** These projects give students a chance to create documents, spreadsheets, database objects, and presentations by entering information. Steps provide all the how-to information needed to complete a project.
- **Apply.** Each lesson concludes with a project that challenges students to apply what they have learned through steps that tell them what to do, without all the how-to information. In the Apply projects, students must show they have mastered each skill set.
- Each chapter ends with two assessment projects: **Critical Thinking** and **Portfolio Builder**, which incorporate all the skills covered throughout the chapter.

Working with Data and Solution Files

As you work through the projects in this book, you'll be creating, opening, and saving files. You should keep the following instructions in mind:

- For many of the projects, you will use data files. The data files can be accessed from the Companion Web site (www.pearsonhighered.com/learningseries). Other projects will ask you to create new documents and files and then enter text and data into them, so you can master creating documents from scratch.

- The data files are used so that you can focus on the skills being introduced—not on keyboarding lengthy documents.
- When the project steps tell you to open a file name, you open the data file provided.
- All the projects instruct you to save the files created or to save the project files under a new name. This is to make the project file your own and to avoid overwriting the data file in the storage location. Throughout this book, when naming files and folders, replace *xx* with your name or initials as instructed by your teacher.

- Follow your instructor's directions for where to access and save the files on a network, local computer hard drive, or portable storage device such as a USB drive.

- Many of the projects also provide instructions for including your name in a header or footer. Again, this is to identify the project work as your own for grading and assessment purposes.

- Unless the book instructs otherwise, use the default settings for text size, margin size, and so on when creating a file. If someone has changed the default software settings for the computer you're using, your exercise files may not look the same as those shown in this book. In addition, the appearance of your files may look different if the system is set to a screen resolution other than 1024 × 768.

Companion Web Site (www.pearsonhighered.com/learningseries)

The Companion Web site includes additional resources to be used in conjunction with the book and to supplement the material in the book. The Companion Web site includes:

- Data files for many of the projects
- Glossary of all the key terms from the book
- Bonus material
- Puzzles correlated to the chapters in the book

Navigating the Textbook and Supplemental Print Resources

Lesson 8

Working with Page Settings, Columns, and Guides

Software Skills

Each lesson begins with an introduction to the computer skills that will be covered in the lesson.

Words to Know

Vocabulary terms are listed at the start of each lesson for easy reference and appear in bold in the text on first use.

What You Can Do

The technology concepts are introduced and explained.

➤ What You Will Learn

Choosing a Page Size
Choosing Publication and Paper Settings
Adjusting Margins
Working with Layout Guides
Placing Ruler Guides
Working with Columns

WORDS TO KNOW

Baseline guides
Yellow nonprinting lines on a page that help position text baselines.

Grid guides
Blue nonprinting lines on a page that show column and/or row margins in a multicolumn or multirow layout.

Layout guides
A generic term for grid guides and margin guides collectively.

Margin guides
Blue nonprinting lines on a page that show the page margins.

Orientation
The direction that the text runs on a page. Orientation can be portrait (text runs across the short edge) or landscape (text runs across the long edge).

Ruler guides
Green nonprinting vertical or horizontal lines that you can display temporarily to help you align objects with one another.

Software Skills So far in this book, you've been working with normal 8.5 × 11 inch portrait-orientation pages, but there are many more possibilities. You can create publications with small page sizes (such as business cards or labels), large page sizes (such as banners), or anything in between.

What You Can Do

Choosing a Page Size

- When you create a publication from a template, the appropriate page size has already been selected.
- If you must set up a publication from scratch (that is, from a blank design), you may need to specify the page size.
- Use the Size command in the Page Setup group on the PAGE DESIGN tab to select a different page size from a gallery of standard sizes.
- You can also choose to create a custom page size, view more preset page sizes, or open the Page Setup dialog box for more options.
- If you choose to create a new page size, the Create New Page Size dialog box opens, as shown in Figure 8-1 on the next page.

  ✓ Note that if you choose the Page Setup command on the Size drop-down menu, or click the Page Setup dialog box launcher on the PAGE DESIGN tab, Publisher displays the Page Setup dialog box with options virtually identical to those in the Create New Page Size dialog box.

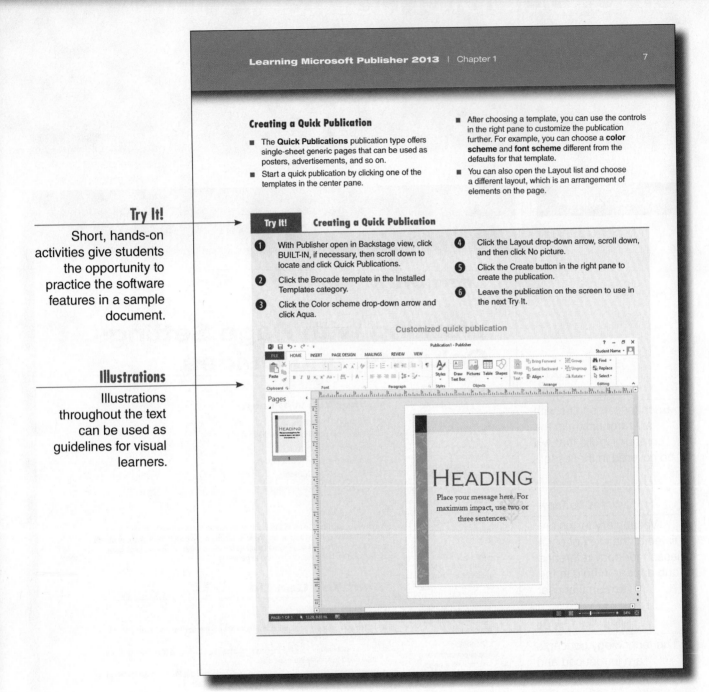

Creating a Quick Publication

- The **Quick Publications** publication type offers single-sheet generic pages that can be used as posters, advertisements, and so on.
- Start a quick publication by clicking one of the templates in the center pane.

- After choosing a template, you can use the controls in the right pane to customize the publication further. For example, you can choose a **color scheme** and **font scheme** different from the defaults for that template.
- You can also open the Layout list and choose a different layout, which is an arrangement of elements on the page.

Try It!   **Creating a Quick Publication**

1. With Publisher open in Backstage view, click BUILT-IN, if necessary, then scroll down to locate and click Quick Publications.
2. Click the Brocade template in the Installed Templates category.
3. Click the Color scheme drop-down arrow and click Aqua.
4. Click the Layout drop-down arrow, scroll down, and then click No picture.
5. Click the Create button in the right pane to create the publication.
6. Leave the publication on the screen to use in the next Try It.

Customized quick publication

Try It!

Short, hands-on activities give students the opportunity to practice the software features in a sample document.

Illustrations

Illustrations throughout the text can be used as guidelines for visual learners.

Lesson 10—Apply

In this exercise, you complete the Greenwood Conservancy publication. You adjust the text boxes and add a page to flow the text properly so that all content displays.

DIRECTIONS

1. Start Publisher, if necessary, and open **PB10Apply** from the data files for this lesson.
2. Save the publication as **PB10Apply_xx** in the location where your teacher instructs you to store the files for this lesson.
3. Delete the text box at the bottom of the left column.
4. Resize the text box at the top of the left column to extend all the way to the bottom margin guide.
5. Add a page to the publication.
6. Draw a text box about 3 inches tall at the top of page 2, from margin to margin. Specify two columns for the text box with 0.2 inch spacing between columns.
7. Link the text box in the right column of page 1 to the text box on page 2. Text flows from page 1 to the linked text box on page 2 and fills both columns, but there is still text in overflow.
8. Adjust the depth of the text box on page 2 until all text is displayed and a roughly equal amount of text displays in each column.
9. **With your teacher's permission**, print the publication. Page 1 should look similar to Figure 10-4. Page 2 should look similar to Figure 10-5.
10. Close the publication, saving changes, and exit Publisher.

Figure 10-4

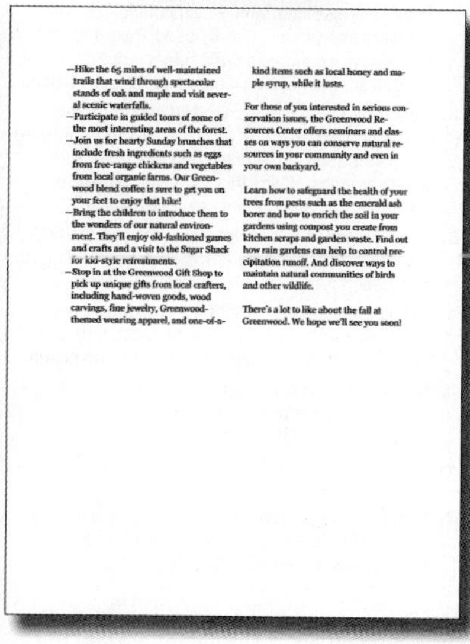

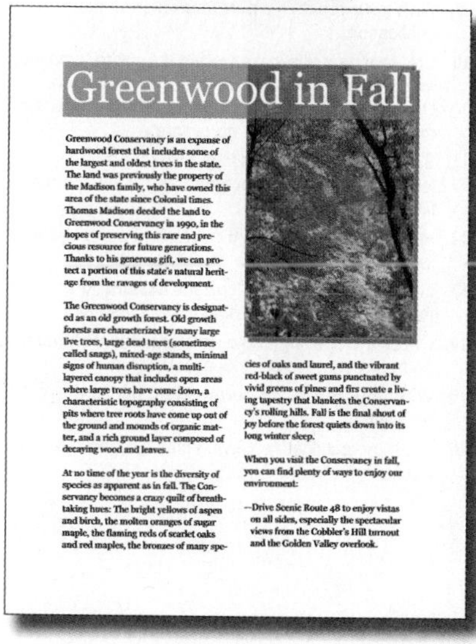

Greenwood in Fall

Greenwood Conservancy is an expanse of hardwood forest that includes some of the largest and oldest trees in the state. The land was previously the property of the Madison family, who have owned this area of the state since Colonial times. Thomas Madison deeded the land to Greenwood Conservancy in 1990, in the hopes of preserving this rare and precious resource for future generations. Thanks to his generous gift, we can protect a portion of this state's natural heritage from the ravages of development.

The Greenwood Conservancy is designated as an old growth forest. Old growth forests are characterized by many large live trees, large dead trees (sometimes called snags), mixed-age stands, minimal signs of human disruption, a multi-layered canopy that includes open areas where large trees have come down, a characteristic topography consisting of pits where tree roots have come up out of the ground and mounds of organic matter, and a rich ground layer composed of decaying wood and leaves.

At no time of the year is the diversity of species as apparent as in fall. The Conservancy becomes a crazy quilt of breathtaking hues: The bright yellows of aspen and birch, the molten oranges of sugar maple, the flaming reds of scarlet oaks and red maples, the bronzes of many species of oaks and laurel, and the vibrant red-black of sweet gums punctuated by vivid greens of pines and firs create a living tapestry that blankets the Conservancy's rolling hills. Fall is the final shout of joy before the forest quiets down into its long winter sleep.

When you visit the Conservancy in fall, you can find plenty of ways to enjoy our environment:

—Drive Scenic Route 48 to enjoy vistas on all sides, especially the spectacular views from the Cobbler's Hill turnout and the Golden Valley overlook.

Figure 10-5

—Hike the 65 miles of well-maintained trails that wind through spectacular stands of oak and maple and visit several scenic waterfalls.
—Participate in guided tours of some of the most interesting areas of the forest.
—Join us for hearty Sunday brunches that include fresh ingredients such as eggs from free-range chickens and vegetables from local organic farms. Our Greenwood blend coffee is sure to get you on your feet to enjoy that hike!
—Bring the children to introduce them to the wonders of our natural environment. They'll enjoy old-fashioned games and crafts and a visit to the Sugar Shack for kid-style refreshments.
—Stop in at the Greenwood Gift Shop to pick up unique gifts from local crafters, including hand-woven goods, wood carvings, fine jewelry, Greenwood-themed wearing apparel, and one-of-a-kind items such as local honey and maple syrup, while it lasts.

For those of you interested in serious conservation issues, the Greenwood Resources Center offers seminars and classes on ways you can conserve natural resources in your community and even in your own backyard.

Learn how to safeguard the health of your trees from pests such as the emerald ash borer and how to enrich the soil in your gardens using compost you create from kitchen scraps and garden waste. Find out how rain gardens can help to control precipitation runoff. And discover ways to maintain natural communities of birds and other wildlife.

There's a lot to like about the fall at Greenwood. We hope we'll see you soon!

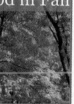

End-of-Lesson Projects

Each lesson includes two hands-on projects where students can use all of the skills that they have learned in the lesson.

End-Result Solutions

Students can refer to solution illustrations to make sure that his or her work is on track.

End-of-Chapter Activities

Topics include a variety of business, career, and college-readiness scenarios. Critical-thinking skills are required to complete the project.

End-of-Chapter Activities

➤ Publisher Chapter 1—Critical Thinking

Making Business Communications More Accurate

Vanessa Bradley, Senior Consultant at Bradley & Cummins, has noticed recently that written communications at the Realty have suffered from some inaccuracies in word choice. She has also noticed that annoying phrases such as "you know" and "like" are creeping into verbal communications with clients. She has asked you to prepare some small posters to remind agents and other staff that business communications should be as accurate and pleasant as possible.

In this project, you will research words that are often misused—such as "alright" instead of "all right"—as well as words and phrases that are considered to be annoying or otherwise troublesome. You will prepare two posters, one for a misused word and one for an annoying phrase.

Directions

Projects challenge students to apply what they have learned through steps that tell what needs to be done, without all the how-to information.

DIRECTIONS

1. **With your teacher's permission**, search the Web for information about words that are commonly used incorrectly in place of other words. Write down one example, with an explanation of how the word should be correctly used. If your word is frequently used in place of another word or words, include all the misused words and their definitions.

2. Perform a second search to find information on words and phrases that most people find annoying in conversation. Write down one example, with an explanation of why this particular phrase is considered to be unnecessary or irritating.

3. Start Publisher and select a template for the first poster (the misused word poster). Choose a quick publication template that will catch the eye.

4. Select a color scheme that will stand out from a distance and, if desired, select a different font scheme. Choose the layout option with no picture.

5. Create the publication and save it as PBCT01A_xx in the location where your teacher instructs you to store the files for this chapter.

6. In the heading placeholder, insert the word or words that are misused.

7. In the message area, insert explanations of what each word means, so that it will be clear to viewers how the words should actually be used.

8. Edit the explanation text in Word, making any adjustment to alignment or spacing that you think will better present the information. Illustration 1A on the next page shows an example.

9. **With your teacher's permission**, print the publication.

10. Create a new publication using the same template, with a different color scheme and font scheme. Use the same layout option to display the heading and message area, but no picture.

11. Save the publication as PBCT01B_xx in the location where your teacher instructs you to store files for this chapter.

12. Insert the annoying word or phrase as the heading in the new publication.

13. In the message area, insert the explanation of why the phrase might be grating or troublesome.

14. Check the spelling and grammar in the document and correct errors as necessary.

15. **With your teacher's permission**, print the publication.

16. Close the publication, saving changes, and exit Publisher.

Teacher's Manual

The Teacher's Manual includes teaching strategies, tips, and supplemental material.

Lesson 5   Working with Business Information

What You Will Learn
✓ Creating a Business Information Set
✓ Editing and Inserting Business Information
✓ Inserting the Current Date and Time
✓ Using AutoCorrect

Words to Know
AutoCorrect   Date code
Business information set   Time code

Tips, Hints, and Pointers

Creating a Business Information Set
- Discuss the concept of a *business information set*. This feature can be a great time-saver for a user who frequently creates publications that contain contact information such as a business name, address, phone number, and e-mail address. The information can be input once and then used over and over whenever necessary.

- Step through the process of creating a new business information set when starting a new publication, and discuss why a person might need more than one set. For example, you might need one for work, one for personal use, and one for an organization to which you belong.

- Demonstrate how, when you start a publication using a template that includes placeholders for business information, the data from the selected business information set is filled in automatically.

- **Try It! Creating a Business Information Set:** Because students are opening a data file rather than creating a new publication from scratch, they must use the Edit Business Information option on the Info tab in Backstage view to access the Business Information dialog box, and then use the Edit button to create the new business information set. Explain that this task is a little more straightforward if creating a new business information set at the same time as creating a new publication, but the process of supplying the information is the same in both cases. Students will have a chance to create business information along with a new publication in the Practice exercise.

- In step 5 of the Try It, students are given the information to type for the business information set. For most of the information boxes, they can delete the sample text and replace it with the new information. For the Phone, fax, and e-mail box, however, you may want to point out that they can leave the Phone, Fax, and E-mail sample text in the box, replacing only the numbers and e-mail address. If they do this, they will not have to type the words Phone, Fax, and E-mail as shown in the step.

Editing and Inserting Business Information
- Explain that business information can be edited at any time using the same command students used to set up business information in the previous Try It.

- Show how to use the Business Information command on the INSERT tab to insert data from the current set. Note that each bit of information displays in its own text box if you do not click inside a text box first; if you do click inside a text box, then the information is added within that box.

- Explain that a business information set will always be available for new publications until it is deleted. If your students are sharing computers, business information sets should be deleted so that a student will not find the set already created. Step through the process of deleting a business information set.

Tips, Hints, and Pointers
These items help explain the content and provide additional information for instructors to use in the classroom.

Try It! Notes
Teaching strategies and troubleshooting hints are correlated to specific exercises in the book.

Test Book with TestGen CD-ROM

Print tests include a pretest, posttest, and two application tests for each chapter in the student edition. Accompanying CD-ROM includes test-generator software so that instructors can create concept tests correlated to the chapters in the book.

Directions

Steps tell students what to do, without all of the how-to detail, so critical-thinking skills must be used.

Publisher 2013 Application Test 2B	Chapter 2: Changing the Design and Layout • Change the Color Scheme • Create a New Color Scheme • Change the Font Scheme • Adjust Margins • Place Ruler Guides • Link Text Boxes • Insert Building Blocks • Add Items to the Master Page • Insert a Footer • Insert a Page • Move Pages

✓ **DIRECTIONS:**

Use Publisher to complete the exercise below. Carefully follow all directions and check your results. (Time: 30 minutes. Point Scale: –5 per formatting error; –2 per typographical error.)

The Forest Park Aquatic Center needs to mail a flyer that will advertise two-for-one admission during the month of July. The flyer has been started. You will improve it by changing some of the layout, font, color, and page options. You will then create a page that can easily be customized for other specials.

Open and Save a Publication with a New Name

1. Start Publisher, if necessary.
2. Open ⊘ **PB2B.pub**. Save the file as **PB2B_xx** in the location where your teacher instructs you to store the files.

Modify the Font and Color Schemes

1. Change to the Tidepool color scheme.
2. Create a new color scheme called July based on the Tidepool color scheme, but change the Accent 3 color to Aqua.
3. Change to the Civic font scheme.

Work with Guides and Text Boxes

1. Change the top margin only to 0.7 inch. Drag down the top edge of the wavy border object to align it with the new top margin. Drag up the page heading text box (if necessary) to align with the top margin.
2. Insert the following ruler guides:
   a. Drag a vertical ruler guide to align with the left ends of the two aqua lines (at 1.05 inches).
   b. Drag another vertical ruler guide to align with the other ends of the aqua lines (about 7.85 inches).
   c. Drag a horizontal ruler guide to 7 inches.
3. Insert a text box that starts at the intersection of the 7-inch horizontal guide and the 1.05-inch vertical guide. Size the text box to 1.6 inches tall by 4.4 inches wide.
4. Link the text box above the photo to the text box below the photo.
5. You still have overflow text after linking. Click the Overflow button and click to the right of the text box below the photo.

6. Align the top of the new text box with the 7-inch ruler guide and the right side of the text box with the 7.85-inch vertical ruler guide. Shorten the text box to just below the last bullet.
7. If necessary, select the bulleted text and apply the Small Bullets format.

Add Building Blocks

1. Open the Advertisements Building Blocks gallery, click More Advertisements, and then search in the Building Blocks Library for a 2 for 1 Attention Getter.
2. Insert the attention getter in the publication and resize and position it as desired. Use the Shape Fill command on the Drawing Tools Format tab to change the fill color of the object to a scheme color.
3. Insert the Diamond Line bar from the Borders & Accents Building Blocks gallery. Position it at the intersection of the 1.05 vertical ruler guide and the bottom margin and drag the center selection handle to the right margin. Then use the DRAWING TOOLS FORMAT > Shape Height box to change the height to 0.3 inch. Move the bar back down to the bottom margin guide.

Work with Masters and Pages

1. Press Ctrl + A to select all items on the page, and then move the selected items to Master Page A.
2. Display Master Page view.
3. Show the footer text box, press Tab, and then insert the Forest Park business tagline, **Have a Splashing Good Time!** Apply Best Fit text fitting.
4. On the master page, select and send these items to the foreground: the page heading (*Hot July Specials*), the three text boxes, and the 2 for 1 attention getter. Close master page view. Your page should look similar to Illustration A.

49

| Solutions Manual | Contains final solution illustrations for all of the projects in the student textbook. Accompanying CD-ROM contains solution files in electronic format. |

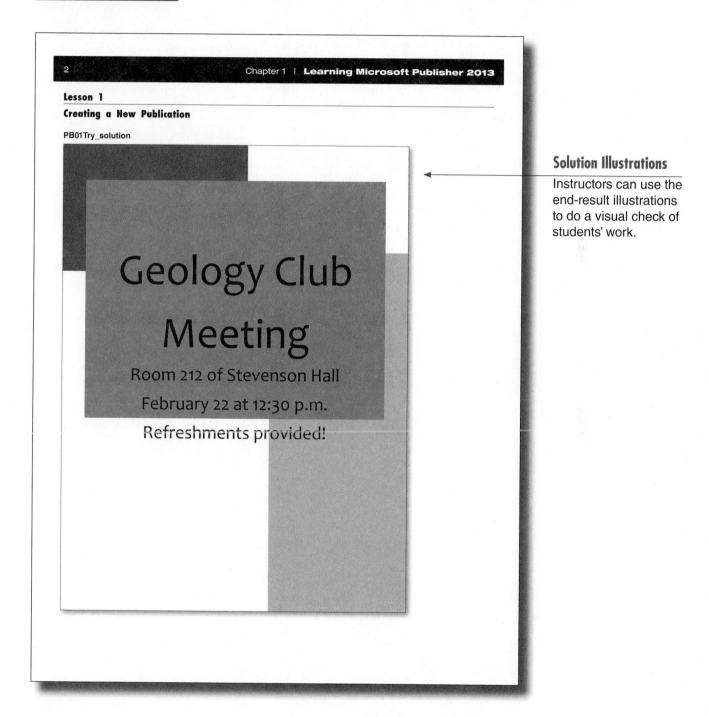

Solution Illustrations

Instructors can use the end-result illustrations to do a visual check of students' work.

Learning
Microsoft®
Publisher 2013

(Courtesy Blend Images/Shutterstock)

Getting Started with Publisher

Lesson 1
Creating a New Publication

- Starting and Exiting Publisher
- Exploring Backstage View
- Creating a Quick Publication
- Working with the Publisher Interface
- Inserting Text in a Placeholder
- Saving and Closing a Publication
- Opening an Existing Publication

Lesson 2
Working with Objects

- Selecting Objects
- Zooming In and Out
- Resizing Objects
- Moving Objects
- Deleting Objects
- Previewing and Printing a Publication

Lesson 3
Working with Text Boxes

- Placing a New Text Box
- Controlling Automatic Copyfitting
- Inserting Symbols
- Checking Spelling
- Using Research and Language Options

Lesson 4
Basic Text Handling

- Selecting Text
- Deleting Text
- Copying and Moving Text
- Using Undo and Redo

Lesson 5
Working with Business Information

- Creating a Business Information Set
- Editing and Inserting Business Information
- Inserting the Current Date and Time
- Using AutoCorrect

Lesson 6
Working with Text from Other Applications

- Opening a File from Another Program
- Opening a Word Document
- Inserting Text from Other Programs
- Customizing the Ribbon
- Editing a Story in Word

End-of-Chapter Activities

Lesson 1

Creating a New Publication

➤ What You Will Learn

Starting and Exiting Publisher
Exploring Backstage View
Creating a Quick Publication
Working with the Publisher Interface
Inserting Text in a Placeholder
Saving and Closing a Publication
Opening an Existing Publication

WORDS TO KNOW

Color scheme
A collection of colors designed to work well together.

Contextual tab
A Ribbon tab that is available only in a certain context or situation.

Font scheme
A combination of two fonts that work well together.

Extension
The code (usually three letters) that follows the period in a file's name (such as .pub for a Publisher file).

Gallery
A menu that displays pictures of available options.

Placeholder
Sample text or graphics to guide you in placing your own text or graphics.

Publication
A document created in Publisher.

Quick Access Toolbar
A toolbar containing tools that are used frequently.

Software Skills   Microsoft Office Publisher 2013 is a desktop publishing program (DTP) you can use to create professional publications with all kinds of design elements. It comes with a catalog of project templates to help you get a quick start on your publications. These templates also provide design ideas that you may not have thought of on your own. In most cases, you will want to start with one of these templates rather than create a new publication from scratch.

What You Can Do

Starting and Exiting Publisher

- Start Publisher using the Microsoft Windows Start menu (Windows 7) or screen (Windows 8). You can navigate to the Microsoft Office folder to find the Publisher icon or click the Publisher 2013 tile on the Windows 8 Start screen if Publisher displays on the screen.

- You may also find the Publisher icon on the Windows desktop or taskbar.

  ✓ *If you use Publisher frequently, consider pinning it to the taskbar. To do so, right-click its entry in the menu system and choose Pin this program to taskbar.*

- Exit Publisher when you are finished working with the program.

Try It!	**Starting and Exiting Publisher**

To start Microsoft Publisher in Windows 8:

1 On the Start screen, scroll to see the application tiles toward the right side of the screen and click or tap Publisher 2013.

2 If you do not see the Publisher 2013 tile, swipe up or right-click anywhere on the screen and then click or tap All apps in the lower-right corner.

3 Scroll right to locate the Microsoft Office 2013 apps and then click or tap the Publisher 2013 app.

✓ *For more information on how to use Windows 8's touch screen interface, see the Windows Help files. This text assumes you will be using a mouse interface.*

To start Microsoft Publisher in Windows 7:

1 Click Start 🌀 > All Programs. If necessary, scroll until you see the Microsoft Office folder icon.

✓ *In this text, the symbol > is used to indicate a series of steps. In this case, click Start and then click All Programs.*

2 Click the Microsoft Office folder icon.

3 Click Microsoft Publisher 2013.

To exit Microsoft Publisher:

1 Click the Close button ✕ in the Microsoft Publisher window.

Quick publication
A design category of publications consisting of a single-page flyer with placeholders for a picture and a few simple text blocks.

Ribbon
A collection of tabs that contain commands grouped by task.

Scratch area
The empty space around a publication page where you can store objects you want to use in the publication.

Template
A file that provides basic design elements, such as styles, page layout settings, and graphics.

Exploring Backstage View

■ When Publisher starts, it opens in Backstage view showing a list of recent **publications**. Publisher also displays featured **templates**, including blank page templates.

■ Click BUILT-IN to see categories of templates, such as Advertisements, Brochures, and Flyers.

■ You can use the Search feature to search for online templates.

■ Click a publication type to display designs for that publication type, organized by category. For example, if you choose Flyers, you can select a flyer from categories such as Event, Marketing, and Real estate.

■ A pane opens to the right to show a larger view of the publication with options for customizing it.

■ Use the navigation path at the top of the center pane to return to the Home view of available templates or to go back to a previous category.

■ Redisplay the Publisher 2013 templates to start a new publication at any time by clicking the FILE tab and then New.

Try It!   **Exploring Backstage View**

1 Start Microsoft Publisher 2013.

2 Click BUILT-IN to display Publisher's built-in templates, and then click Brochures.

3 Click the Bounce template in the Informational category.

4 Click Home at the top of the center pane to redisplay the built-in templates.

5 Leave Publisher open in this view to use in the next Try It.

Built-in templates in Publisher

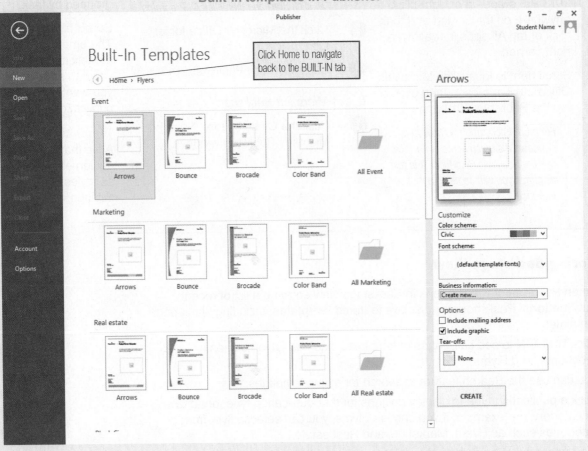

Creating a Quick Publication

- The **Quick Publications** publication type offers single-sheet generic pages that can be used as posters, advertisements, and so on.
- Start a quick publication by clicking one of the templates in the center pane.

- After choosing a template, you can use the controls in the right pane to customize the publication further. For example, you can choose a **color scheme** and **font scheme** different from the defaults for that template.
- You can also open the Layout list and choose a different layout, which is an arrangement of elements on the page.

Try It!   Creating a Quick Publication

1. With Publisher open in Backstage view, click BUILT-IN, if necessary, then scroll down to locate and click Quick Publications.

2. Click the Brocade template in the Installed Templates category.

3. Click the Color scheme drop-down arrow and click Aqua.

4. Click the Layout drop-down arrow, scroll down, and then click No picture.

5. Click the Create button in the right pane to create the publication.

6. Leave the publication on the screen to use in the next Try It.

Customized quick publication

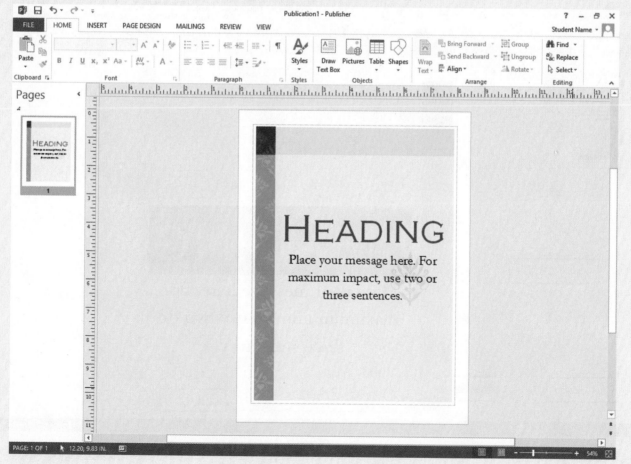

Working with the Publisher Interface

- Figure 1-1 shows the Publisher 2013 window elements:
  - The **Ribbon** displays buttons for accessing features and commands.
  - The Ribbon is organized into tabs based on activities, such as working with page design or inserting content. On each tab, commands are organized into groups. Click a tab such as INSERT or VIEW to see commands related to those activities.
    - ✓ *Note that the way items display on the Ribbon tabs may depend on the width of the program window.*

- The **Quick Access Toolbar** displays buttons for commonly used commands. This toolbar is always visible in the upper-left corner of the window. You can customize the Quick Access Toolbar to display buttons you use frequently.

- In addition to the standard Ribbon tabs, Figure 1-1 shows two contextual tabs: DRAWING TOOLS FORMAT and TEXT BOX TOOLS FORMAT. **Contextual tabs** are only available when certain types of content are selected in the publication. In Figure 1-1, selecting the text in the Heading text box results in the display of the contextual tabs that contain tools you need to work with the text box.

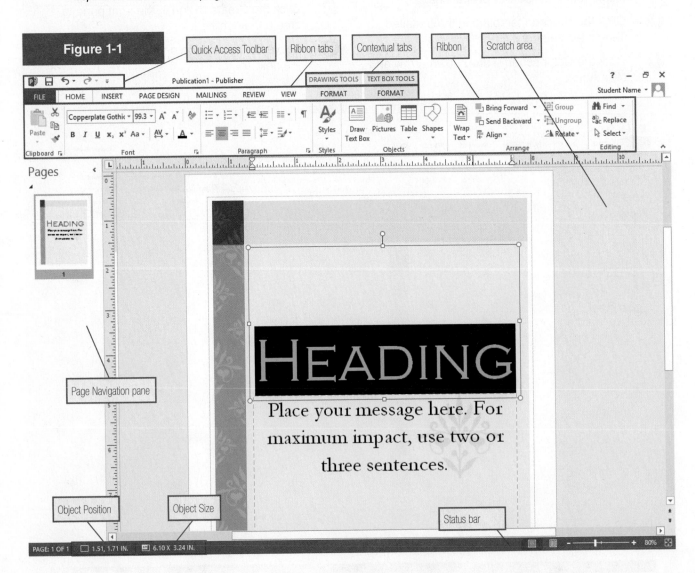

Figure 1-1

- You do your work in the publication area, where the current publication displays. The Page Navigation pane at the left of the window allows you to view and work with the publication's pages. The **scratch area** around the publication page can be used to store objects you have not yet placed on a page.

- Vertical and horizontal rulers display by default to help you adjust object sizes and position objects on the publication page. As you move or size an object, tick marks move on the rulers to show you size and position.

- You can also use the Object Position and Object Size information in the status bar at the lower-left corner of the screen to check the current position and size of an object.

- Figure 1-2 shows a closer view of the PAGE DESIGN Ribbon tab. Note that the Ribbon tab is divided into groups; each group has a name, such as Template, Page Setup, or Schemes. Each group contains a number of related commands.

- If a command displays a drop-down arrow, you can click the arrow to display a menu or **gallery** with further options. Some galleries have more options available than can be displayed on the Ribbon. You can click the More button to see the entire gallery.

- You can see more information about a command by resting the mouse pointer on it to display a ScreenTip.

- Some groups have a dialog box launcher button that you can click to display a dialog box with more options.

- Note that the way items display on the Ribbon may depend on the width of the program window.
  - If the window is wide enough, groups expand to display all items.
  - If the window is not wide enough, groups collapse to a single group button. Click the button to display the commands in the group.
  - The size of icons in a group may vary depending on the width of the window.

- If your program window is narrower or wider than the one used in this book, the Ribbon on your screen may look different from the one in the figures.

- In addition, the steps you must take to complete a procedure may vary slightly.
  - If your screen is narrower than the one in this book, you may have to click a group button to display the commands in that group before you can complete the steps in the procedure.
  - If your screen is wider, you may be able to skip a step for selecting a group button and go directly to the step for selecting a specific command.

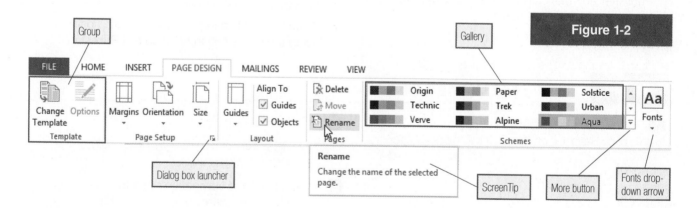

Figure 1-2

Inserting Text in a Placeholder

- Most publications include sample text to show you where you should type your own text. These bits of sample text are text **placeholders**.

- Insert your own text in a placeholder by selecting the sample text and then typing over it.

- With most placeholder text boxes, you can simply click anywhere on the text to select the entire block of text. You can also select text with the mouse by dragging over it.

- Selected text appears in reverse colors (for example, white on black instead of black on white).

- As text is entered, the font size of the text may change so that the text fits attractively in the placeholder.

Try It!   Inserting Text in a Placeholder

1   With the new publication open in Publisher, click the Heading text placeholder to select the placeholder and its text.

2   Type **Focus Group Sessions**.

3   Click the text placeholder with the sample text that begins *Place your message here.*

4   Type the following text:

Session 1: Madison Room

Session 2: Jefferson Room

Session 3: Adams Room

5   Leave the document on the screen for the next Try It.

Saving and Closing a Publication

- If you want to have a publication available for future use, you must save it to a storage device.

- Clicking the Save button on the Quick Access Toolbar or Save on the FILE tab displays the Save As tab in Backstage view.

- In Windows 8, this tab gives you options for saving to your SkyDrive or the computer.

- If you choose to save to your computer, you can select a recent folder or click Browse to open the Save As dialog box.

- In the Save As dialog box, you can provide a name and select the location where you want to store the publication.

- Publisher automatically adds a .pub **extension** to a saved publication file's name.

- After you save a file for the first time, you save changes to the file in order to make sure you do not lose any work. Use the Save button on the Quick Access Toolbar for quick saves as you work.

- When you save the same document subsequent times, Publisher does not prompt for a file name or location; it saves using the same one you originally specified.

- You can save a copy of the file with a different name, or in a different location, with the Save As command on the FILE tab. This command allows you to open the Save As dialog box for an already saved file.

- Close a publication using the Close button on the publication window or the Close command on the FILE tab. If you have made any changes, you will be prompted to save them.

- If you have only one publication open, closing it using the Close button will also exit Publisher.

Try It!   Saving and Closing a Publication

1   With the new publication open on the screen, click Save 🖫 on the Quick Access Toolbar.

    OR

    a. Click FILE.

    b. Click Save.

2   On the Save As tab in Backstage view, click Computer and then click Browse.

3   Select the File name text box if it is not selected already.

4   Type **PB01Try_xx**.

    ✓ *Replace the xx with your initials or your full name, as instructed by your teacher.*

5   Use the Page Navigation pane to navigate to the location where your teacher instructs you to store the files for this lesson. Create a new folder, if necessary.

6   Click Save or press ENTER .

7   Click FILE > Close to close the publication and leave Publisher open for the next Try It.

Opening an Existing Publication

- Open a saved publication when you want to view, edit, and/or print it.

- You can open a file you have used recently by clicking its file name on the Open tab in Backstage view.

- Or, you can use the Open Publication dialog box to locate and open an existing file.

Try It! **Opening an Existing Publication**

1 With Publisher open displaying Backstage view, click Open to see a list of files you have recently used.

2 Click Computer to see folders on your computer.

3 Click the folder where you stored the file you closed in the previous Try It.

4 Double-click **PB01Try_xx** to open it.

OR

a. Click **PB01Try_xx**.

b. Click Open.

5 Click the Close button ☒ to close the publication and exit Publisher.

Open Publication dialog box

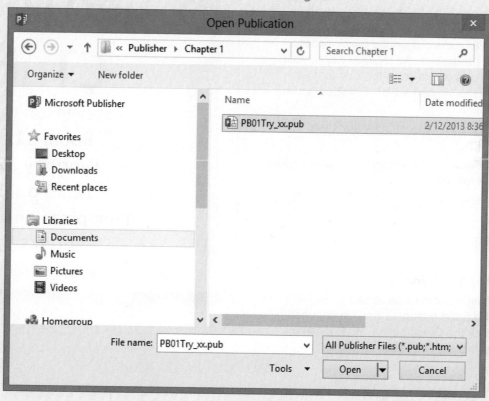

Lesson 1—Practice

The Geology Club at Cutler College is having an informational meeting to recruit new members. In this exercise, you create a flyer for the club president to review.

DIRECTIONS

1. Start Publisher, if necessary.
2. Click BUILT-IN and then click **Quick Publications**.
3. Click the **Bounce** template.
4. In the Customize box in the right pane, click the **Color scheme** drop-down arrow and then click **Citrus**.
5. In the Customize box in the right pane, click the **Layout** drop-down arrow, scroll down, and click **No picture**.
6. Click the **Create** button.
7. Click the **Save** button 🖫 on the Quick Access Toolbar and navigate to the location where your teacher instructs you to store the files for this lesson. Type the file name **PB01Practice_xx** and click **Save**.
8. Click in the *Heading* placeholder and type **Geology Club**.
9. Click in the *Place your message here* placeholder and type the following:

   Stevenson Hall

   Room 212

   February 22

   12:30 p.m.

   Free pizza and soft drinks

10. Your publication should look similar to Figure 1-3. Click the **Save** button 🖫 to save changes, and then click the Close button ✕ to close the publication and exit Publisher.

Figure 1-3

Geology Club

Stevenson Hall
Room 212
February 22
12:30 p.m.
Free pizza and soft drinks

Lesson 1—Apply

In this exercise, you work on an alternate publication for the Geology Club meeting to give the club president a different choice.

DIRECTIONS

1. Start Publisher, if necessary, and choose to create a new quick publication.
2. Choose the **Blocks** template, with a color scheme of **Civic** and the **Concourse** font scheme.

   ✓ *You will find the Blocks template in the More Installed Templates section.*

3. Change the layout to remove the picture if necessary and then create the publication.
4. Save the file as **PB01Apply_xx** in the location where your teacher instructs you to store the files for this lesson.
5. Type the text shown in Figure 1-4.
6. Close the publication, saving changes, and exit Publisher.

Figure 1-4

Geology Club Meeting

Room 212 of Stevenson Hall

February 22 at 12:30 p.m.

Refreshments provided!

Lesson 2

Working with Objects

> ### ➤ What You Will Learn

Selecting Objects

Zooming In and Out

Resizing Objects

Moving Objects

Deleting Objects

Previewing and Printing a Publication

WORDS TO KNOW

Aspect ratio
The ratio of width to height for an object.

Object
Any free-floating content on a publication layout, usually bounded by a rectangular border.

Rotation handle
The symbol at the top of a selected object, used to rotate the object.

Selection handles
Circle and squares on the border of a selected object.

Zoom
The magnification at which the publication appears on-screen.

Software Skills   Publisher objects hold text and graphics. You can resize, move, and even delete the objects themselves, as well as change the contents of an object. Use the Zoom feature to adjust the magnification at which you work. Print your publication when you have finished.

What You Can Do

Selecting Objects

- Publications can include many types of **objects**: text boxes, graphics, WordArt, drawn lines or shapes, and so on.

- Each object holds a single type of content, and in most cases a single item. The exception is a text box. A text box may hold any amount of text.

  ✓ *Objects can overlap. By default, the most recently placed object is "on top" and the contents of the object beneath it wrap around the top one. You will learn how to change the stacking order of overlapping objects later in this book.*

- To select an object, click on it. You see **selection handles** around the border of a selected object; these are circles (at the corners) and squares (at the centers of the left and right sides and the top and bottom) that help you resize the object.

- To select more than one object at once, hold down the ⇧SHIFT key as you click on each one. You can then move, copy, or delete them as a group.

- To deselect an object, click on some other object, or click away from all objects.

- If an object contains a graphic or other non-text item, you can select it by clicking anywhere on (or in) the object.

- When an object is selected or when the insertion point lies inside it, you see a border around it. This border does not print.

- A circle appears at the top of a selected object. This is a **rotation handle**, used to rotate the object.
- When a publication contains a text placeholder, you can click on the text in the placeholder to select all the text in the placeholder.

- You can select the text box by clicking on the outside border. To work with text in a text box, click inside the text box to position the insertion point; you can then use familiar word processing techniques to select text.

Try It!   **Selecting Objects**

1 Start Publisher and open **PB02Try** from the data files for this lesson.

2 Save the file as **PB02Try_xx** in the location where your teacher instructs you to store the files for this lesson.

3 Move the mouse pointer near the *HOPKINS TECHNICAL SERVICES* text box at the top of the page until the pointer turns to a four-headed arrow and you see a dashed line around the text box. Click to select the text box object.

4 Click away from the text box to deselect it.

5 Move the mouse pointer to the upper-left corner of the dark brown box and click. Notice the selection border that surrounds all three colored objects.

✓ *The three objects have been grouped. You will work with groups later in this course.*

6 Click on the computer graphic to see the selection border around the graphic.

7 Click in the middle of the text paragraph below the main heading to see the selection border around the placeholder.

8 Click on the *BUSINESS NAME* placeholder in the lower-left corner of the page, hold down SHIFT , click the *Primary Business Address* placeholder, and then click the *Phone* placeholder. Click outside the page to deselect.

9 Leave the publication open to use in the next Try It.

Three placeholders selected in a publication

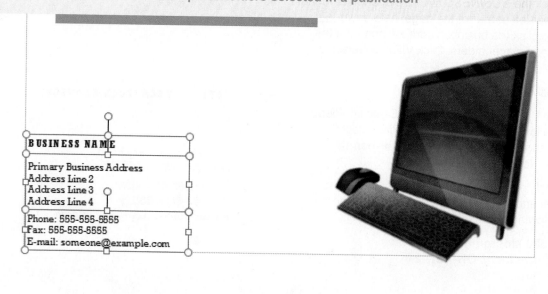

Zooming In and Out

- The **Zoom** feature lets you change your view of the publication on-screen by enlarging or reducing it. As some text elements in Publisher templates use small font sizes, changing the zoom can help you work more easily with text.

- Zooming does not affect the size at which a publication is printed; it is for on-screen viewing purposes only.

- The larger the zoom number, the larger the publication appears. For example, a zoom of 200% focuses closely on one area of the publication.

- Options in the Zoom group on the VIEW tab allow you to adjust the zoom setting in several ways:
  - Use the 100% option to see a publication at its full size.
  - The Zoom list lets you choose a zoom percentage from 10% to 800%.

- The Whole Page option sets the zoom to the largest percentage possible while still showing the entire page. This percentage may vary depending on the screen size.

- The Page Width zoom option sets the zoom to the largest number possible while still showing the entire width of the page from left to right.

- The Selected Objects option zooms in on whatever object is selected (text box, graphic, etc.) and resizes it to completely fill the publication area width.

- You can also use the Zoom In and Zoom Out buttons in the lower-right corner of the Publisher window to quickly zoom in and out by increments of 10 percent, or you can drag the Zoom slider to select an exact zoom percentage.

Try It!　　**Zooming In and Out**

1 In the **PB02Try_xx** file, click VIEW > Page Width to make the publication as wide as the publication pane.

2 Click the VIEW > Zoom drop-down arrow and click 75%.

3 Click the *BUSINESS NAME* placeholder in the lower-left corner of the page, hold down [SHIFT] , and click the business address and then the phone placeholders. Click VIEW > Selected Objects.

4 Click VIEW > 100%.

5 Click in the *BUSINESS NAME* placeholder in the lower-left corner of the page, select the existing text, and type **Hopkins Technical Services**.

6 Click inside the *Primary Business Address* placeholder, select the text, and type the following address:

11580 Montgomery Road
Montgomery, OH 45242

7 Save the changes to **PB02Try_xx**, and leave it open to use in the next Try It.

Zoom in to make it easier to work with objects

HOPKINS TECHNICAL SERVICES

11580 Montgomery Road
Montgomery, OH 45242

Phone: 555-555-5555
Fax: 555-555-5555
E-mail: someone@example.com

Resizing Objects

- You have several options for resizing objects, and the one you choose will depend on how precise you want the size to be.

- If precise size is not important, you can simply drag a selection handle to change an object's size by eye. Drag a side handle to adjust width, a top or bottom handle to adjust height, or a corner handle to adjust both width and height at the same time.

- If exact size is important, you can specify width and height precisely using one of these options:

  - The Object Size information in the lower-left corner of the Publisher window (the second set of numbers to the left of the page numbers) shows the width and height of a selected object. As you draw or adjust the size of an object, these numbers change to show the current width (the first number of the pair) and height (the second number of the pair).

- You can click the Object Size icon to display the Measurement toolbar, a free-floating panel that lets you control a number of different kinds of measurements, including the width and height of the currently selected object. You can click in the Width or Height box and type a precise measurement, or you can click the Width or Height spin arrows to set the measurement.

  - ✓ If desired, you can dock this toolbar beneath the Ribbon or at the left, right, or bottom of the screen so it is always available.

- You can also use the selected object's contextual tab to set a specific size for an object. For example, use the DRAWING TOOLS FORMAT tab's Shape Width and Shape Height boxes to set a precise size for an object. Use the PICTURE TOOLS FORMAT tab to specify a size for a picture.

- Be careful when resizing graphic objects that you do not distort the image by changing its **aspect ratio**, the ratio of width to height for an object.

- To maintain the aspect ratio for an object as you resize it, hold down the [SHIFT] key as you drag a corner selection handle.

Try It!   **Resizing Objects**

1 In the **PB02Try_xx** file, click the computer graphic in the lower-right corner.

2 Point to the upper-left corner selection handle, hold down [SHIFT], and drag toward the lower-right corner about one-half inch to resize the graphic.

3 Size the graphic exactly:

  a. With the graphic still selected, click the Object Size icon [xy] to display the Measurement toolbar.

  b. Click in the Width box and type **2.8**.

  c. Click in the Height box and type **2.8**.

  d. Click the Measurement toolbar's close button **✕** .

4 Click in the text paragraph below the heading to select the placeholder, click on the right side selection handle, and drag it to the right until the right border of the placeholder aligns with the right side of the tan object.

  ✓ A purple guide displays when the text box placeholder aligns with the tan object's right side.

5 Click on the business address placeholder to select it, then click on the bottom center selection handle and drag upward about one-quarter inch.

6 Save the changes to **PB02Try_xx**, and leave it open to use in the next Try It.

Moving Objects

- You have several alternatives for moving objects, depending how precisely you want to position the moved object.

- To move to an approximate position, hover the mouse pointer over the object so that it turns into a Move pointer ✛ and then drag the object to a new location.

- With a text box, the mouse pointer turns into a Move pointer when pointing to a border of the object but not to a selection handle.

- With a nontext object, the mouse pointer turns into a Move pointer when positioned *anywhere* over the object except over a selection handle.

- Selecting a graphic object also displays the mountain icon in the center of the object. Click the mountain icon and drag to move the graphic.

- As you drag an object, you can make use of one of Publisher 2013's object alignment options: purple guidelines that show you when the selected object aligns with other objects on the page or regions of the page, such as the vertical and horizontal center of the page.

  ✓ *You saw this feature at work in the last Try It when you aligned an object with another object.*

- If you need to move an object to a precise position, you can use the Object Position information in the status bar at the lower-left corner of the window. These numbers show the position on the page of the upper-left corner of the selected object, using an X-Y coordinate system similar to the way values are plotted on a graph.

  - The first number of the pair (the X coordinate) indicates the horizontal distance from the left side of the page.

  - The second number (the Y coordinate) indicates the vertical distance from the top of the page.

- You can use the coordinates as a guide while you move an object. Or, you can click the Object Position icon to display the Measurement toolbar and set exact values using the X (Horizontal Position) and Y (Vertical Position) boxes.

- If an object isn't exactly where you want it, but close, you can "nudge" the object into place using the arrow keys.

Try It!   Moving Objects

1 In the **PB02Try_xx** file, select the *Phone* placeholder in the lower-left corner of the page by clicking its outside border.

2 Drag the placeholder up about one-quarter inch to fit more closely beneath the address placeholder. The Object Position coordinates should be 0.50, 9.50.

3 Click anywhere in the computer graphic and drag upward until the bottom of the graphic aligns with the bottom of the placeholder you just moved. Drag slightly to the left to align the right side of the graphic with the right margin guide.

  ✓ *A purple guide displays when the two objects align at the bottom.*

4 Select the *Master Your Computer* text box. Specify an exact position by clicking the Object Position icon ▭ to display the Measurement toolbar; click in the X box and type **4.75**, and then click in the Y box and type **5.8**. Click the Measurement toolbar's close button **✕** .

5 Save the changes to **PB02Try_xx**, and leave it open to use in the next Try It.

(continued)

Try It!   **Moving Objects** *(continued)*

Move objects by dragging or setting precise measurements

Master Your Computer

Organization

HOPKINS TECHNICAL SERVICES

11580 Montgomery Road
Montgomery, OH 45242

Phone: 555-555-5555
Fax: 555-555-5555
E-mail: someone@example.com

Deleting Objects

- Delete an object when you don't need it in a publication. Most templates include a number of placeholders and other objects that you may not need for a particular publication.

- To delete an object, select it and then press the `DEL` key, or right-click it and choose Delete from the shortcut menu.

  ✓ *A shortcut menu appears when you right-click on an object. The shortcut menu contains commands you can select to act upon that object; the commands vary depending on the object chosen.*

- To delete a text placeholder, make sure you have selected the placeholder itself and not moved the insertion point into the box; otherwise, pressing `DEL` removes a single character at the insertion point instead of deleting the whole text box.

- You can also right-click the text box and choose Delete Object from the shortcut menu.

Try It!   **Deleting Objects**

1 In the **PB02Try_xx** file, click the object containing the pyramid graphic and the word *Organization*.

2 Right-click and select Delete Object.

3 Select the *HOPKINS TECHNICAL SERVICES* placeholder in the lower-left corner of the page, and press ⌷DEL⌷.

✓ *Make sure you have selected the placeholder so the solid selection outline displays.*

4 Save the changes to **PB02Try_xx**, and leave it open to use in the next Try It.

Previewing and Printing a Publication

- Most publications are designed to be printed on paper or card stock (heavy paper on which cards are printed).

- In Publisher 2013, you preview and print documents using the Print tab in Backstage view.

- Options on the Print tab let you select the number of copies to print, choose the printer, select which pages to print, and select other settings specific to your printer.

- The preview area gives you a number of options for displaying the preview. You can show or hide rulers that show the page size, change the zoom setting, page through a publication that has multiple pages, and show multiple pages at the same time.

- Ask your teacher for permission before printing any file.

Try It!   **Previewing and Printing a Publication**

1 In the **PB02Try_xx** file, click FILE.

2 Click Print. The publication displays in the preview pane.

3 **With your teacher's permission,** click Print.

✓ *Make sure your printer displays as the default printer.*

4 Close the publication, saving changes, and exit Publisher.

Lesson 2—Practice

Jaime Cruz, owner of Cruz Art, has asked you to create a flyer to advertise art classes. In this exercise, you create the flyer and adjust the position of some of the publication's objects.

DIRECTIONS

1. Start Publisher, if necessary, and choose to start a new quick publication.

2. Click the **Circles** template in the More Installed Templates category. Click the **Color scheme** drop-down arrow, and click the **Oriel** color scheme. If the Font scheme box does not show (default template fonts), click the drop-down arrow, scroll up, and click (**default template fonts**). Click the Layout drop-down arrow, scroll down, and click **No picture**.

3. Create the publication.

4. Save the publication as **PB02Practice_xx** in the location where your teacher instructs you to store the files for this lesson.

5. In the *Heading* placeholder, type **Art Classes**.

6. In the *Place your message here* placeholder, type the following lines:

   Join us at Cruz Art for our new art classes:

   Painting with Oils

   Watercolor Techniques

   Working with Pastels

7. Select a very small gray circle near the right border of the publication, about halfway down the page, and delete it.

8. Select a small black circle near the left margin about halfway down the page and delete it.

9. Select the text placeholder that contains the art class information and drag it slightly to the left, deselect it, and then click on the outside border of the white rectangle behind the text placeholders to select it.

10. Drag the white rectangle's right side selection handle to the right until the border aligns with the blue margin line.

11. Drag the left side selection handle to the left until the border aligns with the blue margin line.

12. Drag the art class text placeholder back to the right to re-center it on the white rectangle.

13. **With your teacher's permission**, print the document. It should look similar to Figure 2-1.

14. Close the publication, saving changes, and exit Publisher.

Figure 2-1

Lesson 2—Apply

In this exercise, you continue to work on the Cruz Art publication. You adjust object positions and sizes and add more text to the publication.

DIRECTIONS

1. Start Publisher, if necessary, and open **PB02Apply** from the data files for this lesson.

2. Save the file as **PB02Apply_xx** in the location where your teacher instructs you to store the files for this lesson.

3. Select the placeholder that contains the *Art Classes* heading. Drag the bottom border upward about 1 inch. The height should be 2.6 in the Object Size area.

   ✓ *Click the Object Position button to display the Measurement toolbar if desired to set measurements in this project exactly.*

4. Select both the art class placeholder and the *Primary Business Address* placeholder and move them upward until the bottom of the *Primary Business Address* placeholder aligns with the bottom of the white shape behind the placeholders.

5. Select the business address placeholder and zoom in on this object. Type the following address:

   326 Ludlow Avenue

   Cincinnati, OH 45220

6. Zoom to Whole Page view. Select the gray ellipse that you see at the lower-left corner of the page (most of it is behind the white rectangle). Drag the left side selection handle to the left until you can see the left side of the ellipse. The object width should be 1.5 inches.

7. Click the dark gray circle at the top center of the page, hold down SHIFT, and drag the lower-right corner about half an inch.

8. Select the dark gray circle about one-quarter of the way down the left side of the page and drag it straight down until the circle aligns at the top with the first line of the *Join us* text.

9. **With your teacher's permission**, print the document. It should look similar to Figure 2-2.

10. Close the publication, saving changes, and exit Publisher.

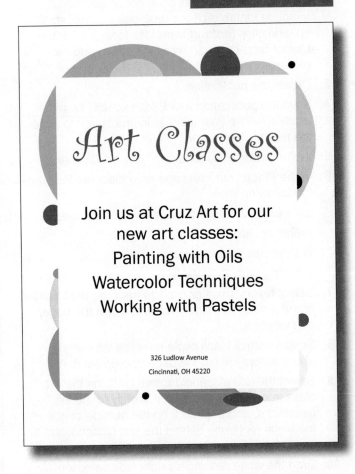

Figure 2-2

Lesson 3

Working with Text Boxes

➤ What You Will Learn

Placing a New Text Box
Controlling Automatic Copyfitting
Inserting Symbols
Checking Spelling
Using Research and Language Options

Software Skills   You can do a lot with the text boxes provided by Publisher's templates, but you may sometimes want to create your own text boxes to type in. You should always check your spelling to make sure you haven't made any mistakes. At times you may want to insert special typographical symbols that do not appear on your keyboard.

What You Can Do

Placing a New Text Box

- Create a new text box whenever you want to place a block of text in a spot where there is not already a text box.
- A text box can hold as much text as you want, so there is no need to create a separate text box for each paragraph; create a new box only when you want to separate one block of text from another.
- Use the Draw Text Box command in the Objects group on the HOME tab to create a new text box.

    ✓ You can also find this command on the INSERT tab.

WORDS TO KNOW

Story
The text in a text box plus any text boxes that are linked to it.

Symbol
Any character that is not a letter or number (such as # or @).

Try It!   Placing a New Text Box

1 Start Publisher and open **PB03Try** from the data files for this lesson.

2 Save the publication as **PB03Try_xx** in the location where your teacher instructs you to store the files for this lesson.

✓ *Don't worry about the typographical errors you see in this publication. You will correct them later in the lesson.*

3 Click HOME > Draw Text Box. The pointer changes to a crosshair.

4 Draw a text box as shown in the illustration at right to the left of the *Come out and get* text box in the center of the page. The text box should be about 2.5 inches wide and high (Your text box will not show a border unless it is selected.)

5 Type **This event benefits the Cutler College Women's Rugby Club** in the new text box.

6 Save the changes to **PB03Try_xx**, and leave it open to use in the next Try It.

Type text in the new text box

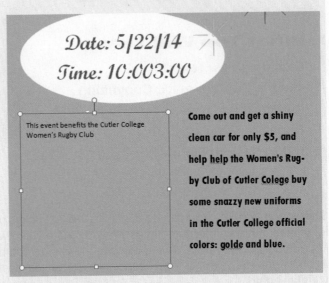

Controlling Automatic Copyfitting

- You will learn in Chapter 3 how to set a specific size for text, but you have additional options for controlling how text fits in a text box.

- You can allow Publisher to resize text automatically to fit in a text box, as long as the text box is not linked to any other text boxes.

- Use the Text Fit command in the Text group on the TEXT BOX TOOLS FORMAT tab to control automatic copyfitting.

- Select any of these options to turn on automatic copyfitting:
  - Use the Best Fit option to enlarge or reduce text size to fill the text box as you type. If you change the text box size, the text will adjust also.
  - Use the Shrink Text On Overflow option to reduce text size so that all text will fit in the box without overflowing it.
  - Use the Grow Text Box to Fit option to expand the text box to hold all the text without overflowing any.

- If you do not want to use automatic copyfitting, select the Do Not Autofit option on the Text Fit menu.

Try It!   **Controlling Automatic Copyfitting**

① In the **PB03Try_xx** file, click anywhere inside the new text box to select it. The TEXT BOX TOOLS FORMAT tab displays.

② Click TEXT BOX TOOLS FORMAT > Text Fit 🔲 > Best Fit to enlarge the text to fill the text box.

③ Click just to the left of the hyphenated word *Rugby* in the text box at the left and press SHIFT + ENTER to insert a line break. Repeat this process for any other hyphenated words.

> ✓ *You will learn in a later lesson how to control hyphenation in a publication.*

④ Save the changes to **PB03Try_xx**, and leave it open to use in the next Try It.

Fit the text to the text box size

This event benefits the Cutler College Women's Rugby Club

Come out and get a shiny clean car for only $5, and help help the Women's Rugby Club of Cutler Colege buy some snazzy new uniforms in the Cutler College official colors: golde and blue.

Inserting Symbols

- You can insert common **symbols** from the keyboard, but as you create more complex publications, you will need to insert many symbols that cannot be found on the keyboard, such as the em dash (—), the en dash (–), and the copyright symbol (©).

- You may also want to include decorative symbols such as diamonds, check marks, and arrows; math symbols; and language symbols such as é or ¿.

- Use the Symbol command in the Text group on the INSERT tab to display a gallery of recently used symbols. Use the More Symbols command to open the Symbol dialog box to find additional symbols.

Try It!   **Inserting Symbols**

① In the **PB03Try_xx** file, zoom to 100% if necessary.

② In the ellipse that gives date and time information, click between the numbers *10:00* and *3:00*.

③ Click INSERT > Symbol Ω > More Symbols. The Symbol dialog box opens.

④ Click the Special Characters tab in the Symbol dialog box.

⑤ Click En Dash and then click Insert and Close.

> ✓ *En dashes are typically used in ranges of numbers.*

⑥ Click in the *Location* text box following the word *Crafts*.

⑦ Click INSERT > Symbol Ω > More Symbols.

⑧ Scroll down until you see the trademark symbol (™), click the symbol, click Insert, and click Close.

⑨ Save the changes to **PB03Try_xx**, and leave it open to use in the next Try It.

Checking Spelling

- Publisher automatically checks your spelling as you type and marks any words that are not in its dictionary with a wavy red underline.

- To correct a red-underlined word, right-click it and choose the correct spelling from the shortcut menu.

- Not all red-underlined words are necessarily misspelled. Many proper names and brand names are erroneously marked as errors because they are not in Publisher's dictionary.

- If the correct spelling does not appear, you can correct the spelling manually, as you would edit any other text.

- You can also run a complete spelling check with Publisher's Check Spelling feature. Click Spelling in the Proofing group on the REVIEW tab to begin checking spelling.

- If the Check Spelling feature identifies a misspelled word, you may add it to the dictionary, ignore it, or correct it.

- A full spelling check looks for misspellings in the current **story**. You can check all stories in the entire publication by clicking in the Check all stories check box.

- If you have not marked the Check all stories check box, Publisher asks after checking the current story whether you want to check the rest of the publication.

- If you choose *Yes*, Publisher remembers your answer and does not ask again unless you clear the Check all stories check box when running the spell check. If you choose *No*, it re-asks each time you check spelling.

Try It!   **Checking Spelling**

1 In the **PB03Try_xx** file, right-click the word *Winford*, which is marked with a wavy red underline as a word Publisher does not recognize.

2 Click Ignore All on the shortcut menu.

3 Click REVIEW > Spelling ✓. Publisher indicates that it has finished checking the current story and asks to check the rest of the publication. Click Yes. The Check Spelling dialog box displays.

4 Click Delete to remove the repeated word, and click Change to correct *Colege*.

5 Select *gold* from the Suggestions list to correct *golde* and click Change.

6 Click OK.

7 Save the changes to **PB03Try_xx**, and leave it open to use in the next Try It.

Using Research and Language Options

- The REVIEW tab offers several additional commands that can be helpful as you are creating the text for a publication.

- Clicking the Research command opens the Research task pane at the right side of the window. You can use this task pane to look up information on a word or phrase using dictionaries or Internet search sites.

- Use the Thesaurus command to find synonyms for a selected word. Synonyms display in the Thesaurus task pane. Click an item to see words similar to that item. Use the drop-down arrow on a word to insert it in place of a selected word.

- Use the Translate Selected Text command to translate a selected word or phrase into any of over 20 languages. You have the option to select the language to translate into in the Research task pane. The translation then appears in that task pane.

Try It!   Using Research and Language Options

1 In the **PB03Try_xx** file, select the word *shiny* in the text box at the right side of the page.

2 Click **REVIEW** > Thesaurus 📖 .

3 Point to the word *sparkly* in the Research task pane to display a drop-down arrow to the right of the word.

✓ *If you click the word* sparkly *rather than the drop-down arrow, click the Back arrow above the word list to return to the previous list of synonyms.*

4 Click the drop-down arrow and click Insert.

5 If necessary, click between the word *sparkly* and the word *clean* and press SPACEBAR .

6 Close the publication, saving changes, and exit Publisher.

Lesson 3—Practice

You continue to work with the Geology Club's flyer. The club president has asked you to replace the Geology Club Meeting text box that you removed during an edit and has suggested that you add more explanation about the club's purpose and activities.

DIRECTIONS

1. Start Publisher, if necessary, and open **PB03Practice** from the data files for this lesson.

2. Save the file as **PB03Practice_xx** in the location where your teacher instructs you to store the files for this lesson.

3. Click **HOME** > **Draw Text Box** 🄰. Starting about 2.5 inches from the top of the page, draw a text box as wide as the existing text box and **2.5 inches** high.

4. Zoom in on the selected object and type the following text in the text box. Type the text exactly as it appears; you will correct errors later in this exercise.

Think geology is is boring? Think again! Come meet new friends and discover what the Geoloogy Club has planned for this semester, including

Geode hunts

Discovery expeditions

Merchandise giveaways from Cool Rockz

Fossil swaps

Rock polishing equipment demonstrations

A chance to attend the NGA convention as a degelate

5. Click after the word *Rockz*, click **INSERT** > **Symbol Ω** > **More Symbols**, and scroll down to locate the registered symbol (®).

✓ *If you see the registered symbol in the gallery of symbols after you click INSERT > Symbol, click it to insert it.*

6. Click the symbol to select it, click **Insert**, and click **Close**.

7. Right-click the word *Geloogy* and click **Geology** on the shortcut menu.

8. Right-click the word *Rockz* and click **Ignore All** to allow this spelling in this document only.

9. Click **REVIEW** > **Spelling**. Click **Change** to correct the spelling of *degelate*. Click **Delete** to remove the repeated word *is*.

10. Click **Yes** when asked if you want to check the rest of the document, and then click **OK** when the spelling check is complete.

11. **With your teacher's permission**, print the publication. It should look similar to Figure 3-1.

12. Close the publication, saving changes, and exit Publisher.

Figure 3-1

Think geology is boring? Think again! Come meet new friends and discover what the Geology Club has planned for this semester, including

Geode hunts

Discovery expeditions

Merchandise giveaways from Cool Rockz®

Fossil swaps

Rock polishing equipment demonstrations

A chance to attend the NGA convention as a delegate

Stevenson Hall, Room 212
February 22
12:30 p.m.
Free pizza and soft drinks

Lesson 3—Apply

In this exercise, you continue to work with the Geology Club announcement. You revise the publication by adding a new text box, modifying an existing text box, and editing text.

DIRECTIONS

1. Start Publisher, if necessary, and open **PB03Apply** from the data files for this lesson.

2. Save the file as **PB03Apply_xx** in the location where your teacher instructs you to store the files for this lesson.

3. Starting about 1 inch below the top of the page, draw a new text box the same width as the text boxes below and about **1 inch** high.

4. Type the text **Discover Geology!** in the new text box.

5. Apply the Best Fit text fitting option to this text box.

6. Position the insertion point following the word *delegate* in the last line of the second text box and press ⌷ENTER⌷ .

7. Insert an em dash symbol (—) from the Special Characters tab of the Symbol dialog box.

8. Without inserting a space following the dash, type **and much more!**

9. Resize the text box you are working in by dragging the bottom selection handle down close to the top of the third text box on the page.

10. Select the word *boring* in the second text box and use the Thesaurus to find a synonym for this word.

11. Change the text fitting option for the second text box on the page to **Best Fit**.

12. **With your teacher's permission**, print the document. It should look similar to Figure 3-2 on the next page.

13. Close the publication, saving changes, and exit Publisher.

Figure 3-2

Discover Geology!

Think geology is unexciting? Think again! Come meet new friends and
discover what the Geology Club has planned for this semester, including

Geode hunts

Discovery expeditions

Merchandise giveaways from Cool Rockz®

Fossil swaps

Rock polishing equipment demonstrations

A chance to attend the NGA convention as a delegate

—and much more!

Stevenson Hall, Room 212
February 22
12:30 p.m.
Free pizza and soft drinks

Lesson 4

Basic Text Handling

➤ What You Will Learn

Selecting Text
Deleting Text
Copying and Moving Text
Using Undo and Redo

Software Skills   As you work with text in publications, you will have need of basic text-handling skills such as selecting text. Editing a publication may require you to delete text, copy text, or move text to a new location. The Undo and Redo features can be invaluable in helping you to recover from undesired edits.

What You Can Do

Selecting Text

- **Selecting** text marks it so that whatever command you issue next affects it. For example, you might select a block of text and then issue the Copy command.
- You can select any amount of text, from a single character to the entire contents of a text box. Deselect by clicking outside the text box.
- You can select a single word (and the space after it) by double-clicking it, or a single paragraph by triple-clicking it.
- Or, drag across text using the I-beam text pointer to select text.
- Selected text appears in reverse colors. For example, if the text is normally black on white, it appears white on black when selected.
- When you select text, the Mini toolbar displays very faintly. You can use the Mini toolbar to make a variety of formatting changes to selected text.

  ✓ *You learn more about the Mini toolbar in Chapter 3.*

Deleting Text

- Delete individual text characters by placing the insertion point and then using BACKSPACE or DEL to remove characters to the left or right of the insertion point, respectively.
- To delete more than one character at a time, select the text you want to delete, and then press the DEL key.

WORDS TO KNOW

Clipboard
A temporary holding area used by Windows programs to move or copy text.

Redo
To reverse an Undo action.

Select
To highlight something (usually text or a frame) so that whatever command you issue applies to it.

Undo
To reverse an action or command.

Try It!   Selecting and Deleting Text

1 Start Publisher and open **PB04Try** from the data files for this lesson.

2 Save the publication as **PB04Try_xx** in the location where your teacher instructs you to store the files for this lesson.

3 Double-click the word *Art* in the heading placeholder to select it. Deselect the text.

4 Triple-click in the *Join us at Cruz Art* paragraph to select the entire paragraph.

5 Use the I-beam pointer to drag across the last item in the list of classes.

6 Press DEL.

7 Position the insertion point to the left of the *P* in *Pastels* and press BACKSPACE four times to remove the word *Oil* and a space.

8 Save the changes to **PB04Try_xx**, and leave it open to use in the next Try It.

Drag with the I-beam to select text

Join us at Cruz Art for our
new art classes:
Painting with Oils
Watercolor Techniques
Working with Pastels
Basic Drawing
Drawing with Pen & Ink

Copying and Moving Text

- You can use HOME tab commands or the mouse to move or copy text.

- You will find commands for moving and copying in the Clipboard group on the HOME tab.

  - Copy selected text by clicking the Copy button. This action places the copied text on the **Clipboard**, an area in computer memory where items are stored until you need them.

  - Use the Paste button to insert copied text at the location of the insertion point.

  - Move selected text by clicking the Cut button to remove text from the publication and store it on the Clipboard. To complete the move, position the insertion point and click the Paste button.

    ✓ *Unlike deleting, cutting text does not remove text permanently from the publication. Cut text resides on the Clipboard until you turn the computer off.*

- To use the mouse to move text, select it and then drag selected text to its new location. To copy text instead of moving it, hold down CTRL as you drag the selection to a new spot.

- When you paste a selection, you can click the Paste button's drop-down arrow to display paste options that control how the pasted text appears. These options vary depending on whether the text is being copied and pasted in the same publication or between different publications.

- Paste options also display at the lower-right corner of pasted text. Click the drop-down arrow to see the paste options available.

Using Undo and Redo

- **Undo** allows you to reverse the last action you took. Use the Undo button on the Quick Access Toolbar to undo the most recent action, or click the button's drop-down arrow to select a number of actions to undo.
- The **Redo** command, also on the Quick Access Toolbar, reverses an Undo action. You can redo as many actions as you have undone, as long as you have not done anything else in the interim. This command is not available if you have not undone anything.

Try It! Copying and Moving Text and Using Undo and Redo

1. In the **PB04Try_xx** file, select the *Basic Drawing* list item and drag it up just to the left of the word *Painting* in the first list item.
2. Select the *Painting with Oils* list item and click HOME > Copy.
3. Click to place the insertion point just to the left of *Watercolor Techniques*.
4. Click HOME > Paste. Then select the word *Oils* in the copied item and type **Acrylics**.
5. Click just to the left of the number *326* in the address box at the bottom of the page and press ENTER.
6. Select the words *Cruz Art* from the first paragraph in the text box and click HOME > Copy.
7. Click in the blank paragraph above the street address, and then click HOME > Paste. The pasted text fills the text box, causing text to overflow.
8. Click the Paste Options button (Ctrl) at the lower-right corner of the text box and note that the Keep Source Formatting option has been selected. Click the Paste option on the Paste Options gallery.
9. Click the Undo button in the Quick Access Toolbar to reverse the paste.
10. Click the Redo button to reverse the Undo.
11. Click the drop-down arrow on the Paste button, and then click Keep Text Only. The formatting of the copied text is removed.
12. Close the publication, saving changes, and exit Publisher.

Pasted text has same format as other text in the text box

Art Classes
Join us at Cruz Art for our new art classes:
Basic Drawing
Painting with Oils
Painting with Acrylics
Watercolor Techniques
Working with Pastels
Cruz Art
326 Ludlow Avenue
Cincinnati, OH 45220

Lesson 4—Practice

Vanessa Bradley, at Bradley & Cummins Realty, has asked you to work on a publication for a house she has just signed. In this exercise, you add text to the publication and then use the tools you learned about in this lesson to select, delete, move, and copy text to improve the publication.

DIRECTIONS

1. Start Publisher, if necessary, and open **PB04Practice** from the data files for this lesson.

2. Save the publication as **PB04Practice_xx** in the location where your teacher instructs you to store the files for this lesson.

3. Click the text box below the house that currently contains directions for describing the house. Type the following description:

   You can be the proud owner of this fabulous house, new this week on the market. Located in an area of well-cared-for older homes in the heart of historic Athens, this home has stayed in one family since it was built in 1896. Period details abound, from cherry woodwork to stained-glass windows.

4. Select the text in the heading, *Welcome to Your New Home!*

5. Click **HOME > Copy** 🗐.

6. Click at the end of the description text, press [SPACEBAR], and click **HOME > Paste** 📋.

7. Click the **Paste Options** button 📋 (Ctrl) ▾ near the lower-right corner of the text box and click **Keep Text Only**.

8. In the pasted text, select the capital letters in the words *Your New Home* and replace them with lowercase letters.

9. In the description text, select the words *in 1896* and press [DEL] . If you have a space between the word *built* and the period, press [BACKSPACE] to remove it.

10. In the description text, select the words *this week* in the first line and drag this text to follow the word *market* in the next line. Click between *market* and *this* and then press [SPACEBAR] . If there is an extra space between the word *week* and the period at the end of the sentence, position the insertion point to the left of the period and press [BACKSPACE] .

11. In the description text, select the text *in an area of well-cared-for older homes* and delete this text.

12. Click the **Undo** button ↶ on the Quick Access Toolbar.

13. Click the **Redo** button ↷ on the Quick Access Toolbar.

14. In the bulleted text, select the word *Excellent* in the second bullet item and delete the word.

15. Check and correct the spelling in the document, and then save the changes.

16. **With your teacher's permission**, print the publication. It should look similar to Figure 4-1 on the next page.

17. Close the publication, saving changes, and exit Publisher.

Figure 4-1

Welcome to Your New Home!

You can be the proud owner of this fabulous house, new on the market this week. Located in the heart of historic Athens, this home has stayed in one family since it was built. Period details abound, from cherry woodwork to stained-glass windows. Welcome to your new home!

$425,000

- Built in 1896
- Tudor exterior details
- New wiring
- 4 bedrooms

- 3 full baths
- 3 full stories
- Detached garage
- Lot 125 x 320

- Full stone basement
- 16 rooms
- 3 WB fireplaces

Bradley & Cummins Realty
Vanessa Bradley: 555 555 5555

2828 N. Court Street
Suite 3
Athens, OH 45701

Phone: 555-555-5555
Fax: 555-555-5555
E-mail: info@bradleycummins.com

Lesson 4—Apply

In this exercise, you continue working with the Bradley & Cummins flyer. You use text handling options to revise and finalize the flyer's text.

DIRECTIONS

1. Start Publisher, if necessary, and open **PB04Apply** from the data files for this lesson.

2. Save the file as **PB04Apply_xx** in the location where your teacher instructs you to store the files for this lesson.

3. In the heading text box, select the text *to Your New* and then delete this text.

4. Copy the bulleted text item *4 bedrooms* and paste it, keeping the words only, before the word *home* in the second sentence of the house description. Delete the letter *s* at the end of the pasted word *bedrooms*.

5. In the bulleted text area, select the *Lot* entry and drag it just to the left of *New wiring* to move the bullet item.

6. Move the *16 rooms* item before the *4 bedrooms* item.

7. Move the *Detached garage* item to follow the *Lot* item, then Undo this change.

8. Select Vanessa Bradley's phone number (at the lower-left corner of the page) and type **740-555-1212**.

9. Select the phone number in the lower-right corner text box and type **740-555-1200**.

   ✓ *You may want to zoom to the selected object to make it easier to type the phone number.*

10. Copy this phone number and paste it in place of the default Fax number, and then change the last digit to **1**.

11. **With your teacher's permission**, print the publication. It should look similar to Figure 4-2 on the next page.

12. Close the publication, saving changes, and exit Publisher.

Figure 4-2

Welcome Home!

You can be the proud owner of this fabulous house, new on the market this week. Located in the heart of historic Athens, this 4 bedroom home has stayed in one family since it was built. Period details abound, from cherry woodwork to stained-glass windows. Welcome to your new home!

$425,000

- Built in 1896
- Tudor exterior details
- Lot 125 x 320
- New wiring

- 16 rooms
- 4 bedrooms
- 3 full baths
- 3 full stories

- Detached garage
- Full stone basement
- 3 WB fireplaces

Bradley & Cummins Realty
Vanessa Bradley: 740-555-1212

2828 N. Court Street
Suite 3
Athens, OH 45701

Phone: 740-555-1200
Fax: 740-555-1201
E-mail: info@bradleycummins.com

Lesson 5

Working with Business Information

➤ What You Will Learn

Creating a Business Information Set
Editing and Inserting Business Information
Inserting the Current Date and Time
Using AutoCorrect

WORDS TO KNOW

AutoCorrect
A program feature that attempts to "guess" your intentions for typing and formatting and applies a change automatically.

Business information set
Stored information about yourself, your job, your company, and how to contact you.

Date code
A code placed in the publication that automatically inserts the current date from your computer's clock whenever the publication is saved or printed.

Time code
Same as the date code, except it shows the current time.

Software Skills You may find yourself typing the same information, such as your name and address, the current date, or your company's name or motto, over and over in different publications. You can save time by inserting such boilerplate text automatically. You will also learn how to save time correcting typing mistakes with the AutoCorrect feature.

What You Can Do

Creating a Business Information Set

- Publisher maintains contact information in **business information sets**. You can create as many different sets as you like, and use them to quickly insert contact information in each publication you create.

- Some publication templates have placeholders for business information predefined; you can also insert pieces of information manually into any publication.

- You can choose to create a new business information set when you start a new publication, or you can create the business information set later by editing the current information from Backstage view.

- Only one set can be associated with the publication at a time. To change that set, select the set to change to and then click Update Publication.

Try It!   **Creating a Business Information Set**

1 Start Publisher and open **PB05Try** from the data files for this lesson.

2 Save the publication as **PB05Try_xx** in the location where your teacher instructs you to store the files for this lesson.

3 Click the FILE tab to display the Info page for the current publication.

4 Click Edit Business Information 🖼 and then click the Edit button if necessary to open the Edit Business Information Set dialog box.

5 Type the following information in the dialog box.

Individual name: **Vanessa Bradley**

Job position or title: **Senior Consultant**

Organization name:
Bradley & Cummins Realty

Address:
**2828 N. Court Street
Suite 3
Athens, OH 45701**

Phone, fax, and e-mail:
**Phone: 740-555-1200
Fax: 740-555-1201
E-mail: info@bradleycummins.com**

6 Type the set name **BradleyCummins** and click Save. Click Update Publication.

7 Click the ⬅ button to see the publication updated with the new business information.

8 Save the changes to **PB05Try_xx**, and leave it open to use in the next Try It.

Business information has been
added to the publication

Bradley & Cummins Realty

2828 N. Court Street
Suite 3
Athens, OH 45701

Phone: 740-555-1200
Fax: 740-555-1201
E-mail: info@bradleycummins.com

Business Tagline or Motto

Editing and Inserting Business Information

- You can edit business information at any time using the Edit Business Information button on the Info tab in Backstage view.

- You can also choose to edit business information by clicking the Business Information command on the INSERT tab and selecting Edit Business Information.

- Some templates insert business information automatically for you in certain spots in the publication. You can choose to insert additional business information from the set if there is not a placeholder for it.

- Click an item of information on the Business Information gallery to add it to the publication.

- If you no longer need a business information set, you can delete it in the Business Information dialog box. The information in the document remains the same, but you no longer have access to the information fields for the set you deleted.

Try It!   Editing and Inserting Business Information

1 In the **PB05Try_xx** file, click INSERT > Business Information 🖼 > Edit Business Information.

2 Click the Edit button.

3 Select the text in the Tagline or motto box and type **Home Is Where the Heart Is**.

4 Click Save and then click Update Publication.

5 Click INSERT > Business Information 🖼, click the Individual name field, and drag the inserted field to the right side of the business information box and then position precisely: Click the Object Position icon ▣ to display the Measurement toolbar and type **4** in the X box and **7.9** in the Y box.

6 Click INSERT > Business Information 🖼, click the Job position or title field, and drag the inserted field just beneath the *Vanessa Bradley* object. In the Measurement toolbar, type **4** in the X box and **8.1** in the Y box.

7 Save the changes to **PB05Try_xx**, and leave it open to use in the next Try It.

Edited business information

Bradley & Cummins Realty

2828 N. Court Street
Suite 3
Athens, OH 45701

Phone: 740-555-1200
Fax: 740-555-1201
E-mail: info@bradleycumminse.com

Vanessa Bradley
Senior Consultant

Home Is Where the Heart Is

Inserting the Current Date and Time

- You can choose to insert the current date and time in your publication to let readers know when it was created or updated. Use the Date & Time command in the Text group on the INSERT tab to add the date and/or time to a publication.

- The date or time you insert is current as of the computer's clock at the moment you insert it. If you want the date to be updated each time the publication is saved or printed, make sure you mark the Update automatically check box in the Date and Time dialog box. When this box is checked, Publisher places a **date code** or **time code** in the document.

- You can choose from among many date/time formats from many countries. The default is English (U.S.), but you can select any language.

Try It!   Inserting the Current Date and Time

1 In the **PB05Try_xx** file, click INSERT > Draw Text Box 🅰 and use the crosshair pointer to draw a text box about 2 inches wide and as tall as the white stripe below the black *New Listing* border at the top of the page.

2 Position the text box so its right edge aligns with the right margin guide.

3 Click INSERT > Date & Time 🖼. Click the format that inserts the date and time similar to 11/9/2014 12:46 PM.

4 Save the changes to **PB05Try_xx**, and leave it open to use in the next Try It.

Using AutoCorrect

- **AutoCorrect** is a feature that maintains a list of commonly misspelled words; whenever you make one of the misspellings, it automatically fixes the error.

- AutoCorrect works automatically; you do not need to do anything special to enable it.

- When AutoCorrect makes a correction, a small blue minus sign appears below the corrected text when your mouse pointer is over it.

- When you point to that minus sign, an AutoCorrect Options button ⬛ ▾ appears. You can click on that button to open a menu, from which you can choose how you want this and other similar situations to be handled.

- You can add your own entries to the AutoCorrect list of words you commonly misspell. You display the AutoCorrect dialog box by clicking AutoCorrect Options in the Publisher Options dialog box.

- You can also use the AutoCorrect list to insert shortcuts for text you type frequently. When you type the shortcut, AutoCorrect replaces the shortcut with the full word or phrase.

- Delete an AutoCorrect entry by selecting it and clicking Delete in the AutoCorrect dialog box.

Try It!   **Using AutoCorrect**

1 In the **PB05Try_xx** file, click FILE > Options to open the Publisher Options dialog box.

2 Click Proofing in the left pane and then click AutoCorrect Options in the main pane.

3 Click in the Replace box and type **bnc**. Then click in the With box and type **Bradley & Cummins**.

4 Click Add, and then click OK twice.

5 In the house description above the picture, select the word *Charming* and then type this replacement text: **bnc presents a charming**. AutoCorrect should replace the *bnc* text with the Bradley & Cummins company name.

6 Click FILE > Options, click Proofing, and click AutoCorrect Options. Scroll down in the AutoCorrect list to locate the *bnc* entry. Select it and then click Delete. Click OK twice.

7 Click INSERT > Business Information ⬛ > Edit Business Information. If necessary, click BradleyCummins from the Select a Business Information set drop-down list, and then click Delete.

8 Click Yes to confirm, and then click Close.

9 Close the publication, saving changes, and exit Publisher.

Lesson 5—Practice

The Geology Club at Cutler College has asked you to be their official publication designer. To prepare for this responsibility, you create a business information set for the club and modify Publisher's AutoCorrect settings. You also start a new flyer that will be handed out at the club's first meeting and insert some of the data from the personal information set on it, along with the current date and time.

DIRECTIONS

1. Start Publisher, if necessary. In Backstage view, click BUILT-IN and then click the **Flyers** category. Click the **All Event** folder, scroll down to the More Installed Templates section, and click the **Axis** template in the first row of Informational templates.

2. Customize the flyer as follows:

   a. Click the **Color scheme** drop-down arrow and select **Concourse**.

   b. Click the **Font scheme** drop-down arrow and select **Basis**.

   c. Click the **Business information** drop-down arrow and click **Create new . . .**

3. Insert the following business information in the Create New Business Information Set dialog box:

   Individual name: **Sue Murphy**

   Job position or title: **President**

   Organization name: **Cutler College**

   Address:
   Geology Club
   202 Stevenson Hall
   34881 Langley Street
   Cutler, IL 62550

   Phone, fax, and e-mail:
   Phone: 217-555-7640
   Fax: 217-555-7641
   E-mail: suemurphy@cutlercollege.edu

   Tagline or motto: **We rock!**

   Logo: No logo

   Business set name: **SueMurphy**

4. After you finish typing the business set name, click **Save**, and then click **Create**.

5. Save the publication as **PB05Practice_xx** in the location where your teacher instructs you to store the files for this lesson.

6. Click in the center of the page to select a picture box. Click DEL to delete it.

7. Click the sample text object and drag it straight up to where the picture box was. (See Figure 5-1.)

8. Click INSERT > **Draw Text Box** and use the crosshair pointer to draw a new text box in the lower-right corner of the page, where the right and bottom margin guides intersect. The text box should be about **1.5 inches** wide and **0.5 inch** high.

9. Type **Last update:** and then press SPACEBAR.

10. Click INSERT > **Date & Time**, select the first date format in the Available formats list, click **Update automatically**, and click **OK**.

11. Click FILE > **Options**, click **Proofing**, and click **AutoCorrect Options**.

12. Click in the Replace box and type **gelogy**. Click in the With box and type **geology**.

13. Click **Add**, and then click **OK** twice.

14. Select the title placeholder text (*Product/Service Information*) and type **Gelogy Club**.

    ✓ *Be sure to type the word Gelogy to see AutoCorrect fix the error.*

15. Click the placeholder in the center of the page and type the following text just as shown:

    Gelogy Club news and information goes in this space. Adjust text size and expand the text box as necessary to fit information.

16. With the insertion point still in this text box, click **TEXT BOX TOOLS FORMAT** > **Text Fit** > **Best Fit**.

17. **With your teacher's permission**, print the publication. It should look similar to Figure 5-1 on the next page.

18. Close the publication, saving changes, and exit Publisher.

Figure 5-1

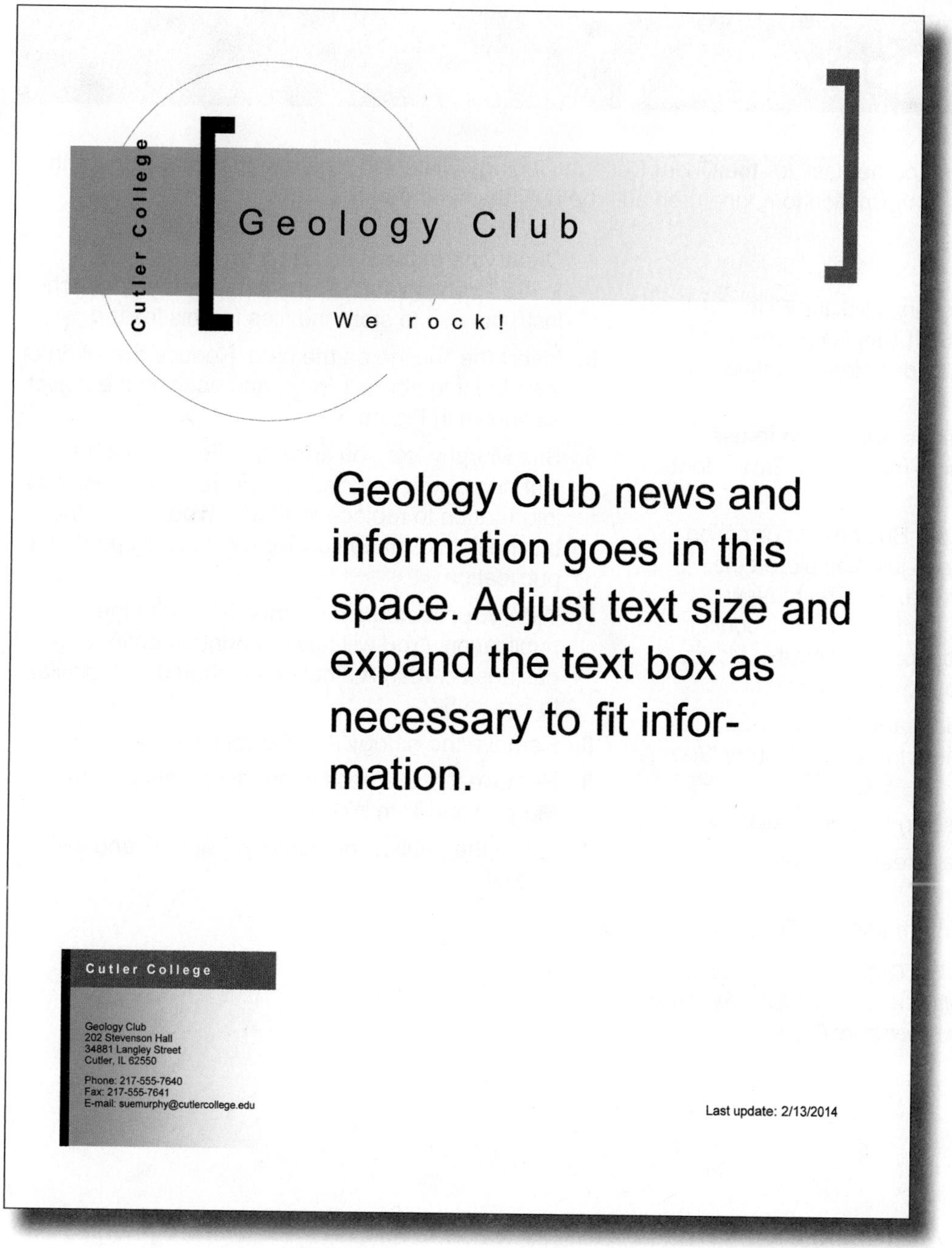

Cutler College

Geology Club

We rock!

Geology Club news and information goes in this space. Adjust text size and expand the text box as necessary to fit information.

Cutler College

Geology Club
202 Stevenson Hall
34881 Langley Street
Cutler, IL 62550

Phone: 217-555-7640
Fax: 217-555-7641
E-mail: suemurphy@cutlercollege.edu

Last update: 2/13/2014

Lesson 5—Apply

In this exercise, you perform another task for the Cutler College Geology Club. You create a business card for the vice-president, add business information to it, and then edit the business information.

DIRECTIONS

1. Start Publisher, if necessary, click the **Business Cards** category in the BUILT-IN templates, and click the **Axis** template under More Installed Templates.

2. If necessary, customize the publication to use the **Concourse** color scheme and the **Basis** font scheme.

3. Click **Create new…** in the Business information drop-down list. If you have just completed the Lesson 5 Practice exercise, the Create New Business Information Set dialog box will contain the business information for Sue Murphy. Modify this information as follows:

   a. Change the Individual name to **Tom Wolf**. (You will need to delete the existing entry, *Sue Murphy*.)

   b. Change the Job position to **Vice-President**.

   c. Change the e-mail address to **tomwolf@ cutlercollege.edu**.

   d. Save the business information as **TomWolf**.

   ✓ *If you do not see the Geology Club business information when you open the Create New Business Information dialog box, enter the information given in the Practice exercise.*

4. Create the publication and then save it as **PB05Apply_xx** in the location where your teacher instructs you to store the files for this lesson.

5. Insert the Tagline on the card. Reduce the width of the object to about **1 inch**, and position the object as shown in Figure 5-2.

6. Sue Murphy lets you know that Tom spells his last name with two o's. Edit the TomWolf business information to replace *Wolf* with *Woolf*. Save the business information as TomWoolf and update the publication.

7. **With your teacher's permission**, print the publication. (You will have to print an entire page of business cards.) A single card should look similar to Figure 5-2.

8. Remove the *gelogy* AutoCorrect entry.

9. Remove the business information sets for Sue Murphy and Tom Woolf.

10. Close the publication, saving changes, and exit Publisher.

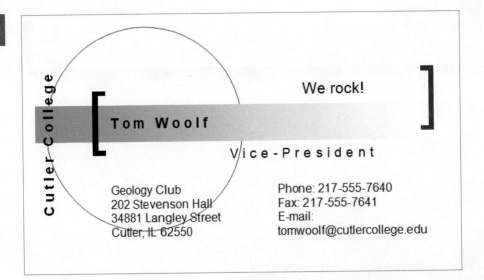

Figure 5-2

Lesson 6

Working with Text from Other Applications

➤ What You Will Learn

Opening a File from Another Program
Opening a Word Document
Inserting Text from Other Programs
Customizing the Ribbon
Editing a Story in Word

Software Skills   Sometimes you may want to include text in a publication that has already been typed in another program. You can either open a file created in another program (and save it as a new publication), or insert a text file from another program as a story in your existing publication. In addition, Publisher allows you to apply templates to imported Word documents.

What You Can Do

Opening a File from Another Program

■ Publisher can open files of several types. Besides its native format (.pub), it can also open Microsoft Word files (.docx), Web files (.htm and .mht), and plain text files (.txt), among others.

■ When you open a document from another program, Publisher converts the document content to a Publisher publication.

■ The imported document will likely need some formatting work to resemble the original; you will learn about text formatting in Chapter 3. You may find that the document will retain some of the functionality of its original source; for example, an imported Web page can be viewed in a browser and will retain its hyperlink functionality.

WORDS TO KNOW

Autoflow
A feature that allows a story to continue into linked text boxes when the original text box is too small to hold it.

Import
To bring something in (e.g., text or a graphic) from another program or format.

Overflow
Text that does not fit in a text box; Publisher automatically creates additional pages and text boxes to display the overflow text.

Try It!   **Opening a File from Another Program**

1   Start Publisher and open **PB06TryA.mht** from the data files for this lesson. Publisher converts the single-file Web document to a publication.

2   Click FILE > Share > Email Preview, and then click Email Preview to see the publication in your browser.

3   Click the link *About Barkley*. This is a dummy link that will open the Office.com Web page.

4   Close the browser.

5   Save the document as **PB06TryA_xx** in the location where your teacher instructs you to store the files for this lesson, and then close the publication. Leave Publisher open for the next Try It.

Opening a Word Document

- If the document you want to open is a Word file, you can **import** the file using the Import Word Documents option among the BUILT-IN templates.

- After selecting this option, you can choose a template to apply to the Word document, as well as choose to customize the template with a new color scheme and font scheme. You can also choose page size, include a title page, and specify number of columns for the imported text.

- After clicking Create, you select the document to open and Publisher converts it, applying the formats you chose.

- If the document is too long to fit on a single page, multiple pages are created, each with a single text box, and the document text flows automatically (using **autoflow**) from box to box via text box links.

✓ *You learn more about linking text boxes in Chapter 2.*

Try It!   **Opening a Word Document**

1   In Backstage view in Publisher, click BUILT-IN > Import Word Documents.

2   Click the Layers template.

3   Click the Color scheme drop-down arrow and select Civic.

4   Click the Page size drop-down arrow and click One-sided portrait.

5   Click Create.

6   In the Import Word Document dialog box, navigate to the data files for this lesson and click **PB06TryB.docx**.

7   Click OK. Publisher converts the document and displays it as a new publication.

8   Click on each page in the Page Navigation pane to see the content in the publication area.

9   Save the publication as **PB06TryB_xx** in the location where your teacher instructs you to store the files for this lesson, and then close it. Leave Publisher open to use in the next Try It.

Inserting Text from Other Programs

- You may prefer to insert the contents of a text file as a story within an existing publication rather than placing it in its own new publication.

- You can insert text in a text box using the Insert File command in the Text group on the INSERT tab to locate the file you want to insert.

- If the imported text is too lengthy to fit in the text box, the text **overflows** the text box. Publisher automatically creates the necessary pages and text boxes to display all the text. Additional text boxes are linked to the first text box so that text flows from text box to text box.

- You can then adjust text box size after the text has been placed in the text boxes.

- The Insert File command will insert only text files. If you want to include material such as an Excel chart, you have to use Copy and Paste. The pasted object appears in its own container rather than the currently selected text box.

Try It!   **Inserting Text from Other Programs**

1 Open **PB06TryC** from the data files for this lesson and then save the file as **PB06TryC_xx** in the location where your teacher instructs you to store the files for this lesson.

2 Click INSERT > Draw Text Box 🄰 and use the crosshair pointer to draw a text box beneath the heading, as wide as the heading and about 2 inches high.

3 Click INSERT > Insert File 📄 and navigate to the location where the data files for this lesson are stored.

4 Click **PB06TryD.docx** and then click OK. The imported text fills up the text box you created, and Publisher adds a page and a text box to display the overflow text.

　✓ *The Next ▶ and Previous ◀ arrow pointers attached to the text boxes allow you to quickly jump from one text box to another to work with the text.*

5 Click page 1 in the Page Navigation pane, click the text box that contains the inserted text, and drag the bottom selection handle down to just above the computer graphic.

6 Click the Next arrow pointer attached to the text box to display the text box on page 2. Press DEL to remove the empty text box. Then click PAGE DESIGN > Delete 🗙 in the Pages group to remove the blank page.

7 Save the changes to **PB06TryC_xx**, and leave it open to use in the next Try It.

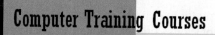

Text has been imported into the text box

Computer Training Courses

Do you need to create documents such as letters and reports? How about presentations for meetings and marketing opportunities? Has someone asked you recently to "crunch some numbers" in a spreadsheet, and you don't have any idea what that means? Do you look blank when your boss mentions putting together a client database?

Hopkins Technical Services specializes in training courses for those who have little or no previous computer experience but must be computer-literate for their jobs. If you find yourself answering any of the above questions with "Yes!" then Hopkins can help you. We start from the ground up with an introduction to the hardware and proceed to hands-on training in the most widely used business software applications.

Software applications include Microsoft Office Word 2013, Microsoft Office Excel 2013, Microsoft Office Access 2013, Microsoft Office PowerPoint 2013.

Master your computer—don't let your computer master you!

11580 Montgomery Road
Montgomery, OH 45242

Phone: 555-555-5555
Fax: 555-555-5555
E-mail: someone@example.com

Customizing the Ribbon

- You can customize the Ribbon by adding commands you use frequently or removing commands you rarely use.

- You can create new groups on a Ribbon tab to hold commands you select, and you can even create a completely new tab with new groups.

- You use the Customize Ribbon tab of the Publisher Options dialog box to create new tabs or groups and add commands to them.

Try It!   Customizing the Ribbon

1 In the **PB06TryC_xx** file, click FILE > Options to open the Publisher Options dialog box.

2 Click Customize Ribbon in the left pane to display the Customize the Ribbon settings.

3 On the right side of the dialog box, in the list of Main Tabs, click Review and then click the New Group button below the list.

4 Click the Rename button and type the display name **Editing**. Click OK.

5 Near the left side of the dialog box, click the Choose commands from drop-down arrow and click All Commands.

6 Scroll down to locate the Edit Story in Microsoft Word command, select the command, click Add, and then click OK.

7 Save the changes to **PB06TryC_xx**, and leave the publication open for the next Try It.

Editing a Story in Word

- You may prefer to edit text in Microsoft Word because of Word's superior editing capabilities. For example, Word includes a grammar checker and many other features that Publisher does not.

- When you edit in Word, the entire story appears there (that is, the current text box and all the text from any linked text boxes). Save your changes and close the document to see your edits in Publisher.

- The Edit Story in Microsoft Word command does not appear on any Ribbon tab by default. You can take advantage of Publisher's ability to customize the Ribbon to make this command available.

Try It!   Editing a Story in Word

1 In the **PB06TryC_xx** file, click in the text box and then click REVIEW > Edit Story in Microsoft Word to open the story in Word.

   ✓ *If the command is grayed out, click the text box to select it. The command should then be available.*

2 At the end of the third paragraph, click to the left of the period and type **, and Microsoft Office Publisher 2013**.

3 Click FILE > Save and then close the document and Word. Notice the story has been updated in Publisher.

4 With the insertion point still in the text box, click TEXT BOX TOOLS FORMAT > Text Fit 🔲 > Best Fit.

5 Close the publication, saving changes, and exit Publisher.

Lesson 6—Practice

Sue Murphy, president of the Geology Club, has typed some text she wants you to put on the flyer you began in the preceding lesson. She has provided it to you in Microsoft Word format. In this exercise, you import that file into the publication.

DIRECTIONS

1. Start Publisher, if necessary, and open **PB06PracticeA** from the data files for this lesson.

2. Save the publication as **PB06PracticeA_xx** in the location where your teacher instructs you to store the files for this lesson.

3. In the Last update text box, insert the current date.

4. Click in the text box in the center of the page and select the text.

5. Click **INSERT** > **Insert File** 🗐.

6. Navigate to the location where data files are stored for this lesson, click **PB06PracticeB.docx**, and click **OK**.

7. Click **REVIEW** > **Edit Story in Word**.

8. Select the text in the first line, *Spring Semester Calendar of Events*, and then click **HOME** > **Bold B** in the Font group.

9. Select *April 21* and type **April 23**.

10. Click **FILE** > **Save** and then close the file and exit Word.

11. With the text box still selected, click the bottom selection handle and drag the text box border down until it aligns with the top of the *Cutler College* text box.

12. **With your teacher's permission**, print the publication. It should look similar to Figure 6-1 on the next page.

13. Close the publication, saving changes, and exit Publisher.

Figure 6-1

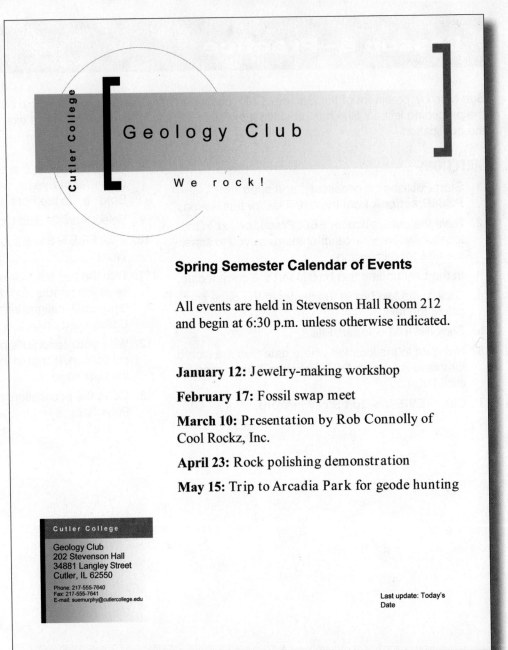

Cutler College

Geology Club

We rock!

Spring Semester Calendar of Events

All events are held in Stevenson Hall Room 212 and begin at 6:30 p.m. unless otherwise indicated.

January 12: Jewelry-making workshop

February 17: Fossil swap meet

March 10: Presentation by Rob Connolly of Cool Rockz, Inc.

April 23: Rock polishing demonstration

May 15: Trip to Arcadia Park for geode hunting

Cutler College

Geology Club
202 Stevenson Hall
34881 Langley Street
Cutler, IL 62550

Phone: 217-555-7640
Fax: 217-555-7641
E-mail: suemurphy@cutlercollege.edu

Last update: Today's Date

Lesson 6—Apply

Sue Murphy wants you to send a letter to Geology Club members. She has created the text in Word. In this exercise, you import the text into Publisher and then edit it in Word.

DIRECTIONS

1. Start Publisher, if necessary, click **BUILT-IN**, click the **Import Word Documents** category, and click the **Axis** template under Installed Templates.

2. If necessary, customize the publication to use the **Concourse** color scheme and the **Basis** font scheme.

3. Select the **One-sided portrait** page size and click **Create**.

4. Navigate to the location where data files are stored for this lesson and open **PB06Apply.docx**.

5. Save the publication as **PB06Apply_xx** in the location where your teacher instructs you to store the files for this lesson.

6. Select the *Document Title* text box at the top of the page and delete it.

7. Select the text box that contains the body of the letter. Choose to edit the story in Word and make these changes:

   a. Delete all the blank paragraphs above the date and the blank paragraphs below Sue Murphy's title.

   b. Remove two blank paragraphs below the date.

   c. Change the date of the rock polishing demonstration to **April 23**.

8. Save changes, close the story, and return to Publisher.

9. Resize the text box containing the letter so the top of the text box is 2 inches from the top edge of the page, the left and right sides are 1 inch from the left and right edges of the page, and the bottom of the text box is 2 inches from the bottom of the page.

10. Delete the unnecessary text box on page 2, and click **PAGE DESIGN** > **Delete** ⟨x⟩ to remove the blank page. Click **Yes** when asked if you want to delete the page.

11. Use Best Fit to increase the text size on page 1.

12. **With your teacher's permission**, print the publication.

13. Close the publication, saving changes, and exit Publisher.

End-of-Chapter Activities

➤ Publisher Chapter 1—Critical Thinking

Making Business Communications More Accurate

Vanessa Bradley, Senior Consultant at Bradley & Cummins, has noticed recently that written communications at the Realty have suffered from some inaccuracies in word choice. She has also noticed that annoying phrases such as "you know" and "like" are creeping into verbal communications with clients. She has asked you to prepare some small posters to remind agents and other staff that business communications should be as accurate and pleasant as possible.

In this project, you will research words that are often misused—such as "alright" instead of "all right"—as well as words and phrases that are considered to be annoying or otherwise troublesome. You will prepare two posters, one for a misused word and one for an annoying phrase.

DIRECTIONS

1. **With your teacher's permission**, search the Web for information about words that are commonly used incorrectly in place of other words. Write down one example, with an explanation of how the word should be correctly used. If your word is frequently used in place of another word or words, include all the misused words and their definitions.

2. Perform a second search to find information on words and phrases that most people find annoying in conversation. Write down one example, with an explanation of why this particular phrase is considered to be unnecessary or irritating.

3. Start Publisher and select a template for the first poster (the misused word poster). Choose a quick publication template that will catch the eye.

4. Select a color scheme that will stand out from a distance and, if desired, select a different font scheme. Choose the layout option with no picture.

5. Create the publication and save it as **PBCT01A_xx** in the location where your teacher instructs you to store the files for this chapter.

6. In the heading placeholder, insert the word or words that are misused.

7. In the message area, insert explanations of what each word means, so that it will be clear to viewers how the words should actually be used.

8. Edit the explanation text in Word, making any adjustment to alignment or spacing that you think will better present the information. Illustration 1A on the next page shows an example.

9. **With your teacher's permission**, print the publication.

10. Create a new publication using the same template, with a different color scheme and font scheme. Use the same layout option to display the heading and message area, but no picture.

11. Save the publication as **PBCT01B_xx** in the location where your teacher instructs you to store files for this chapter.

12. Insert the annoying word or phrase as the heading in the new publication.

13. In the message area, insert the explanation of why the phrase might be grating or troublesome.

14. Check the spelling and grammar in the document and correct errors as necessary.

15. **With your teacher's permission**, print the publication.

16. Close the publication, saving changes, and exit Publisher.

their, there, they're

their—belonging to them; "give them *their* keys"

there—in a place; "meet them *there*"

they're—contraction of they are; "*they're* meeting you at the house"

➤ Publisher Chapter 1—Portfolio Builder

Foster Home Flyer

Pet Rescue, a local charity, is looking for volunteers to provide foster homes for dogs and cats while they await permanent homes. You have been asked to create a flyer that explains the responsibilities and rewards of the job, to be handed out at events animal-lovers are likely to attend.

DIRECTIONS

1. Start Publisher, if necessary, and begin a new quick publication based on the Bars template.

   a. Use a color scheme of your choice.

   b. Use the **Basis** font scheme.

   c. For the Layout, choose **No picture**.

   d. Create a new business information set as follows:

   Individual name: **Rashelle James**

   Job or position title: **Volunteer Coordinator**

   Organization name: **Pet Rescue**

   Address: **2077 W. 166th Street**
   Indianapolis, IN 46240

   Phone/fax/e-mail:
   Phone: **212-555-9191**
   Fax: **212-555-9089**
   E-mail: **rjames@petrescueindy.org**

   Tag line or motto:
   Loving and Caring for Companion Animals

   Save as: **PetRescue**

2. Create the publication and save it as **PBPB01_xx** in the location where your teacher instructs you to store the files for this chapter.

3. Replace the *Heading* placeholder with **Pet Foster Homes Needed!**

   ✓ *If the heading text fills the placeholder without autofitting, click Text Fit > Do Not Autofit, and then click Text Fit > Best Fit.*

4. Drag the heading text box toward the top of the page, and then drag the bottom border of the heading text box up, making the text box shorter so that the text occupies only two lines, as in Illustration 1B, shown on the next page. The text box should be about 2 inches tall.

5. Resize the message frame as shown in Illustration 1B and type the following text:

   Pet Rescue has dozens of cats and dogs who need temporary homes while we are finding them permanent ones. Foster "parents" receive a weekly pet care stipend and are eligible for monthly drawings and prizes.

   If you would like more information about the foster care program, please contact Rashelle James at (212) 555-9191.

   ✓ *If the area code is separated from the phone number on the last two lines in the text box, click to the left of* (212) *and press* SHIFT + ENTER *to insert a line break*

6. At the bottom of the page, insert a new text box 0.4 inches tall and the full width of the page between the margin guides. Set the Text Fit to Shrink Text On Overflow. Insert the organization name, address, and phone/fax/e-mail information from the business information set.

7. Delete any line breaks so all the information is on one line. Delete the Fax information, and separate the pieces of information with a round circle from the Symbol font, as in Illustration 1B.

8. Choose to edit the message story in Word. Delete the text *and are eligible for monthly drawings and prizes.*

9. Check the spelling for the entire publication.

10. Zoom out to Whole Page view and examine your work. Make any changes to the positions of text boxes if needed for a more attractive layout.

11. **With your instructor's permission**, print the publication. Your publication should look similar to Illustration 1B on the next page.

12. Open the Publisher Options dialog box and choose to customize the Ribbon. Expand the Review tab under Main Tabs, and then expand the Editing group.

13. Remove the Edit Story in Microsoft Word command and then remove the Editing group.

14. Delete the PetRescue business information set.

15. Close the publication, saving changes, and exit Publisher.

Illustration 1B

Pet Foster Homes Needed!

Pet Rescue has dozens of cats and dogs who need temporary homes while we are finding them permanent ones. Foster "parents" receive a weekly pet care stipend.

If you would like more information about the foster care program, please contact Rashelle James at (212) 555-9191.

Pet Rescue • 2077 W. 166th Street Indianapolis, IN 46240 • Phone: 212-555-9191 • E-mail: rjames@petrescueindy.org

Chapter 2

(Courtesy Yuri Arcurs/Shutterstock)

Changing the Design and Layout

Lesson 7

Customizing Template Elements

> ## What You Will Learn

Changing the Design and Layout
Applying a Different Color Scheme
Creating a New Color Scheme
Applying a Different Font Scheme
Creating a New Font Scheme
Deleting Custom Schemes

WORDS TO KNOW

Design
The appearance theme of the publication.

Layout
The arrangement of placeholder elements on the page (such as Heading, Picture, and Message).

Software Skills   As you work on a publication, you may decide that it would look better with a different design, or you may want colors or fonts that you cannot find in the default color and font schemes. You can customize both color and font schemes to suit your needs.

What You Can Do

Changing the Design and Layout

- Even blank publications have a **design**. (They have a design called Blank.) There are dozens of designs available to choose from in Publisher. Each design is represented by a template.

- You can apply any design to a publication, at any time. Changing the design does not change any text in the publication; it merely arranges items differently and places different background graphics.

- Use the Change Template command in the Template group on the PAGE DESIGN tab to apply a different design.

- The Change Template dialog box looks similar to the Backstage view of available templates you use to create a new publication.

- You have the same options to select a template, a color scheme, and a font scheme. Depending on the template chosen, you may have other options to select from, such as **layout**, page size, tear-offs, and so on.

- The layout specifies which placeholder elements will appear (picture, heading, sidebar heading, message, and so forth) and where each will be placed.

  ✓ *If you just want to change the color scheme or font scheme, you can select from the Schemes options on the PAGE DESIGN tab rather than open the Change Template dialog box.*

- After you change the publication design, some of your content might have shifted; rearrange objects if needed.

- If you change to a template that does not contain the same placeholders as the current publication, Publisher will not be able to place the current content in the new placeholders. Publisher displays the Extra Content task pane (Figure 7-1) to indicate what content does not appear in the new template. Use this task pane to reinsert the missing objects.

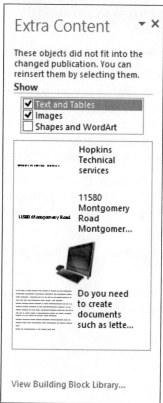

Figure 7-1

Try It!　　**Changing the Design and Layout**

1. Start Publisher and open **PB07Try** from the data files for this lesson.

2. Save the publication as **PB07Try_xx** in the location where your teacher instructs you to store the files for this lesson.

3. Click PAGE DESIGN > Change Template.

4. Click the Brocade template in the first row of installed templates.

5. Click the Layout drop-down arrow and select Large picture at top, if necessary.

  ✓ *Make sure the color scheme and font scheme are both set to default options.*

6. Click OK, then click Apply template to the current publication, and click OK. The Extra Content task pane opens to show content that has not automatically been placed in the new design.

7. Move the *6600 Jefferson Pike* text box up into the light-gray shaded rectangle at the top of the page. Reduce the height of the text box to about the same height as the light-gray rectangle.

8. Move the mouse pointer over the empty space above the heading to reveal the picture box. Then click the picture in the Extra Content task pane, click the drop-down arrow attached to the picture, and click Insert.

(continued)

9 Move the inserted picture to about the location of the picture box.

✓ *Do not drag the picture by the mountain icon in the center, or you will leave behind the graphic placeholder.*

10 Inserting the picture may crowd the heading placeholder so the heading *Flora* is reduced in size. If necessary, click the heading text box and drag the top center selection handle down below the picture until the text regains its full size.

11 You still have one piece of content to place, the message. Drag it from the Extra Content task pane and position the text box below the heading.

12 Click the Close button ✕ on the Extra Content task pane to close it.

13 Save the changes to **PB07Try_xx**, and leave it open to use in the next Try It.

Publication design and layout have been changed

Applying a Different Color Scheme

■ The colors used for various objects on the page come from the chosen color scheme. By applying a different color scheme, you recolor everything formatted with one of these placeholder colors.

■ You can change the color scheme from the PAGE DESIGN tab by selecting a scheme in the Schemes gallery. Click the More button on the gallery to see all available color schemes.

■ As you rest the mouse pointer on one of these color schemes, the publication displays those colors. This Live Preview makes it easier to select a new color scheme because you don't have to guess how the scheme will look when applied—you can see the colors even before you choose a scheme.

■ Note that after you select a new color scheme to customize a publication, that color scheme is selected as the color scheme for the next publication you create. If you want to see the default color scheme for a new publication, choose (default template colors) from the Color scheme drop-down list on the New tab.

Applying a Different Color Scheme

1 In the **PB07Try_xx** file, click PAGE DESIGN.

2 Rest the mouse pointer on several of the color schemes you can see in the Schemes gallery to see the colors applied to the publication.

3 Click the More button ⏷ to see all color schemes, and then click the Ivy color scheme.

4 Save the changes to **PB07Try_xx**, and leave it open to use in the next Try It.

Creating a New Color Scheme

■ You can create your own color schemes by modifying existing ones. When creating a new color scheme, you need to keep in mind how the eight colors that make up a color scheme are used.

- The Main color is generally used for the body text of a publication.

- The Accent colors are used for text, graphic objects, object fill colors, and shadows. Accent 1, for example, is often used for the main heading in a publication, and Accents 2 and 3 are used as fill colors for the most important graphic objects on the page.

- The Hyperlink colors are used to format hyperlinks you may insert in a publication. Hyperlink is the color before the link is clicked; Followed hyperlink is the color after the link has been used.

■ Knowing how color scheme colors work in a template can prevent a lot of trial and error. It wouldn't usually be a good choice, for example, to specify a light yellow for Accent 1, because this color is often used for major headings. (It might be appropriate if you are using a dark page background, however.)

■ Use the Create New Color Scheme command at the bottom of the Schemes gallery to open the Create New Color Scheme dialog box and start the process of creating a custom color scheme.

■ Choose a new color by clicking the color's New drop-down arrow to display a color palette of standard colors.

■ If you do not find a color you like on this palette, click More Colors to open the Colors dialog box, where you can choose an existing color on the Standard tab or create your own color on the Custom tab.

  ✓ *If your publication is to be professionally printed, you can also choose a color from the PANTONE color matching system used by professional print suppliers.*

■ You can save the new color scheme by typing a name in the Color scheme name box and clicking the Save button.

■ This new scheme will appear on the Custom area of the Schemes gallery.

■ You can edit a custom scheme by right-clicking it and selecting Edit Scheme. You cannot edit a built-in scheme.

Try It!   Creating a New Color Scheme

1 In the **PB07Try_xx** file, click PAGE DESIGN, if necessary, click the Schemes More button ⤓, and click Create New Color Scheme.

2 Click the Accent 2 New drop-down arrow, and then click More Colors.

3 Click the Custom tab, and then type the following values: Red, **228**; Green, **144**; Blue, **174**.

4 Click OK.

5 Click the Accent 3 New drop-down arrow, and then click More Colors.

6 Click the Custom tab, and then type the following values: Red, **236**; Green, **202**; Blue, **207**.

7 Click OK.

8 Type the new color scheme name **Flora**, and then click Save.

9 Save the changes to **PB07Try_xx**, and leave it open to use in the next Try It.

New color scheme applied

Applying a Different Font Scheme

■ Like the other schemes, a font scheme applies a predefined set of formatting. In this case, they apply a set of fonts that are chosen to look good together.

  ✓ If you select some text and apply a specific font to that text, that choice overrides the font scheme for that text only. This is called applied formatting. If some text does not change fonts when you apply a new font scheme, it may be the result of applied formatting. You can strip off the applied formatting by pressing CTRL + SPACEBAR.

■ You apply font schemes from the PAGE DESIGN tab. Click the Fonts drop-down arrow to display the gallery of font schemes.

■ Resting the mouse pointer on a font scheme adjusts the fonts in the publication so that you can see how each font scheme would look if you selected it.

■ To fine-tune how the font scheme works, use the Font Scheme Options command to display the Font Scheme Options dialog box. Options in this dialog box let you specify how comprehensively the font scheme will be applied.

■ By default, new fonts are applied to all text, even text that has been specifically formatted in some other way, such as with text formatting or a style. Clearing the check boxes in the dialog box allows certain text to remain formatted with its own font choices.

■ As for color schemes, if you choose to apply a new font scheme to a publication, that font scheme becomes the default scheme for new publications. Choose (default template fonts) to restore a publication template's default fonts.

Try It!   Applying a Different Font Scheme

1 In the **PB07Try_xx** file, click the HOME tab. Then click in each text box on the page and look at the Font box on the HOME tab to see the name of the font. In this publication, the address text is Tw Cen MT, the heading is Copperplate Gothic, and the message text is Garamond.

✓ *Copperplate Gothic and Garamond are the default fonts for the Brocade template. The Tw Cen MT font was applied to the address to match a font in the original publication.*

2 Click PAGE DESIGN > Fonts [Aa].

3 Scroll down the Scheme Fonts gallery and rest the pointer on a few font schemes to see how the publication changes.

4 Click Font Scheme Options at the bottom of the Scheme Fonts gallery and review the selected options. Note the second option, which indicates that a new font scheme will override applied text formatting.

5 Click OK to close the dialog box. Then click PAGE DESIGN > Fonts [Aa], and click the Civic font scheme to apply the Georgia font to both the heading and the message text.

✓ *Note that the applied formatting in the address text block has been overridden by the new Georgia font.*

6 Save the changes to **PB07Try_xx**, and leave it open to use in the next Try It.

Creating a New Font Scheme

■ You can create your own font schemes that specify any two fonts: one for headings and one for body text.

■ When creating a new font scheme, consider how the heading and body fonts complement each other and the purpose of the publication. As a general rule, the two fonts should either be very similar (or even the same) or quite different. You can use the fonts in built-in font schemes as a guideline for choosing your own.

■ Use the Create New Font Scheme command on the Scheme Font gallery to open the Create New Font Scheme dialog box, where you can select the fonts you want to use and specify a scheme name.

Try It!   Creating a New Font Scheme

1 In the **PB07Try_xx** file, click PAGE DESIGN > Fonts [Aa] > Create New Font Scheme.

2 Click the Heading font drop-down arrow, scroll down the font list, and click Constantia.

3 Click the Body font drop-down arrow, scroll down the font list, and click Lucida Calligraphy.

4 Click in the Font scheme name box, type **Flora**, and click Save.

5 Click in the message text box, and click TEXT BOX TOOLS FORMAT > Text Fit [ⓐ] > Best Fit.

6 Save the changes to **PB07Try_xx**, and leave it open to use in the next Try It.

New font scheme applied to publication

Flora

Introducing Flora, the garden supply store for the discriminating gardener. From rare cultivars to the native plants that thrive in our climate, you'll find whatever you need at Flora.

Deleting Custom Schemes

■ Custom schemes display in the Custom area of the color schemes or font schemes gallery, above the built-in schemes.

■ You can delete either a color scheme or a font scheme by right-clicking the scheme and selecting Delete Scheme.

■ The color or font formatting remains in the publication, but the scheme is no longer available to apply to other publications.

Try It!   **Deleting Custom Schemes**

1 In the PB07Try_xx file, click PAGE DESIGN > Fonts Aa to display the Scheme Fonts gallery.

2 Right-click the Flora font scheme in the gallery and click Delete Scheme.

3 Click Yes to confirm.

4 Right-click the Flora color scheme at the upper-left corner of the color schemes gallery and click Delete Scheme.

5 Click Yes to confirm

6 Close the publication, saving changes, and exit Publisher.

Lesson 7—Practice

You have shown your draft publication to the Geology Club members. They like it, but they would like to see some other designs, layouts, and color schemes. In this exercise, you apply a new template, color scheme, and font scheme to the publication.

DIRECTIONS

1. Start Publisher, if necessary, and open PB07Practice from the data files for this lesson.

2. Save the publication as PB07Practice_xx in the location where your teacher instructs you to store the files for this lesson.

3. Click PAGE DESIGN > Change Template 🗐 to open the Change Template dialog box.

4. Click the Arrows template under the Event category.

5. In the Customize box in the right pane, under Options, deselect Include graphic to remove the picture placeholder.

6. Click the Tear-offs drop-down arrow to see the additional layout items that can be added to this template. Click Coupon to see how the layout changes in the sample.

7. Click the Tear-offs drop-down arrow and click None.

8. Click OK, click Apply template to the current publication, and then click OK.

9. In the Extra Content task pane, click the Last update object, click the drop-down arrow attached to it, and click Insert.

10. Drag the inserted text box to the lower-right corner of the publication, aligned with the bottom of the e-mail address and the right side of the blue graphic bar. Insert today's date.

11. Hover the mouse pointer over several color schemes visible in the Schemes gallery, and then click Equity.

12. Click PAGE DESIGN > Fonts Aa, scroll down, and click the Trek font scheme.

13. **With your teacher's permission**, print the document. It should look similar to Figure 7-2 on the next page.

14. Close the publication, saving changes, and exit Publisher.

Figure 7-2

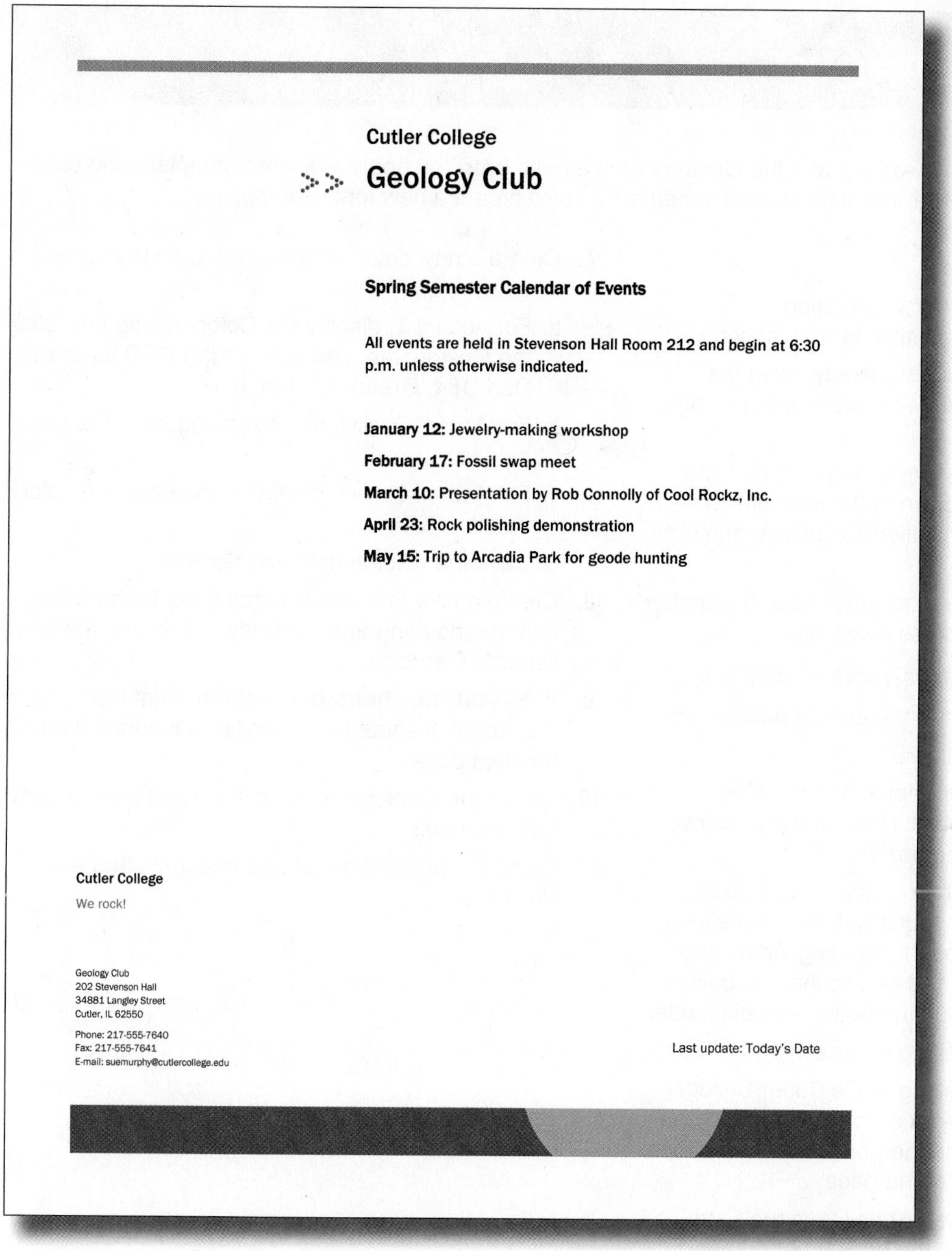

Cutler College

Geology Club

Spring Semester Calendar of Events

All events are held in Stevenson Hall Room 212 and begin at 6:30 p.m. unless otherwise indicated.

January 12: Jewelry-making workshop

February 17: Fossil swap meet

March 10: Presentation by Rob Connolly of Cool Rockz, Inc.

April 23: Rock polishing demonstration

May 15: Trip to Arcadia Park for geode hunting

Cutler College

We rock!

Geology Club
202 Stevenson Hall
34881 Langley Street
Cutler, IL 62550

Phone: 217-555-7640
Fax: 217-555-7641
E-mail: suemurphy@cutlercollege.edu

Last update: Today's Date

Lesson 7—Apply

In this exercise, you continue working with the Geology Club events flyer. You apply a different template and color scheme, then customize the layout and the color scheme. You also create a new font scheme.

DIRECTIONS

1. Start Publisher, if necessary, and open **PB07Apply** from the data files for this lesson.

2. Save the publication as **PB07Apply_xx** in the location where your teacher instructs you to store the files for this lesson.

3. Open the Change Template dialog box, click the All Event folder, scroll down to the Informational category under More Installed Templates, and click **Mobile**.

4. Change the color scheme to **Solstice** and select the Include mailing address check box.

   ✓ *Make sure the Include graphic check box is not selected.*

5. Apply the new template to the current publication.

6. Modify the layout as follows:

   a. Click the small picture box below the blue arrowhead and delete it. (Move the pointer over this area to locate the box.)

   b. Adjust the width of the events text box so the right side of the box aligns with the right side of the brown box behind the heading. Adjust the height of the events text box so that the bottom border of the box is on the bottom margin guide.

   c. Apply Best Fit copyfitting to the events text box.

   d. Apply Best Fit copyfitting to the Cutler College text box in the lower-left corner of the page, the address text box, and the phone/fax/e-mail text box at the lower-left of the page.

   e. Drag the Last update text box from the Extra Content task pane to the upper-right corner of the page, and insert the current date.

   f. Delete page 2 of the publication.

7. Create a new color scheme based on the current one:

   a. For Accent 1, display the Colors dialog box, click the Custom tab, and change the RGB values to Red, **184**, Green, **0**, Blue, **0**.

   b. For Accent 2, click the **Aqua** square in the color palette.

   c. For Accent 3, click the **Gold** square in the color palette.

   d. Save the color scheme as **Geology**.

8. Create a new font scheme that uses Tahoma for both the heading and the body text. Name the font scheme **Geology**.

9. **With your teacher's permission**, print the document. It should look similar to Figure 7-3 on the next page.

10. Delete the Geology color scheme and the Geology font scheme.

11. Close the publication, saving changes, and exit Publisher.

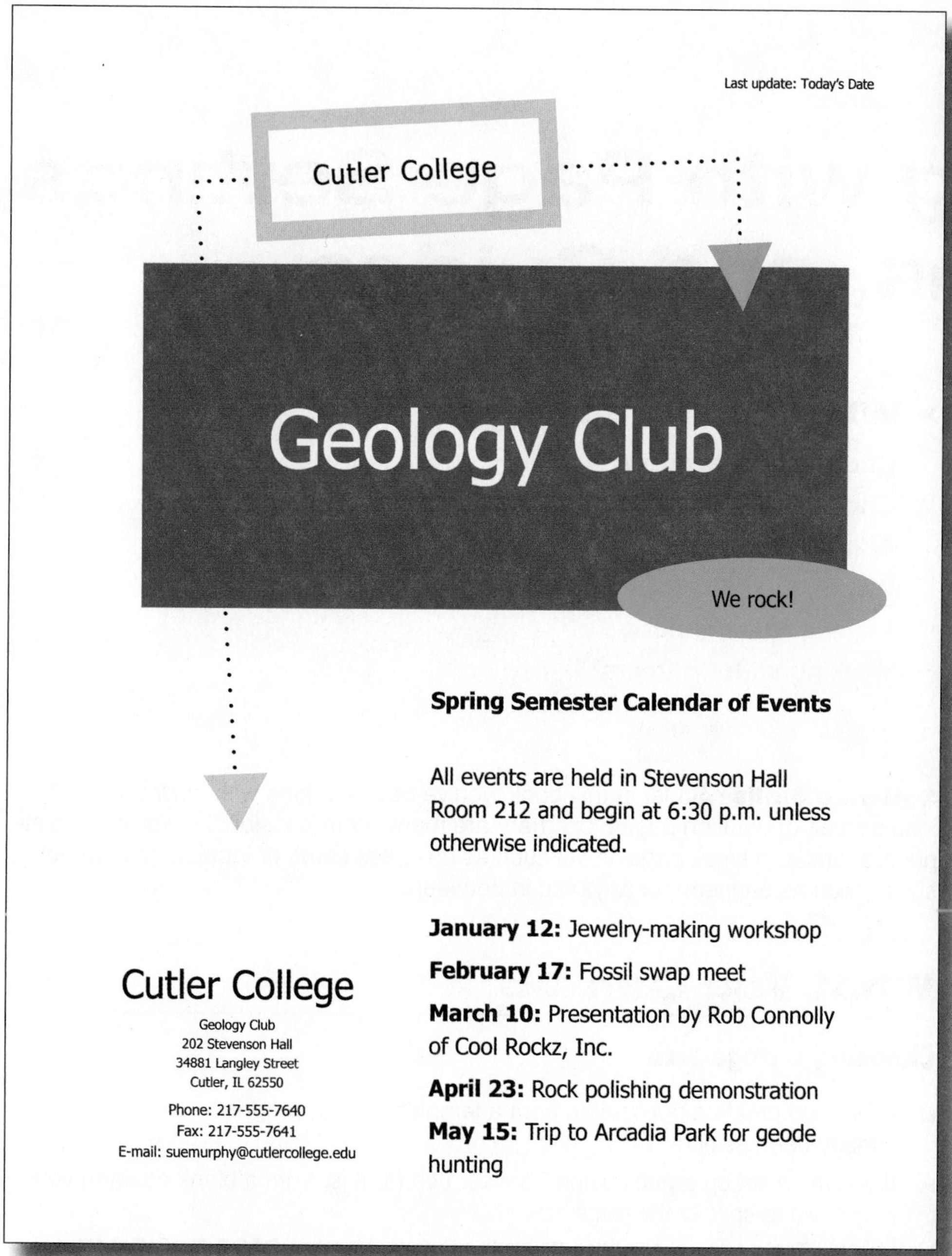

Figure 7-3

Last update: Today's Date

Cutler College

Geology Club

We rock!

Spring Semester Calendar of Events

All events are held in Stevenson Hall Room 212 and begin at 6:30 p.m. unless otherwise indicated.

January 12: Jewelry-making workshop

February 17: Fossil swap meet

March 10: Presentation by Rob Connolly of Cool Rockz, Inc.

April 23: Rock polishing demonstration

May 15: Trip to Arcadia Park for geode hunting

Cutler College

Geology Club
202 Stevenson Hall
34881 Langley Street
Cutler, IL 62550

Phone: 217-555-7640
Fax: 217-555-7641
E-mail: suemurphy@cutlercollege.edu

Lesson 8

Working with Page Settings, Columns, and Guides

WORDS TO KNOW

Baseline guides
Yellow nonprinting lines on a page that help position text baselines.

Grid guides
Blue nonprinting lines on a page that show column and/or row margins in a multicolumn or multirow layout.

Layout guides
A generic term for grid guides and margin guides collectively.

Margin guides
Blue nonprinting lines on a page that show the page margins.

Orientation
The direction that the text runs on a page. Orientation can be portrait (text runs across the short edge) or landscape (text runs across the long edge).

Ruler guides
Green nonprinting vertical or horizontal lines that you can display temporarily to help you align objects with one another.

Software Skills　So far in this book, you've been working with normal 8.5 × 11 inch portrait-orientation pages, but there are many more possibilities. You can create publications with small page sizes (such as business cards or labels), large page sizes (such as banners), or anything in between.

What You Can Do

Choosing a Page Size

- When you create a publication from a template, the appropriate page size has already been selected.

- If you must set up a publication from scratch (that is, from a blank design), you may need to specify the page size.

- Use the Size command in the Page Setup group on the PAGE DESIGN tab to select a different page size from a gallery of standard sizes.

- You can also choose to create a custom page size, view more preset page sizes, or open the Page Setup dialog box for more options.

- If you choose to create a new page size, the Create New Page Size dialog box opens, as shown in Figure 8-1 on the next page.

  ✓ *Note that if you choose the Page Setup command on the Size drop-down menu, or click the Page Setup dialog box launcher on the PAGE DESIGN tab, Publisher displays the Page Setup dialog box with options virtually identical to those in the Create New Page Size dialog box.*

■ You can choose a layout type, such as one page per sheet of paper, envelope, booklet, and so on. The page width and height adjust for each layout type, and the Preview shows the selection.

■ If there is no layout type that matches the size you want, select one that is similar and then change its width and height in the Page area of the dialog box.

■ Each page size preset also has margin guide presets. These do not affect the page content; they simply display guides onscreen to help with layout.

■ You can change the positions of the margin guides in the Margin Guides area of the dialog box.

   ✓ *You learn more about margin guides later in this lesson.*

■ If you choose Multiple pages per sheet from the Layout type list, you can choose a target sheet size separately from the page size. This is useful for publications with small page sizes, such as mailing labels, because it enables you to print multiple pages per sheet.

■ For a layout with multiple pages per sheet, you can specify margins for the sheet itself (Side margin and Top margin); this determines where the first copy of the publication starts on the sheet.

■ You can also specify a horizontal and vertical gap; these dictate the amount of space between copies.

■ If you choose Folded card as the layout type, you can select a sheet fold setting. This determines how many times the sheet will be folded (quarter or half) and whether the fold will be on the side or at the top.

■ As you are working with page settings, keep in mind that page size is not the same as paper size. A page in Publisher can be letter-sized, or it can be the size of a business card or greeting card. Knowing this distinction can make it easier to understand how several pages can fit on a single sheet of paper.

Figure 8-1

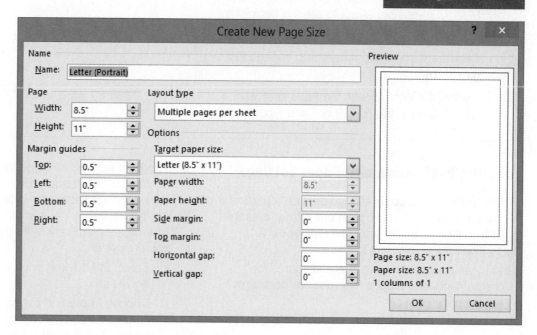

Try It!   Choosing a Page Size

1 Start Publisher and select the Blank 8.5 x 11" template.

2 Save the publication as **PB08Try_xx** in the location where your teacher instructs you to store the files for this lesson.

3 Draw a text box in the upper-left corner of the page, where the left and top margin guides intersect, 1.5 inches wide by 1.0 inches high. Type **Insert text here to describe new features.**

4 Click TEXT BOX TOOLS FORMAT > Text Fit ⊞ > Best Fit.

5 Click PAGE DESIGN > Size ▢ > Create New Page Size.

6 Click the Layout type drop-down list and click One page per sheet to see the settings for this layout type.

7 Click the Layout type drop-down list and click Multiple pages per sheet to see the settings for this layout type.

8 Click the Vertical gap up arrow to change the gap to 0.5".

9 Click in the Width box in the Page section and type **5**. Click in the Height box and type **3**.

10 Click OK. You will see the text box in the scratch area, but you will not be able to see the actual page.

11 Zoom to 100% to see the page. Use the vertical and horizontal scroll bars to move the page to the center of the screen. Move the text box near the upper-left corner of the page, as shown in the illustration below.

12 Save the changes to **PB08Try_xx**, and leave it open to use in the next Try It.

Page size changed

Insert text here
to describe new
features.

Choosing Publication and Paper Settings

- You can set up a publication to print on a particular printer, if you have more than one printer available. This makes it easy to print different types of publications on different printers.

- You can also set a paper size and source for the print job, and a page **orientation** (portrait or landscape).

- The Print tab in Backstage view offers settings for controlling how a publication prints. Figure 8-2 on the next page shows the location of the following settings. You may not see all of these settings, or you may see different settings, depending on what you are printing.

  - Select the desired printer from the Printer drop-down list.

  - Choose to print all pages, a selection, the current page, or a custom range (such as pages, 1, 3, and 4).

- The print imposition setting lets you specify how pages are positioned on the sheet of paper on which the publication will be printed. For small items such as cards, for example, you can specify multiple copies of a page on one sheet of paper.

- Choose a paper size such as Letter or Legal.

- Some page setups will allow you to select Portrait or Landscape orientation as part of the print settings.

- If your printer allows you to automatically print on both sides of the paper, you can choose one-sided or two-sided printing. If your printer does not offer this feature, you can choose to manually print on two sides of the paper.

- Choose to print in color or grayscale.

- The Save settings with publication option allows you to save any print settings you have specified along with the publication, so you don't have to specify them again the next time you print the publication.

■ You can also change orientation using the Orientation command on the PAGE DESIGN tab.

■ If you change the orientation of the publication, you will probably need to reposition some of the content on the page(s).

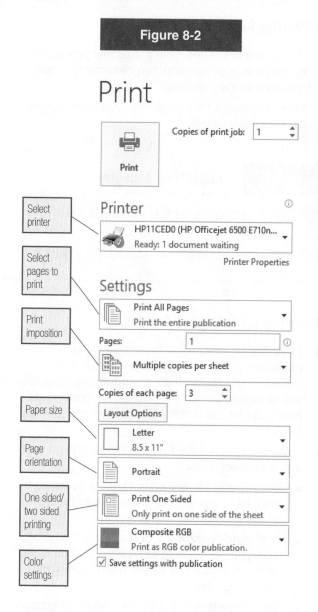

Figure 8-2

---

1. In the **PB08Try_xx** file, click FILE > Print to see the Print tab.

2. Click the Print imposition drop-down arrow and select Multiple copies per sheet if necessary. The preview at the right side of the screen shows three pages on the same sheet.

3. Click the Orientation drop-down arrow and select Landscape. The preview changes to show four pages on the same sheet.

4. Click ⬅ to return to the publication.

5. Save the changes to **PB08Try_xx**, and leave it open to use in the next Try It.

Adjusting Margins

- Publisher's templates have preset margins suitable for the type of publication. You can modify these margin settings if desired.
- When creating a new page size, you must specify the margins yourself.

- Use the Margins command in the Page Setup group on the PAGE DESIGN tab to display a gallery of margin settings you can apply to any publication.
- For more control over the margins, choose Custom Margins to open the Layout Guides dialog box, which is discussed in the next section.

Try It!   **Adjusting Margins**

1 In the **PB08Try_xx** file, click PAGE DESIGN > Margins ▦ > Wide.

2 Click PAGE DESIGN > Margins ▦ > Narrow.

3 Click PAGE DESIGN > Margins ▦ > Moderate.

4 Save the changes to **PB08Try_xx**, and leave it open to use in the next Try It.

Working with Layout Guides

- Publisher provides several different kinds of guidelines to help you with page layout. These guidelines are called **layout guides**. Layout guides are especially useful in multipage publications to help you place objects in a consistent way on each page.
- Layout guides include margin guides, grid guides, and baseline guides.
  - **Margin guides**, shown in Figure 8-3, define the margins of a page and display as a blue border all the way around the page.
  - **Grid guides** show the borders of columns or rows you have added to a page to divide it into sections. Figure 8-3 shows both column and row grid guides.
  - **Baseline guides** display as a series of horizontal yellow lines over the entire publication. You can use these guides to align text when you have multiple text boxes on a page.

    ✓ The baseline of text is the imaginary horizontal line on which the text characters sit. In publishing, text is measured vertically from one baseline to the next.

- You can control all of these layout guides in the Layout Guides dialog box. There are several ways to get to this dialog box. You can click Custom Margins on the Margins gallery, or you can select Grid and Baseline Guides on the Guides command on the PAGE DESIGN tab.

    ✓ You can also modify margin guides in other dialog boxes, such as Page Setup or Create New Page Size.

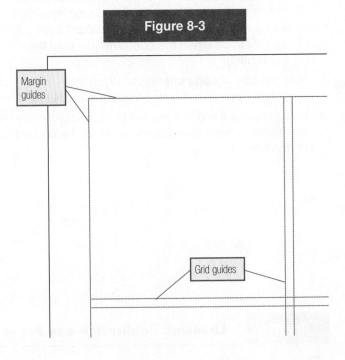

Figure 8-3

Margin guides

Grid guides

- When setting the position of margin guides, you can have separate layout settings for left and right pages if your publication is two-sided. Clicking the Two-page master check box changes the Left and Right margins to Inside and Outside boxes. You can also have different settings for all four margins if desired.

- Use grid guides to divide the page into multiple equal-sized sections. For example, if you wanted a page divided into eight equal sections, you could set up the grid guides to show where those sections should be. This is not the same as setting up text columns on a page. You learn about creating columns in a text box later in this lesson.

- For baseline guides, you can set spacing and offset. Spacing is the space between the guides, and offset is the distance between the top margin guide and the first horizontal baseline below it. If you want text to snap to the baseline guides, you can choose Align text to baseline guides in the Paragraph dialog box.

- Margin and grid guides display by default. Deselect the Guides check box on the VIEW tab to hide the guides. You must select Baselines on the VIEW tab to display the baseline grid; deselect the check box to hide the grid.

- Guides help you in aligning objects by highlighting when an object intersects the guide. If you move a text box so the top border of the text box intersects the top margin guide, for example, the margin guide changes color, comes to the front of the display, and extends all the way across the page. This feature makes it easier to snap objects to guides for precise alignment.

Try It!   Adjusting Margin and Grid Guides

1. In the **PB08Try_xx** file, click PAGE DESIGN > Guides ⬚ > Grid and Baseline Guides to open the Layout Guides dialog box.

2. Click the Margin Guides tab.

3. Select the number in the Left box and type **0.25**.

4. Press TAB and type **0.25** in the Right box; press TAB and type **0.25** in the Top box; press TAB and type **0.25** in the Bottom box.

5. Click the Grid Guides tab.

6. Click the Columns up arrow to change the number of columns from 1 to 2.

7. Click OK. Move the text box to the intersection of the left and top margin guides and note how the guides highlight when the text box aligns to them.

8. Save the changes to **PB08Try_xx**, and leave it open to use in the next Try It.

Try It!   Applying the Baseline Grid

1. In the **PB08Try_xx** file, click PAGE DESIGN > Guides ⬚ > Grid and Baseline Guides.

2. Click the Baseline Guides tab.

3. Click the Spacing up arrow to change spacing to 20pt. Click the Offset up arrow to change the offset to 20pt. Click OK.

4. Click VIEW > Baselines. Click the text box and adjust its position so that the bottom of the first line of text sits on the first yellow baseline guide below the top margin guide.

5. With the insertion point in the text box, click HOME > Paragraph dialog box launcher ⬎.

6. Click to select the Align text to baseline guides check box, and click OK. Note that all lines in the text box are now aligned to baseline guides. The font size has changed to allow for this alignment.

7. Copy the text box, paste the copy, and move it into the right column. When you release the mouse button after moving, the text in the text box snaps to a baseline guide so text aligns across the page.

(continued)

Try It!   **Applying the Baseline Grid** *(continued)*

8   Click VIEW > Baselines to hide baseline guides.

9   Click in the text of each text box, click HOME > Paragraph, and deselect Align text to baseline guides.

10   Save the changes to **PB08Try_xx**, and leave it open to use in the next Try It.

Text aligns to the baseline grid

Insert text here to describe new features.	Insert text here to describe new features.

Placing Ruler Guides

- **Ruler guides** are straight vertical or horizontal lines that you can temporarily place on your screen to assist you in aligning objects on a page. They do not print, and they can be easily removed at any time. Ruler guides are green to differentiate them from margin guides or grid guides.

- Place a ruler guide by moving the mouse pointer over a ruler, clicking, and dragging toward the center of the page. Release the left mouse button to drop the ruler guide where you want to position it.

- The Guides command on the PAGE DESIGN tab has a gallery of pre-positioned guides you can select, or you can click a command to add a horizontal or vertical ruler guide.

- You can move ruler guides after placement by dragging them to a new position. Remove a ruler guide by dragging it off the page.

- As for margin and grid guides, ruler guides become highlighted when an object snaps to the guide.

Try It!   **Placing Ruler Guides**

1   In the **PB08Try_xx** file, position the mouse pointer on the horizontal ruler. The pointer changes shape to a double-pointed arrow ⬍.

2   Drag downward, watching the vertical ruler, until you see the moving tick mark at 1.5 inches. Drop the ruler guide by releasing the left mouse button.

   ✓ *You can also check the position of the ruler guide in the Object Position area of the status bar. The numbers will read 0.00, 1.50 when the ruler guide is in the correct position.*

3   Click on the ruler guide and drag it upward 0.25 inch.

4   Position the mouse pointer on the vertical ruler and drag to the left until the moving tick mark is on the 0.5 inch mark on the horizontal ruler. Drop the ruler guide.

5   Click in the text box in the left column of the page, click its outside border, and drag it until it aligns to the vertical ruler guide and the top margin guide.

(continued)

Try It!   **Placing Ruler Guides** *(continued)*

6 Click in the text box in the right column, click its outside border, and drag it until it aligns at the top with the ruler guide and on the left with the column grid guide.

7 Save the changes to **PB08Try_xx**, and leave it open to use in the next Try It.

Align objects to ruler guides.

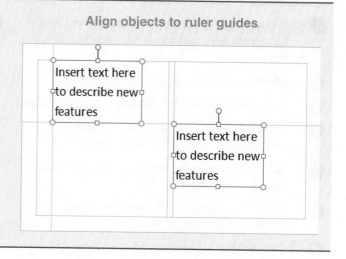

Working with Columns

- You have seen in this lesson one way to create columns on a page: by setting up grid guides and then creating text boxes that align to those guides.

- This is an acceptable practice when text boxes will not contain much text, or when they contain non-related text. If you have a considerable amount of text to place in columns, however, you should use the Columns command to divide a single text box into multiple columns.

  ✓ *Another option is to link text boxes, which you will learn to do in Lesson 10.*

- The Columns command in the Paragraph group on the HOME tab offers a gallery of three column setup options to specify one, two, or three columns. You can also click the More Columns option to open the Columns dialog box, where you can choose the number of columns and the spacing between columns.

  ✓ *You will also find a Columns command on the TEXT BOX TOOLS FORMAT tab, which makes this feature easy to access if you have just drawn a new text box.*

- Placing text in multiple columns in a single text box has distinct advantages over creating multiple text boxes. As you type or import text, it flows automatically from one column to the next. You can easily balance the columns by adjusting the depth of the text box to move lines from column to column, or you can use the keyboard shortcut SHIFT + CTRL + ENTER to create a column break that will move text to the next column.

- When a text box is divided into multiple columns, you have no visual guidelines for the column dimensions. You can, however, adjust grid guide settings to be the same as the column settings so you can see column margins as you work.

Try It!   Working with Columns

1 In the **PB08Try_xx** file, drag the vertical and horizontal ruler guides off the page to remove them.

2 Delete the text box in the right column.

3 Click PAGE DESIGN > Margins ▦ > Moderate.

4 Move the text box to align at the upper-left corner with the left and top margin guides.

5 Select the text in the text box, and then click HOME > Font Size 11 ▾ > 10.

6 Resize the text box to fill the entire area inside the margin guides.

7 Click HOME > Columns ▦ ▾ > Three Columns.

8 Type the following text, replacing the currently selected text.

You can read about many new features in Publisher in the Publisher 2013 Help files. To access the Help files, click the ? button at the upper-left corner of the Publisher window. The Help feature opens and gives you the option of browsing through topics or searching for a specific topic. You can access Help topics on Office.com to see tutorials and blog posts that cover many features of this dynamic software.

✓ *Hover the mouse pointer over the word* Button *to display the AutoCorrect Options button, click it, and click Undo Automatic Capitalization.*

9 Click HOME > Columns ▦ ▾ > More Columns. In the Columns dialog box, click the Spacing up arrow once to change spacing to 0.18. Click OK.

10 Click PAGE DESIGN > Guides ▯ > Grid and Baseline Guides. On the Grid Guides tab in the Layout Guides dialog box, click the Columns up arrow once to specify 3 columns. Then select the value in the Spacing box and type **0.18**. Click OK. The grid guides now match the column spacing, making it easy to see the dimensions of each column.

11 Click the bottom selection handle of the text box and drag upward to move more lines into the third column to distribute lines more evenly among the three columns.

12 Close the publication, saving changes, and exit Publisher.

Column text has been adjusted for balance

You can read about many new features in Publisher in the Publisher 2010 Help files. To access the Help files, click the ? button at the upper-left corner of the	Publisher window. The Help feature opens and gives you the option of browsing through topics or searching for a specific topic. You can access Help topics	on Office.com to see tutorials and blog posts that cover many features of this dynamic software.

Lesson 8—Practice

Anderson Farms is a fruit and vegetable farm that hosts special promotional events throughout the year. The owner, Jean Anderson, wants to create a flyer on special orange-colored paper she has ordered (8 × 10 inches) announcing an upcoming pumpkin-carving contest. In this exercise, you help her by creating a new publication and setting up the nonstandard paper size and orientation, margin guides, and grid guides. Then you import text for the flyer content.

DIRECTIONS

1. Start Publisher, if necessary, and select the **Blank 8.5 × 11"** template.

2. Save the publication as **PB08Practice_xx** in the location where your teacher instructs you to store the files for this lesson.

3. Click **PAGE DESIGN > Page Setup dialog box launcher** ⌐.

4. Type **8** in the Page Width box, press TAB, and type **10** in the Height box.

5. Select the current Top margin guide measurement and type **0.8**. Press TAB and type **0.8**, press TAB and type **0.8**, and press TAB and type **0.8**.

6. Press TAB twice to select the Side margin value and type **0.3**. Press TAB and type **0.5**.

7. Click **OK**.

8. Position the mouse pointer over the vertical ruler and drag a ruler guide to the **1.5 inch** mark on the horizontal ruler. Drag another vertical ruler guide to the **6.5 inch** mark.

   ✓ *If you're having trouble setting the ruler guide at the correct position, it helps to zoom in.*

9. Position the mouse pointer over the horizontal ruler and drag a ruler guide to the **2 inch** mark on the vertical ruler. Drag another horizontal ruler guide to the **5.5 inch** mark.

10. Click **INSERT > Draw Text Box** 🄰 and position the crosshair at the intersection of the 1.5 inch vertical ruler guide and the 2 inch horizontal ruler guide. Drag the crosshair to the 6.5 inch vertical ruler guide and then down to create a box about 1.5 inches high.

11. Type **Pumpkin Carving Contest** in the text box.

12. With the insertion point in the text box, click **TEXT BOX TOOLS FORMAT > Text Fit** 🄰 **> Best Fit**.

13. Click **INSERT > Draw Text Box** 🄰. Position the crosshair at the intersection of the 1.5 inch vertical ruler guide and the 5.5 inch horizontal ruler guide and draw a text box to the intersection of the bottom margin guide and the 6.5 inch vertical ruler guide.

14. Click **TEXT BOX TOOLS FORMAT > Columns** ▤ **> Two Columns**.

15. With the insertion point in the text box, click **INSERT > Insert File** 🗐, navigate to the data files for this lesson, click **PB08Practice_import.docx**, and click **OK**.

16. Click **HOME > Columns** ▤ ▾ **> More Columns**. Click the **Spacing** up arrow twice to change spacing to **0.28**, and then click **OK**.

17. Drag the bottom border of the text box up to move the *Refreshments* paragraph to the next column. Your page should look similar to Figure 8-4 on the next page.

18. **With your teacher's permission**, print the publication.

19. Close the publication, saving changes, and exit Publisher.

Figure 8-4

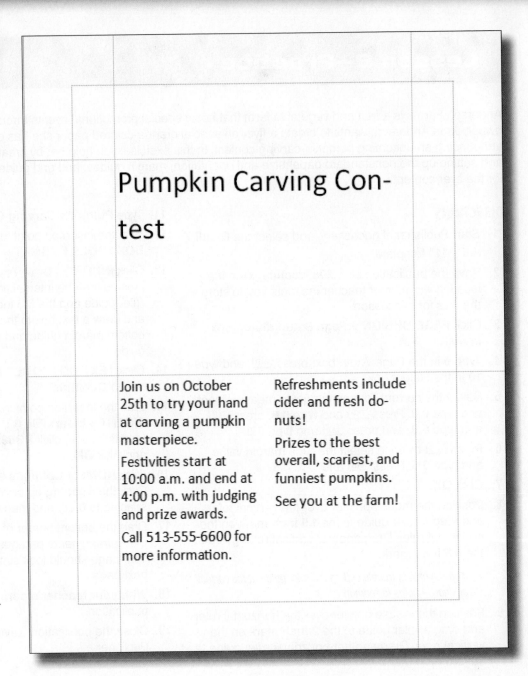

Pumpkin Carving Con-test

Join us on October 25th to try your hand at carving a pumpkin masterpiece.

Festivities start at 10:00 a.m. and end at 4:00 p.m. with judging and prize awards.

Call 513-555-6600 for more information.

Refreshments include cider and fresh do-nuts!

Prizes to the best overall, scariest, and funniest pumpkins.

See you at the farm!

Lesson 8—Apply

You continue to work for Anderson Farms to prepare a pumpkin-carving publication. In this exercise, you adjust guides and move content to align with those guides. Then you align content using the baseline grid.

DIRECTIONS

1. Start Publisher, if necessary, and open **PB08Apply** from the data files for this lesson.

2. Save the publication as **PB08Apply_xx** in the location where your teacher instructs you to store the files for this lesson.

3. In the Layout Guides dialog box, on the Grid Guides tab, specify **2** columns for the publication.

4. Still in the Layout Guides dialog box, click the **Baseline Guides** tab and set Spacing to **26pt** and Offset to **6pt**. Click **OK**.

5. Drag a horizontal ruler guide to the **1.75 inch** mark on the vertical ruler. Drag another horizontal ruler guide to the **5.25 inch** mark.

6. Click the *Pumpkin Carving Contest* text box and drag it off the page into the scratch area, and then move the *Anderson Farms Presents* text box up so the bottom of the text box sits on the 1.75 inch ruler guide you just inserted. Resize the text box so that it extends from the left margin guide to the right margin guide.

7. Move the *Join us* text box so that the top of the text box aligns with the 5.25 inch ruler guide in the left column. Move the *Refreshments include* text box to align the top of the text box with the 5.25 inch ruler guide in the right column.

8. Move the *Scary* text box so that the bottom of the text box aligns with the 5.25 inch ruler guide. Center the text box on the page by moving the box horizontally until you see a purple vertical alignment guide that indicates the center of the page.

9. Move the *Pumpkin Carving Contest* text box so that the top of the text box aligns with the 1.75 inch ruler guide and the text box is centered on the page.

10. Display the baseline grid. Make sure that the *Join us* text is sitting on a baseline guide. Then move the *Refreshments include* text box down one guideline in the right column.

11. Hide all guidelines.

12. **With your teacher's permission**, print the document. It should look similar to Figure 8-5 on the next page.

13. Close the publication, saving changes, and exit Publisher.

Figure 8-5

Anderson Farms Presents
the 17th Annual

Pumpkin Carving
Contest

Scary? Mean? Happy?
Mischievous? What kinds of
faces do you like to make?

Join us on October 25th to try
your hand at carving a
pumpkin masterpiece.

Refreshments include cider
and fresh donuts!

Festivities start at 10:00 a.m.
and end at 4:00 p.m. with
judging and prize awards.

Prizes to the best overall,
scariest, and funniest
pumpkins.

Call 513-555-6600 for more
information.

See you at the farm!

Lesson 9

Inserting Pages, Headers/Footers, and Page Numbers

➤ What You Will Learn

Inserting and Deleting Pages
Viewing As a Two-Page Spread
Working with Headers and Footers
Inserting Page Numbers

Software Skills A publication can have as many pages as you like. You may even lay out an entire book in Publisher. When you begin working with multipage publications, special challenges arise, such as how to keep repeated elements identical on every page and how to number the pages.

What You Can Do

Inserting and Deleting Pages

- You can insert any number of pages, either before or after the current page.
- Use the Page command in the Pages group on the INSERT tab to quickly insert a blank page or a duplicate page. Or, click Insert Page to open the Insert Page dialog box, where you can choose to insert a left or right page (if your template has left and right pages), insert the page before or after the current page, or choose other options, such as inserting a text box on each new page.
- If an existing page already contains text boxes in the locations you want on the new page(s), you can duplicate all the objects from a particular page as you create the new ones.
- If you choose to duplicate objects on an existing page, that duplication includes any layout guides, ruler guides, and other page settings.

WORDS TO KNOW

Footer
Text that is repeated at the bottom of each page in a multipage document.

Header
Text that is repeated at the top of each page in a multipage document.

Spread
A set of two pages (a left page and a right page) viewed together on-screen.

- Delete a page using the Delete command on the PAGE DESIGN tab. When you delete a page, all objects on that page are deleted, too. You can delete only one page at a time.

- If the page you're deleting contains a text box that is part of a chain of linked text boxes, the text that was in that text box moves to the connected text boxes on the other pages.

  ✓ *You learn how to work with linked text boxes in the next lesson.*

Try It!   **Inserting and Deleting Pages**

1 Start Publisher and open **PB09Try** from the data files for this lesson.

2 Save the publication as **PB09Try_xx** in the location where your teacher instructs you to store the files for this lesson.

3 With page 1 selected, click INSERT > Page ☐ > Insert Page.

4 Click Create one text box on each page, and then click OK.

5 Scroll down in the Page Navigation pane to display page 7, and then click on the page to select it.

6 Click PAGE DESIGN > Delete ⬚, and then click Yes to confirm the deletion.

7 Save the changes to **PB09Try_xx**, and leave it open to use in the next Try It.

Viewing As a Two-Page Spread

- When creating a publication that will be printed double-sided with facing pages, such as a booklet, it may be helpful to see the pages in pairs, or **spreads**. In a spread of facing pages, the left and right pages often have different settings and position objects in different ways.

- For example, page numbers may display at the far left side of a left page and the far right side of a right page. A left page may have a wider margin at the right side of the page to allow for binding; on a right page, the wider margin will be at the left side of the page.

- Use the Two-Page Spread command on the VIEW menu to view two pages at a time. Page 1 will be by itself, and the remaining pages in the publication will pair up. The last page in the publication may also stand alone, if there aren't enough pages for all to display in spreads.

- You can view a publication as single pages by clicking the Single Page command on the VIEW tab.

Try It!   **Viewing As a Two-Page Spread**

1 In the **PB09Try_xx** file, click VIEW > Two-Page Spread 📖.

2 Click each spread in the Page Navigation pane to see the left and right pages of each spread.

3 Save the changes to **PB09Try_xx**, and leave it open to use in the next Try It.

Working with Headers and Footers

- The **header** and **footer** areas of a page enable you to enter text that you want to appear at the top or bottom of every page in the publication, such as the publication title, for example.

- Insert a header or footer from the INSERT tab. The MASTER PAGE Ribbon tab displays and the display changes to show the master page elements with the Header or Footer area displayed, as shown in Figure 9-1.

  ✓ *You will work with master pages in Lesson 11.*

- You type the desired header text in the header text box. If you are working with two-page spreads, you can enter the header text on both the left and right pages. You can use the same information for both pages or different information for each.

- You can move the header or footer text box to a different location on the page if desired. Delete a header by dragging it off the page.

- If you are working in the header area, you can display the footer area by clicking the Show Header/Footer command on the MASTER PAGE tab, and vice versa.

- The Header & Footer group on the MASTER PAGE tab allows you to insert other standard information in the header or footer, such as a page number, the date, or the time.

- To leave the header/footer and return to working normally with the document, click the Close Master Page button.

- By default, headers and footers apply to all pages in a publication. If you do not want a header or footer on a page, such as on the first page of a publication, you can tell Publisher not to display the master page items on that page. Click the Master Pages command on the PAGE DESIGN tab and select the None option.

Figure 9-1

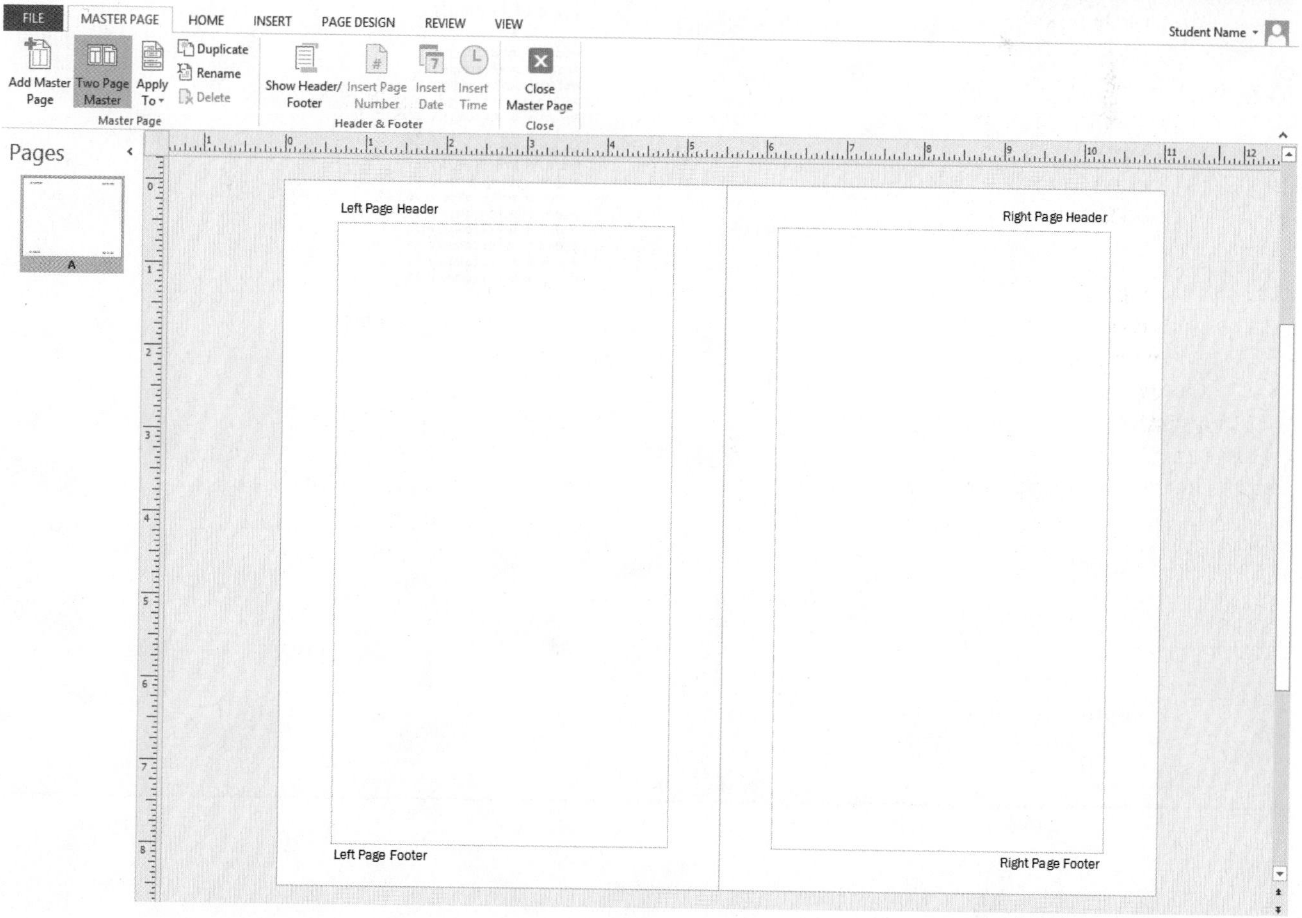

Try It!   Working with Headers and Footers

1 In the **PB09Try_xx** file, click INSERT > Header 🗋. The master page displays with the Header text box active on the left page.

2 Type **Flora Spring Catalog**.

3 Click in the header area on the right page and type **Distinctive Plants and Plant Supplies**.

4 Click HOME > Align Right ≡. (Find this command in the Paragraph group.)

5 Click MASTER PAGE > Show Header/Footer 📄.

6 Click in the footer area on the left page and click MASTER PAGE > Insert Date 🗓.

7 Click MASTER PAGE > Close Master Page ⊠.

8 Click page 1 if necessary in the Page Navigation pane. Note that the right-page header displays on the catalog's first page.

9 Click PAGE DESIGN > Master Pages 🗋 > None. Then click pages 2–3 in the Page Navigation pane to see the headers and footer on the spread.

10 Save the changes to **PB09Try_xx**, and leave it open to use in the next Try It.

Headers and footer display on two-page spread

Flora Spring Catalog

Distinctive Plants and Plant Supplies

Table of Contents

Product or service category 1
Product or service category 2
Product or service category 3
Product or service category 4
Product or service category 5
Product or service category 6
Product or service category 7
Product or service category 8
Product or service category 9
Product or service category 10
Product or service category 11
Product or service category 12
Product or service category 13
Product or service category 14
Product or service category 15

2/15/2014

Inserting Page Numbers

- If your publication includes headers and/or footers, the easiest way to insert a page number is to do so in the header or footer text box.

- A page number inserted in the header or footer text box displays as a # symbol. This symbol is replaced with the correct page number when you exit the master page area.

- The Page Number command on the INSERT tab gives you additional options for inserting a page number.

  - Use one of the gallery options to insert the page number at the top left, center, or right, or the bottom left, center, or right. Page numbers display immediately in the header or footer areas of the pages, without your having to display the master pages.

- You can draw a text box, and then use the Insert in Current Text Box command to insert the page number at the insertion point.

- You can use the Format Page Numbers command to open the Page Number Format dialog box, where you can choose a number format different from the default Arabic numbers and choose the number to start from.

- You can select Show Page Number on First Page if you want automatic numbers to appear on the first page of a publication as well as all the other pages.

Try It! Inserting Page Numbers

1. In the **PB09Try_xx** file, click the page 2–3 spread in the Page Navigation pane.

2. Double-click the header to open the Header text box in the master page area.

3. Click to the left of the word *Flora* in the left page header. Click MASTER PAGE > Insert Page Number ⬚, and then press SPACEBAR two times.

4. Click to the right of the word *Supplies* in the right page header and press SPACEBAR two times. (You may not see these spaces until you insert the page number in the next step.)

5. Click MASTER PAGE > Insert Page Number ⬚.

6. Click MASTER PAGE > Close Master Page ⬚.

7. Click page 1 in the Page Navigation pane and draw a small text box near the center of the page, beneath the bottom margin guide.

8. Click INSERT > Page Number ⬚ > Insert in Current Text Box. (You will not see the page number until you complete the next step.)

9. Click INSERT > Page Number ⬚ > Show Page Number on First Page. The number 1 should display in the text box.

10. Click INSERT > Page Number ⬚ > Format Page Numbers.

11. Click the Number format drop-down arrow and click the A, B, C format; click OK. The numbering scheme changes throughout the publication to capital letters.

12. Close the publication, saving changes, and exit Publisher.

Page number displays on first page

SHOP FLORA FOR

- High-quality plant stock
- Pots and planters
- Soils and mulches

A

Lesson 9—Practice

Marcela Lopez is a computer consultant who has been hired by a local dentist to research the availability of office management software. She has created the main report in Publisher and a separate cover sheet in Word. In this exercise, you help her by combining the two publications and by setting up page numbering for her publication.

DIRECTIONS

1. Start Publisher, if necessary, and open **PB09Practice** from the data files for this lesson.

2. Save the publication as **PB09Practice_xx** in the location where your teacher instructs you to store the files for this lesson.

3. Click page **3** in the Page Navigation pane.

4. Click **PAGE DESIGN** > **Delete** ✗, and then click **Yes** to confirm the deletion.

5. Click page 1 in the Page Navigation pane.

6. Click **INSERT** > **Page** ☐ > **Insert Page**.

7. In the Insert Page dialog box, click **Before current page** and **Create one text box on each page**. Click **OK**.

8. Click in the text box on the new page 1, and then click **INSERT** > **Insert File** ▤. Navigate to the data files for this lesson, click **PB09Practice_import.docx**, and click **OK**.

9. Click in the text box on page 1 to select it and drag the top border down to the **3 inch** mark on the vertical ruler so that the text appears centered vertically on the page.

10. Click **INSERT** > **Page Number** ▣ > **Bottom Center**. If the page number appears on page 1, click **INSERT** > **Page Number** ▣ and deselect **Show Page Number on First Page**.

11. **With your teacher's permission**, print the publication.

12. Close the publication, saving changes, and exit Publisher.

Lesson 9—Apply

In this exercise, you add headers and footers to Marcela Lopez's report publication. You also change the view to see the pages in two-page spreads.

DIRECTIONS

1. Start Publisher, if necessary, and open **PB09Apply** from the data files for this lesson.

2. Save the publication as **PB09Apply_xx** in the location where your teacher instructs you to store the files for this lesson.

3. View the pages in two-page spreads.

4. Insert a header that reads **Report created by Marcela Lopez on** and then insert the date.

5. Click **HOME** > **Center** ≡ to apply center alignment to the heading.

6. Click the **Show Header/Footer** button ▤ on the MASTER PAGE tab to move to the footer area. The page number currently appears as a code in the center of the footer area.

7. Click in the footer text box and press ⟨TAB⟩ twice to move the page number code to the right side of the text box.

8. Click at the left side of the footer text box to position the insert point and type **Computer System Purchase for Dental Office**.

9. Remove the header and footer display from the first page of the report using the None option on the **PAGE DESIGN** > **Master Pages** gallery.

10. **With your teacher's permission**, print the document. Pages 2 and 3 should look similar to Figure 9-2. (Your date will be different.)

11. Close the publication, saving changes, and exit Publisher.

Figure 9-2

Figure 9-2 (document pages 2 and 3)

Page 2:

Report created by Marcela Lopez on Today's Date

Goals

- Computerized scheduling
- Computerized billing
- Electronic insurance filing
- Computer-printed reminder cards

Hardware Recommended

I recommend a Windows-based PC, not necessarily top-of-the-line but current enough that it will not need upgrading for at least 2 years. A suitable configuration would be:

- 500MHz or higher Windows-based PC
- 256MB (or more) of memory
- 160G or more hard disk
- DVD-ROM and RW
- 15" or 17" monitor
- Integrated networking

Total computer cost: $1000 to $3000, depending on options chosen

A printer will also be required. Some dental practice management software requires a certain printer model; others can use any printer. The model required by some programs is a LaserJet 2100, at around $500. Cheaper printers are available, as low as $150.

Software

There are many inexpensive programs that will take care of the four goals individually—one program for scheduling, one program for billing, one program for reminders, etc. However, this would require maintaining four separate customer databases on the computer, and might actually be *more* work than the current paper-based system for the staff.

An integrated program that handles all four functions would be best. There are many such programs available on the market, tailored specifically for dental offices.

I am in the process of researching various dental practice management programs. These range in cost from $450 to $6000. Within 3 weeks I will have demos of several programs to review with you, so a decision can be made. Some possible programs are covered below.

Dentrix
Web site: http://www.dentrix.com
I have requested a demo CD. NOTE: This seems to be a first-class operation with good support. I do not have pricing information.

SoftDent
Web site: http://www.softdent.com
I have requested a demo CD. This seems to be a very full featured package. I do not have pric-

Computer System Purchase for Dental Office   2

Page 3:

Report created by Marcela Lopez on Today's Date

ing information.

PracticeWorks
Local sales rep., $4600 includes training, support, installation, etc. I have requested a demo CD and literature.

WinDent
Web site: http://www.windent.com
$5000 to purchase or $300/mo lease. Free phone support for the first year, after that $1000 a year. 1-800-555-9661. Salesperson: Kevin King. Demo disk is being sent to me.

HPS - Dental 2000
Web site: http://www.hpsnets.com
$3995, minus $500 if bought based on demo being sent. Can take 4 months to pay. 3 months support free. Demo disk being sent to me. 901-424-3999. Salesperson: James Prince.

Practisoft Advanced Dental Practice Accounting
Web site: http://www.medicserve.com
$450. I have downloaded a demo for this program; however it appears to have some bugs in it that prevent it from working well. This is a bad sign, if their demo has errors.

DentalWorks
Web site: http://www.bitesoft.com
$1500; I have downloaded a demo of this program, and will show it to you when we meet to review all the demos.

Dental Office Manager II
Web site: http://www.dom2.com
$750; I have requested a demo to be sent to me.

Dental Details
Web site: htttp://www.dentaldetails.com
$395 for full version; $35 for a demo CD that can be used for 6 months as a trial. I was not able to get a demo of this program without paying the $35 for it.

Autopia
Web site: http://www.autopia.com
I have requested a demo CD.

Consulting Fees

Time spent developing this proposal and gathering the software demos is covered by a barter agreement, and will not be billed.

Additional services can be purchased at $85/hour:

- **Software evaluation and demonstration**: I can install each of the demos on my laptop PC, figure out how they work, and demonstrate them to you, helping you make an informed choice in selecting a practice management program. I estimate that this would

Computer System Purchase for Dental Office   3

Lesson 10

Linking Text Boxes

➤ What You Will Learn

Creating Linked Text Boxes
Controlling Text Flow in Linked Text Boxes
Adjusting Linked Text Boxes

WORDS TO KNOW

Link
To join two text boxes
together so that any text
that does not fit in the
first one will flow into the
second one.

Overflow
The situation where there
is more text in a text box
than the text box can
display.

Unlink
To break a link between
text boxes.

Software Skills　Some Publisher templates, such as Newsletter templates,
include text boxes that are linked so that stories will flow from one text box to
another throughout the publication. You can also manually link text boxes to create
a publication where text flows from page to page.

What You Can Do

Creating Linked Text Boxes

- In some publications, you will not be able to display all of a story's text in one text
  box or on one page. In this situation, you can **link** text boxes so that text will flow
  from a full text box into another box, or even several additional boxes.

- Some Publisher templates, such as those for Newsletters, have text boxes
  already linked so that a story you place in the first text box will fill a series of text
  boxes on various pages of the publication.

  ✓ *You work with newsletters in Chapter 5.*

- If you do not want to use a Newsletter template, you can link text boxes yourself.
  Use the Create Link command in the Linking group on the TEXT BOX TOOLS
  FORMAT tab to create a link between text boxes.

- With a text box selected, click the Create Link command; the pointer changes
  shape to a pitcher pouring letters, as shown in Figure 10-1. Click in another text
  box, or simply click on a page, to establish the link.

- Linked text boxes display arrows attached to the selection border that point
  forward or backward to indicate how the boxes are linked.

Figure 10-1

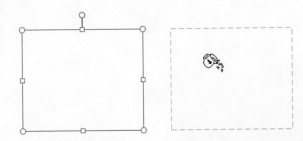

Try It!   **Creating Linked Text Boxes**

1 Start Publisher and open **PB10Try** from the data files for this lesson.

2 Save the publication as **PB10Try_xx** in the location where your teacher instructs you to store the files for this lesson.

3 Click HOME > Draw Text Box and position the crosshair at the intersection of the 2.5 inch horizontal ruler guide and the 3.2 inch vertical ruler guide.

4 Draw a text box that ends at the intersection of the right margin guide and the 6 inch ruler guide.

5 Click INSERT > Page to add a page.

6 Click INSERT > Draw Text Box and draw a text box that starts at the intersection of the left and top margin guides and is about 3 inches high and wide.

7 Click page 1 in the Page Navigation pane and click in the text box you drew on this page.

8 Click TEXT BOX TOOLS FORMAT > Create Link. The mouse pointer changes to a pitcher icon.

9 Click page 2 in the Page Navigation pane and click in the text box you drew on this page. The pointer changes to the pouring pitcher when over the text box on page 2. Note the left-pointing arrow at the upper-left side of the text box that indicates it is linked to the previous text box.

10 Click page 1 again and click in the text box to see the right-pointing arrow that indicates the link to the next text box.

11 Save the changes to **PB10Try_xx**, and leave it open to use in the next Try It.

Linked text box displays a right-pointing arrow

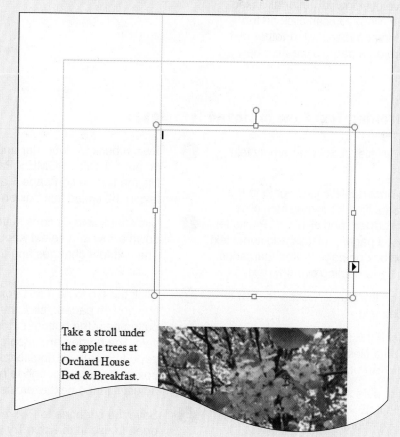

Take a stroll under the apple trees at Orchard House Bed & Breakfast.

Controlling Text Flow in Linked Text Boxes

■ You learned in Chapter 1 that if you import text using the Insert File command, Publisher will automatically add pages to place any text that does not fit in the text box into which you import the text. By default, Publisher places the extra text in full-page text boxes.

■ If you want more control over how text is placed, you can copy the text in its original file and then paste it in a Publisher text box.

■ When a text box contains more text than will display, the selection handles turn red to indicate there is **overflow** text—more text that needs to be placed. The Text in Overflow button displays near the lower-right corner of the full text box, as shown in Figure 10-2.

■ Overflow text is stored in the overflow area until you either increase the size of the current text box or link the current text box to another one so that the text can flow into the new text box.

■ If you have linked text boxes before pasting the text, the text will flow automatically into all linked text boxes. If you still have overflow text after all linked text boxes have been filled, you can click on the Text in Overflow button and then click another text box or click anywhere on a page to create a new text box.

■ You can easily move from text box to text box by clicking the Go to next text box or Go to previous text box arrow buttons attached to the linked text boxes.

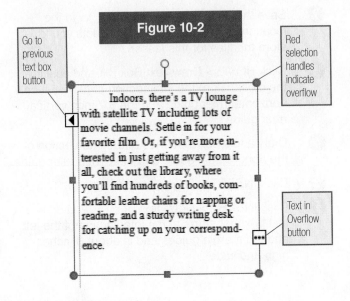

Figure 10-2

Go to previous text box button

Red selection handles indicate overflow

Indoors, there's a TV lounge with satellite TV including lots of movie channels. Settle in for your favorite film. Or, if you're more interested in just getting away from it all, check out the library, where you'll find hundreds of books, comfortable leather chairs for napping or reading, and a sturdy writing desk for catching up on your correspondence.

Text in Overflow button

Try It!   **Controlling Text Flow in Linked Text Boxes**

1 In the **PB10Try_xx** file, click in the empty text box on page 1.

2 Click INSERT > Insert File 📄, navigate to the location of the data files for this lesson, click **PB10Try_import.docx**, and click OK. Publisher fills the text box on page 1, places additional text in the linked text box on page 2, and then adds a page to hold the remaining overflow text.

3 Click Undo ↺ on the Quick Access Toolbar to remove all placed text.

4 Open Word, click FILE > Open, navigate to the location of the data files for this lesson, click **PB10Try_import.docx**, and click Open.

5 Press CTRL + A to select all text in the document, and then click HOME > Copy 📋. Then close the document and exit Word.

6 Switch back to Publisher and click in the text box on page 1. Click HOME > Paste 📋. Publisher fills the text box on page 1 and places additional text in the linked text box on page 2.

7 Click the Paste Options button's 📋 (Ctrl) ▾ drop-down arrow and select Keep Source Formatting. The text font changes and the text box on page 1 displays.

8 Click the Go to next text box button to select the text box on page 2, click the Text in Overflow button near the bottom of the right text box selection border, and then click anywhere on the page to create an additional linked text box. The box is not large enough to place all text; you will adjust it in the next exercise.

9 Save the changes to **PB10Try_xx**, and leave it open to use in the next Try It.

Adjusting Linked Text Boxes

- You control the amount of text that appears in any linked text box by adjusting the size of the text box.

- Enlarge a text box to display more text. Reduce a text box's size to push more of the text to the next linked text box.

- If you delete a linked text box, the text in it does not disappear. It moves to the next or previous linked text box.

- If at some point you do not want text boxes to flow text freely back and forth, you can **unlink** the text boxes using the Break Link command on the TEXT BOX TOOLS FORMAT tab. You break links from the first text box in the chain. This action causes text to fill the first text box, with overflow text going to the overflow area.

Try It!   **Adjusting Linked Text Boxes**

1 In the **PB10Try_xx** file, click the first text box on page 2 and notice the wording in the first line of text.

2 Press DEL to delete the text box. Note the text in the first line of the second text box on page 2 now begins with the same wording.

3 Click Undo ↶.

4 Enlarge the first text box to about 4 inches wide. More of the text from the second text box now appears in the first one.

5 Enlarge the second text box on page 2, if necessary, until the Text in Overflow button disappears, indicating that all text is now displayed.

6 Click the Go to previous text box arrow in the first text box on page 2 to select the text box on page 1, and then click TEXT BOX TOOLS FORMAT > Break ⛓. Note that text has been removed from the text boxes on page 2 and the text box on page 1 shows red overflow handles and the Text in Overflow button.

7 Close the publication, saving changes, and exit Publisher.

Lesson 10—Practice

The Greenwood Conservancy has asked you to create a publication about seasonal happenings at the Conservancy. Rather than use a Publisher template, you create a publication using linked text boxes.

DIRECTIONS

1. Start Publisher, if necessary, and open **PB10Practice** from the data files for this lesson.

2. Save the publication as **PB10Practice_xx** in the location where your teacher instructs you to store the files for this lesson.

3. On page 1, click **HOME > Draw Text Box** 🄰 and draw a text box in the left column of the publication between the 2.25 inch ruler guide and the 6 inch ruler guide.

4. Draw a text box in the left column below the 6.25 inch ruler guide that fills the column and extends down to the bottom margin guide.

5. Draw a similar text box in the right column below the 6.25 inch ruler guide.

6. Click in the first text box at the top of the page, click **TEXT BOX TOOLS FORMAT > Create Link** ⛓, and then click in the second text box at the bottom of the left column.

7. Click **TEXT BOX TOOLS FORMAT > Create Link** again ⛓ and click in the text box at the bottom of the right column.

8. Open Word, if necessary, click **FILE** > **Open**, and navigate to the location where data files are stored for this lesson.

9. Select **PB10Practice_import.docx** and click **Open**.

10. Press CTRL + A to select all text in the document.

11. Click **HOME** > **Copy** 📄. Then close the document and exit Word.

12. Click in the first text box in the publication and click **HOME** > **Paste** 📋. The text flows into the linked text boxes, but there is still overflow text to place. You will finish placing the text in the next project.

13. **With your teacher's permission**, print the publication. It should look similar to Figure 10-3.

14. Close the publication, saving changes, and exit Publisher.

Figure 10-3

Greenwood in Fall

Greenwood Conservancy is an expanse of hardwood forest that includes some of the largest and oldest trees in the state. The land was previously the property of the Madison family, who have owned this area of the state since Colonial times. Thomas Madison deeded the land to Greenwood Conservancy in 1990, in the hopes of preserving this rare and precious resource for future generations. Thanks to his generous gift, we can protect a portion of this state's natural heritage from the ravages of development.

The Greenwood Conservancy is designated as an old growth forest. Old growth forests are characterized by many large live trees, large dead trees (sometimes called snags), mixed-age stands, minimal signs of human disruption, a multi-layered canopy that includes open areas where large trees have come down, a characteristic topography consisting of pits where tree roots have come up out of the ground and mounds of organic matter, and a rich ground layer composed of decaying wood and leaves.

At no time of the year is the diversity of species as apparent as in fall. The Conservancy becomes a crazy quilt of breathtaking hues: The bright yellows of aspen and birch, the molten oranges of sugar maple, the flaming reds of scarlet oaks and red maples, the bronzes of many species of oaks and laurel, and the vibrant red-black of sweet gums punctuated by vivid greens of pines and firs create a living tapestry that blankets the Conservancy's rolling hills. Fall is the final shout of joy before the forest quiets down into its long winter sleep.

When you visit the Conservancy in fall, you can find plenty of ways to enjoy our environment:

—Drive Scenic Route 48 to enjoy vistas on all sides, especially the spectacular views from the Cobbler's Hill turnout and the Golden Valley overlook.

Lesson 10—Apply

In this exercise, you complete the Greenwood Conservancy publication. You adjust the text boxes and add a page to flow the text properly so that all content displays.

DIRECTIONS

1. Start Publisher, if necessary, and open **PB10Apply** from the data files for this lesson.

2. Save the publication as **PB10Apply_xx** in the location where your teacher instructs you to store the files for this lesson.

3. Delete the text box at the bottom of the left column.

4. Resize the text box at the top of the left column to extend all the way to the bottom margin guide.

5. Add a page to the publication.

6. Draw a text box about 3 inches tall at the top of page 2, from margin to margin. Specify two columns for the text box with 0.2 inch spacing between columns.

7. Link the text box in the right column of page 1 to the text box on page 2. Text flows from page 1 to the linked text box on page 2 and fills both columns, but there is still text in overflow.

8. Adjust the depth of the text box on page 2 until all text is displayed and a roughly equal amount of text displays in each column.

9. **With your teacher's permission**, print the publication. Page 1 should look similar to Figure 10-4. Page 2 should look similar to Figure 10-5.

10. Close the publication, saving changes, and exit Publisher.

Figure 10-4

Greenwood in Fall

Greenwood Conservancy is an expanse of hardwood forest that includes some of the largest and oldest trees in the state. The land was previously the property of the Madison family, who have owned this area of the state since Colonial times. Thomas Madison deeded the land to Greenwood Conservancy in 1990, in the hopes of preserving this rare and precious resource for future generations. Thanks to his generous gift, we can protect a portion of this state's natural heritage from the ravages of development.

The Greenwood Conservancy is designated as an old growth forest. Old growth forests are characterized by many large live trees, large dead trees (sometimes called snags), mixed-age stands, minimal signs of human disruption, a multi-layered canopy that includes open areas where large trees have come down, a characteristic topography consisting of pits where tree roots have come up out of the ground and mounds of organic matter, and a rich ground layer composed of decaying wood and leaves.

At no time of the year is the diversity of species as apparent as in fall. The Conservancy becomes a crazy quilt of breath-taking hues: The bright yellows of aspen and birch, the molten oranges of sugar maple, the flaming reds of scarlet oaks and red maples, the bronzes of many spe-

cies of oaks and laurel, and the vibrant red-black of sweet gums punctuated by vivid greens of pines and firs create a living tapestry that blankets the Conservancy's rolling hills. Fall is the final shout of joy before the forest quiets down into its long winter sleep.

When you visit the Conservancy in fall, you can find plenty of ways to enjoy our environment:

—Drive Scenic Route 48 to enjoy vistas on all sides, especially the spectacular views from the Cobbler's Hill turnout and the Golden Valley overlook.

Figure 10-5

—Hike the 65 miles of well-maintained trails that wind through spectacular stands of oak and maple and visit several scenic waterfalls.

—Participate in guided tours of some of the most interesting areas of the forest.

—Join us for hearty Sunday brunches that include fresh ingredients such as eggs from free-range chickens and vegetables from local organic farms. Our Greenwood blend coffee is sure to get you on your feet to enjoy that hike!

—Bring the children to introduce them to the wonders of our natural environment. They'll enjoy old-fashioned games and crafts and a visit to the Sugar Shack for kid-style refreshments.

—Stop in at the Greenwood Gift Shop to pick up unique gifts from local crafters, including hand-woven goods, wood carvings, fine jewelry, Greenwood-themed wearing apparel, and one-of-a-

kind items such as local honey and maple syrup, while it lasts.

For those of you interested in serious conservation issues, the Greenwood Resources Center offers seminars and classes on ways you can conserve natural resources in your community and even in your own backyard.

Learn how to safeguard the health of your trees from pests such as the emerald ash borer and how to enrich the soil in your gardens using compost you create from kitchen scraps and garden waste. Find out how rain gardens can help to control precipitation runoff. And discover ways to maintain natural communities of birds and other wildlife.

There's a lot to like about the fall at Greenwood. We hope we'll see you soon!

Lesson 11

Using Master Pages

➤ What You Will Learn

About Master Pages
Placing Objects on the Master Page
Using Multiple Master Pages
Applying a Master Page
Naming Pages
Moving Pages

WORDS TO KNOW

Foreground
The "normal" part of the publication, where you place the text, graphics, and other objects that are unique to each page.

Master page
The backdrop on which you place elements that should repeat on every page of the publication to which that master page is applied.

Software Skills   You can ensure consistency among the pages of a publication with a background template called a master page. Most publications have a single master page, but Publisher enables you to create and use multiple master pages in a single publication if desired.

What You Can Do

About Master Pages

- Each publication has a **master page**, on which you place any objects that you want to repeat the same way on every page in the publication. You can think of the master page as the solid "sheet" beneath each page, and each page as a kind of transparency overlaid on top of it. Objects not included on the master page are on the **foreground**.

- The header and footer text boxes exist on this master page; when you were working with the header and footer, you were actually displaying and editing text boxes on the master page.

- You can place any object anywhere on the master page to make it repeat on each page. This could include text boxes, graphics, or other objects.

- Creating masters can speed your work on long publications because you can set up the layout once and use it over and over. For publications that have a number of different types of page layouts, setting up a master for each layout makes it far easier for you to ensure consistency among pages.

- Switch between master page and the foreground using the Master Page command on the VIEW tab. Make sure you don't inadvertently add items to the background that belong on an individual page.

  ✓ Use the ⟨CTRL⟩ + ⟨M⟩ shortcut to quickly switch back and forth between the master page and the foreground.

- By default the master page is blank; it contains content only if you placed any there, either manually or by using the Header and Footer or Page Number commands.

Placing Objects on the Master Page

- You can easily send objects back and forth between the master page and the foreground.

- Select the object(s) and then click Master Pages in the Page Background group on the PAGE DESIGN tab and select Send to Master Page.

- If there are multiple master pages in the publication (see the next section), and you use Send to Master Page, the object is sent to the master page that is currently applied to that page.

- When viewing the master page, you can select objects and choose PAGE DESIGN, Send to Foreground from the Master Pages menu to return them to the main publication.

- You can also place objects on the master page by inserting text boxes or graphics while viewing the master page.

Try It!   **Placing Objects on the Master Page**

1 Start Publisher and open **PB11Try** from the data files for this lesson.

2 Save the publication as **PB11Try_xx** in the location where your teacher instructs you to store the files for this lesson.

3 Press ⟨CTRL⟩ + ⟨A⟩ to select all objects on the page.

4 Click PAGE DESIGN > Master Pages ⊡ > Send to Master Page. Then click OK to confirm.

5 Click VIEW > Master Page ⊡. Note that all objects you selected are now part of the master page for the publication.

6 Click INSERT > Draw Text Box ⊡ and draw a text box at the top of the page from the left margin guide to the right margin guide and about 1.25 inches high.

7 Type **Orchard House**. Click TEXT BOX TOOLS FORMAT > Text Fit ⊡ > Best Fit.

8 Click in the main text box on the page (*Guest Comforts*), and then click PAGE DESIGN > Master Pages ⊡ > Send to Foreground. Click OK.

9 Click in the figure caption text box to the left of the picture at the bottom of the page, and then click PAGE DESIGN > Master Pages ⊡ > Send to Foreground. Click OK.

✓ You send these two objects to the foreground so that you can change the text if desired. The Orchard House *text box remains on the master because it will not need to be changed.*

10 Save the changes to **PB11Try_xx**, and leave it open to use in the next Try It.

The master page now displays a heading and a picture

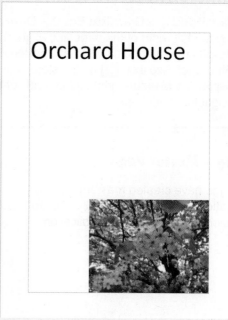

Using Multiple Master Pages

■ A publication can use more than one master page. You may, for example, want to create a master page for the first page of a report or newsletter, and then create one or more additional master pages for other parts of the publication.

■ The default master page is called Master A. Additional masters are designated as Master B, Master C, and so on.

✓ *You can change the Page ID character from B to any other character, such as a number. You can also rename a master at any time by clicking the Rename button in Master Page view.*

■ Use the Add Master Page command to insert a new master page.

■ Use the Duplicate button to create a new master identical to the currently selected one. This is a good option if the new master will be very similar to the current master.

■ You can delete master pages, as long as at least one remains. (You cannot delete the last one.) With the master selected that you want to delete, click the Delete button.

Try It!   **Using Multiple Master Pages**

1 In the **PB11Try_xx** file, in Master Page view, click MASTER PAGE > Add Master Page 🗋.

2 Click OK to accept the new ID and description.

3 Click PAGE DESIGN > Margins ▥ > Wide.

4 Click PAGE DESIGN > Guides ▤ > Grid and Baseline Guides. In the Layout Guides dialog box, type **2** to change the number of columns from 1 to 2. Click the Spacing up arrow to change spacing to 0.2". Click OK.

5 Drag a horizontal ruler guide to the 1.5 inch mark on the vertical ruler.

6 Click INSERT > Draw Text Box Ⓐ. Draw a text box the full width of the page and aligned at the top with the ruler guide you just inserted. Click the Object Size icon 🔳 on the status bar to display the Measurement toolbar and set the height to 3.3 inches.

7 Click TEXT BOX TOOLS FORMAT > Columns ▤ > More Columns. Click the Number up arrow to change the number of columns to 2. Press TAB and type **0.2**. Click OK.

8 Click MASTER PAGE > Close Master Page ☒. You now have an additional page in the publication with the elements of Master Page A applied.

9 Save the changes to **PB11Try_xx**, and leave it open to use in the next Try It.

Applying a Master Page

■ Once you have created master pages for a publication, you can easily apply them to ensure consistency throughout the publication.

■ You can apply the master page from the master page area using the Apply To command to apply the master to all pages or the current page, or you can click Apply Master Page on the Apply To menu to open a dialog box in which you can select all pages, a range of pages, or the current page.

■ You can also use the Master Pages gallery on the PAGE DESIGN tab to apply a master to a page.

Try It!   Applying a Master Page

1 In the PB11Try_xx file, click page 2 in the Page Navigation pane, and then click PAGE DESIGN > Master Pages 📄 > Master Page B.

2 Click VIEW > Master Page 📄 to display Master Page B.

3 Click the text box on the master page to select it, and then click PAGE DESIGN > Master Pages 📄 > Send to Foreground. Click OK to confirm that the text box will move to page 2.

4 Click MASTER PAGE > Close Master Page ✖ .

5 Click the Text in Overflow button on page 1 and click in the text box on page 2 to display all text.

6 Save the changes to PB11Try_xx, and leave it open to use in the next Try It.

Naming Pages

- Each page of your publication can have a unique name. This name does not show up when the publication is printed.

- The main purpose of a page name is to help you keep track of which page is which when you are constructing the publication and arranging pages.

- You will see the page name when you hover the mouse pointer over a page in the Page Navigation pane.

- Use the Rename command in the Pages group on the PAGE DESIGN tab to name a page. If the page you want to rename is part of a two-page spread, you have the option of naming both the left and right pages.

Try It!   Naming Pages

1 In the PB11Try_xx file, click page 1 in the Page Navigation pane.

2 Click PAGE DESIGN > Rename 📄 in the Pages group.

3 Type Opener Page and click OK.

4 Click INSERT > Page 📄 to insert a new page following page 1. Click PAGE DESIGN > Master Pages 📄 > None to remove the Master Page A elements.

5 Click PAGE DESIGN > Rename 📄, type Mailing Page, and click OK.

6 Click page 3, click PAGE DESIGN > Rename 📄, type Body Page, and click OK.

7 Hover the mouse pointer over each page in the Page Navigation pane to see the page names.

8 Save the changes to PB11Try_xx, and leave it open to use in the next Try It.

Moving Pages

- You can rearrange the pages in your publication by dragging the page thumbnails in the Page Navigation pane.

- You can also rearrange pages using the Move command in the Pages group on the PAGE DESIGN tab. In the Move Page dialog box, select a page, choose whether to display it before or after, and then select the page it should appear before or after.

- If you have named pages as described in the previous section, the page names display in the Move Page dialog box. This makes it easy to relocate pages when you have more than a few pages in a publication.

- If pages are shown as spreads, the Move Page dialog box allows you to choose whether to move both pages, only the left page, or only the right page.

Try It!   Moving Pages

1 In the **PB11Try_xx** file, select the blank page 2 (Mailing Page) in the Page Navigation pane and drag it above page 1 (Opener Page).

2 Click PAGE DESIGN > Move 🔄. In the Move Page dialog box, make sure that Page 1. Mailing Page is selected.

3 Click the After option, if necessary, and then click Page 3. Body Page. Click OK.

4 Close the publication, saving changes, and exit Publisher.

Lesson 11—Practice

Martha Sieberling, the owner of Flora, has asked you to create master pages for the catalog being prepared for spring to make it easy to create not just this version but future catalogs. In this exercise, you name and reorder pages and then create and apply new master pages.

DIRECTIONS

1. Start Publisher, if necessary, and open **PB11Practice** from the data files for this lesson.

2. Save the publication as **PB11Practice_xx** in the location where your teacher instructs you to store the files for this lesson.

3. Click page 1 in the Page Navigation pane. Then click **PAGE DESIGN > Rename** 🔖, type **Title Page**, and click **OK**.

4. Click page 2 in the Page Navigation pane. Then click **PAGE DESIGN > Rename** 🔖, type **End Page**, and click **OK**.

5. With page 2 still selected, click **PAGE DESIGN > Move** 🔄. Click **Page 8. Page Title**, and then click **OK**.

6. Click page 7 and drag it up in the Page Navigation pane to just below page 1.

7. Click page 1 and then click **VIEW > Master Page** 🔖. Note that Master Page A is a two-page master, but you want to create a master page for the title page that is a single page.

8. Click **MASTER PAGE > Add Master Page** 🔖. Type the description **Title Page**, and deselect **Two-page master**. Click **OK**.

9. Click **MASTER PAGE > Apply To** 🔖 > **Apply to Current Page**.

10. Click **MASTER PAGE > Close Master Page** ✖.

11. With page 1 selected, press `CTRL` + `A` to select all objects on the page.

12. Click **PAGE DESIGN > Master Pages** 🔖 > **Send to Master Page**. Click **OK** to confirm that the objects have been sent to the Title Page master.

13. Click **VIEW > Two-Page Spread** 📖, and then click on the pages 6–7 spread.

14. Click **VIEW > Master Page** 🔖.

15. Click **MASTER PAGE > Duplicate** 🔖. Type the description **Catalog Page**, and click **OK**.

16. Click **MASTER PAGE > Apply To** 🔖 > **Apply Master Page**. In the Apply Master Page dialog box, click **Pages**, then type **6** in the from box and **7** in the to box. Click **OK**.

17. Click **MASTER PAGE > Close Master Page** ✖.

18. Display pages 6–7. Click `CTRL` + `A` to select all objects on the spread. Click **PAGE DESIGN > Master Pages** 🔖 > **Send to Master Page**. Click **OK** to confirm that the objects have been sent to the Catalog Page master.

19. Close the publication, saving changes, and exit Publisher.

Lesson 11—Apply

You continue to work on the Flora catalog. In this exercise, you rename the remaining pages, add two new master pages, and then adjust content for both the catalog and master pages.

DIRECTIONS

1. Start Publisher, if necessary, and open **PB11Apply** from the data files for this lesson.

2. Save the publication as **PB11Apply_xx** in the location where your teacher instructs you to store the files for this lesson.

3. Rename the remaining pages as follows:

   a. Click the pages 2–3 spread, and rename the left page **Inside Blank** and the right page **TOC**.

   b. Click the pages 4–5 spread and rename the left page **Intro Page** and the right page **Special Page**.

   c. Click the pages 6–7 spread and rename both pages **Catalog Page**.

4. Click the pages 2–3 spread and then open Master Page view and create a new master page for these introductory pages.

   a. Duplicate Master Page A and rename the duplicate **Front Matter**.

   b. Remove the header and footer from the left page.

   c. Remove the header on the right page.

   d. Display the footer area of the right page, press TAB once, and insert the page number.

   e. Apply the Front Matter master to pages 2 and 3, and then close the master page.

5. Click page 8 and then open Master Page view and create a new master page for the last page of the publication:

   a. Duplicate Master Page A and rename the duplicate **End Page**.

   b. Deselect the **Two Page Master** button 📖 on the MASTER PAGE tab to make the new master page a single page master. Click **OK** when warned about removing the left page.

   c. Apply the master page to the current page.

   d. Send all content from page 8 to the End Page master page.

6. Select page 1. Return to Master Page view and make the following changes to the masters:

   a. Delete the page number text box at the bottom of the page.

   b. Send the *Spring Catalog* and the *Date* text boxes to the foreground.

7. Select the pages 6–7 spread and open Master Page view. Make the following changes:

   a. Press CTRL + A to select all objects on the master pages.

   b. Holding down SHIFT, click on the headers on both pages, the footer on the left page, and the eight horizontal lines above and below the catalog copy.

   c. Send the remaining selected items to the foreground.

   d. To make sure that your catalog master pages will show only the headers, footers, and horizontal lines between items, insert a new page following page 7 and apply the Catalog Page master page.

8. **With your teacher's permission**, print the publication. Pages 2 and 3 should look like Figure 11-1 on the next page.

9. Close the publication, saving changes, and exit Publisher.

Figure 11-1

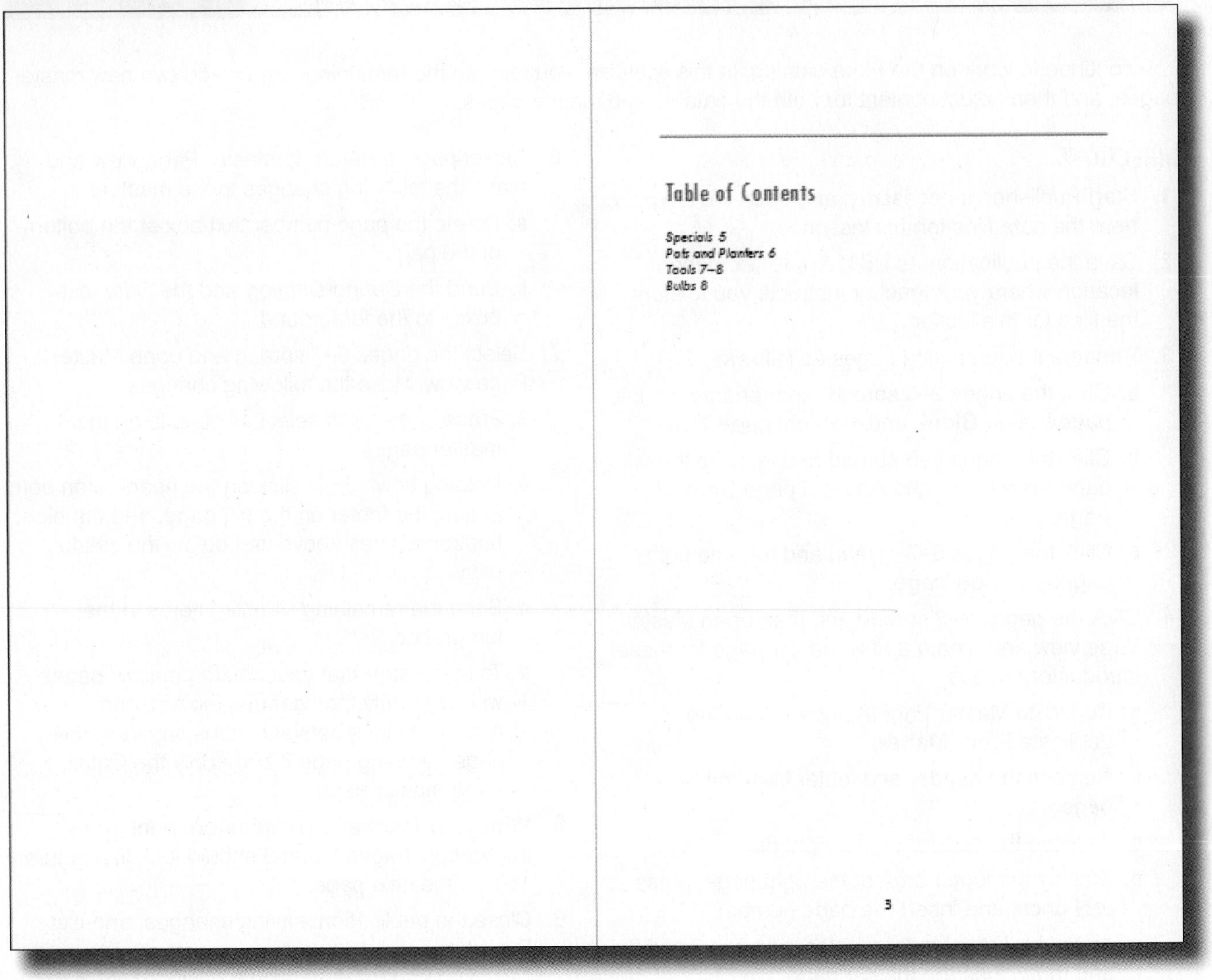

Table of Contents

3

Lesson 12

Working with Building Blocks

➤ What You Will Learn

Inserting Building Blocks
Saving an Object As a Building Block

Software Skills   You can use building blocks to add content in the form of page parts, decorative items, and even advertisement components to quickly create a page layout or customize an existing template. You can save your own objects to the Building Block Library to make them available for other projects.

What You Can Do

Inserting Building Blocks

- In this chapter, you have learned how to create publications by drawing text boxes and positioning them where desired on a blank page. In this lesson, you learn how to create much more sophisticated publications from scratch using **building blocks**.

- Building blocks include page parts such as headings, stories, **pull quotes**, and **sidebars**; calendars; graphic borders and accents; and preconstructed advertisement elements such as coupons and attention getters.

- You will find the building block galleries in the Building Blocks group on the INSERT tab. Insert a building block by simply clicking it on the gallery.

- If you don't find a building block you like, you can click the More command at the bottom of any gallery to open the Building Block Library for that category. You will find an expanded selection of building blocks, some available from Office.com.

- You can add a building block to any publication, or you can construct a new publication entirely from building blocks. Building blocks such as stories, headings, and sidebars include placeholders into which you can insert your own text, just as in a template.

- Once you have inserted a building block, you can modify it as you would modify other objects. You can resize it or move it; if you change the font scheme or color scheme, the building block will reflect those changes.

WORDS TO KNOW

Building block
A text element or graphic object that you can insert in any publication.

Pull quote
A portion of a story that has been "pulled out" of the story and placed in a text box within the story for emphasis.

Sidebar
Text content such as information related to the main story that is positioned in a text box that displays beside the main story.

Try It!   **Inserting Building Blocks**

1 Start Publisher and click Blank 8.5 × 11" to start a new blank document.

2 Save the publication as **PB12Try_xx** in the location where your teacher instructs you to store the files for this lesson.

3 Click INSERT > Borders & Accents ▛ to display the Design Accents Gallery. Click the Awning Stripes building block in the Bars category.

4 Position the graphic in the upper-left corner of the page. Then click the lower-right selection handle and drag to the right until the crosshair reaches the right margin guide without increasing the height of the object.

5 Click INSERT > Page Parts ▤ to display the Page Parts Gallery. Click the Convention heading building block.

6 Position the building block just below the stripes element at the left margin guide. Click the lower-right selection handle and drag to the right margin.

7 Click the *TITLE TEXT* placeholder text and type **BRADLEY & CUMMINS**. Click the *SUBTITLE TEXT* placeholder text and type **WHAT'S NEWS?**

8 Click INSERT > Page Parts ▤. Click the Pure (Layout 2) sidebar building block and then position it at the right margin beneath the heading.

9 Click the *TITLE TEXT* placeholder text and type **GARDEN TOUR**. Click the message text placeholder and type the following text:

Bradley & Cummins is proud to be a sponsor of the 12th Annual Athens Garden Tour. Join us in viewing some of the finest gardens of your town!

10 Click in the text you just typed, click TEXT BOX TOOLS FORMAT > Text Fit ▣ > Best Fit.

11 Click INSERT > Advertisements ▣ > More Advertisements. In the Building Block Library, scroll down to the Attention Getters category and click Brackets. Click Insert.

12 Resize the building block to a width of about 2.5 inches, and position it below the sidebar.

13 Click the placeholder text and type **Buy 1 ticket, get 1 free!**

14 Click PAGE DESIGN > Equity to change the color scheme. Click PAGE DESIGN > Fonts Aa > Metro to change the font scheme.

15 Save the changes to **PB12Try_xx**, and leave it open to use in the next Try It.

Building blocks add content
to a blank publication

Saving an Object As a Building Block

- You can create your own reusable objects and store them in the building block galleries.

- These objects can either be items you create "from scratch" or existing building block objects that you have customized with your own information.

- Save an object as a building block by selecting it and then clicking the command of the building block category to which you want to add the object. To add a design to the Design Accents gallery, for example, click Borders & Accents and then Add Selection to Design Accents Gallery.

- The Create New Building Block dialog box allows you to specify a title for the new building block, add a description if desired, select the gallery in which the building block will be stored, and choose a category.

- Your building blocks appear in the category to which you saved them. You insert a building block you have saved the same way you insert any other building block.

- You can delete a custom building block at any time by right-clicking it on the gallery and selecting Delete.

Try It!   **Saving an Object As a Building Block**

1 In the **PB12Try_xx** file, click on the title building block to which you added the *Bradley & Cummins* title.

2 Click INSERT > Page Parts ▤ > Add Selection to Page Parts Gallery.

3 Type the title **B&C Heading**. Press TAB and type the description **Newsletter heading**.

4 Click the Category drop-down arrow and select Headings, and then click OK.

5 Click INSERT > Page Parts ▤ and view the Headings category. Your building block should appear as the first building block in the Headings category.

6 Right-click the B&C Heading building block and click Delete.

7 Close the publication, saving changes, and exit Publisher.

Lesson 12—Practice

John Lowery of The Hendricks Inn wants to create a one-page flyer, including some quotations from happy customers and a coupon, to mail to potential customers. None of the Publisher templates have exactly what he wants, so in this exercise, you build one that meets his exact specifications using building blocks.

DIRECTIONS

1. Start Publisher, if necessary, and open **PB12Practice** from the data files for this lesson.

2. Save the publication as **PB12Practice_xx** in the location where your teacher instructs you to store the files for this lesson.

3. Click **INSERT** > **Page Parts** 📄 > **More Page Parts**. In the Building Block Library, click the **All Headings** folder.

4. Click **Capsules** and then click **Insert**.

5. Move the heading to the top of the page, with the upper-left corner at the intersection of the left and top margin guides.

6. Add text to the heading as follows:

   a. Select the business name placeholder text and type **The Hendricks Inn**.

   b. Select the newsletter date and type today's date.

   c. Select the newsletter title and type **Hendricks Gazette**.

7. Move the *Springtime Is Garden Time* text box upward to sit just below the heading (see Figure 12-1 on the next page).

8. Click **INSERT** > **Page Parts** 📄, and then click the **Pure** pull quote. Repeat this step to insert the **Portal** and the **Geometric** pull quotes, and position them as shown in Figure 12-1. Use the Geometric pull quote's selection handles to resize the shape as shown.

9. Insert text in the pull quotes as follows, resizing the shapes as necessary to display all text:

   a. In the Pure pull quote, type:

   "Sitting on the deck at The Hendricks Inn in the evenings watching the fireflies was the highlight of our vacation."
   —Sheila and Rob Roberson, Dallas, TX

   b. In the Portal pull quote, type:

   "We try to visit The Hendricks Inn in the spring, summer, and fall because the gardens are so different in each season, each beautiful in its own way."
   —Larry Meyer, Tulsa, OK

   c. In the Geometric pull quote, type:

   "We had seen pictures of the perennial gardens on the Web site, but they were even more spectacular in person."
   —Ann West, San Diego, CA

10. Click **INSERT** > **Advertisements** 📧, and click the **Open Background** coupon. Position the coupon near the bottom of the page, centered horizontally.

11. Insert text in the coupon as follows, (You may want to zoom in on the selected object to make these changes.)

   a. Replace the text *Name of Item or Service* with **One Night's Stay**.

   b. Replace *00% OFF* with **50% OFF**.

   c. Replace *Organization Name* with **The Hendricks Inn**.

   d. Replace *Describe your location* with **1478 W. 86th St., Hendricks, KY**.

   e. Replace the telephone number with **Tel: (327) 555-1987**.

   f. Replace the expiration date with **12/31/2015**.

12. Check spelling in all stories.

13. **With your teacher's permission**, print the publication. It should look similar to Figure 12-1 on the next page.

14. Close the publication, saving changes, and exit Publisher.

Figure 12-1

The Hendricks Inn

Volume 1, Issue 1

Today's Date

Hendricks Gazette

Springtime Is Garden Time!

The flowers are blooming, and the grass is a bright emerald green on the hills surrounding The Hendricks Inn. Come stroll through our gardens and orchard and discover the unique beauty of our property. Relax on the deck overlooking the bird feeders, where an array of bird life regularly appears including woodpeckers, hummingbirds, and finches.

Come see us at The Hendricks Inn and save 50%!

"Sitting on the deck at The Hendricks Inn in the evenings watching the fireflies was the highlight of our vacation."
—Sheila and Rob Roberson, Dallas, TX

"We try to visit The Hendricks Inn in the spring, summer, and fall because the gardens are so different in each season, each beautiful in its own way."
—Larry Meyer, Tulsa, OK

"We had seen pictures of the perennial gardens on the Web site, but they were even more spectacular in person."
—Ann West, San Diego, CA

One Night's Stay

50% OFF

The Hendricks Inn
1478 W. 86th St., Hendricks, KY
TEL: (327) 555-1987

Expiration Date: 12/31/2015

Lesson 12—Apply

You continue to work with the newsletter design for The Hendricks Inn. In this exercise, you add more design features and then save the customized building blocks so you can easily create a new version of the newsletter.

DIRECTIONS

1. Start Publisher, if necessary, and open **PB12Apply** from the data files for this lesson.

2. Save the publication as **PB12ApplyA_xx** in the location where your teacher instructs you to store the files for this lesson.

3. Change the color scheme to **Mulberry**.

4. Insert a building block bar accent of your choice, such as Argyle, and position it to the left of the coupon. Adjust the size if needed to align with the left margin and still leave some space between the building block and the coupon. Insert another instance of the same building block on the right side of the coupon.

5. Select the heading and save it as a new building block in the Page Parts gallery. Use the title **Hendricks Title**, a description of your choice, and the **Headings** category.

6. Select the coupon and the two accent bars and save the selection as a new building block in the Advertisements gallery. Use the title **Hendricks Coupon with Bars**, a description of your choice, and the **Coupons** category.

7. **With your teacher's permission**, print the publication. It should look similar to Figure 12-2 on the next page.

8. Close the publication, saving changes.

9. Start a new publication using the 8.5 × 11" blank template.

10. Save the publication as **PB12ApplyB_xx** in the location where your teacher instructs you to store the files for this lesson.

11. Insert the **Hendricks Title** building block and move it to the top of the page.

    ✓ *Because scheme colors are used for the building blocks, the colors change in the new document to the equivalent colors for this template.*

12. Insert the **Hendricks Coupon with Bars** building block.

13. **With your teacher's permission**, print the publication. It should look similar to Figure 12-3 on the next page.

14. Delete the Hendricks Title building block.

15. Delete the Hendricks Coupon with Bars building block.

16. Close the document, saving changes, and exit Publisher.

Figure 12-2

Figure 12-3

End-of-Chapter Activities

➤ Publisher Chapter 2—Critical Thinking

Workplace Communication

Vanessa Bradley was pleased with the posters you made to display improper word usage and unnecessary verbal phrases; everyone at the Realty is taking more care over their written and verbal communications. Now Vanessa has decided to address another subject that she believes will make the Realty a better place to work: communications between colleagues and clients. She has in mind a poster or newsletter about effective workplace communication—"just the basics!"

In conversation with Vanessa, you have determined the basics to be a discussion of active listening, verbal and nonverbal communications, and conflict resolution. In this project, you will research information on these topics and then create a publication that provides information about them.

DIRECTIONS

1. **With your teacher's permission**, search the Web for information about active listening, verbal and nonverbal communications, and conflict resolution in the workplace. Take notes on paper or in a word processing program, taking care to record the Web addresses of the sites where you find information.

2. Start Publisher, select **More Blank Page Sizes** on the New tab, and then select **Tabloid (Portrait) 11 x 17"**. Choose a color scheme and font scheme, and then create the publication.

3. Save the publication as **PBCT02_xx** in the location where your teacher instructs you to store the files for this chapter.

4. Select a heading page part to place at the top of the publication and insert the title **Improving Communications**, with the subtitle **A Publication by Bradley & Cummins Realty**.

5. Insert another heading page part below the publication title and use the title **Basic Business Communications**.

6. Spend a few moments mocking up the page to determine how you will present the information you researched. You may decide at this point that a two-page newsletter approach would be a better way to present the information. If so, change the page size and then readjust the position and sizes of the building blocks you have added so far.

7. Adjust margins as necessary and insert layout guides and ruler guides to help you lay out the publication.

8. Insert page parts and text boxes as necessary to contain the information you intend to present. If necessary, add a page to the publication and link text boxes on the first page to continuations on the second page. You may set text in columns to make it easier to read. If you recorded information in a word processing file, you may import the text using the Insert File command or copy and paste it into the text boxes. Your publication should contain the following parts:

   a. The publication title given in step 4 and the topic title given in step 5.

   b. An introduction to the topics that will be covered and an explanation of why workplace communication is important.

   c. An explanation of active listening and how it is helpful in the workplace.

   d. An explanation of both verbal and nonverbal communications, and how an understanding of both methods of communication can improve interactions between colleagues and between realty staff and clients.

   e. An explanation of what causes conflict and how to resolve conflicts in the workplace.

   f. A list of sources you consulted to find the information you have presented.

9. Insert your full name, page number, and the date in a footer on all pages.

10. Check the spelling in the publication and correct errors as necessary.

11. **With your teacher's permission**, print the publication.

12. Close the publication, saving changes, and exit Publisher.

➤ Publisher Chapter 2—Portfolio Builder

Newsletter Design

Pet Rescue would like you to design a newsletter they can send to friends of the shelter. You will use what you have learned about templates, designs, color schemes, and other objects to do this.

DIRECTIONS

1. Start Publisher and select the blank 8.5 × 11" page template. Save the publication as **PBPB02_xx** in the location where your teacher instructs you to store files for this chapter.

2. Insert a building block heading of your choice. Use **Pet Rescue** as the business name, **Happenings** as the newsletter title, and **Autumn** for the newsletter date.

3. Insert a building block border at the bottom margin that extends from left margin to right margin.

4. Send all items on the page to the master page.

5. On the master page, click the heading and then click **DRAWING TOOLS FORMAT** > **Ungroup** ⬚ to ungroup the items that make up the heading. Deselect all objects, and then select and send the *Autumn* and *Volume 1* text boxes to the foreground so you can easily change them in the next issue. Close Master Page view.

6. Place a horizontal ruler guide at 3 inches and a vertical ruler guide at about 2 inches (or a position that aligns with some part of your heading). At the intersection, insert a heading building block, and then draw a text box beneath the heading to fill the rest of the page. Insert some sample text in the text box so the person who creates the newsletter will know where to place text.

7. Add a new master page. Change the top margin on this master to 1 inch, leaving other margins at their default settings. Use grid guides to create two columns.

8. Insert a header of your choice at the top of the page and the page number centered in the footer area.

9. Add a page to the publication and apply the Master Page B master. Draw a text box the full width of the page, from the top margin to about the 6 inch mark on the vertical ruler. Specify two columns in the text box, with the spacing between columns the same as for the grid guides. Link the text box on page 1 to the text box on page 2.

10. Create new color and font schemes to customize the publication.

11. **With your teacher's permission**, print the publication. Illustration 2A, on the next page, shows one way the publication could look.

12. Delete the custom color scheme and font scheme.

13. Close the publication, saving changes, and exit Publisher.

Illustration 2A

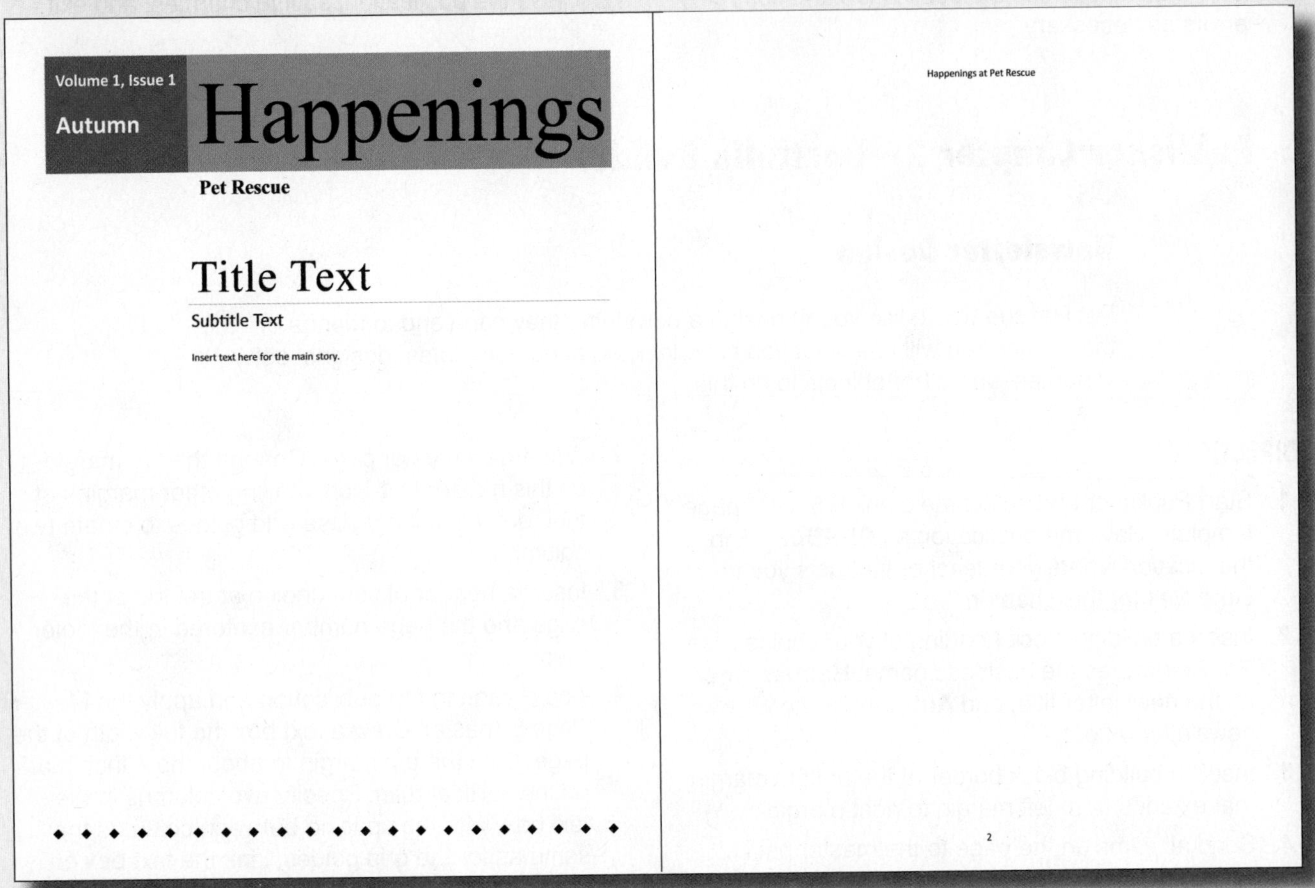

Volume 1, Issue 1

Autumn

Happenings

Pet Rescue

Title Text

Subtitle Text

Insert text here for the main story.

Happenings at Pet Rescue

2

Chapter 3

(Courtesy donatas1205/Shutterstock)

Working with Fonts and Styles

Lesson 13
Changing Font Formatting

- Changing Font, Font Size, Font Color, and Font Style
- Applying Text Effects and WordArt Styles
- Changing Character Spacing
- Creating a Drop Cap

Lesson 14
Applying Object Borders and Fills

- Applying Object Borders
- Changing an Object's Fill Color
- Working with Grouped Objects
- Applying Shape Styles and Other Effects

Lesson 15
Applying Special Border and Fill Effects

- Applying a Patterned Border
- Using BorderArt
- Using Fill Effects

Lesson 16
Applying Paragraph Formats

- Aligning Text Horizontally and Vertically
- Changing Line and Paragraph Spacing

Lesson 17
Controlling Text with Tabs and Indents

- Using Tab Stops
- Setting, Modifying, and Removing Tab Stops
- Using Tab Leaders
- Applying Indents
- Adjusting Text Box Margins

Lesson 18
Working with Lists

- Creating Bulleted Lists
- Creating Numbered Lists

Lesson 19
Working with Styles

- Controlling Line and Paragraph Breaks
- Copying Text Formatting
- Applying a Style
- Creating a Style
- Modifying and Deleting Styles
- Importing Styles from Other Publications

Lesson 20
Working with Typographic Features

- Using OpenType Fonts
- Selecting Number Styles
- Applying Ligatures
- Applying Stylistic Sets, Swashes, and Stylistic Alternates

Lesson 21
Inserting Tables

- Creating a Table
- Typing in a Table
- Selecting Cells and Ranges
- Inserting or Deleting Rows or Columns
- Changing Cell Height and Width

Lesson 22
Formatting Tables

- Merging and Splitting Cells
- Changing Text Direction
- Adjusting Cell Margins
- Using Diagonals
- Applying Table Styles
- Applying Table Fills and Borders
- Changing Table Alignment
- Turning Off Automatic Hyphenation

End-of-Chapter Activities

Lesson 13

Changing Font Formatting

➤ What You Will Learn

Changing Font, Font Size, Font Color, and Font Style
Applying Text Effects and WordArt Styles
Changing Character Spacing
Creating a Drop Cap

WORDS TO KNOW

Character spacing
The space between each letter in a block of text.

Drop cap
An ornamental capital letter at the beginning of a paragraph that is much larger than surrounding letters and that "drops" into the lines beneath it or rests on the baseline.

Fixed color
A color that does not change when the color scheme changes. Publications do not use any fixed colors by default, but you can specify a fixed color for any object.

Font
A typeface; a style of lettering.

Font style
A change in appearance of a font, such as bold or italic.

Software Skills   Publisher's templates provide consistent font formatting for a publication, but sometimes you will want to format text manually, applying a specific font, size, color, and so on. You may also want to manually adjust the spacing between letters, or make the first letter of a paragraph stand out with a drop cap.

What You Can Do

Changing Font, Font Size, Font Color, and Font Style

■ The commands for changing font, font size, font color, and font style can be found in the Font group on the HOME tab or the TEXT BOX TOOLS FORMAT tab. Changing font formatting is an easy process of choosing the desired formatting option from drop-down menus and galleries.

■ You can also use the **Mini toolbar** to select font formatting options. The Mini toolbar, shown in Figure 13-1, displays faintly when you select text, and darkens as you move the pointer toward it. You can click options on the Mini toolbar just as you would on the HOME tab.

■ To choose a different **font**, select the text and then choose a font from the Font drop-down list. The font names display using the actual font formatting, so it is easy to see how the font will look when applied to text.

■ You can also set the font from the Font dialog box; to display the dialog box, click the Font dialog box launcher. This dialog box also allows you to choose font style, font size, font color, and text effects such as Superscript, Shadow, and All caps.

✓ *You learn more about text effects in the next section.*

Figure 13-1

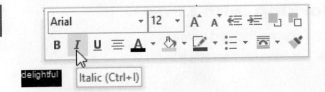

■ To choose a different font size, select the text and then choose from the Font Size drop-down list in the Font group. Or, select the font size in the Font dialog box.

✓ *You can also simply type the size you want in the Font Size box.*

■ Fonts are measured in points. A **point** is $1/72$ of an inch. A typical size for body text is 10 or 12 points.

■ In addition, the Font group has Increase Font Size and Decrease Font Size buttons. Each time you click one of these buttons, you increase or decrease the size of selected text by one size on the Font Size list.

■ **Font style** is a change in appearance applied to text, such as *italic*, **bold**, or ***bold italic***. The font style buttons are located beneath the Font box on the HOME or TEXT BOX TOOLS FORMAT tab.

■ Publisher also offers an Underline font style. You can apply a single underline using the Underline button on a Ribbon tab. The Font dialog box lets you select from additional underline formatting, such as a double or dotted underline.

■ You set the font color using the Font Color palette on a Ribbon tab or the Color palette in the Font dialog box.

✓ *The color that displays in the Font Color command is the current color; you can click this sample to apply it to an object or selected text.*

■ When changing font colors, you must decide whether you want to use **scheme colors** (which will change if you change the color scheme in use) or **fixed colors**.

    ● Using scheme colors ensures that the entire publication uses consistent colors. Scheme colors display at the top of the palette, as shown in Figure 13-2. Below the scheme colors are percentages of each color that are lighter or darker than the scheme color. These percentages give you a broader palette of colors to choose among that will all work well together visually. Note that colors are named according to their function (such as Accent 2); with the color values of the current color model (such as RGB (173, 194, 153)); and with the percentage lighter or darker, if you have chosen one of the percentage colors below the scheme colors.

    ● Using a fixed color gives you more colors to choose from and ensures that the color will not change regardless of later color scheme changes you make.

■ The Standard Colors palette displays eight fixed colors you can apply quickly. If you have chosen colors recently for text or an outline or fill, they will display in the Recent Colors section of the palette. You can also choose More Colors to display the Colors dialog box. You can click a colored hexagon on the Standard tab to choose from among many basic colors.

Sidebar

Kerning
The spacing between certain characters based on their shapes and the way they fit together side-by-side.

Mini toolbar
A toolbar containing frequently used formatting commands that displays when you select text.

Point
$1/72$ of an inch, a font size measurement.

Scaling
The width of characters in relation to a fixed default setting of 100%.

Scheme color
A color placeholder that is defined by the chosen color scheme for the publication; it changes when you change the color scheme.

Tracking
The spacing between the characters for a selected text box.

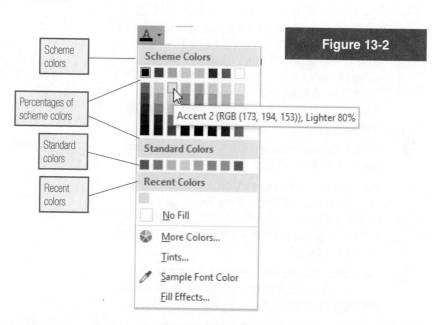

Figure 13-2

Scheme colors

Percentages of scheme colors

Standard colors

Recent colors

Scheme Colors

Accent 2 (RGB (173, 194, 153)), Lighter 80%

Standard Colors

Recent Colors

No Fill

More Colors...

Tints...

Sample Font Color

Fill Effects...

- Instead of Standard colors, you can click the Custom tab and then enter a color by its numeric code in any of a variety of color models or matching schemes, such as RGB, CMYK, and PANTONE. Being able to select an exact color can be useful in professional publications such as those for a company that uses specific colors as part of its branding.

- Choosing Fill Effects from the Font Color drop-down list opens the Format Shape dialog box. With the TEXT OPTIONS settings active, you can choose a solid fill or a gradient fill. For a solid fill, click the Color box to display scheme colors and the Tints option, where you can select a tint for the chosen color. For example, if you choose Red, you may select a bright red, a dark red, a pale red (pink), etc. This is useful if you want to use a scheme color but also want a more customized look.

Try It!   Changing Font, Font Size, Font Color, and Font Style

1 Start Publisher and open **PB13Try** from the data files for this lesson.

2 Save the publication as **PB13Try_xx** in the location where your teacher instructs you to store files for this lesson.

3 Select the caption text to the left of the picture. Click HOME > Increase Font Size A˄ twice to enlarge the text to 22 point.

4 With the text still selected, click HOME > Font Times New Roman ▾ and scroll up to locate a script font such as Brush Script MT. Click the font name to apply it.

5 Select the text again and move the pointer toward the Mini toolbar to view its commands. Click the Font Color drop-down arrow A ▾ and select Accent 2 (RGB (173, 194,153)), the third square from the left on the top row of scheme colors.

6 The Mini toolbar should still be displayed. Click the Font Color drop-down arrow A ▾ again and click Fill Effects. Click the Fill Color box ◇ ▾ and click Tints. On the Tint tab, click the Base color down arrow and click Accent 2 (RGB (173, 194, 153)). Then click the third color box from the right in the second row, 90% Shade. Click OK and then click OK again.

7 Select the words *Guest Comforts* in the main text box. Click HOME > Font Size 11 ▾ > 22.

8 With the text still selected, click HOME > Bold B . Then click HOME > Font Color A ▾ and click the Accent 1 (RGB (51, 102, 0)) scheme color (the second square from the left in the top row of the palette).

9 Select the *Orchard House* text, and then click HOME > Font dialog box launcher ⬕ to open the Font dialog box.

10 Click the Font drop-down arrow, scroll down, and select Brush Script MT. Click in the Font size box and type **85**. Click the Font color drop-down arrow and select Accent 4 (RGB (204, 204, 204)), Darker 50%. Click OK to apply all changes.

11 Save the changes to **PB13Try_xx**, and leave it open to use in the next Try It.

New fonts, font sizes, font colors, and font styles

Applying Text Effects and WordArt Styles

- When a text box is selected, the TEXT BOX TOOLS FORMAT contextual tab is active, giving you access to many commands you need to work with text. You will find that some commands are duplicated on this tab from the HOME tab. The entire Font group, for example, appears on both the HOME tab and the TEXT BOX TOOLS FORMAT tab.

- The TEXT BOX TOOLS FORMAT tab also displays the WordArt Styles group, which allows you to apply to text the same formatting options available when you insert a WordArt object. Click any of these styles to apply preformatted fill, outline, and other effects to text.

- Or, use the Text Fill, Text Outline, and Text Effects buttons to customize text appearance.

  ✓ You work with WordArt graphics in Chapter 4.

Try It! Applying Text Effects and WordArt Styles

1 In the **PB13Try_xx** file, select the Orchard House heading.

2 On the TEXT BOX TOOLS FORMAT tab, click the WordArt Styles More button ⬇, and click Gradient Fill - Gray.

3 Click TEXT BOX TOOLS FORMAT > Text Outline 🅰 and click Accent 3 (RGB (214, 224, 204)), Darker 25%.

4 Click TEXT BOX TOOLS FORMAT > Text Effects 🅰 > Shadow > Inside Left (the first effect in the second row under Inner).

5 Save the changes to **PB13Try_xx**, and leave it open to use in the next Try It.

Changing Character Spacing

- As you would expect, **character spacing** is the amount of space between text characters.

- The Character Spacing command in the Font group on the HOME tab (or the TEXT BOX TOOLS FORMAT tab) displays a drop-down menu you can use to quickly set the space between characters from Very Tight to Very Loose.

- If you want more control over character spacing, you can click More Spacing at the bottom of the Character Spacing menu to open the Character Spacing dialog box. You can choose among three additional options for adjusting character spacing and appearance.

  - **Scaling** sets the width of selected characters to more or less than the default (100%). For example, if you selected a capital A and then set its scaling to 200%, it would be twice as wide as normal, but the same height.

- **Tracking** controls the spacing between letters for a selected text box. You can set tracking to one of the presets (Normal, Very Tight, Tight, Loose, Very Loose) or to a specific percentage amount.

- **Kerning** fine-tunes the spacing between certain characters based on their shapes. For example, when a capital V and a capital A appear next to one another, the spacing between them can be decreased without the letters running into each other because of the shape of the letters. Automatic pair kerning is turned on by default to kern text whenever the font size is 14 point and above (or whatever size you specify).

- The Character Spacing dialog box contains a Show Toolbar button you can click to display the Measurement toolbar. When text is selected, the Measurement toolbar gives you information on scaling, tracking, and kerning as well as other object information.

Try It!   **Changing Character Spacing**

1 In the **PB13Try_xx** file, select the *Guest Comforts* heading.

2 Click TEXT BOX TOOLS FORMAT > Character Spacing $\overset{AV}{\longleftrightarrow}$ ▾ > Loose.

3 Select the *Orchard House* heading. Click TEXT BOX TOOLS FORMAT > Character Spacing $\overset{AV}{\longleftrightarrow}$ ▾ > More Spacing.

4 Click the Scaling down arrow to change scaling to 90%.

5 Click the Tracking drop-down list, click Tight, and then click the By this amount up arrow one time to change the percentage to 92.5%.

6 Click Show Toolbar to display the Measurement toolbar. Click the Tracking $\overset{aaa}{\longleftrightarrow}$ up arrow twice to change tracking to 94%. Close the Measurement toolbar.

7 Save the changes to **PB13Try_xx**, and leave it open to use in the next Try It.

Creating a Drop Cap

- A **drop cap** is a large first letter in a paragraph. You have probably seen this text design in books at the beginning of a chapter. Publisher can create a variety of drop cap effects.

- Use the Drop Cap command on the TEXT BOX TOOLS FORMAT tab to display a gallery of drop cap styles from which you can choose. You do not have to select the first letter of a paragraph to apply drop cap formatting—just click anywhere in the paragraph.

- Remove a drop cap by displaying the Drop Cap gallery and selecting the No Drop Cap style.

- Click the Custom Drop Cap command on the Drop Cap gallery to display the Drop Cap dialog box, where you have more options to choose among, such as specifying that the cap stick up rather than drop down, selecting the number of lines the cap will drop down and the number of letters to drop, and other font and color options.

Try It!   **Creating a Drop Cap**

1 In the **PB13Try_xx** file, click in the paragraph below the *Guest Comforts* heading.

2 Click TEXT BOX TOOLS FORMAT > Drop Cap $\overset{A}{\equiv}$. Hover the mouse over some of the gallery options to see how the drop caps look in the publication.

3 Click Drop Cap Style 9.

4 Click TEXT BOX TOOLS FORMAT > Drop Cap $\overset{A}{\equiv}$ > Custom Drop Cap. In the Drop Cap dialog box, click the Lines down arrow until 0 displays.

5 Click the Color drop-down arrow and select Followed Hyperlink (Blue-Gray). Click OK.

6 Close the publication, saving changes, and exit Publisher.

Final font formatting

Orchard House

Guest Comforts

Being travel enthusiasts ourselves, we know how important it is to have a comfortable bed to sleep in, so all of our rooms have the best in bedding and linens. You'll enjoy luxurious pillow-top mattresses with firm support, 100 percent cotton sheets, and cozy quilts and comforters, as well as thick, absorbent bathrobes and large, fluffy towels.

Each room is furnished with Mission-style furniture typical of the Arts and Crafts movement of the early twentieth century. We have a passion for this style of furnishing, and it shows throughout the house.

Indoors, there's a TV lounge with satellite TV including lots of movie channels. Settle in for your favorite film. Or, if you're more interested in just get-

Lesson 13—Practice

The Hendricks Inn flyer you created in the last lesson is a good start, but some of the text is too small, the fonts are inconsistent, and there is not much variety in the text formatting. In this exercise, you format the text to make it more readable and attractive.

DIRECTIONS

1. Start Publisher, if necessary, and open **PB13Practice** from the data files for this lesson.

2. Save the publication as **PB13Practice_xx** in the location where your teacher instructs you to store the files for this lesson.

3. Select the text *Springtime Is Garden Time*. Click **Bold** **B** on the Mini toolbar. Then, with the Mini toolbar still displayed, click **Font Color** **A ▾** and click the **Hyperlink (RGB (153, 0, 0))** square in the top row of scheme colors.

4. Select the two paragraphs below the heading you just formatted. Click **HOME** > **Font** Times New Roman ▾ , scroll up, and select **Arial**.

5. With the text still selected, click **HOME** > **Decrease Font Size** A˅ one time to reduce the font size to **11 point**.

6. With the text still selected, click **HOME** > **Character Spacing** AV ▾ > **More Spacing**. Click the **Tracking** up arrow twice to set tracking to **110%**. Click **OK**.

7. Click in the first paragraph of the text you just formatted, and then click **TEXT BOX TOOLS FORMAT** > **Drop Cap** ▤ . Click **Drop Cap Style 7**.

8. Click **TEXT BOX TOOLS FORMAT** > **Drop Cap** ▤ > **Custom Drop Cap**. Click the **Color** drop-down arrow and select the **Hyperlink (RGB (153, 0, 0))** square to make the drop cap the same color as the heading above it. Click **OK**.

9. Select *The Hendricks Inn* text at the top of the page, and then click **TEXT BOX TOOLS FORMAT** > **Increase Font Size** A˄ twice to increase the font size to **16 point**.

10. With the text still selected, click **TEXT BOX TOOLS FORMAT** > **Character Spacing** AV ▾ > **Loose**.

11. Select the *Volume 1, Issue 1* text, display the Mini toolbar, click the **Font** drop-down arrow Times New Roman ▾ , and click **Arial**. Repeat this process to change the date font to **Arial**.

12. **With your teacher's permission**, print the document. It should look similar to Figure 13-3 on the next page.

13. Close the publication, saving changes, and exit Publisher.

Figure 13-3

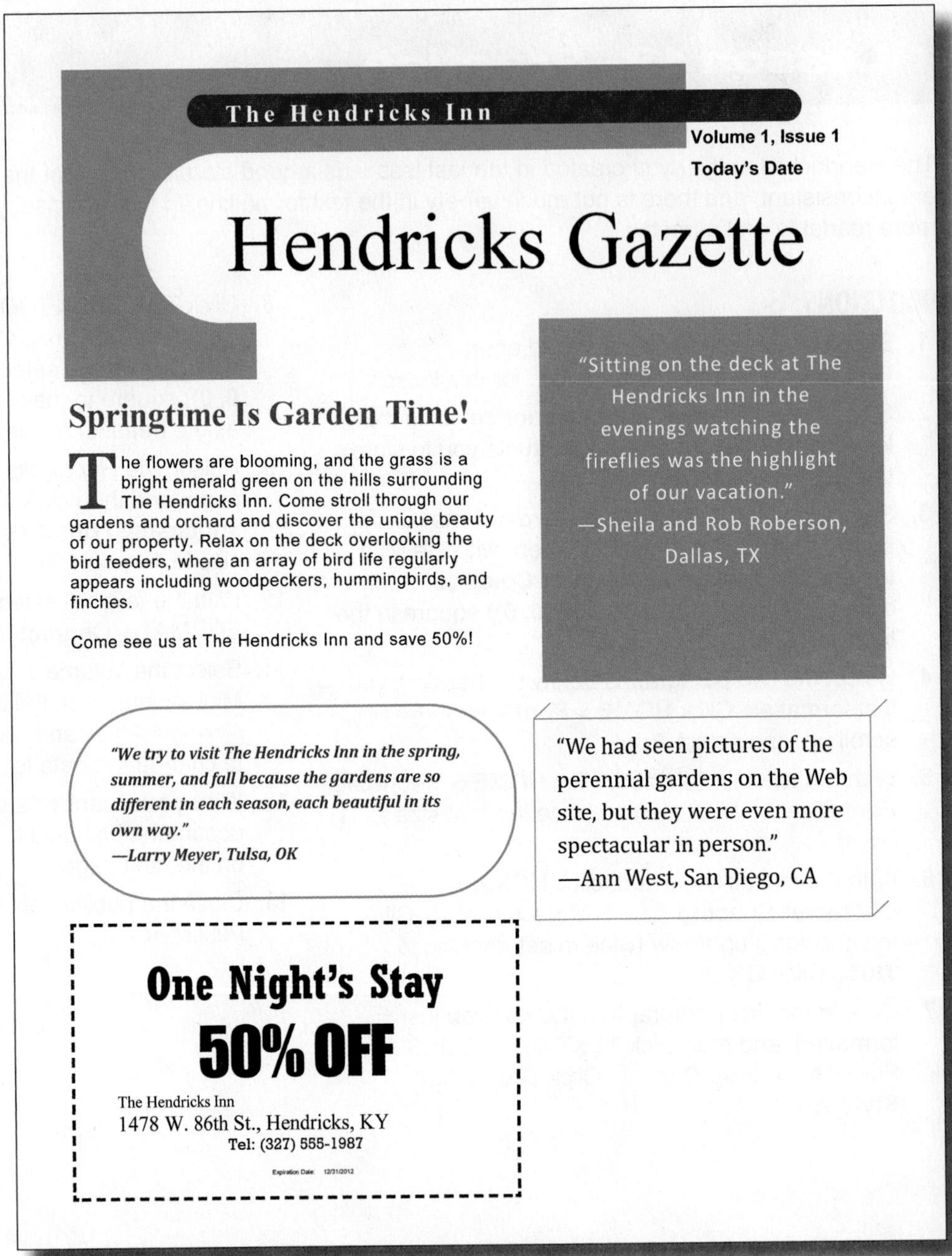

The Hendricks Inn

Volume 1, Issue 1
Today's Date

Hendricks Gazette

Springtime Is Garden Time!

The flowers are blooming, and the grass is a bright emerald green on the hills surrounding The Hendricks Inn. Come stroll through our gardens and orchard and discover the unique beauty of our property. Relax on the deck overlooking the bird feeders, where an array of bird life regularly appears including woodpeckers, hummingbirds, and finches.

Come see us at The Hendricks Inn and save 50%!

"Sitting on the deck at The Hendricks Inn in the evenings watching the fireflies was the highlight of our vacation."
—Sheila and Rob Roberson, Dallas, TX

"We try to visit The Hendricks Inn in the spring, summer, and fall because the gardens are so different in each season, each beautiful in its own way."
—Larry Meyer, Tulsa, OK

"We had seen pictures of the perennial gardens on the Web site, but they were even more spectacular in person."
—Ann West, San Diego, CA

One Night's Stay
50% OFF

The Hendricks Inn
1478 W. 86th St., Hendricks, KY
Tel: (327) 555-1987

Expiration Date: 12/31/2012

Lesson 13—Apply

In this exercise, you complete the newsletter. You adjust font formats and then apply a different color sch___ the final step.

DIRECTIONS

1. Start Publisher, if necessary, and open **PB13Apply** from the data files for this lesson.

2. Save the publication as **PB13Apply_xx** in the location where your teacher instructs you to store the files for this lesson.

3. Select the text in the green text box and change the font to **Times New Roman**. Change the font size to **16 point** and apply Italic *I* font style.

4. Select the text in the rounded rectangle and change the font to **Times New Roman**. Change the font size to **12 point** and remove bold formatting. If you have overflow text, shorten the *Springtime* text box and increase the height of the rounded rectangle pull quote until all text displays.

5. Choose a different font color for this text.

6. Select the text in the remaining pull quote and change it to **Times New Roman, 16 point**.

7. Select the coupon and zoom in on it. Make t___ following changes:

   a. Select *One Night's Stay* and change the font ___ **Arial** and the font size to **24 point**. Change the font color to the **Dark Red** standard color.

   b. Select the text in the three text boxes beneath *50% OFF* and change the text to **Arial 12 point**.

   c. Change the expiration date text and the date to **Arial 9 point**.

8. Apply the **Field** color scheme. Notice that colors of shapes and text change throughout the page, except for the *One Night's Stay* text, which you formatted with a fixed color.

9. **With your teacher's permission**, print the document. It should look similar to Figure 13-4 on the next page.

10. Close the publication, saving changes, and exit Publisher.

Figure 13-4

The Hendricks Inn

Volume 1, Issue 1
Today's Date

Hendricks Gazette

Springtime Is Garden Time!

The flowers are blooming, and the grass is a bright emerald green on the hills surrounding The Hendricks Inn. Come stroll through our gardens and orchard and discover the unique beauty of our property. Relax on the deck overlooking the bird feeders, where an array of bird life regularly appears including woodpeckers, hummingbirds, and finches.

Come see us at The Hendricks Inn and save 50%!

"Sitting on the deck at The Hendricks Inn in the evenings watching the fireflies was the highlight of our vacation."
—Sheila and Rob Roberson, Dallas, TX

"We try to visit The Hendricks Inn in the spring, summer, and fall because the gardens are so different in each season, each beautiful in its own way."
—Larry Meyer, Tulsa, OK

"We had seen pictures of the perennial gardens on the Web site, but they were even more spectacular in person."
—Ann West, San Diego, CA

One Night's Stay

50% OFF

The Hendricks Inn
1478 W. 86th St., Hendricks, KY
Tel: (327) 555-1987
Expiration Date: 12/31/2015

Lesson 14

Applying Object Borders and Fills

❯ **What You Will Learn**

Applying Object Borders
Changing an Object's Fill Color
Working with Grouped Objects
Applying Shape Styles and Other Effects

Software Skills   Text boxes are transparent by default, so that the background on which they are placed shows through. However, sometimes you might want to give a text box a colored background. You also can apply a line border in any thickness, line style, and color you want. In this lesson, you will work with text boxes, but these same skills apply to any type of object.

What You Can Do

Applying Object Borders

- By default, you see the edges of text boxes only if you click in the text box to select it. A selected text box displays the selection border with its selection handles.

- If you want to see the edges of text boxes when they are not selected, you can select the Boundaries option on the VIEW menu. Boundaries display as dotted lines around text boxes and other **objects** such as pictures. Displaying boundaries can help you keep track of overlapping objects or objects that would otherwise not appear, such as empty text boxes.

  ✓ *For a less cluttered look when working with a number of objects, many designers turn boundaries off.*

- Boundaries do not print. If you want to print an outline around an object, you must apply an outline, or **border**, to the object.

- Border formatting is available on the DRAWING TOOLS FORMAT tab when an object is selected. The Shape Outline command displays a menu that gives you a number of border options:

WORDS TO KNOW

Border
A line around the outside of an object that is visible when the publication is printed.

Group
Multiple objects linked together so that they can be selected or formatted as a single object.

Object
A generic term for any text box, picture, drawing, or other piece of data in a publication that is separately movable and resizable.

Opaque
Unable to be seen through; the opposite of transparent. An object's opacity is the measurement of how nontransparent it is.

Sample
Pick up a color from an image in the publication.

Shape style
Preformatted fill and border styles that can be applied with a single click from the Shape Styles gallery.

- Select a border color from the scheme or standard colors palettes, or click More Outline Colors to display the Colors dialog box where you can click a standard color hexagon or create a color by entering color values. You can also select a color from the Recent Colors palette that shows colors you have applied recently.

- Choose to **sample** a color for the border. Selecting this option changes the mouse pointer to an eyedropper that you can click on any color on the screen, including any area of the window as well as images in the publication. The eyedropper picks up the color and applies it to the border.

- Select the Weight option to see a gallery of weights, or line thicknesses.

- Select the Dashes option to see a gallery of plain, dashed, and dotted lines.

- Click the Pattern option to open the Patterned Lines dialog box. You learn more about patterns in the next lesson.

  ✓ *You can also apply a border as part of a shape style. You learn about shape styles later in this lesson.*

- To remove a border from an object, select No Outline from the Shape Outline menu.

- Once you have selected a border color, it displays on the Shape Outline command so you can easily apply that color to other object borders.

- For more control over border lines, click More Lines on the Weight or Dashes gallery to open the Colors and Lines tab of the Format Text Box dialog box (Figure 14-1). (If you are working with a type of object other than text box, the dialog box name will be different.) This dialog box enables you to choose attributes such as color, width, line type, and dash option without having to repeatedly click the Shape Outline command.

  ✓ *You can also right-click an object and select a command to format the object, such as Format Text Box, on the shortcut menu. The Mini toolbar also displays when you right-click the object.*

- A transparency slider allows you to adjust the transparency of the border lines.

- The dialog box also allows you to choose which edges of the object receive a border. You can specify a border to appear only at the top of a text box, for example, or only on the left side.

- By default, the border is applied to all edges of the object. Deselect all the border icons and then select only the ones for the edge where you want the border to appear. Selected border icons are blue, as shown in Figure 14-1.

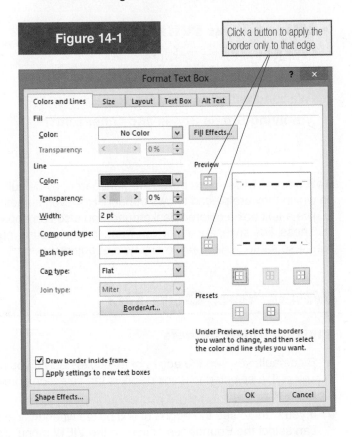

Figure 14-1

Click a button to apply the border only to that edge

Try It! Applying Object Borders

1 Start Publisher and open **PB14Try** from the data files for this lesson.

2 Save the publication as **PB14Try_xx** in the location where your teacher instructs you to store files for this lesson.

3 Click VIEW > Boundaries to see the dotted line boundaries around all objects in the publication.

4 On page 1, click the picture caption to select the text box.

5 Click DRAWING TOOLS FORMAT > Shape Outline ✎, and then click the Accent 1 (RGB (51, 102, 0)) square in the top row of scheme colors.

6 Click Shape Outline ✎ > Weight and click the 2¼ pt line.

7 Click Shape Outline ✎ > Sample Line Color. With the eyedropper pointer, click on a light green leaf anywhere in the picture.

8 Right-click the *Orchard House* text box and select Format Text Box.

9 Click the top ⊞, left ⊞, and right ⊞ border icons to deselect them, leaving only the bottom border icon ⊞ selected (it is shaded blue when selected).

10 Click the Color drop-down arrow and click Accent 4 (RGB (204, 204, 204)), Darker 50% scheme color.

11 Click the Dash type drop-down arrow and click Dash.

12 Click the Width up arrow until 3 pt displays. Click OK.

13 Save the changes to **PB14Try_xx**, and leave it open to use in the next Try It.

Borders applied to text boxes

Changing an Object's Fill Color

- By default, a text box is transparent, so whatever background is behind it shows through. You can set the background to be any color, however, including solid (**opaque**) white.

- Use the Shape Fill command on the DRAWING TOOLS FORMAT tab to apply a fill. You can choose from these options:

  - Choose a solid color from the scheme colors or standard colors palettes, or click More Fill Colors to select a color from the Colors dialog box. You can also choose a color from the Recent Colors palette.

  - You can sample a fill color from any location on the screen.

  - You can choose a picture to apply as a fill.

  - You can apply a gradient, texture, or pattern fill. You learn about these fill effects in the next lesson.

- To remove the fill from an object, choose No Fill.

- If you choose a color from the Colors dialog box, you can set a transparency for it using the slider at the bottom of the dialog box.

- A transparency of 0% (the default) shows the color at its full strength. Dragging the Transparency slider to the right decreases opacity, allowing objects beneath to show through.

- You can also specify a fill color in a Format dialog box, such as the Format Text Box dialog box. As you select a fill color, the preview area shows the fill along with any border options you have selected. You can adjust color transparency in this dialog box.

- If you right-click a text box to access a command such as Format Text Box, you will also see a Mini toolbar displayed with the shortcut menu. The Shape Fill and Shape Outline commands are available on this toolbar; it can be faster to apply a fill or outline in this way than to use the DRAWING TOOLS FORMAT tab or a dialog box.

Try It!   **Changing an Object's Fill Color**

1 In the **PB14Try_xx** file, right-click the figure caption text box and then click Format Text Box.

2 In the Fill area of the dialog box, click the Color drop-down arrow and click the Accent 2 (RGB (173, 194, 153)) scheme color.

3 Click the Transparency slider and drag to the right until 60% displays in the percentage box. Click OK.

4 Click the *Orchard House* text box, click DRAWING TOOLS FORMAT > Shape Fill, and click Accent 2 (RGB (173, 194, 153)), Lighter 80%.

5 Save the changes to **PB14Try_xx**, and leave it open to use in the next Try It.

Working with Grouped Objects

- Building blocks that contain text, such as headers and pull quotes, consist of several **grouped** objects. A sidebar building block, for example, may include one or more text boxes as well as one or more rectangular shapes, and sometimes other graphic elements, all of which have been combined into one object.

  ✓ *You will learn how to group and ungroup objects in the next chapter.*

- Formatting a grouped object requires some special attention because you need to be sure which part of the object you have selected before applying a format.

- Clicking the outline of a grouped object displays the selection handles you are used to seeing for selected text boxes. When these handles display, any format you apply will apply to all objects in the group: A fill will fill each object in the group; a border will surround each object in the group.

- With a grouped object selected, you can click on any of the objects that make up the group to display small gray selection handles, each with an x in their center (see Figure 14-2).

- When the individual object's gray selection handles display, formatting will apply to that object only.

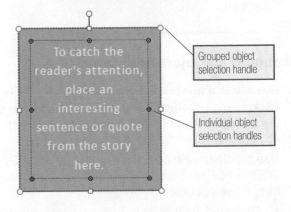

Figure 14-2

Try It! Working with Grouped Objects

1 In the **PB14Try_xx** file, click page 2 in the Page Navigation pane.

2 Click VIEW > Boundaries to turn off the display of boundaries.

3 Move the pointer near the bottom of the *Spring Events* heading building block and then click the dashed border to select the entire grouped object. Click DRAWING TOOLS FORMAT > Shape Fill 🖎, and then click Accent 2 (RGB (173, 194, 153)), Lighter 80%. The fill applies to the entire object.

4 Click on the top border of the object to display the gray selection handles around the *Spring Events* text box.

✓ *You may have to click twice to display the gray selection handles.*

5 Right-click the selected text box and click Format Text Box.

6 Deselect all border icons except the bottom border icon ⊞. Click the Color drop-down arrow and select No Outline to remove the border from the bottom of the text box.

7 Click the bottom border icon ⊞ to deselect it, and then click the top border icon ⊞ to select it. Click the Color drop-down arrow and click Accent 1 (RGB (51, 102, 0)). Click the Width up arrow until 3 pt displays. Click OK. The border applies only to the selected text box.

8 Click the entire object again if necessary to display the selection handles, and then click on the bottom outline to select only the text box that contains the *March—April—May* text.

9 Click DRAWING TOOLS FORMAT > Shape Fill 🖎, and then click Accent 1 (RGB (51, 102, 0)). The fill applies only to the selected text box.

10 Save the changes to **PB14Try_xx**, and leave it open to use in the next Try It.

Border and fill applied to a grouped object

Spring Events
March—April—May

Applying Shape Styles and Other Effects

- Applying borders and fills using the Shape Outline and Shape Fill commands can be a fairly labor-intensive process. You can instead apply a **shape style** from the Shape Styles gallery on the DRAWING TOOLS FORMAT tab.

- Shape styles are combinations of border and fill designs that can add sophisticated formatting to an object without your having to build the appearance yourself. Some styles also include shadow formatting.

- The Shape Styles gallery shows only a few options on the tab. To see all options, click the gallery's More button. Hover the mouse pointer over each style to see a live preview of the style on the currently selected object.

- Shape styles are created using five colors from the current color scheme (the main color plus the four accent colors).

- The Shape Effects command allows you to apply a wider selection of effects than you find with shape styles.

- You can apply shadows, reflections, glows, soft edges, bevels, and 3-D rotation options by clicking styles on galleries.

- Each gallery of effects includes an Options command you can use to open the Format Shape dialog box, where you can customize effects.

Try It!   Applying Shape Styles and Other Effects

1 In the **PB14Try_xx** file, click page 1 in the Page Navigation pane.

2 Click the *Guest Comforts* text box to select it. Click the DRAWING TOOLS FORMAT tab, if necessary, to display it.

3 Click the More button ▾ on the Shape Styles gallery, and then click the Diagonal Gradient – Accent 1 shape style.

4 Click the *Orchard House* text box, click the More button ▾ on the Shape Styles gallery, and then click the Linear Up Gradient – Accent 2 shape style.

5 With the text box still selected, click DRAWING TOOLS FORMAT > Shape Effects 🔾, point to Shadow, and then click Shadow Options at the bottom of the gallery to display the Format Shape dialog box.

6 Click the Shadow Presets button ☐ ▾, and then click the Offset Diagonal Bottom Right option (the first under Outer).

7 In the Shadow options, drag the Distance slider to the right until 8 pt displays in the Distance box.

8 Click OK.

9 Close the publication, saving changes, and exit Publisher.

Shape styles applied to text boxes

Guest Comforts

Being travel enthusiasts ourselves, we know how important it is to have a comfortable bed to sleep in, so all of our rooms have the best in bedding and linens. You'll enjoy luxurious pillow-top mattresses with firm support, 100 percent cotton sheets, and cozy quilts and comforters, as well as thick, absorbent bathrobes and large, fluffy towels.

Each room is furnished with Mission-style furniture typical of the Arts and Crafts movement of the early twentieth century. We have a passion for this style of furnishing, and it shows throughout the house.

Indoors, there's a TV lounge with satellite TV including lots of movie channels. Settle in for your

Lesson 14—Practice

The Hendricks Inn flyer could benefit from some dressing up with text box formatting. In this exercise, you work with the borders and fills on some of the text boxes.

DIRECTIONS

1. Start Publisher, if necessary, and open **PB14Practice** from the data files for this lesson.

2. Save the publication as **PB14Practice_xx** in the location where your teacher instructs you to store the files for this lesson.

3. Click the *Sitting on the deck* pull quote to select the object, and then click on the text box to display the gray sizing handles that indicate you have selected an individual object rather than the grouped object.

4. Right-click on the selected text box and click **Format Text Box** on the shortcut menu. Modify text box formats as follows:

   a. In the Fill area of the Colors and Lines tab, click the **Color** drop-down arrow and click the **Accent 2 (RGB (204, 153, 51)), Lighter 40%** scheme color.

   b. In the Line area of the tab, click the **Color** drop-down arrow and click the **Hyperlink (RGB (102, 51, 0))** scheme color.

   c. Click the **Dash type** drop-down arrow and click the **Long Dash** dash.

   d. Click the **Width** up arrow until **1.5 pt** displays.

   e. Click **OK**.

   f. Select the text in the quote, and then click **HOME > Font Color △ ▾ > Hyperlink (RGB (102, 51, 0))**.

5. Click the outside border of the Geometric pull quote (*We had seen pictures*), and then click again until you see the gray selection handles at the outer border on the top and right side of the object.

   ✓ *You may find it helpful to click slightly inside the object selection border to select the rectangle shape that is behind the text.*

6. Click **DRAWING TOOLS FORMAT > Shape Outline ✎**, and then click the **Accent 2 (RGB (204, 153, 51)), Lighter 60%** scheme color.

7. Click the 50% off coupon, and then click the *50% Off* text box to select only that text box. Click the **DRAWING TOOLS FORMAT > Shape Styles More** button ▾ to display the entire Shape Styles gallery.

8. Click **Diagonal Gradient – Dark**. With the text box still selected, click **DRAWING TOOLS FORMAT > Shape Outline ✎ > No Outline**.

9. **With your teacher's permission**, print the publication. Your publication should look similar to Figure 14-3 on the next page.

10. Close the publication, saving changes, and exit Publisher.

Figure 14-3

The Hendricks Inn

Volume 1, Issue 1
Today's Date

Hendricks Gazette

Springtime Is Garden Time!

The flowers are blooming, and the grass is a bright emerald green on the hills surrounding The Hendricks Inn. Come stroll through our gardens and orchard and discover the unique beauty of our property. Relax on the deck overlooking the bird feeders, where an array of bird life regularly appears including woodpeckers, hummingbirds, and finches.

Come see us at The Hendricks Inn and save 50%!

"Sitting on the deck at The Hendricks Inn in the evenings watching the fireflies was the highlight of our vacation."
—Sheila and Rob Roberson, Dallas, TX

"We try to visit The Hendricks Inn in the spring, summer, and fall because the gardens are so different in each season, each beautiful in its own way."
—Larry Meyer, Tulsa, OK

"We had seen pictures of the perennial gardens on the Web site, but they were even more spectacular in person."
—Ann West, San Diego, CA

One Night's Stay
50% OFF

The Hendricks Inn
1478 W. 86th St., Hendricks, KY
Tel: (327) 555-1987
Expiration Date: 12/31/2015

Lesson 14—Apply

In this exercise, you complete your work on the Hendricks Inn newsletter. You apply additional formatting to some of the newsletter's text boxes for special visual interest.

DIRECTIONS

1. Start Publisher, if necessary, and open **PB14Apply** from the data files for this lesson.

2. Save the publication as **PB14Apply_xx** in the location where your teacher instructs you to store the files for this lesson.

3. Click the rounded rectangle pull quote to select it. Change the border to **Accent 1 (RGB (0, 102, 51))**. Change the border weight to **2¼ pt**.

4. Click the main text box on the page (*Springtime Is Garden Time*). Apply the **Diagonal Gradient – Accent 2** shape style, and then add a border of **2¼ pt Accent 2 (RGB (204, 153, 51))**.

5. Turn on boundaries so you can see the edges of the text boxes in the heading building block.

6. Click the heading building block to select it, and then click at the left end of the dark green rounded rectangle behind *The Hendricks Inn*. Change the fill to the **Dark Red** standard color.

7. With the object still selected, click **Shape Effects** ▢ > **Shadow** > **Offset Diagonal Top Right**.

8. With the object still selected, click **Shape Effects** ▢ > **Shadow** > **Shadow Options** to open the Format Shape dialog box.

9. Click the **Color** box ▢▾ and select the **Hyperlink (RGB (102, 51, 0))** scheme color. Adjust the Distance measurement as desired to give the shadow a pleasing appearance.

10. Select the *Volume 1* text box and apply a shape style of your choice. Apply the same style to the date text box. (When you apply the shape styles, the *Hendricks Gazette* text may change size; this is okay.)

11. Select the rounded rectangle shape behind the *Hendricks Gazette* text box and apply the **Colored Outline – Accent 2** shape style.

    ✓ *If the* Hendricks Gazette *text did not change size in step 8, the rounded rectangle may cut through the text. Adjust the text size to look similar to that in Figure 14-4.*

12. Hide boundaries.

13. **With your teacher's permission**, print the publication. It should look similar to Figure 14-4 on the next page.

14. Close the publication, saving changes, and exit Publisher.

Figure 14-4

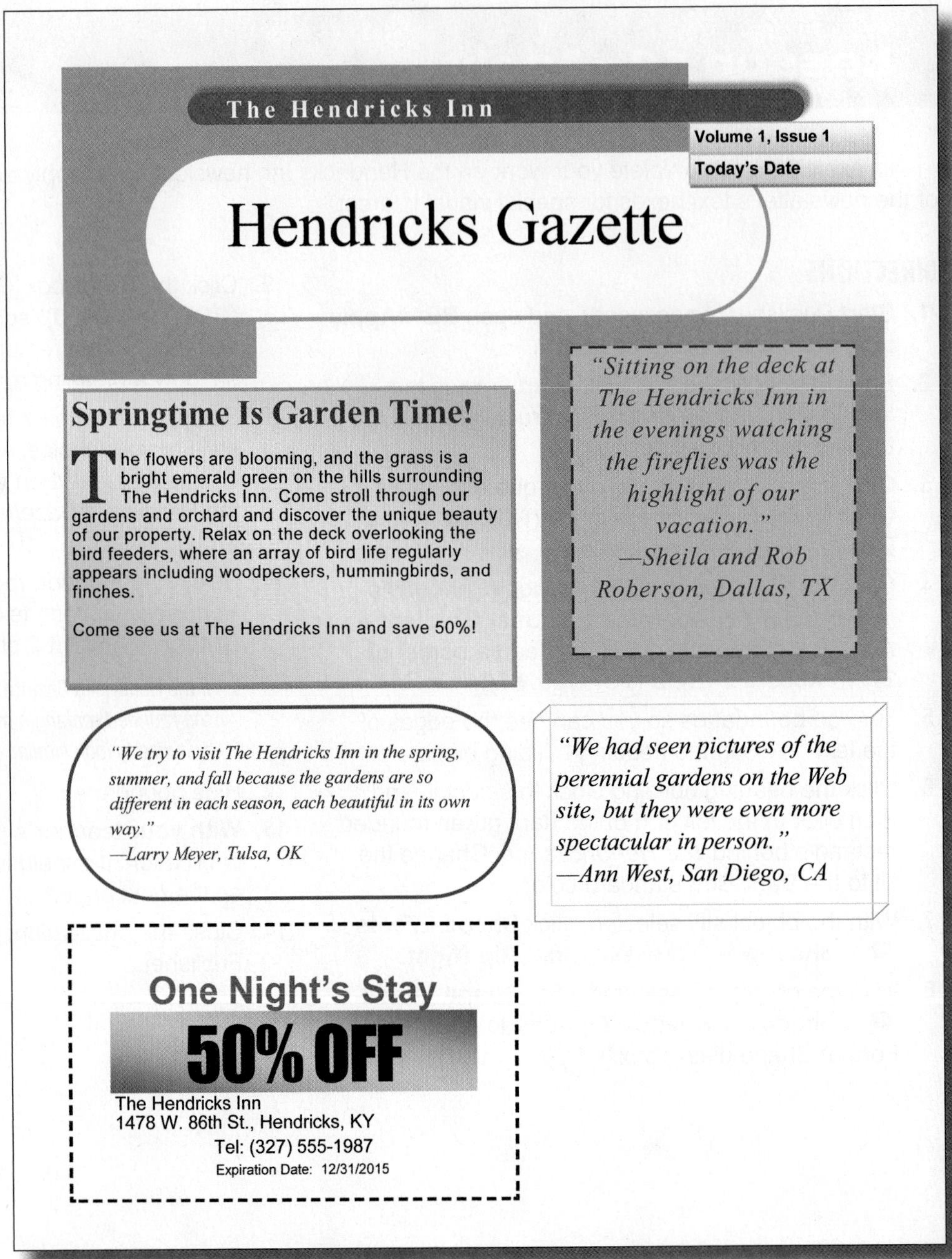

The Hendricks Inn

Volume 1, Issue 1

Today's Date

Hendricks Gazette

Springtime Is Garden Time!

The flowers are blooming, and the grass is a bright emerald green on the hills surrounding The Hendricks Inn. Come stroll through our gardens and orchard and discover the unique beauty of our property. Relax on the deck overlooking the bird feeders, where an array of bird life regularly appears including woodpeckers, hummingbirds, and finches.

Come see us at The Hendricks Inn and save 50%!

"Sitting on the deck at The Hendricks Inn in the evenings watching the fireflies was the highlight of our vacation."
—Sheila and Rob Roberson, Dallas, TX

"We try to visit The Hendricks Inn in the spring, summer, and fall because the gardens are so different in each season, each beautiful in its own way."
—Larry Meyer, Tulsa, OK

"We had seen pictures of the perennial gardens on the Web site, but they were even more spectacular in person."
—Ann West, San Diego, CA

One Night's Stay

50% OFF

The Hendricks Inn
1478 W. 86th St., Hendricks, KY
Tel: (327) 555-1987
Expiration Date: 12/31/2015

Lesson 15

Applying Special Border and Fill Effects

➤ What You Will Learn

Applying a Patterned Border
Using BorderArt
Using Fill Effects

Software Skills Publisher comes with a wide array of special effects that can dress up a publication. In addition to the standard borders that you learned about in Lesson 14, you can also apply patterned lines and BorderArt. To fill a frame, in addition to using solid colors, you can apply any of several fill effects.

What You Can Do

Applying a Patterned Border

- When selecting border options from the Shape Outline menu, one of your choices is Pattern.
- Choosing Pattern opens the Patterned Lines dialog box.
- The Pattern tab in this dialog box offers 40 patterns you can choose among to apply to a border. The patterns are shown in their default view of black foreground on white background.
- You can click the Foreground and Background drop-down arrows to select different foreground and background colors. For an emphatic pattern, choose colors that contrast strongly with each other. For a more subtle approach, choose colors that are more similar to each other.
- Patterned lines do not make much of a visual statement unless the border is very thick.

    ✓ *You may find patterns more useful as fill effects. You learn more about fill effects later in this lesson.*

WORDS TO KNOW

BorderArt
A small graphic that is repeated around the edge of an object, forming a border.

Gradient
A fill effect that gradually progresses from one color to another.

Gradient stop
Point at which a gradient changes from one color to another color.

Try It!   Applying a Patterned Border

1 Start Publisher and open **PB15Try** from the data files for this lesson.

2 Save the publication as **PB15Try_xx** in the location where your teacher instructs you to store the files for this lesson.

3 Right-click the *Cutler College* text box, and then click Format Text Box.

4 Click the Width up arrow until the border weight is 11 pt, and then click OK.

5 Click DRAWING TOOLS FORMAT > Shape Outline 🖉 > Pattern.

6 Click the first pattern in the second row of the pattern gallery (the pattern name is 10%).

7 Click the Background drop-down arrow and click the Accent 3 (Gold) scheme color. Click OK.

8 Save the changes to **PB15Try_xx**, and leave it open to use in the next Try It.

Using BorderArt

- **BorderArt** is a repeated picture that serves as a border around a text box or other object.

- Click the BorderArt button in the Format Text Box dialog box (on the Colors and Lines tab) to open the BorderArt dialog box.

- The available borders list includes graphics that can be used for a multitude of occasions, such as holiday themes, birds and other animals, flowers, and many other decorative patterns.

- BorderArt can be overwhelming for individual text boxes. Use it sparingly.

- The Stretch pictures to fit option makes each copy of the picture slightly wider or taller if needed to minimize the amount of blank space between pictures.

- If you leave the Always apply at default size check box marked, the BorderArt picture will remain the same size regardless of the frame size. When applied to a very small frame, this can result in only a few copies of the picture on each side of the frame.

- If you clear this check box, you can then specify a picture size in the Width box of the Format Text Box dialog box to control the size of the BorderArt border.

Try It!   Using BorderArt

1 In the **PB15Try_xx** file, right-click the red text box and click Format Text Box.

2 On the Colors and Lines tab, click the BorderArt button.

3 In the BorderArt dialog box, scroll down in the Available Borders list to locate Checked Bar. Make sure that Always apply at default size and Stretch pictures to fit are selected.

4 Click OK twice to apply the border.

5 Save the changes to **PB15Try_xx**, and leave it open to use in the next Try It.

Decorative borders applied to two objects

Cutler College

Geology Club

Using Fill Effects

- Fill effects create special backgrounds in whatever object they are applied to (such as a text box). Fill effects you can choose from include Picture, Gradient, Texture, and Pattern.

Applying a Picture Fill

- You have two options for inserting a picture in an object.
  - Click Picture on the Shape Fill menu and navigate to the location of the picture file. Clicking Open places the picture in the selected object.
  - Display the Format Text Box (or the format box for the selected object) and click the Fill Effects button on the Colors and Lines tab. Click Picture or texture fill, then click File and navigate to the picture file.

- The latter option is usually the better choice, because the Format Shape dialog box allows you to adjust offset, scaling, and alignment to fit the picture as desired in the object. You can also choose an option to rotate the picture with the object.

- If you use a picture as a fill for a text box, you may need to adjust the transparency setting to "wash out" the picture so the text can be easily read. You can make this adjustment if you insert the picture from a dialog box rather than the Shape Fill menu.

Try It!   **Applying a Picture Fill**

1 In the **PB15Try_xx** file, right-click the aqua ellipse and click Format AutoShape.

     ✓ *The ellipse was created by drawing a shape. You can use the same steps, however, to fill a text box with a picture.*

2 Click the Fill Effects button on the Colors and Lines tab, and then click Picture or texture fill in the Format Shape dialog box.

3 Click File, and then navigate to the location of the data files for this lesson.

4 Click **PB15Try_image.jpg**, and then click Insert.

5 Click OK. Click OK again.

6 Save the changes to **PB15Try_xx**, and leave it open to use in the next Try It.

Applying a Gradient Fill

- A **gradient** fill effect creates a sensation of movement, with one color fading into another. You can choose from a variety of gradient "directions" and specify the colors that will comprise it.

- For a simple gradient that uses the currently selected fill color to create a variety of light and dark gradient options, click Gradient on the Shape Fill menu and select from the pop-out gallery of gradients.

- For more control over the gradient, click More Gradients to open the Format Shape dialog box with the Gradient fill options active.

  - You can choose preset gradients that use scheme colors.
  - You can create your own gradient by selecting **gradient stops** and then choosing colors for those points on the gradient.

- You can fine-tune a gradient by selecting the gradient type, the direction the gradient will flow, and the gradient angle. You can also adjust the transparency of the gradient.

- As for a picture fill, you can choose to rotate the gradient fill if the object is rotated. You will learn about rotating objects in Chapter 4.

Try It!   Applying a Gradient Fill

1 In the **PB15Try_xx** file, select the ellipse that is currently filled with the rock picture.

2 Click DRAWING TOOLS FORMAT > Shape Fill 🖌, and select the Accent 2 (Aqua) scheme color.

3 Click DRAWING TOOLS FORMAT > Shape Fill 🖌 > Gradient > More Gradients.

✓ *Note that even though the current color is aqua, the default gradients on the Gradient gallery are always shown using a medium blue. If you applied one of these gradients, it would be created using the current color, aqua.*

4 In the Format Shape dialog box, click the Preset gradients box 🔲 ▾ and select Bottom Spotlight - Accent 2.

5 Click the Direction button 🔲 ▾ and select Linear Down. Click OK.

6 Save the changes to **PB15Try_xx**, and leave it open to use in the next Try It.

Applying a Texture and a Pattern Fill

■ A texture fill enables you to apply a graphic as a background that resembles a certain type of material, such as paper, cloth, or wood.

■ Selecting Texture on the Shape Fill menu displays a pop-out gallery of textures. Hover the mouse over a texture to see its name.

■ You can click More Textures to display the Format Shape dialog box with the Texture options active. You can select a texture from the same pop-out gallery, navigate to a file, or search online for a texture.

■ You can apply a pattern as a fill by clicking the Pattern option on the Shape Fill menu. You select the pattern, foreground, and background colors from the Format Shape dialog box.

Try It!   Applying a Texture and a Pattern Fill

1 In the **PB15Try_xx** file, click the red text box, and then click DRAWING TOOLS FORMAT > Shape Fill 🖌 > Texture.

2 On the pop-out gallery, click the Granite texture.

3 Click the *Cutler College* text box, and then click DRAWING TOOLS FORMAT > Shape Fill 🖌 > Pattern.

4 In the Format Shape dialog box with Pattern fill selected, click the Foreground drop-down arrow and click the Accent 3 (Gold) scheme color. Then click the first pattern in the first row. Click OK.

5 Close the publication, saving changes, and exit Publisher.

All objects have special fills

Cutler College

Geology Club

We Rock!

Lesson 15—Practice

Anderson Farms would like you to improve the basic pumpkin-carving flyer you created in the last chapter. In this exercise, you add an artistic border and several fills to improve the appearance of the publication.

DIRECTIONS

1. Start Publisher, if necessary, and open **PB15Practice** from the data files for this lesson.

2. Save the publication as **PB15Practice_xx** in the location where your teacher instructs you to store the files for this lesson.

3. Right-click the *Pumpkin Carving Contest* text box and click **Format Text Box**.

4. Click the BorderArt button.

5. Scroll down in the list of Available Borders and select **Candy Corn**. Make sure **Always apply at default size** and **Stretch pictures to fit** are selected. Click **OK** and then click **OK** again.

6. Click the left text box at the bottom of the page. Click **DRAWING TOOLS FORMAT** > **Shape Fill** > **Gradient** > **More Gradients**.

7. In the Format Shape dialog box, click **Preset gradients** and select **Bottom Spotlight - Accent 2**.

8. Click the **Direction** box and select **Linear Diagonal - Top Left to Bottom Right**.

9. On the Gradient stops bar, click the stop at the right (it currently shows the darkest color in the gradient), and then click the **Color** box and click **Accent 3 (Gold)**. Click **OK**.

10. Click the right text box at the bottom of the page. Follow steps 6–9 to apply and adjust a gradient fill, but choose the **Linear Diagonal - Top Right to Bottom Left** gradient direction.

11. Right-click the *Anderson Farms* text box, and then click **Format Text Box**.

12. Click the **Fill Effects** button, and then click the **Picture or texture fill** option. Click the **Texture** box.

13. Click the **Denim** texture, and then click the **Transparency** slider and drag to change the transparency to **25%**. Click **OK** twice.

14. **With your teacher's permission**, print the publication. It should look similar to Figure 15-1 on the next page.

15. Close the publication, saving changes, and exit Publisher.

Figure 15-1

**Anderson Farms Presents
the 17th Annual**

Pumpkin Carving
Contest

Join us on October 25th
to try your hand at carving
a pumpkin masterpiece.

Festivities start at 10:00
a.m. and end at 4:00 p.m.
with judging and prize
awards.

Call 513-555-6600 for
more information.

Refreshments include
cider and fresh donuts!

Prizes to the best overall,
scariest, and funniest
pumpkins.

See you at the farm!

Lesson 15—Apply

You continue to work with the Anderson Farms flyer. In this exercise, you modify fill and border effects to create a different version of the flyer.

DIRECTIONS

1. Start Publisher, if necessary, and open **PB15Apply** from the data files for this lesson.

2. Save the publication as **PB15Apply_xx** in the location where your teacher instructs you to store the files for this lesson.

3. Click in the *Anderson Farms* text box and apply a fill using the **Accent 3 (Gold)** scheme color. Then apply the **Linear Up** gradient from the Light Variations category on the pop-out Gradient gallery.

4. Right-click the *Pumpkin Carving Contest* text box and open the Format Text Box dialog box. Modify fill and border as follows:

   a. Click the **Compound type** drop-down arrow and select **6 pt** to turn off the BorderArt.

   b. In the Width box, type **12 pt**.

   c. Click the **Fill Effects** button and select the **Picture or texture fill** option. Click **File** and navigate to the data files for this lesson. Select **PB15Apply_image.jpg** and click **Insert**. Lock the picture aspect ratio. Change Transparency of the picture to **75%**, and then click **OK** twice.

   d. With the text box still selected, choose to apply a pattern border. Select the **90%** pattern (the last pattern in the second column), and set the foreground color to **Accent 2 (Orange), Darker 25%**.

5. Apply a checkerboard pattern fill to the two text boxes at the bottom of the page, using a variation of the Accent 3 (Gold) scheme color as the foreground and white as the background. Apply a 2 point outline to the top of each text box only, using a color of your choice.

6. **With your teacher's permission**, print the document. Your publication should look similar to Figure 15-2 on the next page.

7. Close the publication, saving changes, and exit Publisher.

Figure 15-2

Anderson Farms Presents
the 17th Annual

Pumpkin Carving Contest

Join us on October 25th to try your hand at carving a pumpkin masterpiece.

Festivities start at 10:00 a.m. and end at 4:00 p.m. with judging and prize awards.

Call 513-555-6600 for more information.

Refreshments include cider and fresh donuts!

Prizes to the best overall, scariest, and funniest pumpkins.

See you at the farm!

Lesson 16

Applying Paragraph Formats

➤ What You Will Learn

Aligning Text Horizontally and Vertically
Changing Line and Paragraph Spacing

Software Skills Text alignment within a text box can make a big difference in the look of a publication. Publisher lets you adjust the spacing between paragraphs and between lines of an individual paragraph, as well as set alignment options for text both vertically and horizontally.

What You Can Do

Aligning Text Horizontally and Vertically

- **Horizontal alignment** controls how text is positioned between the left and right sides of a text box. See Figure 16-1 for examples of these alignments.
  - Left alignment lines text up at the left side of a text box.
  - Center alignment positions text so that each line is centered between the left and right sides of the text box.
  - Right alignment lines text up at the right side of a text box.
  - **Justified** alignment lines text up at both the left and right sides of a text box.
- The default horizontal alignment is left for manually placed text boxes; for placeholder boxes, the alignment varies depending on the template.

Figure 16-1

This paragraph uses left horizontal alignment, so all text lines up at the left side of the text box, and lines end raggedly at the right.

This paragraph uses center horizontal alignment, so all text lines up evenly between the left and right sides of the text box.

This text uses right horizontal alignment, so all text lines up at the right side of the text box, and lines end raggedly at the left.

This text uses justified horizontal alignment, so text lines up at both the left and right sides of the text box.

WORDS TO KNOW

Horizontal alignment
The horizontal position of text between the left and right sides of a text box.

Justified
Text stretched out with extra spacing as needed so that all lines align evenly on both the right and left.

Line spacing
The space between lines.

Paragraph spacing
The space before or after paragraphs.

Vertical alignment
The vertical positioning of text between the top and bottom edges of a text frame.

- Change horizontal alignment by clicking in the paragraph you want to align and selecting an alignment option from the Paragraph group on the HOME tab. To format more than one paragraph at once, select the paragraphs first.

- You also can select a horizontal alignment from the Paragraph dialog box. Choose from its Alignment drop-down list on the Indents and Spacing tab. This list offers two additional alignment options, Distributed and Distribute All Lines. Distributed aligns text in the same way that justified alignment does. Distribute All Lines justifies all text, even short lines at the end of a paragraph.

- **Vertical alignment** refers to the vertical position of the text within the text frame. The default vertical alignment is Top, but Publisher offers Center or Bottom as well.

- The Alignment group on the TEXT BOX TOOLS FORMAT tab gives you options for applying both horizontal and vertical alignment at the same time. Choose the Align Center command, for example, to apply both horizontal and vertical center alignment. Choose Align Bottom Right to position the text at the bottom right side of the text frame.

- These alignment options make it easy for you to decide on an alignment without having to select the horizontal alignment and the vertical alignment in separate steps.

Try It! **Aligning Text Horizontally and Vertically**

1. Start Publisher and open **PB16Try** from the data files for this lesson.

2. Save the publication as **PB16Try_xx** in the location where your teacher instructs you to store the files for this lesson.

3. Click in the *Car Wash* heading text, and then click the TEXT BOX TOOLS FORMAT tab. Note that the current alignment is Align Bottom Left. Click the Align Top Center option ▤.

4. Click in the Date text, and then click TEXT BOX TOOLS FORMAT > Align Bottom Right ▤.

5. Click in the Time text, and then click TEXT BOX TOOLS FORMAT > Align Top Right ▤.

6. Click the *This event benefits* text box, and then click TEXT BOX TOOLS FORMAT > Align Center ▤.

7. Select both paragraphs in the *Come out and get* text box, and then click HOME > Justify ▤.

8. Select all the *Location* paragraphs, and then click HOME > Center ▤.

9. Save the changes to **PB16Try_xx**, and leave it open to use in the next Try It.

Horizontal and vertical alignments applied

Changing Line and Paragraph Spacing

- **Line spacing** is the amount of space between the baseline of one line of text and the baseline of the next line. By default, Publisher sets the space between lines at 1.19sp; that is, one line space plus a fraction of another line, so there is enough white space between lines for text to be easily readable.

- You can use the Line Spacing command in the Paragraph group on the HOME tab to quickly change the line spacing, from 1.0 to 3.0sp. Or, you can use the Paragraph dialog box to set the spacing between lines more precisely.

- **Paragraph spacing** is the space before or after a paragraph. By default, Publisher sets the space after paragraphs to 6 points.

- You can use the Paragraph Spacing command in the Paragraph group on the HOME tab to set the space after a paragraph to None, 8 pt, 10 pt, or 12 pt. Or, you can use the Paragraph dialog box to set the space before or after paragraphs to any amount.

- Line and paragraph spacing settings apply only to the paragraph in which the insertion point is located when you make the change. To affect more than one paragraph at once, select them before making the change.

Try It!   **Changing Line and Paragraph Spacing**

1. In the **PB16Try_xx** file, click in the *This event benefits* text, and click HOME > Line Spacing ‡☰ > Line Spacing Options.

2. In the Paragraph dialog box, click the Between lines up arrow once to change the spacing to 1.25sp. Click OK.

3. Select both paragraphs in the *Come out and get* text box, and then click HOME > Line Spacing ‡☰ > 1.5.

4. Click in the *Come out and get* paragraph, and then click HOME > Paragraph Spacing ☴▾ > Paragraph Spacing Options.

5. Click the After paragraphs up arrow seven times to set 7 points of space. Click OK.

6. Select the three paragraphs below the *Location* heading, and then click HOME > Paragraph Spacing ☴▾ > 8 pt.

7. Close the publication, saving changes, and exit Publisher.

Line and paragraph spacing adjusted

Lesson 16—Practice

Anderson Farms would like you to make some additional modifications to the pumpkin-carving flyer, including changing the page size to present the material as a poster. In this exercise, you begin work with another version of the flyer and change a number of text and paragraph formats.

DIRECTIONS

1. Start Publisher, if necessary, and open **PB16Practice** from the data files for this lesson.

2. Save the publication as **PB16Practice_xx** in the location where your teacher instructs you to store the files for this lesson.

3. First, modify the page size and layout and position of guides as follows:

   a. Click **PAGE DESIGN > Size** 🗋 **> More Preset Page Sizes**. Click the **Posters** folder and then click **A3 (Portrait)**. Click **OK**.

   b. Click **PAGE DESIGN > Guides** 🗋 **> Grid and Baseline Guides**. Click the **Columns** up arrow one time to specify **2** columns. Then click the **Spacing** up arrow four times to specify **0.5** inch spacing between columns. Click **OK**.

   c. Move the first horizontal ruler guide up to **2.5** inches. Move the second ruler guide up to **3** inches. Move the third ruler guide to **9.5** inches.

   d. Drag a new ruler guide down from the horizontal ruler and drop it at the **15** inch mark.

4. Adjust the position and size of text boxes as follows:

   a. Move the *Anderson Farms* text box to the top of the page, at the intersection of the left and top margin guides. Resize the text box to fit in the area above the 2.5 inch guide.

   b. Move the *Pumpkin Carving* text box up to align the top of the box with the 3 inch ruler guide. Resize the text box to fit the entire area inside the left and right margins. Pull the bottom of the text box down to the 7.5 inch mark on the vertical ruler.

   c. Move the *Join us* text box to the intersection of the left margin guide and the 9.5 inch ruler guide. Drag the lower-right corner down to the intersection of the column guide and the 15 inch ruler guide.

   d. Move the *Refreshments* text box to the intersection of the column guide and the 9.5 inch ruler guide. Drag the lower-right corner down to the intersection of the right margin and the 15 inch ruler guide.

5. Select the text in the *Join us* text box, and then click **TEXT BOX TOOLS FORMAT > Font Size** [11 ▾] **> 24**. Repeat this step to resize the text in the *Refreshments* text box.

6. Click **TEXT BOX TOOLS FORMAT > Draw Text Box** 🅰 and draw a text box below the *Pumpkin Carving* text box, about **1.3** inches high and **9** inches wide. Click **HOME > Center** ≡ and then type the following text:

   Scary? Mean? Happy? Mischievous? What kinds of faces do you like to make?

7. Select the text, and then click **HOME > Font Size** [11 ▾] **> 26**. Adjust the width of the text box if necessary to avoid hyphenating *faces*, and then drag the text box to center it between the left and right margins.

8. Click in the *Anderson Farms Presents* text. Click **HOME > Line Spacing** ↕≡ **> 1.0**. Then click **HOME > Center** ≡. Your publication should look similar to Figure 16-2 on the next page.

9. Close the publication, saving changes, and exit Publisher.

Figure 16-2

Anderson Farms Presents
the 17th Annual

Pumpkin Carving
Contest

Scary? Mean? Happy? Mischievous? What kinds of
faces do you like to make?

Join us on October 25th to try your hand at carving a pumpkin masterpiece. You'll find all the tools you need for your creation.
Festivities start at 10:00 a.m. and end at 4:00 p.m. with judging and prize awards.
Call 513-555-6600 for more information.

Refreshments include cider and fresh donuts!
Prizes to the best overall, scariest, and funniest pumpkins.
Come in costume and enter our costume contest. Prizes to best overall, scariest, most elaborate, and funniest costumes.
See you at the farm!

Lesson 16—Apply

You continue to fine-tune the Anderson Farms pumpkin-carving poster. In this exercise, you adjust alignments and line and paragraph spacing to make text easier to read.

DIRECTIONS

1. Start Publisher, if necessary, and open **PB16Apply** from the data files for this lesson.

2. Save the publication as **PB16Apply_xx** in the location where your teacher instructs you to store the files for this lesson.

3. In the *Anderson Farms* text box, change alignment to bottom center.

4. In the *Pumpkin Carving* text box, change alignment to center text both horizontally and vertically.

5. Center the text in the *Scary? Mean?* text box horizontally and vertically.

6. Select all paragraphs in the *Join us* text box and make the following changes:

   a. Apply **Justify** horizontal alignment.

   b. Change the line spacing to **1.19sp**.

   c. Change the spacing after each paragraph to **12 pt**.

7. Apply the same formats to the text in the *Refreshments* text box.

8. Draw a text box in the right column below the 15 inch ruler guide the full width of the column, with the bottom of the text box at the bottom margin guide.

9. Type the following lines in the text box:

   Anderson Farms is located on Route 4 in Fairfield, OH.

   Visit us on the web at www.andersonfarms.com.

10. Select the text and change the font size to 14. Apply bottom right alignment. Click in the first paragraph and remove the space after the paragraph. Your page should look like Figure 16-3 on the next page.

11. Close the publication, saving changes, and exit Publisher.

Figure 16-3

Anderson Farms Presents
the 17th Annual

Pumpkin Carving Contest

Scary? Mean? Happy? Mischievous? What kinds of
faces do you like to make?

Join us on October 25th to try your hand at carving a pumpkin masterpiece. You'll find all the tools you need for your creation.

Festivities start at 10:00 a.m. and end at 4:00 p.m. with judging and prize awards.

Call 513-555-6600 for more information.

Refreshments include cider and fresh donuts!

Prizes to the best overall, scariest, and funniest pumpkins.

Come in costume and enter our costume contest. Prizes to best overall, scariest, most elaborate, and funniest costumes.

See you at the farm!

Anderson Farms is located on Route 4 in Fairfield, OH.
Visit us on the web at www.andersonfarms.com.

Lesson 17

Controlling Text with Tabs and Indents

> ## What You Will Learn

Using Tab Stops
Setting, Modifying, and Removing Tab Stops
Using Tab Leaders
Applying Indents
Adjusting Text Box Margins

WORDS TO KNOW

Hanging indent
An indent style in which the first line is set with a negative indent in relation to the rest of the paragraph, so it sticks out farther to the left.

Indent
Extra horizontal space inserted on one or both sides of a paragraph, between the paragraph and the margin.

Leader
A repeated character appearing between some text and the next tab stop that helps the eye follow the text across the page.

Tab stop
A location at which text will align when the Tab key is pressed.

Software Skills   Tabs and indents can be used to align text neatly on a page. If you have worked with a word processing program before, such as Microsoft Word, you may already be familiar with these features; they work the same in Publisher as they do in Word.

What You Can Do

Using Tab Stops

- A **tab stop** marks a certain horizontal location within a text box. Use tab stops to align text at specific locations.
- Publisher offers four types of tab stops:
  - A left tab stop aligns text at the left at the tab stop position.
  - A right tab stop aligns text at the right at the tab stop position.
  - A center tab stop spaces text evenly on each side of the tab stop position.
  - A decimal tab stop aligns the decimal points of numbers at the tab stop position.
- By default, every paragraph in a text box has left tab stops every half inch, although you cannot see these default tab stops on the ruler.

Setting, Modifying, and Removing Tab Stops

- To set a tab stop, click in the paragraph for which you want to set the tab stop and then click the ruler to place a stop at the desired location. You can choose the type of tab stop by clicking the tab selector at the location where the vertical ruler and horizontal ruler meet.

- Custom tab stops display on the ruler with a symbol that represents the type of tab.

- To change a tab stop to a different type, double-click the tab stop symbol to open the Paragraph dialog box with the Tabs tab active, and then choose a different alignment.

- Each paragraph has its own separate tab stop settings. To change the tab stops for more than one paragraph at once, first select the paragraphs.

- To adjust the position of a tab stop, drag the tab stop on the ruler to reposition it.

- To remove a tab stop, drag it off the ruler.

- You also can set, modify, and remove tab stops on the Tabs tab of the Paragraph dialog box (Figure 17-1). To set a tab stop in this dialog box, type a ruler position (in inches) in the Tab stop position box, and then choose an alignment and click Set.

- You can modify a selected tab stop by typing a different position. Remove a tab stop by selecting it and clicking Clear, or click Clear All to remove all tab stops.

- You can also change the spacing between default tab stops on the Tabs tab in the Paragraph dialog box.

✓ You also use this dialog box to specify a tab leader. You learn about tab leaders in the next section.

Figure 17-1

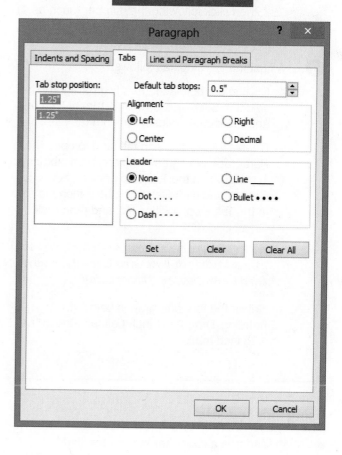

Try It! **Setting, Modifying, and Removing Tab Stops**

1. Start Publisher and open **PB17Try** from the data files for this lesson.

2. Save the publication as **PB17Try_xx** in the location where your teacher instructs you to store the files for this lesson.

3. In the text box at the top of the page, click in the boldfaced column heading paragraph (*RegionQuarterTop Seller*) following the word *Region* and press TAB to move the text following *Region* to a default tab stop.

4. Click following *Quarter* and press TAB; then click following *Top Seller* and press TAB. You have aligned text in this paragraph on Publisher's default tab stops.

5. Select the four paragraphs beneath the paragraph for which you just inserted tab stops.

6. Click at the 1 inch mark on the ruler, at the 2 inch mark, and at the 3 inch mark to set three custom Left tab stops for these paragraphs.

(continued)

Try It!   Setting, Modifying, and Removing Tab Stops (continued)

7 In each of the paragraphs you selected, click after the region (such as *North*) and press TAB; then click following the number (such as *1*) and press TAB; then click following the product (such as *Alta-Clean*) and press TAB.

8 Adjust the tab stops as follows:

a. Click in the boldfaced heading paragraph to select it. Click on the ruler at 1 inch, 2 inches, and 3.5 inches to insert custom tab stops.

b. Double-click the 2 inch tab stop to open the Paragraph dialog box with the Tabs tab active. Type **2.625** in the Tab stop position box, click Center, and click Set. Click the 2 inch tab stop in the Tab stop position list, and then click Clear. Click OK.

✓ *You may find that the tab stops you set on the ruler are not exact to the inch. If you do not have a 2 inch tab stop, select the one closest to 2 inches to clear.*

c. Select the four paragraphs below the heading. Drag the 1 inch Left tab stop to the 1.25 inch mark.

d. Drag the 3 inch Left tab stop to the 4.25 inch mark, and then double-click it to open the Paragraph dialog box with the Tabs tab active.

e. With the 4.25 inch tab stop selected in the Tab stop position list, click Decimal alignment, and then click Set. Click OK.

9 Save the changes to **PB17Try_xx**, and leave it open to use in the next Try It.

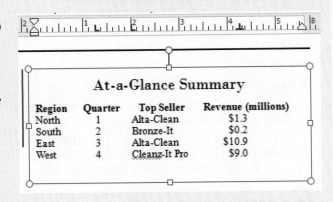

Custom tabs set to control text

At-a-Glance Summary

Region	Quarter	Top Seller	Revenue (millions)
North	1	Alta-Clean	$1.3
South	2	Bronze-It	$0.2
East	3	Alta-Clean	$10.9
West	4	Cleanz-It Pro	$9.0

Using Tab Leaders

■ A tab **leader** is a character that is repeated between text and the next tab stop to the right. Tab leaders help a reader's eye follow the text from one side of the text box to the other; they are often used in tables of contents to "connect" the contents entry to its page number.

■ You set tab leaders on the Tabs tab in the Paragraph dialog box. You have a choice of four leader options: dot, dash, line, and bullet. Dot and line leader characters display at the baseline; dash and bullet characters are centered vertically with text.

Try It!   Using Tab Leaders

1 In the **PB17Try_xx** file, select all the text in the *Table of Contents* text box except for the heading.

2 Click HOME > Paragraph dialog box launcher ⌐, and then click the Tabs tab.

3 Click in the Tab stop position box and type **7**.

4 Click Right alignment.

5 Click the Dot leader, and then click Set. Click OK.

6 Save the changes to **PB17Try_xx**, and leave it open to use in the next Try It.

Applying Indents

- **Indents** increase the amount of white space to the left and/or right of a paragraph. You might want to indent a paragraph, such as a quotation, for emphasis, or you might want to indent the first line of text paragraphs to help the reader identify new paragraphs.

- Indents may also be used when you want to use a fill or border around a text box and don't want the text in the text box to crowd the border.

  ✓ *You learn another way to adjust space between text and the text box border later in this lesson.*

- Do not confuse indents with left/right margins. Margins are for the entire text box or entire page, while indents are for individual paragraphs only.

- You have a number of options for inserting indents. You can use toolbar commands, ruler options, or the Paragraph dialog box.

Applying Indents with the Toolbar and the Ruler

- Use the Increase Indent Position command in the Paragraph group on the HOME tab to quickly insert a 0.5 inch left indent of the currently selected paragraph. You can reverse this indent with the Decrease Indent Position command in the same group.

- Using the indent markers on the ruler gives you more control over indents. Markers display at the left end of the ruler for first-line indent, hanging indent, and left indent (Figure 17-2). The right indent marker displays at the right end of the ruler.

  - The first-line indent marker looks like a downward-pointing triangle. Drag this marker to set the indent for the first line of a paragraph.

  - The hanging indent marker looks like an upward-pointing triangle. Drag this marker to the right of the first-line indent marker, as shown in Figure 17-2, to set a **hanging indent**, in which the first line of the paragraph is further to the left than the remaining lines of the paragraph.

  - The left indent marker looks like a small rectangle attached to the bottom of the hanging indent marker. Drag this marker to move both the first-line indent and hanging indent marker at the same time to create the left indent.

  - The right indent marker looks like an upward-pointing triangle. Drag this marker to set an indent at the right side of the text box.

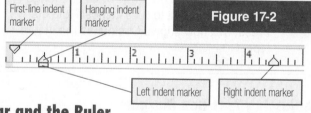

First-line indent marker | Hanging indent marker | **Figure 17-2**

Left indent marker | Right indent marker

Try It!   **Applying Indents with the Toolbar and the Ruler**

1. In the **PB17Try_xx** file, click HOME > Draw Text Box 🔲, and draw a text box about 1 inch high by 5 inches wide, below the *At-a-Glance* table and above the *Table of Contents* text box.

2. Click HOME > Font Size [11 ▾] > 14. Type the following text:

   Executive Summary—Our most profitable seller continues to be Alta-Clean in the East region. Sales of $10.9 million are up substantially for this year. The West region's Cleanz-It Pro ran a close second at $9.0 million.

3. Click DRAWING TOOLS FORMAT > Shape Fill 🎨 and fill the text box with a light gray fill such as Accent 5 (White), Darker 15%.

4. With the insertion point in the paragraph, click HOME > Increase Indent Position ⬕. A 0.5 inch left indent is inserted to the left of the paragraph.

5. Click HOME > Decrease Indent Position ⬔ to remove the indent.

6. Drag the right indent marker to the 4.75 inch mark on the ruler to set a right indent.

7. Click on the left indent marker (the rectangle below the upward-pointing hanging indent marker) and drag to the right to the 0.25 inch mark on the ruler.

8. Click on the first-line indent marker and drag to the right to the 0.5 inch mark on the ruler.

9. Save the changes to **PB17Try_xx**, and leave it open to use in the next Try It.

Right, left, and first-line indent

Executive Summary—Our most profitable seller continues to be Alta-Clean in the East region. Sales of $10.9 million are up substantially for this year. The West region's Cleanz-It Pro ran a close second at $9.0 million.

Applying Indents with the Paragraph Dialog Box

- You also can set indents with the Paragraph dialog box.

- The Preset list makes it easy for you to set frequently used indents such as first-line indents, hanging indents, or quotation indents in which a paragraph is indented from both the left and right margin. These preset indents set the position of the first line, the left indent, and the right indent for you.

- The Sample box shows how indents are applied to the selected lines.

- To remove all indents, choose the Flush Left preset.

- You can also create a custom indent by entering your own Left, First line, and Right settings.

Try It!   **Applying Indents with the Paragraph Dialog Box**

1. In the **PB17Try_xx** file, with the insertion point in the *Executive Summary* paragraph, click HOME > Paragraph dialog box launcher ⌐ .

2. Click the Preset drop-down arrow and click Flush Left to remove all indents from the paragraph.

3. Click the Preset drop-down arrow and click 1st Line Indent. Note the First line box shows a value of 0.25.

4. Click the First line up arrow twice to change the first line indent to 0.45 inches. Note the Preset box now shows Custom as the indent type. Click OK.

5. Click HOME > Paragraph dialog box launcher ⌐ . Click the Preset drop-down list and click Hanging Indent. Note the First line box shows a negative value that indicates the first line is set to the left of the left indent, which is 0.25 inches. Click OK.

6. Save the changes to **PB17Try_xx**, and leave it open to use in the next Try It.

Adjusting Text Box Margins

- Indents are one way to insert space between the text in a text box and the text box's edges. Another way to increase this space is to adjust the margins of the text box.

- Publisher's default margins for text boxes are 0.04 inches on all sides. You can use the Margins command on the TEXT BOX TOOLS FORMAT tab to change the default setting (Narrow) to Moderate or Wide, or to remove all margins.

- Click the Custom Margins command on the Margins menu, or right-click the text box and select Format Text Box, to open the Format Text Box dialog box. On the Text Box tab, you can adjust the margin for each side of a text box, if desired. You can also specify vertical alignment and autofitting behavior for the text box.

Try It!   Adjusting Text Box Margins

1 In the **PB17Try_xx** file, click in the *Executive Summary* paragraph, and then click HOME > Paragraph dialog box launcher ⌐. Click the Preset drop-down arrow and click Flush Left. Click OK.

2 Click TEXT BOX TOOLS FORMAT > Margins [A] > Wide. If text overflows the text box, increase the height slightly to display all text.

3 Click TEXT BOX TOOLS FORMAT > Margins [A] > None to see what the text box looks like with no margins.

4 Click TEXT BOX TOOLS FORMAT > Margins [A] > Custom Margins.

5 Click the Left up arrow twice to set the left margin to 0.2. Click the Right up arrow once. Click in the Top box and type .15. Click OK.

✓ *If necessary, adjust the width of the text box to avoid the hyphen after Cleanz moving to the last line of the paragraph.*

6 Close the publication, saving changes, and exit Publisher.

Tabs, indents, and margin settings complete

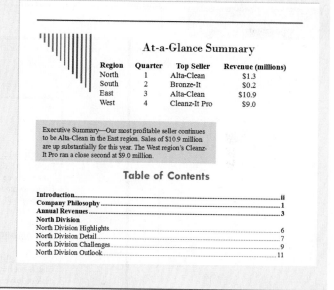

Lesson 17—Practice

The Hendricks Inn has asked you to work on a binder of important information to be placed in each room of the inn. In this exercise, you begin work on several binder pages and format text using tabs and indents to present the information more clearly.

DIRECTIONS

1. Start Publisher, if necessary, and open **PB17Practice** from the data files for this lesson.

2. Save the publication as **PB17Practice_xx** in the location where your teacher instructs you to store the files for this lesson.

3. Click in the text box on page 1 to select the text box.

4. Click **TEXT BOX TOOLS FORMAT** > **Margins** [A] > **Wide**.

5. Click page 2, select the text box, and click **TEXT BOX TOOLS FORMAT** > **Margins** [A] > **Wide**.

6. Click page 1 and select the seven paragraphs below the *Telephone Extensions* heading. Click **HOME** > **Paragraph dialog box launcher** ⌐, and then click the **Tabs** tab.

7. Click in the Tab stop position box and type **4.5**. Click the **Right** alignment option. Click the **Dot** leader option. Click **Set**. Click **OK**.

8. Click just to the left of the extension number in each of the paragraphs you selected (such as **1* or *9*), and then press TAB.

9. Click in the second paragraph below the *Check-Out* heading. Drag the first-line indent marker to the **0.5 inch** mark on the ruler.

10. Click in the *Winter two-for-one* paragraph, click **HOME** > **Paragraph dialog box launcher** ⌐, click the **Preset** drop-down arrow, and click **Quotation**. Click **OK**.

11. Click page 2, and then select the last eight paragraphs under the *Personal Items* heading.

12. Click **HOME** > **Increase Indent Position** ⅀.

13. **With your teacher's permission**, print the publication. Page 1 should look like Figure 17-3.

14. Close the publication, saving changes, and exit Publisher.

Figure 17-3

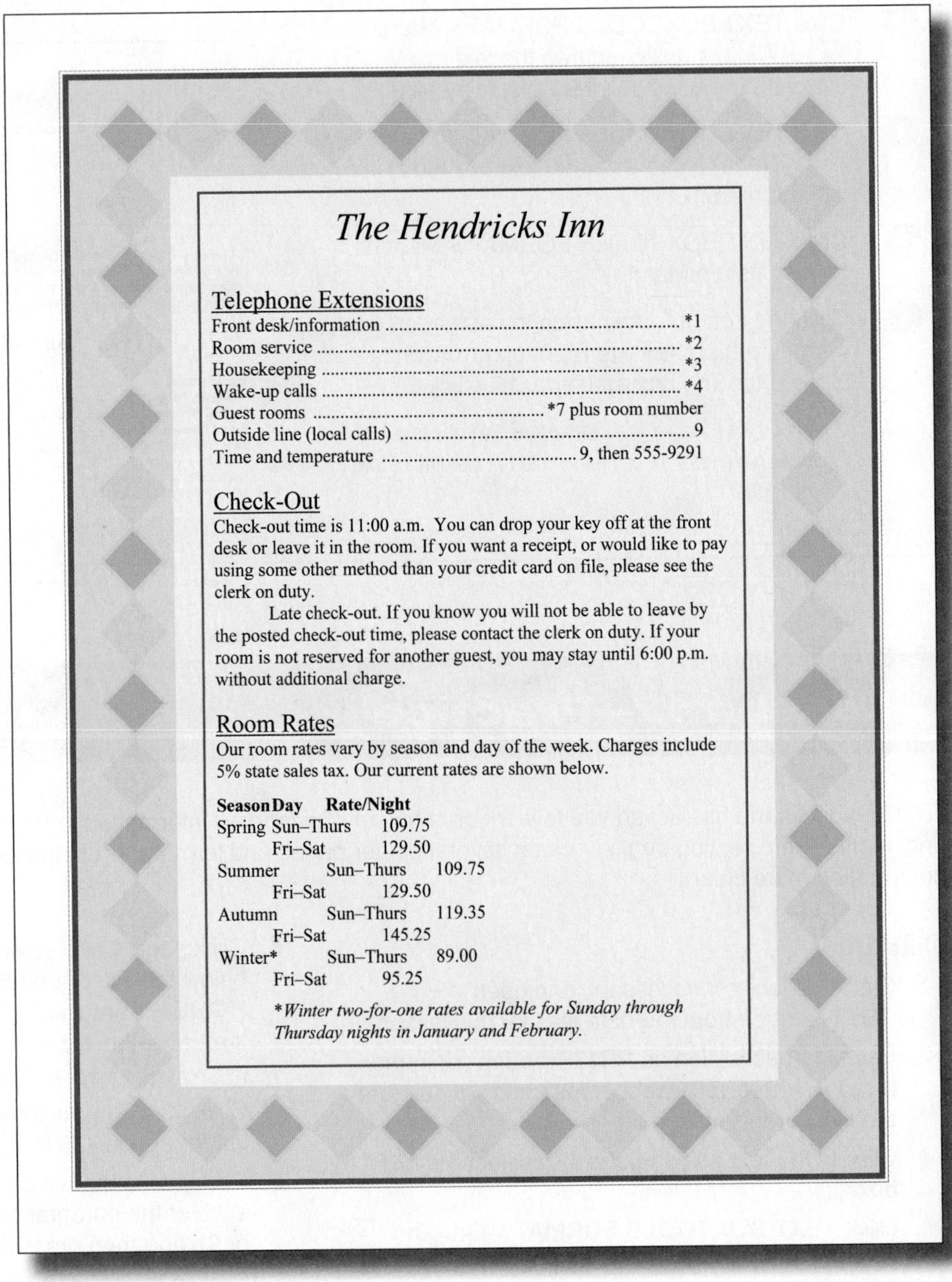

The Hendricks Inn

Telephone Extensions
Front desk/information *1
Room service *2
Housekeeping *3
Wake-up calls *4
Guest rooms .... *7 plus room number
Outside line (local calls) 9
Time and temperature .... 9, then 555-9291

Check-Out
Check-out time is 11:00 a.m. You can drop your key off at the front desk or leave it in the room. If you want a receipt, or would like to pay using some other method than your credit card on file, please see the clerk on duty.

     Late check-out. If you know you will not be able to leave by the posted check-out time, please contact the clerk on duty. If your room is not reserved for another guest, you may stay until 6:00 p.m. without additional charge.

Room Rates
Our room rates vary by season and day of the week. Charges include 5% state sales tax. Our current rates are shown below.

Season	Day	Rate/Night
Spring	Sun–Thurs	109.75
	Fri–Sat	129.50
Summer	Sun–Thurs	109.75
	Fri–Sat	129.50
Autumn	Sun–Thurs	119.35
	Fri–Sat	145.25
Winter*	Sun–Thurs	89.00
	Fri–Sat	95.25

Winter two-for-one rates available for Sunday through Thursday nights in January and February.

Lesson 17—Apply

In this exercise, you continue working on the information pages for The Hendricks Inn. You organize text using tabs and adjust indents to improve appearance.

DIRECTIONS

1. Start Publisher, if necessary, and open **PB17Apply** from the data files for this lesson.

2. Save the publication as **PB17Apply_xx** in the location where your teacher instructs you to store the files for this lesson.

3. Select the tabular material in the *Room Rates* section and apply left and right indents of 0.7 inch.

4. Select the tabular information below the bold column headings paragraph and use the ruler or the Paragraph dialog box to set tabs to align the text. The day items should have a center tab, and the rate entries should be aligned with a decimal tab. Adjust tabs as necessary to align text attractively.

5. Insert tab stops for the boldfaced column headings. The *Day* and *Rate/Night* headings should be centered over their respective columns.

6. On page 2, select the list of things to do below the first paragraph in the *Things to Do* section. Use the Tabs tab in the Paragraph dialog box to set a left tab at 1.3 inches. Then click the Indents and Spacing tab and set a hanging indent that has a first line of -1.3 inches and a left indent of 1.3 inches.

7. Make this list of three items easier to read by adding an 8 pt paragraph space after the first and second items.

8. On page 1, for a final decorative touch, click at the right end of the *Telephone Extensions* heading (just to the right of a space that follows the heading) and set a right tab at about 4.6 inches with a line tab leader. Press TAB after the space at the end of the heading to insert the line leader. Insert similar lines to the right of each heading on the two pages.

   ✓ *Make sure there is no underline formatting on the space after the heading or on the leader.*

9. **With your teacher's permission**, print the publication. Page 1 should look like Figure 17-4 and page 2 should look like Figure 17-5, both shown on the next page.

10. Close the publication, saving changes, and exit Publisher.

Figure 17-4

The Hendricks Inn

Telephone Extensions
Front desk/information *1
Room service *2
Housekeeping *3
Wake-up calls *4
Guest rooms .... *7 plus room number
Outside line (local calls) 9
Time and temperature .... 9, then 555-9291

Check-Out
Check-out time is 11:00 a.m. You can drop your key off at the front
desk or leave it in the room. If you want a receipt, or would like to pay
using some other method than your credit card on file, please see the
clerk on duty.

     Late check-out. If you know you will not be able to leave by
the posted check-out time, please contact the clerk on duty. If your
room is not reserved for another guest, you may stay until 6:00 p.m.
without additional charge.

Room Rates
Our room rates vary by season and day of the week. Cl
5% state sales tax. Our current rates are shown below.

Season	Day	Rate
Spring	Sun–Thurs	109.
	Fri–Sat	129.
Summer	Sun–Thurs	109.
	Fri–Sat	129.
Autumn	Sun–Thurs	119.
	Fri–Sat	145.
Winter*	Sun–Thurs	89.
	Fri–Sat	95.

*Winter two-for-one rates available for Sunday
Thursday nights in January and February.

Figure 17-5

The Hendricks Inn

Restaurant Reservations
We are happy to make suggestions of local restaurants, and to assist
you in making reservations. Ask the front desk clerk or the concierge
(if on duty).

Things to Do
You will find a number of things to do in the area. For more information on any of these topics, ask the front desk clerk or the concierge.

Horseback riding	The Clover Valley Stables offers trail rides in spring, summer, and fall. You can also contact them in winter for lessons in their indoor ring.
Hiking	We are only a few miles from Bedford Forest, a well-maintained natural area crisscrossed with hiking trails that vary from accessible paved paths to strenuous climbs.
Shopping	Berea, with its many craft and antique shops, is only 10 miles from the Inn. Lexington is also an easy drive.

Personal Items
The following personal care items are available at no charge should
you need them. Dial *2 for housekeeping to request them.
    Toothbrush/toothpaste
    Make-up remover towelettes
    Nail clippers
    Tweezers
    Razor
    Comb
    Shoe shine cloth
    Hypoallergenic soap and shampoo

Lesson 18

Working with Lists

➤ What You Will Learn

Creating Bulleted Lists
Creating Numbered Lists

Software Skills   Bulleted and numbered lists are organizational devices that help you present data to your readers in more interesting and readable formats. Both require a hanging indent for the first line, and the Bullets and Numbering features in Publisher set up those indents for you automatically.

What You Can Do

Creating Bulleted Lists

■ A **bullet** is a character used to add emphasis to a list item, such as a plain black dot, a diamond, an arrow, a star, and so on.

■ Use a bulleted list when you want to organize information in a list but the order of items is not important.

■ You can quickly apply bullet formatting to any paragraph by clicking in the paragraph, or selecting multiple paragraphs, and clicking the Bullets command in the Paragraph group on the HOME tab. A gallery of bullets appears from which you can select the desired character.

■ You can also create a bulleted list as you type. Click the Bullets command and select the desired bullet style, and then type your list, pressing ENTER between items. Publisher will continue assigning bullets to each paragraph until you press ENTER twice without typing any text, or click the Bullets button again.

■ You can select a new bullet character, or control the indents for bulleted paragraphs, in the Bullets and Numbering dialog box. The Bullets tab gives you these options:

• Set the size of the bullet in the Size box. By default it is the same size as the paragraph's text.

• Use the Indent list by box to specify how much indent the text should have. This does not affect the bullet character's positioning—only the text.

✓ *To change the bullet character's positioning, adjust the hanging indent for the first line in the Paragraph dialog box.*

WORDS TO KNOW

Bullet
A character that appears to the left of the first line of a paragraph to call attention to that paragraph's beginning point.

Separator character
The character that follows the number in a numbered list item. For example, a period is a common separator character.

- If none of the bullet characters on the Bullets tab appeal to you, you can select a different character by clicking the Character button. In the Bullet Character dialog box, choose a font and then select a character from that font to use as your bullet.

  ✓ *Some useful fonts for bullets include Wingdings, Webdings, Symbol, and Marlett.*

- Once you have applied bullets in a publication, the options you chose display in the Recently Used Bullets section at the top of the Bullets gallery.

Try It!   Creating Bulleted Lists

1 Start Publisher and open **PB18Try** from the data files for this lesson.

2 Save the publication as **PB18Try_xx** in the location where your teacher instructs you to store the files for this lesson.

3 Select the first three paragraphs under the *Fire Extinguisher Guidelines* heading.

4 Click HOME > Bullets ≡ ▾, and then click the Large Bullets option.

5 Click the last three paragraphs under the *Fire Extinguisher Guidelines* heading.

6 Click HOME > Bullets ≡ ▾, and then click the Filled Diamond Bullets option. With the three paragraphs still selected, click HOME > Bullets ≡ ▾ > Bullets and Numbering. Click the Size up arrow until the size is 13pt. Click OK.

7 With the three paragraphs still selected, click HOME > Increase Indent Position ≡ to indent the subordinate bullet items.

8 Select the three paragraphs under the *Emergency Exit Guidelines* heading.

9 Click HOME > Bullets ≡ ▾ > Bullets and Numbering.

10 In the Bullets and Numbering dialog box, click any bullet character shown, and then click the Character button.

11 Click the Font drop-down list `Times New Roman ▾`, scroll down the list of fonts, and click Wingdings.

12 Scroll to the bottom of the Wingdings font display and click the heavy, right-pointing arrow in the second-to-last row. (The number 232 displays in the Character code box.) Click OK, and then click OK again to apply the bullet.

13 Save the changes to **PB18Try_xx**, and leave it open to use in the next Try It.

Bullet characters applied

Safety Procedures

Fire Extinguisher Guidelines

- Check the gauge on each fire extinguisher every 3 months, ensuring it is still functional.
- Do not discharge fire extinguishers except in case of an actual fire.
- Take care to use the correct fire extinguisher class on the fire:
  - ◆ Class A: Paper and wood
  - ◆ Class B: Grease and liquid flammables
  - ◆ Class C: Electrical

Emergency Exit Guidelines

- → Do not block emergency exits with boxes, pallets, or other obstacles.
- → Keep signs for emergency exits clearly visible.
- → Under no circumstances are emergency exits to be chained shut or locked from the inside.

Creating Numbered Lists

- Use a numbered list when the items in a list must be in a specific order. A numbered list starts with a number or a letter.

- Use the Numbering command in the Paragraph group on the HOME tab to create a numbered list. Clicking this button displays a gallery of numbering options, including Arabic numbers (1, 2, 3), roman numerals, and capital and lowercase letters.

- Just as with bullets, you can create a numbered list while you type. Click the Numbering command and select the desired number format to turn numbers on, and then type the list, pressing [ENTER] after each item. Press Enter [ENTER] twice, or click the Numbering command again, to turn numbering off.

- You can adjust formats for the numbered list by clicking Bullets and Numbering on the Numbering gallery.
  - You may choose a different number format from the Format drop-down list.

- You can choose a different **separator character**. The separator character is the character that follows the number. By default, it is a period, but you may choose from a variety of characters (or no character).

- Start at lets you start the numbering at some number other than 1 if desired. This is useful when you are continuing a numbered list from elsewhere in the document, for example.

- Indent list by is the same for numbered lists as for bulleted ones; it specifies where the text should begin. It has no effect on the number or separator character position.

- To change list levels or styles—for example, to change from 1) 2) 3) to a) b) c) for subordinate list entries—first apply None from the Numbering list to remove the current numbering format. Then apply the different format. If you try to change the format for a subordinate item without first applying None, you will change the format for the entire list.

Try It!   **Creating Numbered Lists**

① In the **PB18Try_xx** file, select the three paragraphs below the *Evacuation Procedures* heading.

② Click HOME > Numbering ▤ ▾ > 1.2.3.

③ Select the two paragraphs below the *If care is required for an injury* heading, and then click HOME > Numbering ▤ ▾ > 1) 2) 3).

④ Select the three paragraphs under the *If hurt on the job heading*. Click HOME > Numbering ▤ ▾ > 1) 2) 3).

⑤ Create a second-level numbered list as follows:

   a. Click at the end of the first item in the paragraphs you just numbered and press [ENTER].

   b. Click HOME > Numbering ▤ ▾ > None to turn off number formatting for this item.

   c. Click HOME > Numbering ▤ ▾ > a) b) c).

   d. Type **Supply your supervisor's name.**

   e. Press [ENTER] and type **Briefly describe the circumstances.**

   f. Select the a) and b) paragraphs, and then click HOME > Increase Indent Position ▦.

   g. Click in the next item (the second item 1)), and click HOME > Numbering ▤ ▾ > Bullets and Numbering.

   h. Click the Start at up arrow one time to change the start number to 2. Click OK.

⑥ Close the publication, saving changes, and exit Publisher.

Lists have been numbered

Evacuation Procedures
1. When an emergency alarm sounds, everyone should exit the building in an orderly fashion.
2. After everyone has exited, team captains should account for all personnel in their sections.
3. If a team captain finds anyone is missing, he or she should report it to the emergency coordinator.

Section	Captain	Phone
Accounting	Sally Kirkland	555-2741 x44
Personnel	Grace Baumgartner	555-2741 x410
Housekeeping	Charles Butler	555-2743
Engineering and Design	Margaret Li	555-2741 x15

First Aid Procedures
If hurt on the job:
1) Proceed to the nurse's station to receive care.
   a) Supply your supervisor's name.
   b) Briefly describe the circumstances.
2) Cooperate with the nurse in completing the required paperwork to document the injury.
3) Return to work with a signed copy of the paperwork.

If care is required for an injury not sustained on the job:
1) Proceed to the nurse's station to receive care.
2) Return to work as soon as possible. No paperwork is required.

Lesson 18—Practice

Your client at The Hendricks Inn wants to add some pages to the information binder you started in the last lesson. In this exercise, you use custom bullets to format a room service menu.

DIRECTIONS

1. Start Publisher, if necessary, and open **PB18Practice** from the data files for this lesson.

2. Save the publication as **PB18Practice_xx** in the location where your teacher instructs you to store the files for this lesson.

3. Click **VIEW** > **Boundaries** if necessary so you can see the text boxes on the page.

4. Click in the text box at the top of the page and type **Room Service Breakfast Menu**.

5. Select the text and click **HOME** > **Italic** *I* . Click **HOME** > **Font Size** 11 ▾ > **24**.

6. Click in the left text box beneath the heading and type the entries shown in Figure 18-1 on the next page. Apply bold and italic as shown in the figure.

7. Click in the right text box beneath the heading and type the entries shown in Figure 18-1. Apply bold and italic as shown in the figure.

8. Select the paragraphs under the *Select one coffee* heading and click **HOME** > **Bullets** ▤ ▾ > **Bullets and Numbering**.

9. Define a new bullet character as follows:
   a. Click any bullet and then click **Character**.
   b. Click the **Font** drop-down arrow and scroll down to select the **Wingdings** font.
   c. Click the square box character with the character code of **111**. Click **OK**.
   d. Click the **Size** up arrow three times to set the bullet size to **13pt**. Click **OK**.

10. Apply the same square box bullet to other entries on the menu as follows:
    a. Under *Select one juice,* apply bullets to all four juice choices.
    b. Under *Select one bread*, apply bullets to all entries *except* Toast.
    c. Under *Select one meat*, apply bullets to all choices.
    d. Under *Select up to two main course items*, apply bullets to all items *except* Eggs.
    e. Under *Select as many of the following as desired*, apply bullets to all items *except* Jelly/jam.

11. Adjust the indent for some selections as follows:
    a. Under *Toast* in the left column, select the two italic bread options, click **HOME** > **Paragraph dialog box launcher** ▣ , and click the **Left** indent up arrow twice to set the left indent to **0.45** inches. Click **OK**.
    b. Make the same indent change to the three eggs styles. Adjust the blank line length for *Fried* if necessary to prevent text from setting on two lines.
    c. Make the same indent change to the three choices under *Jelly/jam*.

12. Check spelling. Click **VIEW** > **Boundaries** to turn off boundaries.

13. **With your teacher's permission**, print the publication. It should look similar to Figure 18-2.

14. Close the publication, saving changes, and exit Publisher.

Figure 18-1

Room Service Breakfast Menu

Select one coffee:

Regular

Decaf

Select one juice:

Orange

Grapefruit

Grape

Apple

Select one bread:

Toast:

White

Wheat

Bagel

Muffin

Biscuit

Select one meat:

Sausage links

Sausage patties

Ham

Bacon

Vegetarian "sausage links"

Select up to two main course items:

Biscuits and gravy

Hash browns

Eggs:

Fried (style: _____)

Scrambled

Poached

Pancakes

French toast

Select as many of the following as desired:

Butter

Margarine

Jelly/jam:

Strawberry jam

Grape jelly

Orange marmalade

Ketchup

Salt and pepper

Sugar

Cream

Artificial sweetener

Maple syrup

Cream cheese

Figure 18-2

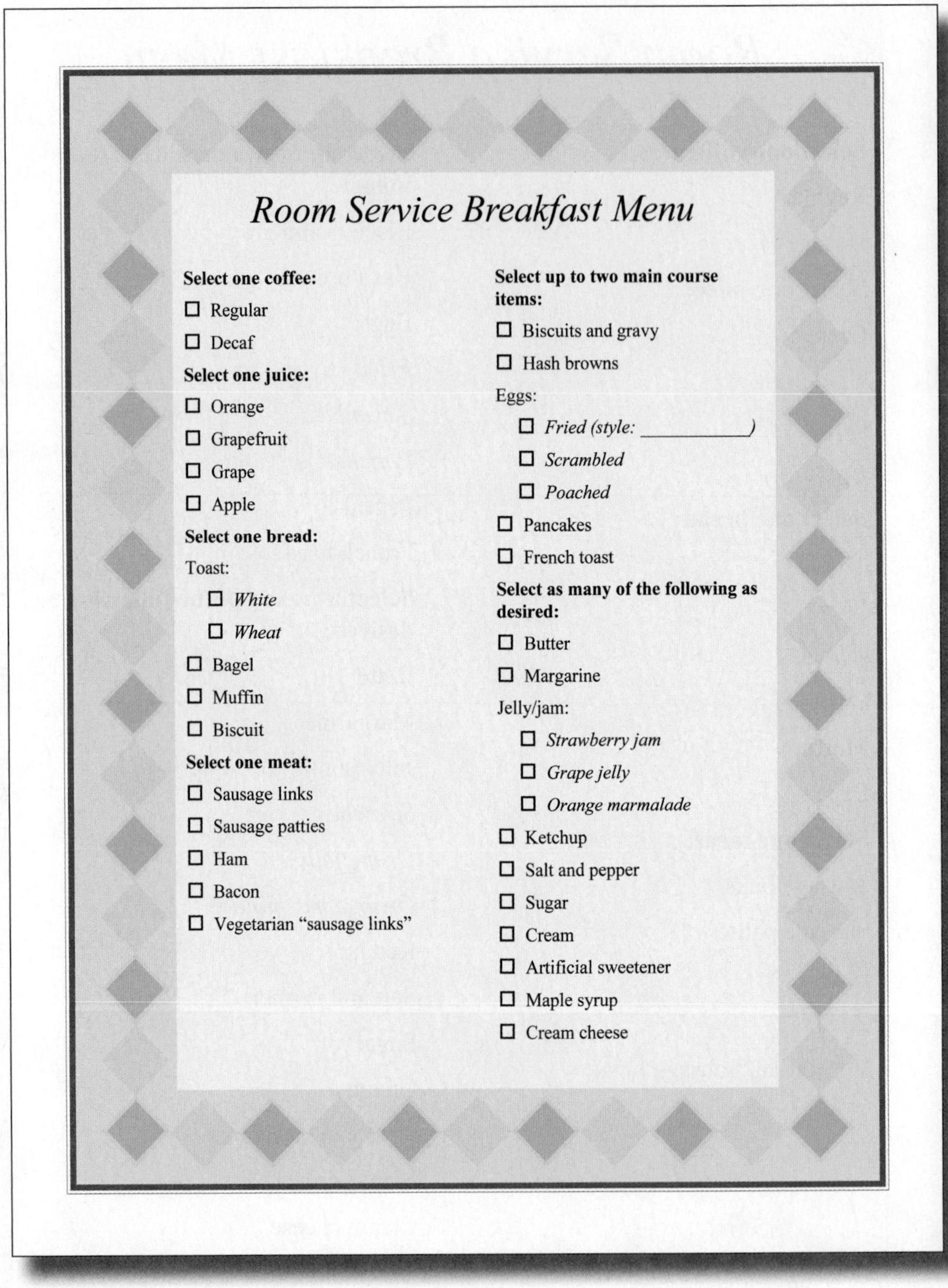

Room Service Breakfast Menu

Select one coffee:

☐ Regular

☐ Decaf

Select one juice:

☐ Orange

☐ Grapefruit

☐ Grape

☐ Apple

Select one bread:

Toast:

 ☐ *White*

 ☐ *Wheat*

☐ Bagel

☐ Muffin

☐ Biscuit

Select one meat:

☐ Sausage links

☐ Sausage patties

☐ Ham

☐ Bacon

☐ Vegetarian "sausage links"

Select up to two main course items:

☐ Biscuits and gravy

☐ Hash browns

Eggs:

 ☐ *Fried (style: _____)*

 ☐ *Scrambled*

 ☐ *Poached*

☐ Pancakes

☐ French toast

Select as many of the following as desired:

☐ Butter

☐ Margarine

Jelly/jam:

 ☐ *Strawberry jam*

 ☐ *Grape jelly*

 ☐ *Orange marmalade*

☐ Ketchup

☐ Salt and pepper

☐ Sugar

☐ Cream

☐ Artificial sweetener

☐ Maple syrup

☐ Cream cheese

Lesson 18—Apply

You continue to work on information sheets for the Hendricks Inn binder. In this exercise, you format an emergency procedures publication using different numbering options.

DIRECTIONS

1. Start Publisher, if necessary, and open **PB18Apply** from the data files for this lesson.

2. Save the publication as **PB18Apply_xx** in the location where your teacher instructs you to store the files for this lesson.

3. Type the page title **Emergency Procedures** in the text box at the top of the page. Apply **24 point italic** formatting.

4. Type the following information in the main text box, applying numbered formats as shown.

   I. **Reporting an Emergency**

      A. **Dial *1 for the front desk**

      B. **State your name, location, and nature of emergency**

   II. **Fire Procedures**

      A. **If the fire is in your room, get out quickly if you can**

         1. **Close the door**

         2. **Notify the front desk when you are safe**

      B. **If the fire is not in your room, place your hand on the door to test for heat**

         1. **If the door is hot:**

            a. **Do not exit; seal the door with wet towels**

            b. **Turn on the air conditioner fan**

            c. **Signal from your window**

         2. **If the door is not hot:**

            a. **Get low to the floor and brace your shoulder against the door**

            b. **Open the door slowly**

            c. **Crawl low to the floor to the nearest exit**

   III. **Tornado Procedures**

      A. **If you hear tornado sirens, stay clear of windows**

      B. **Go to a safe place**

         1. **In your room, the safest place is the bathroom**

         2. **If you are not in your room, go to a hall away from windows**

5. Adjust indents as necessary to align levels attractively.

6. **With your teacher's permission**, print the publication. It should look similar to Figure 18-3 on the next page.

7. Close the document, saving changes, and exit Publisher.

Figure 18-3

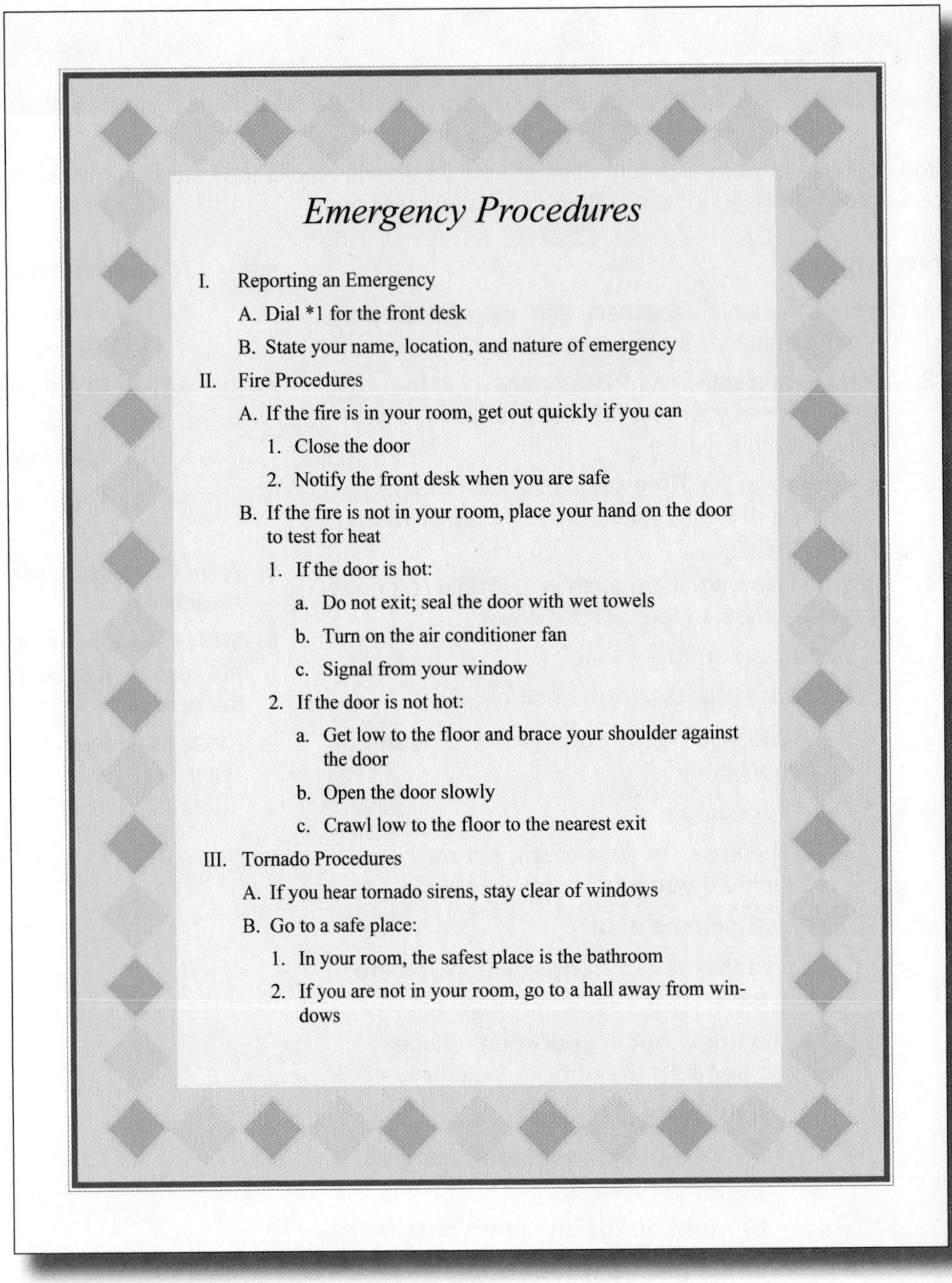

Emergency Procedures

I.   Reporting an Emergency

    A. Dial *1 for the front desk

    B. State your name, location, and nature of emergency

II. Fire Procedures

    A. If the fire is in your room, get out quickly if you can

       1. Close the door

       2. Notify the front desk when you are safe

    B. If the fire is not in your room, place your hand on the door to test for heat

       1. If the door is hot:

          a. Do not exit; seal the door with wet towels

          b. Turn on the air conditioner fan

          c. Signal from your window

       2. If the door is not hot:

          a. Get low to the floor and brace your shoulder against the door

          b. Open the door slowly

          c. Crawl low to the floor to the nearest exit

III. Tornado Procedures

    A. If you hear tornado sirens, stay clear of windows

    B. Go to a safe place:

       1. In your room, the safest place is the bathroom

       2. If you are not in your room, go to a hall away from windows

Lesson 19

Working with Styles

➤ What You Will Learn

Controlling Line and Paragraph Breaks
Copying Text Formatting
Applying a Style
Creating a Style
Modifying and Deleting Styles
Importing Styles from Other Publications

Software Skills   Now that you know how to format text, it's time to learn a few formatting shortcuts. You can copy all the formatting from one text block to another with the Format Painter feature. You can also create named styles that contain groups of formatting specifications, and apply those styles to any text you choose.

What You Can Do

Controlling Line and Paragraph Breaks

■ Sometimes when text flows from one text box to another, paragraphs break in awkward ways. The first line of a paragraph might be left by itself at the bottom of a page (an **orphan**), or the last line carries over by itself to the top of a page (a **widow**).

■ Traditional rules of page layout require at least two lines of a paragraph to appear at the bottom or top of a column or page. Also, a heading should never sit by itself at the bottom of a column or a page. A heading should be accompanied by at least two lines of the paragraph that follows the heading.

■ You can adjust paragraph breaks using the Line and Paragraph Breaks tab in the Paragraph dialog box. This tab gives you four options for controlling how text breaks from one text box to another.

- Widow/Orphan control prevents widows and orphans by keeping at least the first two or last two lines of a paragraph together.

- Keep with next keeps the selected paragraph with the next paragraph.

- Keep lines together keeps all lines of a paragraph in the same text box or column.

- Start in next text box sends a paragraph to the overflow area so that you can place it in a new text box.

WORDS TO KNOW

Format Painter
A feature that enables you to copy the formatting from existing text and "paint" it onto other text.

Orphan
The first line of a paragraph appearing by itself at the bottom of a page.

Style
A set of predefined formatting specifications that you can apply to certain text.

Widow
The last line of a paragraph appearing by itself at the top of a page.

Copying Text Formatting

■ To copy formatting from one section of text to another, select the text that is already formatted correctly, and then click the **Format Painter** command in the Clipboard group on the HOME tab. The mouse pointer becomes a paintbrush. Drag across the text to be formatted, and the formatting is copied.

■ If you click in the paragraph of the text to be formatted instead of dragging over specific text, the entire paragraph receives the formatting.

■ Format Painter copies all attributes of the text: font, size, text effects, underline style, color, and so on.

■ If you double-click the Format Painter button, you can then drag over multiple sections of text. Click the button again to turn the feature off when finished.

Try It!   **Copying Text Formatting and Controlling Paragraph Breaks**

❶ Start Publisher and open **PB19Try** from the data files for this lesson.

❷ Save the publication as **PB19TryA_xx** in the location where your teacher instructs you to store the files for this lesson.

❸ Select the first heading in the left column of text, *What Is Greenwood?*

❹ Click HOME > Font Size [11 ▾] > 14. Then click HOME > Bold **B** . Finally, click HOME > Font Color **A ▾** and click the Accent 3 (RGB (211, 72, 23)) scheme color.

❺ Select the heading text again, and then click HOME > Format Painter .

❻ Drag the Format Painter over the next heading in the column, *Old Growth Forest.*

✓ *To avoid dragging the text box by mistake, try dragging over the text from right to left.*

❼ Click in the first paragraph of text, and click HOME > Justify ≡ .

❽ Click HOME > Paragraph dialog box launcher ⌐ , click the Line and Paragraph Breaks tab, and click Widow/Orphan control. Click OK.

❾ With the insertion point still in the justified paragraph, double-click the Format Painter .

❿ Click in the paragraph below the *Old Growth Forest* heading and in the paragraph below the *Fall Is Spectacular* heading. Then click the Format Painter again to turn the feature off.

⓫ Save the changes to **PB19TryA_xx**, and leave it open to use in the next Try It.

Formatting copied to headings and text

Greenwood in Fall

What Is Greenwood?
Greenwood Conservancy is an expanse of hardwood forest that includes some of the largest and oldest trees in the state. The land was previously the property of the Madison family, who have owned this area of the state since Colonial times. Thomas Madison deeded the land to Greenwood Conservancy in 1990, in the hopes of preserving this rare and precious resource for future generations. Thanks to his generous gift, we can protect a portion of this state's natural heritage from the ravages of development.

Old Growth Forest
The Greenwood Conservancy is designated as an old growth forest. Old growth forests are characterized by many large live trees, large dead trees (sometimes called snags), mixed-age stands, minimal signs of human disruption, a multilayered canopy that includes open areas where large trees have come down, a characteristic topography consisting of pits where tree roots have come up out of the ground and mounds of organic matter, and a rich ground layer composed of decaying wood and leaves.

Fall Is Spectacular
At no time of the year is the diversity of species as apparent as in fall. The Conservancy becomes a crazy quilt of breathtaking hues: The bright yellows of aspen and birch, the molten oranges of sugar maple, the flaming reds of scarlet oaks and red maples, the bronzes of many species of oaks and laurel, and the vibrant red-black of sweet gums punctuated by vivid greens of pines and firs create a living tapestry that blankets the Conservancy's rolling hills. Fall is the final shout of joy before the forest quiets down into its long winter sleep.

What to See and Do
When you visit the Conservancy in fall, you can find plenty of ways to enjoy our environment:

Drive Scenic Route 48 to enjoy vistas on all sides, especially the spectacular views from the Cobbler's Hill turnout and the Golden Valley overlook.

Hike the 65 miles of well-maintained

Applying a Style

- A **style** is a named set of formatting specifications that you can apply with a single command. Using styles saves formatting time and also ensures consistency in a publication.

- If you decide to change style formatting, all paragraphs to which that style applies will automatically be updated.

- A style usually includes a number of formatting options, such as font, font style, paragraph alignment, paragraph spacing, and so on.

- Click in a text box and then click the Styles command on the HOME tab to see a drop-down list of styles currently stored in the publication. Styles are organized under the Styles in use and Font Scheme Styles categories.

- The Styles in use category may show only one or two styles, such as Normal or [Basic Paragraph]. The Font Scheme Styles category will contain all styles you might need to work with the current template, such as Accent Text, Heading 1, Body Text, and Organization Name.

- As you apply styles from the Font Scheme Styles category, they will appear in the Styles in use category at the top of the Styles list.

Try It!   Applying a Style

1 In the **PB19TryA_xx** file, click in the *What Is Greenwood* heading.

2 Click HOME > Styles 𝐀, and then scroll down and click Heading 3.

3 Click in the *Old Growth Forest* heading, click HOME > Styles 𝐀, and then click Heading 3 from the Styles in use category.

4 At the bottom of the right column, click in the last paragraph *(Drive Scenic Route 48)*.

5 Click HOME > Styles 𝐀, and then scroll down and click List Bullet 2.

6 Save the changes to **PB19TryA_xx**, and leave it open to use in the next Try It.

Creating a Style

- You can create a new style based on the current formatting of a paragraph, or you can create a new style from scratch by selecting all formats you want to include in the style. Either way, you start the process of creating the style by clicking New Style on the Styles list to open the New Style dialog box, shown in Figure 19-1 on the next page.

- If you have already applied formatting to the paragraph you are using as a basis for the new style, it displays in the Sample area of the New Style dialog box.

- Use the buttons in the Click to change section to open other dialog boxes to specify font, alignment, spacing, and so on. Note that you can also apply a horizontal rule to appear above or below a paragraph.

- When you define a style, you define it in relation to the Normal style. For example, if you want a style to be just like Normal except center aligned, center alignment is the only style attribute you need to define.

- You can also base a style on another style to pick up basic formats and then add other formats to the style. If you change the style on which another style is based, both styles will be updated.

■ The Style for the following paragraph setting lets you specify what style will be applied to a new paragraph created by pressing 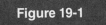 within a paragraph of this style. You will probably want a heading to be followed by a body text style, but you will usually want body text style to be followed by another body text style.

■ Note that even if you create a style based on the existing format of a paragraph, the new style does not automatically apply to that paragraph. You must apply the new style to the paragraph you used to create it.

Figure 19-1

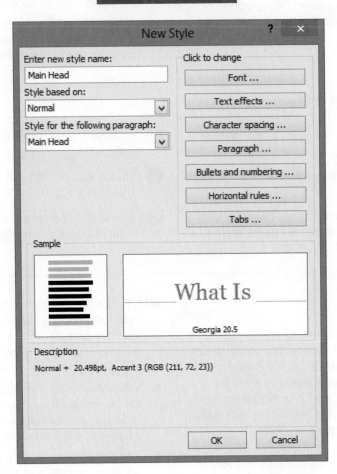

Try It!   Creating a Style

1 In the **PB19TryA_xx** file, select the *What Is Greenwood* heading.

2 Click HOME > Font Color **A** ▾ and click the Accent 3 (RGB (211, 72, 23)) scheme color you applied to this heading previously. (You may still have this color on the Font Color command.)

3 Click HOME > Styles **A** > New Style.

4 In the New Style dialog box, create a style for this heading as follows:

  a. Click in the Enter new style name box and type **Main Head**.

  b. Click the Style for the following paragraph drop-down arrow and click Normal.

  c. Click the Font button, click the Font size drop-down arrow, and then click 16. Click OK.

  d. Click the Paragraph button, click the Line and Paragraph Breaks tab, and click Keep with next. Click OK.

  e. Click OK.

5 With the insertion point in the first heading, click HOME > Styles **A**, and then scroll down to locate Main Head. Click the style to apply it.

6 Click each heading in the publication, on both pages, including those that were previously formatted, and click HOME > Styles **A** > Main Head to apply the style.

7 Click in the first text paragraph on page 1, and then click HOME > Styles **A** > New Style. Type **Body** as the style name.

8 Click the Paragraph button, and click the After paragraphs up arrow until 12pt displays. Click OK and then click OK again.

9 Apply the Body style to all text paragraphs except those that have hanging indents or bullet characters.

10 Click in the paragraph on page 1 to which you previously applied the List Bullet 2 style, and then click HOME > Styles **A** > New Style. Create the new style as follows:

  a. Type **Bullet List** as the style name.

  b. Click the Style based on drop-down arrow and click Body.

  c. Click the Font button, click the Font size drop-down arrow, and click 12. Click OK.

  d. Click the Paragraph button, and click the After paragraphs down arrow to change the space after paragraphs to 6pt. Click OK.

  e. Click the Bullets and numbering button, click the large bullet character on the Bullets tab, and click OK.

  f. Click OK.

11 Click the first bulleted paragraph, click HOME > Styles **A**, scroll down to locate the Bullet List style, and click the style to apply it.

12 Apply the same style to the remaining hanging indent paragraphs.

13 Save the changes to **PB19TryA_xx**, and leave it open to use in the next Try It.

Modifying and Deleting Styles

■ After creating styles, you can modify them at any time or delete them if they are no longer used in the publication.

■ Right-click a style name in the Styles list and choose Modify to open the Modify Style dialog box, which is identical to the New Style dialog box. Make any changes desired and then close the dialog box to apply the changes to the publication.

■ You can modify the Normal style just as you would change any other style. When you change the Normal style, any style you based on the Normal style will also change.

■ You can also choose to rename a style from this shortcut menu.

■ You cannot delete the Normal style, but you can delete any other styles you have created. Choose Delete on the shortcut menu to remove a style.

Try It!   **Modifying and Deleting Styles**

1   In the **PB19TryA_xx** file, click in the *What Is Greenwood* heading.

2   Click HOME > Styles , and then right-click on the Main Head style. Click Modify.

3   Click the Font button, click the Font style drop-down arrow, and click Bold. Click OK twice. Note that the headings change throughout the publication.

4   Click in the first paragraph of text, click HOME > Styles, and then right-click on the Body style. Click Modify.

5   Click the Font button, click in the Font size box, and type **13**. Click OK. Click OK again. Note that the text size changes throughout the publication, and that the Bullet List style also changes because it is based on the Body style.

6   Click HOME > Styles, and then right-click the [Basic Paragraph] style and click Delete. Click Yes to confirm the deletion.

7   Repeat this step to delete each style in the Font Scheme Styles list except the styles you created and the Normal style.

    ✓ *You would not ordinarily need to delete these styles, but doing so will give you further practice on deleting and also make it easier to import styles in the next Try It.*

8   Adjust the text boxes on page 2 to display all text.

9   Close the publication, saving changes, and leave Publisher open to use in the next Try It.

Styles have been modified

Greenwood in Fall

What Is Greenwood?

Greenwood Conservancy is an expanse of hardwood forest that includes some of the largest and oldest trees in the state. The land was previously the property of the Madison family, who have owned this area of the state since Colonial times. Thomas Madison deeded the land to Greenwood Conservancy in 1990, in the hopes of preserving this rare and precious resource for future generations. Thanks to his generous gift, we can protect a portion of this state's natural heritage from the ravages of development.

Old Growth Forest

The Greenwood Conservancy is designated as an old growth forest. Old growth forests are characterized by many large live trees, large dead trees (sometimes called snags), mixed-age stands, minimal signs of human disruption, a multi-layered canopy that includes open areas where large trees have come down, a characteristic topography consisting of pits where tree roots have come up out of the ground and mounds of organic matter, and a rich ground layer composed of decaying wood and leaves.

Fall Is Spectacular

At no time of the year is the diversity of species as apparent as in fall. The Conservancy becomes a crazy quilt of breathtaking hues: The bright yellows of aspen and birch, the molten oranges of sugar maple, the flaming reds of scarlet oaks and red maples, the bronzes of many species of oaks and laurel, and the vibrant red-black of sweet gums punctuated by vivid greens of pines and firs create a living tapestry that blankets the Conservancy's rolling hills. Fall is the final shout

Importing Styles from Other Publications

- If you have styles set up in one publication, you can use them in another publication.

- Use the Import Styles command on the Styles list to navigate to the publication that contains the styles you want to import. All of that publication's styles are instantly transferred to your new publication.

    ✓ *You might want to create a "dummy" publication for the sole purpose of storing styles. Then you can import the styles from that publication each time you need styles in a new publication.*

- When you import styles from one publication to another, you may have to resolve differences between styles. For example, the Normal style you are importing may not match the formats of the Normal style in your current document. Publisher gives you the choice to keep the current Normal style or overwrite it with the imported Normal style. If your publications include any of the same style names, such as Heading 1, Organization Name, and so on, you will have to make a decision on a style-by-style basis whether to keep the current style or use the formats of the imported styles.

Try It!   **Importing Styles from Other Publications**

① In the Backstage view, click the Blank 8.5 × 11" template.

② Save the publication as **PB19TryB_xx** in the location where your teacher instructs you to store the files for this lesson.

③ Draw a text box anywhere on the page and type:

Main Head

Body text

Bulleted text

④ Click HOME > Styles 🅰 > Import Styles.

⑤ Navigate to the location where you have stored solution files for this lesson, click **PB19TryA_xx**, and click OK.

⑥ When asked if you want to keep the current Normal style, click No to change Normal to match the imported styles.

⑦ Apply the imported Main Head, Body, and Bullet List styles to the text you typed.

✓ *Note that because you used a scheme color for the Main Head style, the heading color changes in this document to use the scheme color in the current theme.*

⑧ Close the publication, saving changes, and exit Publisher.

Lesson 19—Practice

Marcela Lopez would like to make some formatting changes to her report for Dr. Green. In this exercise, you create and apply styles that she can use for other reports of a similar nature.

DIRECTIONS

1. Start Publisher, if necessary, and open **PB19Practice** from the data files for this lesson.

2. Save the publication as **PB19Practice_xx** in the location where your teacher instructs you to store the files for this lesson.

3. Click **PAGE DESIGN** > **Schemes More** button ⊟ and select the **Trout** color scheme.

4. Click in the report title on page 1. Click **HOME** > **Styles** 🅰 > **New Style**. Define a new style for the title as follows:

   a. Click in the Enter new style name box and type **Report Title**.

   b. Click the **Font** button. Click the **Font** drop-down arrow, scroll down, and click **Cambria**. Click the **Font style** drop-down arrow and click **Regular**. Click the **Font size** drop-down arrow and click **36**. Click the **Font color** drop-down arrow and click the **Accent 1 (RGB (51, 102, 102))** scheme color. Click OK.

   c. Click **OK**.

   d. Click **HOME** > **Styles** 🅰 > **Report Title** to apply the style to the report title.

5. On page 2, click in the *Goals* heading, and then click **HOME > Styles** A✓ **> New Style**. Define a new heading style as follows:

   a. Type the style name **Head 1**.

   b. Click the **Font** button. Click the **Font** drop-down arrow, scroll down, and click **Calibri**. Click the **Font style** drop-down arrow and click **Regular**. Click the **Font color** drop-down arrow and click the **Hyperlink (RGB (204, 102, 0))** scheme color. Click **OK**.

   c. Click the **Horizontal rules** button. In the Horizontal Rules dialog box, click the **Rule before paragraph** check box. Click the **Thickness** drop-down arrow and click **2pt**. Click the **Color** drop-down arrow and click the same scheme color as the heading. Click the **Before Paragraph** up arrow until **6pt** displays. Click **OK**. Click **OK** again.

   d. Click in each major heading on pages 2 and 3 and click **HOME > Styles** A✓ **> Head 1**.

6. On page 2, click in the first paragraph beneath the *Hardware Recommended* heading. Click **HOME > Styles** A✓ **> New Style**, and define a new style as follows:

   a. Type **Text** for the new style name.

   b. Click the **Font** button, click the **Font** drop-down arrow, and click **Calibri**. Click **OK**.

   c. Click the **Paragraph** button. Click the **After paragraphs** up arrow three times to set the space to **3pt**. Click the **Between lines** up arrow once to set the space to **1.25sp**. Click the **Line and Paragraph Breaks** tab and click **Widow/Orphan control**. Click **OK**.

   d. Click **OK**.

7. Click in each text paragraph on pages 2 and 3 and click **HOME > Styles** A✓ **> Text** to apply the style.

8. Click in the first bullet item under the first heading on page 2, and then click **HOME > Styles** A✓ **> New Style**. Type the style name **Bullet List**, click the **Style based on** drop-down arrow and select **Text**, and then click **OK**.

9. Select each bulleted item in the publication and apply the **Bullet List** style.

   ✓ *Don't worry if text overflows. You will adjust styles to prevent this in a later step.*

10. On page 3, click in the *Dentrix* heading and click **HOME > Styles** A✓ **> New Style**. Define a style for the heading as follows:

    a. Type **Head 2** for the style name.

    b. Click the **Font** button. Click the **Font** drop-down list and click **Cambria**, click the **Font color** drop-down arrow and click the **Followed Hyperlink (Dark Yellow)** scheme color, and click **OK**.

    c. Click the **Paragraph** button, click the **Line and Paragraph Breaks** tab, and click **Keep with next**. Click **OK**.

    d. Click **OK**.

11. Click in each second-level heading on pages 3 and 4 and apply the **Head 2** style.

12. Click in the *Goals* heading, click **HOME > Styles** A✓, right-click the **Text** style, and click **Modify**. Click the **Paragraph** button, and click the **Between lines** down arrow to change the spacing back to **1sp**. Click **OK**. Click **OK** again.

13. **With your teacher's permission**, print the publication. Your second page should look similar to Figure 19-2 on the next page.

14. Close the publication, saving changes, and exit Publisher.

Figure 19-2

Goals

- Computerized scheduling
- Computerized billing
- Electronic insurance filing
- Computer-printed reminder cards

Hardware Recommended

I recommend a Windows-based PC, not necessarily top-of-the-line but current enough that it will not need upgrading for at least 2 years. A suitable configuration would be:

- 500MHz or higher Windows-based PC
- 256MB (or more) of memory
- 160G or more hard disk
- DVD-ROM and RW
- 15" or 17" monitor
- Integrated networking

Total computer cost: $1000 to $3000, depending on options chosen.

A printer will also be required. Some dental practice management software requires a certain printer model; others can use any printer. The model required by some programs is a LaserJet 2100, at around $500. Cheaper printers are available, as low as $150.

Software

There are many inexpensive programs that will take care of the four goals individually—one program for scheduling, one program for billing, one program for reminders, etc. However, this would require maintaining four separate customer databases on the computer, and might actually be *more* work than the current paper-based system for the staff.

An integrated program that handles all four functions would be best. There are many such programs available on the market, tailored specifically for dental offices.

I am in the process of researching various dental practice management programs. These range in cost from $450 to $6000. Within 3 weeks I will have demos of several programs to review with you, so a decision can be made. Some possible programs are covered below.

Dentrix
Web site: http://www.dentrix.com

I have requested a demo CD. NOTE: This seems to be a first-class operation with good support. I do not have pricing information.

2

Lesson 19—Apply

In this exercise, you import the styles you created in the Practice exercise to format a new publication for Marcela Lopez.

DIRECTIONS

1. Start Publisher, if necessary, and open **PB19Apply** from the data files for this lesson.

2. Save the publication as **PB19Apply_xx** in the location where your teacher instructs you to store the files for this lesson.

3. Apply the **Trout** color scheme.

4. Import the styles from **PB19Practice_xx**.

   ✓ If you did not work on the Practice exercise, ask your instructor for the location of a file from which to import styles.

5. Apply the **Report Title** style to the title on page 1. Then apply styles as you did in the Practice exercise.

6. Modify the styles as follows:

   a. The indents are not correct for the bulleted lists, as you can see on page 3. Modify the **Bullet List** style so that the first line is at **-0.25** inches and the left indent is at **0.25** inches.

   b. Modify the **Head 1** style to change the horizontal rule spacing to **2pt** before the paragraph.

   c. Modify the **Head 2** style to add **6 points** of space above the paragraph.

   d. Modify the **Text** style to have **6 points** of space after the paragraph.

   e. There is now too much space between bulleted list items. Modify the **Bullet List** style to have **0pt** of space after paragraphs.

7. **With your teacher's permission**, print the publication. Your second page should look similar to Figure 19-3 on the next page.

8. Close the publication, saving changes, and exit Publisher.

Figure 19-3

Goals

- State-of-the-art computers for five designers
- Software for illustration, photo work, and publication layout

Hardware Recommended

I recommend Macintosh hardware, as Mac is still the industry standard for print-based graphic design. One of these Macs may be configured to boot to both Mac and Windows operating systems.

- Mac Pro
- 2.8GHz Quad-Core processor
- 3GB memory
- 1TB hard drive
- 24 inch monitor
- Integrated networking

Total computer cost: $3000 to $4000, depending on options chosen.

Additional options may include laser printers for output and graphics tablets for input.

Software

For graphics applications, Adobe software has long been the choice of professional designers. Creative Suite 6, the most recent version of Adobe, comes in various packages. The Design Professional suite includes the following programs.

For more information, www.adobe.com.

Adobe Illustrator CS6
Vector graphics illustration package that can also be used to create and export Web graphics.

Adobe Photoshop CS6 Extended
The industry standard for photo retouching and manipulation. Now includes support for 3-D graphics.

Adobe InDesign CS6
Sophisticated page layout that can also be used to create video and Web materials.

Adobe Flash Professional CS6
Industry standard for animation.

Adobe Dreamweaver CS6
A full-featured Web design program that can easily integrate illustrations and animations.

2

Lesson 20

Working with Typographic Features

> ## ➤ What You Will Learn
>
> Using OpenType Fonts
> Selecting Number Styles
> Applying Ligatures
> Applying Stylistic Sets, Swashes, and Stylistic Alternates

WORDS TO KNOW

Ligature
Two or more characters formed into a single character to make text more readable or attractive.

OpenType
An improved version of TrueType, offering all of TrueType's benefits plus additional stylistic features.

TrueType
A Windows- and Macintosh-compatible class of software fonts that can be used at any size and printed on almost any printer.

Software Skills   Publisher's typographic features allow you to modify the appearance of text characters for a more visually interesting appearance.

What You Can Do

Using OpenType Fonts

- Unless you have a wide selection of fonts on your computer, you are most likely using TrueType fonts. **TrueType** fonts have been the most commonly used fonts on both Macintosh and Windows systems for many years.

- **OpenType** fonts, developed by Microsoft and Adobe and based on TrueType fonts, have become increasingly popular and available. OpenType fonts provide more stylistic features than TrueType fonts.

- The typographical features available in Office 2013 applications, including Publisher 2013, require OpenType fonts. Office 2013 includes two fonts that will display many of the new typographic features, Gabriola and Calibri. These fonts do not display all of the typographic options included, however.

- If you have access to Adobe fonts such as Adobe Caslon Pro, Adobe Garamond Pro, or Minion Pro, you can take full advantage of Publisher's typographic features. But note that even OpenType fonts differ in how many typographic features they support.

Selecting Number Styles

- OpenType fonts allow you to make a decision on how to display numbers in your publications. When you insert text with a font that supports alternate number forms, the Number Style command on the TEXT BOX TOOLS FORMAT becomes active, giving you the following options. Samples of some of these options are shown in Figure 20-1.

  - The Default option applies the number style specified for the current font. This style will be the same as one of the other four options on the menu.

  - The Proportional Lining option displays numbers proportionally; that is, the 1 does not take up as much room as the 2. *Lining* means that the characters align with the capital letters of text.

  - The Tabular Lining option displays numbers in equal widths; the 1 takes up as much room as the 2. You might select this option when displaying numbers in a table or report so that they align neatly in columns.

  - The Proportional Old-style option displays numbers proportionally and at the same height as lowercase letters in text. Some numbers, such as the 3, 4, and 5, drop below the baseline.

  - The Tabular Old-style option displays numbers at a fixed width and the same height as lowercase text.

Figure 20-1

Proportional lining: 1 2 3 4 5 6 7 8 9 0

Tabular lining: 1 2 3 4 5 6 7 8 9 0

Proportional old-style: 1 2 3 4 5 6 7 8 9 0

Tabular old-style: 1 2 3 4 5 6 7 8 9 0

- Several standard Office fonts allow you to select a number style: Calibri, Cambria, Constantia, and Corbel.

Applying Ligatures

- **Ligatures** are single characters that combine two or more characters. Figure 20-2 shows several words as they would look without and with ligatures.

- Note that in the second row, the letters *T* and *h* have been joined in the word *The*. In the word *field*, the *f* and the *i* have been joined. In the word *stiff*, the two *f*s have been joined. In the word *quaffle*, the two *f*s and the *l* have been joined into one character.

- The use of ligatures streamlines the text and makes text easier to read or more attractive.

Figure 20-2

The field stiff quaffle

The field stiff quaffle

cast check act stop

- There are several categories of ligatures. The ligatures in the second row of Figure 20-2 are considered to be standard ligatures. They can be used in any text, and most OpenType fonts create them automatically.

- The ligatures in the third row are discretionary ligatures. Because they are more decorative, a designer would usually need to select an option to apply these ligatures.

- In Publisher 2013, the only standard Microsoft font that will display ligatures is Calibri, which is used to display the discretionary ligatures in the third line of Figure 20-2.

- If you want to be able to display the range of ligatures shown in the second and third lines of the figure, you need to acquire Adobe fonts such as Adobe Garamond Pro, which was used to create the ligatures in the second line of the figure.

- To modify the ligatures in selected text, use the Ligatures command on the TEXT BOX TOOLS FORMAT tab. You have the option of applying only standard ligatures, standard and discretionary ligatures, or no ligatures.

Try It!   Applying Number Style and Ligatures

1 Start Publisher and open **PB20Try** from the data files for this lesson.

2 Save the publication as **PB20Try_xx** in the location where your teacher instructs you to store the files for this lesson.

3 Select the last three lines at the bottom of the text box. Click TEXT BOX TOOLS FORMAT > Number Style 12₃ .

4 Watch the appearance of the numbers in the address, Zip code, and phone number as you move the mouse pointer over each option on the Number Style menu. Then click Proportional Old-style.

5 Select the *You must act now* paragraph. Click TEXT BOX TOOLS FORMAT > Ligatures fi > Standard and Discretionary.

6 Save the changes to **PB20Try_xx**, and leave it open to use in the next Try It.

Number style and ligatures applied

Madame Ruth
Spiritual Consultation, Magical
Thinking, and Exquisite Elixirs
Including the Famous
Love Potion No. 9
You must act now to embrace the infinite!
In person: 34th & Vine
               Baton Rouge, LA 70810
Telephone: 225.555.4509

Applying Stylistic Sets, Swashes, and Stylistic Alternates

- A stylistic set changes the look of text by applying different appearances to some or all characters in the font. The number of sets you have to choose from depends on how many sets the font designer created.

- The Gabriola font included with Publisher 2013 has seven stylistic sets available. As shown in Figure 20-3, stylistic sets can differ quite a lot from one another.

- Swashes are further embellishments that can be applied to text, usually in the form of more elaborate capital letters. Text must be italic for swashes to display. There are currently no default fonts in the Publisher 2013 font list that will display swashes.

- Stylistic alternates are different forms of specific characters provided by the font designer. Note in Figure 20-3, for example, the alternate forms of the letter e when it appears at the end of a word.

- If you are using Gabriola, the only default Publisher font that supports stylistic alternates, you select alternates by selecting a different stylistic set. If you are using another OpenType font such as an Adobe Pro font, you can select a letter such as the *e*, click the Stylistic Alternates command, and see a list of alternate forms of the letter from which you can choose.

Figure 20-3

The field stiff quaffle

The field stiff quaffle

The field stiff quaffle

Try It!   **Applying Stylistic Sets**

1 In the **PB20Try_xx** file, select the five paragraphs at the top of the text box, click HOME > Font [Times New Roman ▾], and scroll to select Gabriola.

2 Select the *Madame Ruth* paragraph, click HOME > Font Size [11 ▾], type **40**, and press [ENTER].

3 With the text still selected, click TEXT BOX TOOLS FORMAT > Stylistic Sets *abc*, and click the sixth option in the Individual section of the gallery.

4 Select the next two paragraphs, click HOME > Font Size [11 ▾], type **32**, and press [ENTER].

5 With the text still selected, click TEXT BOX TOOLS FORMAT > Stylistic Sets *abc*, and click the fourth option in the Individual section of the gallery.

6 Select the *Including the Famous* paragraph, and click HOME > Font Size [11 ▾] > 20.

7 With the text still selected, click TEXT BOX TOOLS FORMAT > Stylistic Sets *abc*, and click the third option in the Individual section of the gallery.

8 Select the *Love Potion* paragraph, click HOME > Font Size [11 ▾], type **32**, and press [ENTER].

9 With the text still selected, click TEXT BOX TOOLS FORMAT > Stylistic Sets *abc*, and click the sixth option in the Individual section of the gallery.

10 With the insertion point still in the *Love Potion* paragraph, click HOME > Paragraph dialog box launcher ⬓. Click in the After paragraphs box and type **18pt**. Click OK.

11 Close the publication, saving changes, and exit Publisher.

Stylistic sets applied

Madame Ruth

Spiritual Consultation, Magical Thinking, and Exquisite Elixirs

Including the Famous

Love Potion No. 9

You must act now to embrace the infinite!
In person: 34th & Vine
             Baton Rouge, LA 70810
Telephone: 225.555.4509

Lesson 20—Practice

The Hendricks Inn would like a menu for the tea room. In this exercise, you use typographic features to make the Afternoon Tea menu interesting and attractive.

DIRECTIONS

1. Start Publisher, if necessary, and open **PB20Practice** from the data files for this lesson.

2. Save the publication as **PB20Practice_xx** in the location where your teacher instructs you to store the files for this lesson.

3. Click in the text box below the heading. Click **HOME > Paragraph dialog box launcher** ⌐, click the **Tabs** tab in the Paragraph dialog box, and type **.125** in the Tab stop position box. Click **Set**. Type **.25** in the Tab stop position box and click **Set**. Type **.375** in the Tab stop position box and click **Set**. Click **OK**.

   ✓ *To find the text box, move the pointer near the left margin at about 1.5 inches; when you see the text box outline, move the pointer into the upper-left corner of the text box and click.*

4. Type the following menu. Use the Increase Indent Position and the Decrease Indent Position commands on the HOME tab to adjust indents as shown.

Menu

  Scones

    Accompanied by jam and clotted cream

  Savories

    Warm quiche, dill biscuits, finger sandwiches

  Sweets

    Pastries and tea cookies

Tea or beverage of choice

Adults $20.00 per person; children $14.00 per person

Gratuity and tax included

Tea Is Served

  Monday through Saturday

    2:00 p.m. until 4:30 p.m.

  Sunday

    1:00 p.m. until 3:30 p.m.

5. Select the *Afternoon Tea* heading.
   a. Click **HOME > Font** `Times New Roman ▾` **> Gabriola**.
   b. Click **HOME > Font Size** `11 ▾` **> 28**.
   c. Click **TEXT BOX TOOLS FORMAT > Stylistic Sets** *abc*, and then click the sixth set under Individual.

6. Select the *Menu* paragraph.
   a. Click **HOME > Font** `Times New Roman ▾` **> Gabriola**.
   b. Click **HOME > Font Size** `11 ▾` **> 14**.
   c. Click **TEXT BOX TOOLS FORMAT > Stylistic Sets** *abc*, and then click the fourth set under Individual.
   d. With the text still selected, click **HOME > Format Painter** ❤ and drag the painter over the *Tea Is Served* paragraph.

7. Select the nine paragraphs below the *Menu* heading, and then click **HOME > Font** `Times New Roman ▾` **> Calibri**.

8. With the text still selected, click **TEXT BOX TOOLS FORMAT > Number Style** 12_3 **> Proportional Old-style**. Then click **Ligatures** fi **> Standard and Discretionary**.

9. Select the four paragraphs under the *Tea Is Served* heading and apply the same font, number style, and ligature option.

10. Select the *Gratuity* paragraph, click **HOME > Italic** *I*, and then click **HOME > Font Size** `11 ▾` **> 9**.

11. Check spelling.

12. **With your teacher's permission**, print the publication. Your page should look similar to Figure 20-4 on the next page.

13. Close the publication, saving changes, and exit Publisher.

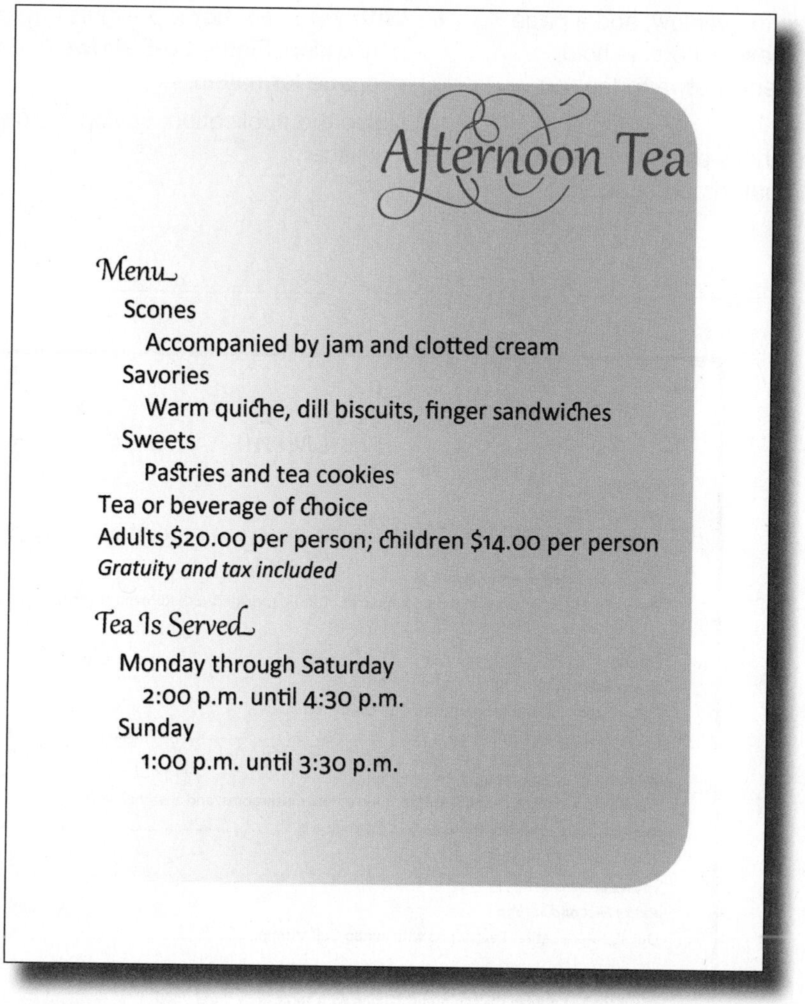

Figure 20-4

Afternoon Tea

Menu
  Scones
    Accompanied by jam and clotted cream
  Savories
    Warm quiche, dill biscuits, finger sandwiches
  Sweets
    Pastries and tea cookies
  Tea or beverage of choice
  Adults $20.00 per person; children $14.00 per person
  Gratuity and tax included

Tea Is Served
  Monday through Saturday
    2:00 p.m. until 4:30 p.m.
  Sunday
    1:00 p.m. until 3:30 p.m.

Lesson 20—Apply

John at The Hendricks Inn is pleased with your work on the Afternoon Tea menu and has asked you to improve the appearance of the fall dinner menu. In this exercise, you use typographic options to add some pizzazz to the menu.

DIRECTIONS

1. Start Publisher, if necessary, and open **PB20Apply** from the data files for this lesson.

2. Save the publication as **PB20Apply_xx** in the location where your teacher instructs you to store the files for this lesson.

3. Make this menu more attractive using features you have learned about in this lesson. For example:

   a. Apply a font that allows you to use stylistic sets. If you have access to Adobe Pro fonts, you may want to use one of those fonts, or use Gabriola.

   b. Apply a font that will allow you to display discretionary ligatures, such as Calibri or another OpenType font.

   c. Apply a font that will allow you to use number styles, such as Calibri, Cambria, Constantia, or Corbel.

   d. If you have access to Adobe OpenType fonts, apply swashes to italic text.

4. If your changes cause text to overflow, add a page to the menu and create a new text box to hold the overflow. Divide text evenly between the two pages.

5. Adjust font sizes and font styles as desired. Modify indents, line spacing, and paragraph spacing if necessary.

6. **With your teacher's permission**, print the publication. Figure 20-5 shows one way the menu might be formatted.

7. Close the publication, saving changes, and exit Publisher.

Figure 20-5

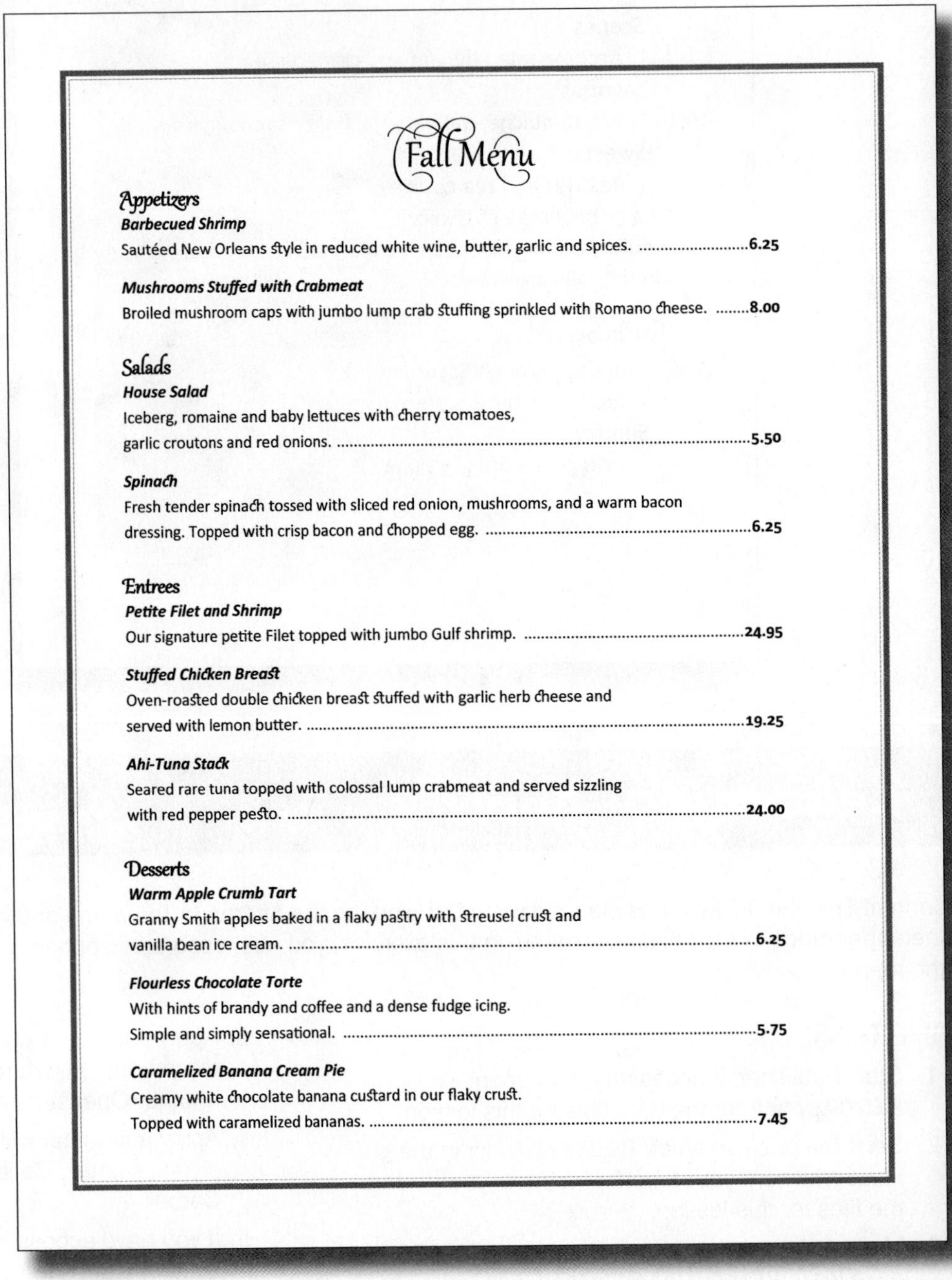

Fall Menu

Appetizers

Barbecued Shrimp
Sautéed New Orleans style in reduced white wine, butter, garlic and spices. **6.25**

Mushrooms Stuffed with Crabmeat
Broiled mushroom caps with jumbo lump crab stuffing sprinkled with Romano cheese. **8.00**

Salads

House Salad
Iceberg, romaine and baby lettuces with cherry tomatoes,
garlic croutons and red onions. **5.50**

Spinach
Fresh tender spinach tossed with sliced red onion, mushrooms, and a warm bacon
dressing. Topped with crisp bacon and chopped egg. **6.25**

Entrees

Petite Filet and Shrimp
Our signature petite Filet topped with jumbo Gulf shrimp. **24.95**

Stuffed Chicken Breast
Oven-roasted double chicken breast stuffed with garlic herb cheese and
served with lemon butter. **19.25**

Ahi-Tuna Stack
Seared rare tuna topped with colossal lump crabmeat and served sizzling
with red pepper pesto. **24.00**

Desserts

Warm Apple Crumb Tart
Granny Smith apples baked in a flaky pastry with streusel crust and
vanilla bean ice cream. **6.25**

Flourless Chocolate Torte
With hints of brandy and coffee and a dense fudge icing.
Simple and simply sensational. **5.75**

Caramelized Banana Cream Pie
Creamy white chocolate banana custard in our flaky crust.
Topped with caramelized bananas. **7.45**

Lesson 21

Inserting Tables

➤ What You Will Learn

Creating a Table
Typing in a Table
Selecting Cells and Ranges
Inserting or Deleting Rows or Columns
Changing Cell Height and Width

Software Skills   Tables help organize data. If you have lists of numbers and text to display, need to make comparisons, and the like, create tables to communicate your content to readers.

What You Can Do

Creating a Table

- You have already learned one way to arrange tabular information in a publication by using tab stops to align text. If you have more than two or three columns or rows, however, you may find that using tabs to organize data becomes a challenge.

- A better alternative for organizing information in this case is to create a **table**. A table's grid of **cells** makes it easy to insert information without having to worry about positioning tab stops.

- Use the Table command in the Tables group on the INSERT tab to insert a new table. You have two options for specifying the number of rows and columns in the table.

  - Clicking the Table command displays a grid. Drag the mouse pointer over the grid to select the number of rows and columns you need.

  - Click in the Insert Table option on the Table menu to display the Create Table dialog box, where you can type the number of rows and columns you want.

- After you specify the number of rows and columns using either of these methods, Publisher displays the columns and rows in a light gray container on the page. The container has resizing handles at the center of each side and in the corners. You can use this container to resize the table or move the table to a new location.

- Columns and rows are separated by dashed gridlines that mark the column and row boundaries. These gridlines do not print. You will learn in the next lesson how to apply borders along the gridlines.

WORDS TO KNOW

Cell
The intersection of a row and a column in a table.

Range
A rectangular block of cells selected as a group.

Table
A grid of rows and columns in which it is easy to insert text and numbers.

Try It!   Creating a Table

1   Start Publisher and open **PB21Try** from the data files for this lesson.

2   Save the publication as **PB21Try_xx** in the location where your teacher instructs you to store the files for this lesson.

3   Click INSERT > Table ⊞ to display the table grid. Drag across to highlight four columns and then drag down to highlight five rows. Click to insert the table on the center of the page.

4   Click on the light gray table container and drag the table so the upper-left corner is at about 3.5 inches on the vertical ruler and 1.5 inches on the horizontal ruler.

5   Click on the sizing handle in the middle of the right side and drag to the right to the 7 inch mark on the horizontal ruler.

6   Save the changes to **PB21Try_xx**, and leave it open to use in the next Try It.

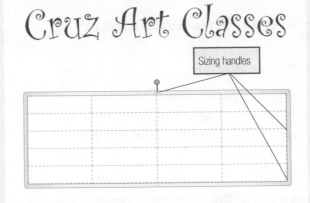

Sizing handles make it easy to resize a table

Typing in a Table

- Click in a cell to move the insertion point there, and then type.
- To move to the next cell (to the right, or to the next row if you are already in the rightmost column), press TAB.
- To move to the previous cell, press SHIFT + TAB.
- If you press TAB while in the lower-right cell in the table, you start a new row.

Try It!   Typing in a Table

1   In the **PB21Try_xx** file, click in the first cell in the table, if necessary.

2   Type **Class**, press TAB, type **Meets**, press TAB, type **Instructor**, press TAB, type **Cost**, and press TAB to move to the second row.

3   Type the remaining table text shown at right, pressing TAB after each entry except the last one.

Painting with Oils	M, W	Cruz	$95.00
Watercolor Techniques	T, Th	Jamison	$125.50
Basic Drawing	W, Sa	Marquette	$75.00
Drawing with Pen & Ink	W, F	Parker	$85.75

4   Save the changes to **PB21Try_xx**, and leave it open to use in the next Try It.

Selecting Cells and Ranges

- Modifying a table requires you to select the part of the table you want to change.

- You can select text in a cell the same way you would select it in a text box: double-click a single word, or drag over multiple words to select.

- To select parts of a table, use these guidelines:
  - To select a cell, click it.
  - To select a **range** of cells in a table, drag across them.
  - To select the entire table, click inside a table cell and then press CTRL + A twice. The first time selects the cell, and the second time selects the whole table.
  - To select an entire row, move the mouse pointer to the left edge of the row, so the mouse pointer becomes a right-pointing arrow ➡, and then click.

- To select an entire column, do the same thing at the top of a column, so the mouse pointer becomes a down-pointing arrow ⬇.

- You also can select various parts of the table with the Select command in the Table group on the TABLE TOOLS LAYOUT tab. This command displays a menu from which you can choose Select Cell, Select Column, Select Row, or Select Table.

- You can format text in a table the same way you format any text in a text box. Select the text to format, or select an entire row or column. Apply different font, font style, font size, and font color using commands on the HOME tab. Adjust horizontal and vertical alignment using tools on the TABLE TOOLS LAYOUT tab.

Try It! Selecting Cells and Ranges and Formatting Text

1. In the PB21Try_xx file, move the mouse pointer just to the left of the first row of the table.

2. When you see the right-pointing arrow ➡, click to select the entire first row.

3. Click HOME > Bold **B** . Click HOME > Font Size 11 > 16.

4. Click in the *Painting with Oils* cell, hold down the left mouse button, and drag to the *$85.75* cell in the lower-right corner of the table.

5. Click HOME > Font Size 11 > 14.

6. Move the mouse pointer above the *Class* column header until you see the down-pointing arrow, click to select the entire column, and click TABLE TOOLS LAYOUT > Align Center Left.

7. Move the mouse pointer above the *Meets* column header until you see the down-pointing arrow, click to select the entire column, and then drag to the right to select the *Meets* column as well as the *Instructor* and *Cost* columns.

8. Click TABLE TOOLS LAYOUT > Align Center.

   ✓ Don't worry if some of the text in your first column disappears. You will adjust column widths later to show all text.

9. Select only the table body cells in the *Cost* column (do not select the column heading), and then click TABLE TOOLS LAYOUT > Align Center Right.

10. Save the changes to PB21Try_xx, and leave it open to use in the next Try It.

Alignments and text formats changed

Class	Meets	Instructor	Cost
Painting with Oils	M, W	Cruz	$95.00
Watercolor Techniques	T, Th	Jamison	$125.50
Basic Drawing	W, Sa	Marquette	$75.00
Drawing with Pen & Ink	W, F	Parker	$85.75

Inserting or Deleting Rows or Columns

- You do not have to worry about choosing the exact number of rows and columns you need when inserting a table because you can always add rows and columns or delete rows and columns you do not need.

- To insert rows or columns, position the insertion point in a cell adjacent to where you want to insert, and then choose an option from the Rows & Columns group on the TABLE TOOLS LAYOUT tab. You can insert a row above or below the row that currently contains the insertion point, or insert a column to the left or right of the current column.

- If you want to insert multiple rows or columns at once, select multiple rows or columns before issuing the Insert command. For example, to insert three rows, select three rows first.

- To delete a row or column, click in the row or column and then use the Delete command in the Rows & Columns group on the TABLE TOOLS LAYOUT tab. Clicking this command displays a menu that allows you to delete the current column, row, or table.

- If you want to delete the entire table, you can also select the table container and press DEL .

Try It!   Inserting or Deleting Rows or Columns

1 In the PB21Try_xx file, click anywhere in the *Instructor* column.

2 Click TABLE TOOLS LAYOUT > Delete ▦ > Delete Columns.

3 Click anywhere in the *Painting with Oils* row, and then click TABLE TOOLS LAYOUT > Insert Below ▦ .

4 Type the following entries in the new row:

Painting with Acrylics   T, W $95.00

5 Save the changes to PB21Try_xx, and leave it open to use in the next Try It.

Changing Cell Height and Width

- By default, each row and column is set to grow automatically to fit the text within it. That means if your cell has a lot of text, or uses a very large font, the cell will expand as needed (usually vertically, by adding more text lines).

- You can turn this behavior off by removing the check mark from the Grow to Fit Text command on the TABLE TOOLS LAYOUT tab.

- You also can manually resize a row or column. Position the insertion point on the divider between two rows or columns. The mouse pointer becomes a double-headed arrow. Drag the row or column to its new size.

- You can also adjust cell height and width by resizing the table. Use the Height and Width boxes in the Size group on the TABLE TOOLS LAYOUT tab to adjust the table size. Columns and rows adjust proportionally as the table is resized.

Try It!   Changing Cell Height and Width

1 In the **PB21Try_xx** file, click anywhere in the table to select it, if necessary.

2 Click **TABLE TOOLS LAYOUT** and type **5.5** in the Width box.

3 Position the mouse pointer on the gridline between the *Class* column and the *Meets* column. The pointer becomes a double-headed arrow. Click and drag to the right until all text is on one line in the first column. The column should be about 2.5 inches wide.

4 Position the mouse pointer on the gridline between the *Meets* column and the *Cost* column. Click and drag to the left until the column is about 1.25 inches wide.

5 Position the mouse pointer just to the left of the right container border to display the double-headed arrow. Drag to the left until the column is about 1.25 inches wide.

6 Position the mouse pointer on the gridline below the column headings and drag upward about an eighth of an inch.

7 Close the publication, saving changes, and exit Publisher.

Drag the right column gridline to resize the column

Click here to select the gridline

Class	Meets	Cost
Painting with Oils	M, W	$95.00
Painting with Acrylics	T, W	$95.00
Watercolor Techniques	T, Th	$125.50
Basic Drawing	W, Sa	$75.00
Drawing with Pen & Ink	W, F	$85.75

Lesson 21—Practice

The Hendricks Inn needs an informational flyer listing some of the local attractions. The owner has experimented with making this a bulleted list, but finds that there are too many items and it looks overwhelming. In this exercise, you work on the table of activities.

DIRECTIONS

1. Start Publisher, if necessary, and open **PB21Practice** from the data files for this lesson.

2. Save the publication as **PB21Practice_xx** in the location where your teacher instructs you to store the files for this lesson.

3. On page 1, click **INSERT** > Table > Insert Table 🏢. Type **5** in Number of rows, press TAB, and type **3** in Number of columns. Click **OK**.

4. Drag the table container so the left edge of the table lines up with the left edge of the *Ask at the front desk* text box, leaving about one-quarter inch of space between the top of the table and the bottom of the text box.

5. Click **TABLE TOOLS LAYOUT** > Height ‡⃞ and type **2**. Click **TABLE TOOLS LAYOUT** > Width 🗔 and type **4.9**.

6. Type the following entries in the table. Press TAB after each entry except the last one.

Activity	Location	Distance
Hiking	Bedford Forest	5 miles
Bicycling	Mission Road Rentals	3 miles
Horseback riding	Clover Valley Stables	10 miles
Golf	Pine Hills Golf Center	4 miles

7. Click anywhere in the *Distance* column. Click **TABLE TOOLS LAYOUT** > Insert Left 🏢.

8. Click on the right side container handle and drag the right border of the table to the left to align with the right side of the text box above.

9. Click in the first cell in the new column and type **Season**. Then type the following entries in the column cells, starting in the cell below the column header.

 All

 Spring, summer, fall

 Summer

 Spring, summer, fall

10. Click anywhere in the *Hiking* row. Click **TABLE TOOLS LAYOUT** > **Insert Below** ▦.

11. Click in the first cell in the new row and type the following entries, pressing TAB after each entry.

 Cross country skiing

 Bedford Meadows

 Winter

 6 miles

12. Click **TABLE TOOLS LAYOUT** > **Select** ⌖ > **Select Table**. Then click **HOME** > **Font Size** > 12.

13. Position the mouse pointer to the left of the first row until it becomes a right-pointing arrow, and then click to select the row.

14. Click **HOME** > **Bold** **B** .

15. Click on the gridline between the *Activity* and the *Location* columns and drag to the right until no entries are hyphenated in the *Activity* column. Repeat this step to drag the gridline between the *Location* and the *Season* columns until no entries are hyphenated in the *Location* column. Click on the right gridline for the *Distance* column and drag to the left until the column aligns at the right with the text box above.

16. Drag over the distance items to select them (do not select the column heading), and then click **TABLE TOOLS LAYOUT** > **Align Top Right** ▤.

17. Drag over all the season items to select them (do not select the column heading), and then click **TABLE TOOLS LAYOUT** > **Align Top Center** ▤.

18. Drag over the *Activity* and *Location* column headings, and then click **TABLE TOOLS LAYOUT** > **Align Center Left** ▤.

19. Click in the *Season* cell, and then click **TABLE TOOLS LAYOUT** > **Align Center** ▤.

20. Click in the *Distance* cell, and then click **TABLE TOOLS LAYOUT** > **Align Center Right** ▤.

21. **With your teacher's permission**, print page 1 of the publication. Your table should look similar to Figure 21-1.

22. Close the publication, saving changes, and exit Publisher.

Figure 21-1

Activity	Location	Season	Distance
Hiking	Bedford Forest	All	5 miles
Cross country skiing	Bedford Meadows	Winter	6 miles
Bicycling	Mission Road Rentals	Spring, summer, fall	3 miles
Horseback riding	Clover Valley Stables	Summer	10 miles
Golf	Pine Hills Golf Center	Spring, summer, fall	4 miles

Lesson 21—Apply

You continue to work on information for The Hendricks Inn. In this exercise, you create a table that lists local dining options.

DIRECTIONS

1. Start Publisher, if necessary, and open **PB21Apply** from the data files for this lesson.

2. Save the publication as **PB21Apply_xx** in the location where your teacher instructs you to store the files for this lesson.

3. On page 2, use the table grid on the **INSERT > Table** ▦ command to insert a table with **3** columns and **5** rows. Move the new table down into the empty area below the *Ask at the front desk* text box.

4. Type the following table text:

Name	Location	Cost
Mateo's Ristorante	Richmond	$$$
Hendricks Grill	Hendricks	$$
Tradewinds	Hendricks	$$
Marley's Pub	Bridgeton	$

5. Insert a row above the *Tradewinds* row and type the following entries.

The Heritage	Greenville	$$$

6. Add a column to the right of the *Location* column and insert the following entries in the column, from top to bottom:

    Cuisine

    Italian

    American

    Continental

    Asian

    American

7. Select the entire table and change the font size to **14 point**. Boldface the column headings.

8. Adjust the column widths so that all entries are on one line and columns display text attractively.

9. Change the height of the table to about **2.7** inches, and then adjust the height of the *Mateo's* row to be the same height as the other rows.

10. Align all entries in the first three columns using **Align Center Left**. Align the dollar sign entries using **Align Center Right**. Align the *Cost* heading using **Align Center**.

11. The Hendrick's Grill has closed. Delete the row with information on this restaurant.

12. **With your teacher's permission**, print page 2 of the publication. Your page should look similar to Figure 21-2.

13. Close the publication, saving changes, and exit Publisher.

Name	Location	Cuisine	Cost
Mateo's Ristorante	Richmond	Italian	$$$
The Heritage	Greenville	Continental	$$$
Tradewinds	Hendricks	Asian	$$
Marley's Pub	Bridgeton	American	$

Figure 21-2

Lesson 22

Formatting Tables

> ### What You Will Learn

Merging and Splitting Cells
Changing Text Direction
Adjusting Cell Margins
Using Diagonals
Applying Table Styles
Applying Table Fills and Borders
Changing Table Alignment
Turning Off Automatic Hyphenation

WORDS TO KNOW

Merge
Combine two or more cells to create a single, larger cell.

Table styles
Combinations of fills and borders that can be applied to an entire table with a single click.

Software Skills   You can greatly improve a table's appearance by applying formatting to it, in much the same way as you apply formatting to a text box and its text. You can use either automatic formatting or manual. Features such as merging, splitting, diagonal borders, and text direction can give your table a custom look. Adjust the position of the table with alignment options, and adjust cell margins to fit text more accurately. To improve text appearance in a table or a text box, turn off automatic hyphenation.

What You Can Do

Merging and Splitting Cells

- You might occasionally want to **merge** two or more cells in a table. The most common reason for this is to create a larger single cell in which you might center a title or column head.

- Use the Merge Cells command in the Merge group on the TABLE TOOLS LAYOUT tab to combine selected cells. Any text in the separate cells is placed together in the new, common cell, separated by spaces.

- Once you have merged cells, you can restore the merged cell to its individual cells using the Split Cells command. Unlike in Word, you cannot split a single cell into additional rows or columns. Split Cells works only on a cell that has previously been merged.

Try It!   **Merging and Splitting Cells**

1 Start Publisher and open **PB22Try** from the data files for this lesson.

2 Save the publication as **PB22Try_xx** in the location where your teacher instructs you to store the files for this lesson.

3 Click anywhere in the first row of the table, and then click TABLE TOOLS LAYOUT > Insert Above.

4 Click in the cell above the *Class A* cell and drag to the right to select the third and fourth cells in the row.

5 Click TABLE TOOLS LAYOUT > Merge Cells.

6 Deselect the merged cell. Then click in the *Class B* column and click TABLE TOOLS LAYOUT > Insert Right. Notice that the first cell in the new column automatically merges with the previously merged cell, but you do not want this cell merged.

7 Click in the merged cell at the right end of the first row, and then click TABLE TOOLS LAYOUT > Split Cells to restore the three separate cells.

8 Click the third cell in the first row and once again drag to the right to select the third and fourth cells. Click TABLE TOOLS LAYOUT > Merge Cells.

9 Click in the merged cell and type **Enrollment**. Click in the first cell of the new column and type **Rate**.

10 Click TABLE TOOLS LAYOUT > Insert Right.

11 Select the first two cells in the new column and then click TABLE TOOLS LAYOUT > Merge Cells.

12 Click in the merged cell in the new column and type **Location**.

✓ *Don't worry that the table is wider than the margins. You will adjust cell and table width later in this lesson.*

13 Select the *Rate* cell, and then click HOME > Font Size 11 > 12.

14 Save the changes to **PB22Try_xx**, and leave it open to use in the next Try It.

Merged cell and new columns

Class		Instructor	Enrollment		Rate	Location
			Class A	Class B		
Basic Word Processing Skills with Microsoft Word		Thompson	35	22		
Advanced Word Processing Skills with Microsoft Word		Jerrod	21	15		
Introduction to Spreadsheets and Microsoft Excel		Tranh	15	10		
Advanced Spreadsheet Topics with Microsoft Excel		Patel	16	15		

Changing Text Direction

- The Text Direction command in the Alignment group on the TABLE TOOLS LAYOUT tab allows you to change the direction of text from horizontal to vertical.

- This command actually rotates text 90 degrees, so that the tops of the letters point to the right.

- Setting text vertically can save horizontal space in a table or a text box.

Adjusting Cell Margins

- You can adjust the margins between text and cell borders for any cell in a table.

- By default, table cell margins are set to Narrow: 0.04 inch on each side. You can use the Cell Margins command in the Alignment group on the TABLE TOOLS LAYOUT tab to remove all cell margins, set the margins to Moderate (0.06 inch on each side), or set the margins to Wide (0.1 inch on each side).

- You can also set custom margins to adjust the margin on any side. The Cell Properties tab in the Format Table dialog box also lets you adjust vertical alignment for the current cell.

Using Diagonals

- You can insert diagonal gridlines to split a cell. This feature allows you to insert information in two different regions in one cell.

- Use the Diagonals command in the Merge group on the TABLE TOOLS LAYOUT tab to insert a diagonal. You can choose whether the gridline should run from the upper-left corner of the cell to the lower-right or from the lower-left corner to the upper-right corner.

- The No Division option lets you remove the diagonal.

Try It!   **Changing Text Direction, Adjusting Cell Margins, and Using Diagonals**

1 In the **PB22Try_xx** file, select the entire column below the *Rate* cell.

2 Click TABLE TOOLS LAYOUT > Diagonals ▦ > Divide Up. Then select the cells you just divided and click HOME > Font Size 11 ▾ > 12.

3 Click on the gridline below the *Class* row and drag downward about one-quarter inch.

4 Click in the left side of the divided cell below the *Rate* cell and type **2014**. Click in the right side of the divided cell and type **2015**.

  ✓ *If you cannot see the entire 2015 entry, increase the height of the row until you can see all four digits.*

5 With the insertion point still in *2015*, click TABLE TOOLS LAYOUT > Align Bottom Right ▤.

6 Type the following entries in the divided cells. Apply Align Bottom Right alignment to the text in the right side of the diagonal.

  $145 $155

  $165 $175

  $145 $155

  $175 $185

7 Click in the *Location* cell, and then click TABLE TOOLS LAYOUT > Text Direction ▥. Then click TABLE TOOLS LAYOUT > Align Center ▤.

8 Type the following entries in the *Location* column:

  Onsite

  HTS

  Onsite

  HTS

9 Select the *Enrollment* and the *Rate* cells, and then click TABLE TOOLS LAYOUT > Align Bottom Center ▤.

10 With the cells still selected, click TABLE TOOLS LAYOUT > Cell Margins ▥ > Custom Margins. In the Bottom box, type **0.05**. Click OK.

11 Save the changes to **PB22Try_xx**, and leave it open to use in the next Try It.

Applying Table Styles

- You can use **table styles** to apply sophisticated color formatting to a table with a single click.

- Click the Table Formats gallery on the TABLE TOOLS DESIGN tab to see a collection of format styles you can apply. Table styles use the colors of the current color scheme in various combinations of fills and borders.

- As the mouse pointer hovers over a table style, the formats are applied to the currently selected table so you can see how the formats will look with your data. Each table style has a number to identify it.

- In addition to applying color fills and borders, table formats apply font styles such as bold for the first column and row. By default, all text is left-aligned. If you want to center or right-align text in a table, it is best to adjust these alignments after applying the table format.

- If you are used to working with the AutoFormats of previous Publisher versions, you can click the Table AutoFormat command at the bottom of the Table Format gallery to open the AutoFormat dialog box. Here you can click a table style to see it applied to a sample, or click [None] to remove all auto formatting.

- Click the Options button at the bottom of the dialog box to display the Formats to apply check boxes. All are marked by default, but you can clear one or more to prevent certain formatting aspects from being applied.

- If you have already applied a table style, you must remove it using the [None] option before any changes you make to the style using the Options settings will take effect.

| **Try It!** | **Applying Table Styles** |

1 In the **PB22Try_xx** file, click anywhere in the table if necessary to select it.

2 Click TABLE TOOLS DESIGN > Table Formats More button ⊡.

3 Locate Table Style 36 and hover the mouse pointer over it to see the styles applied to the table.

4 Scroll down and hover the mouse over Table Style 58.

5 Click Table Style 29 to apply it.

✓ *Note that the center alignment you applied to the Enrollment and Rate cells has been changed to left alignment. The values in the divided cells may also have been truncated.*

6 Select the Enrollment and Rate cells and click TABLE TOOLS LAYOUT > Align Bottom Center ▤.

7 Drag the row gridlines down until the bottom values display in the split cells. Reapply Bottom Right alignment to the values to the right of the diagonals.

Table style applied and alignments adjusted

Class	Instructor	Enrollment		Rate	Location
		Class A	Class B	2014 2015	
Basic Word Processing Skills with Microsoft Word	Thompson	35	22	$145 $155	Onsite
Advanced Word Processing Skills with Microsoft Word	Jerrod	21	15	$165 $175	HTS
Introduction to Spreadsheets and Microsoft Excel	Tranh	15	10	$145 $155	Onsite
Advanced Spreadsheet Topics with Microsoft Excel	Patel	16	15	$175 $185	HTS

(continued)

| **Try It!** | **Applying Table Styles** (continued) |

8 Select the *Class* and *Instructor* cells and click TABLE TOOLS LAYOUT > Align Center Left ▤.

9 Select the *Class A* and *Class B* cells and click TABLE TOOLS LAYOUT > Align Center ▤.

10 Select the cells that contain the enrollment numbers and click TABLE TOOLS LAYOUT > Align Top Center ▤.

11 Click in the *Location* cell and click TABLE TOOLS LAYOUT > Align Center ▤.

12 Save the changes to **PB22Try_xx**, and leave it open to use in the next Try It.

Applying Table Fills and Borders

- If you cannot find a table style you like, you can format the table manually using the fill and borders options available on the TABLE TOOLS DESIGN tab. You can also use these options to adjust the formats of a table style you have already applied.

- Apply a fill to selected cells using the Fill command in the Table Formats group. This command displays the color palette containing scheme colors, standard colors, and the More Fill Colors and Sample Fill Color options that allow you to select a color from the Colors dialog box or by clicking on any color on the screen.

- You can also use the Fill palette to remove fill from selected cells.

- Apply borders using options in the Borders group on the TABLE TOOLS DESIGN tab. You can select a border weight and color and then select an option from the Borders menu to apply the border to selected cells.

- You can also apply fill and border formatting by selecting the cells you want to format, right-clicking, and selecting Format Table. The Format Table dialog box allows you to apply fill and border options at the same time, which can be a more efficient process than using the TABLE TOOLS DESIGN tools.

- Once you have applied border formatting to a table, you may no longer want to view the default gridlines. Turn off the gridline display by selecting View Gridlines on the TABLE TOOLS LAYOUT tab. Turning off gridlines, which do not print, can help you decide if you need to insert additional borders in the table to make the information easy to read and understand.

| **Try It!** | **Applying Table Fills and Borders** |

1 In the **PB22Try_xx** file, select the two blank cells in the top row of the table.

2 Click TABLE TOOLS DESIGN > Fill ⬧ > No Fill.

3 Click TABLE TOOLS LAYOUT > View Gridlines ⊞ to turn off gridline display.

4 Select the *Instructor, Class A, Class B,* and the *2014/2015* cell in the second row. Click TABLE TOOLS DESIGN > Fill ⬧ > Accent 3 (RGB (148, 182, 219)) scheme color.

5 With the cells still selected, click HOME > Font Color **A ·** > Accent 5 (White), and then click HOME > Bold **B** .

6 Select the cells that contain diagonals, right-click, and click Format Table.

7 On the Colors and Lines table of the Format Table dialog box, deselect all the blue border buttons in the Preview area. Then click the diagonal border option ▧ to select it.

(continued)

Try It!   **Applying Table Fills and Borders** (continued)

8 In the Line area, click the Color drop-down arrow and click Accent 5 (White). Click the Width up arrow until the width is 1.5pt. Click OK.

9 Save the changes to **PB22Try_xx**, and leave it open to use in the next Try It.

Fills and borders applied

Class	Instructor	Enrollment		Rate	Location
		Class A	Class B	2014 / 2015	
Basic Word Processing Skills with Microsoft Word	Thompson	35	22	$145 / $155	Onsite
Advanced Word Processing Skills with Microsoft Word	Jerrod	21	15	$165 / $175	HTS
Introduction to Spreadsheets and Microsoft Excel	Tranh	15	10	$145 / $155	Onsite
Advanced Spreadsheet Topics with Microsoft Excel	Patel	16	15	$175 / $185	HTS

Changing Table Alignment

- To this point, you have changed the position of a table on a page by simply dragging it using its container. If you need to be more precise about where you position the table, you can use the Align command in the Arrange group on the TABLE TOOLS LAYOUT tab.

- The Align command displays a menu of options that allow you to align the table at the left, center, right, top, middle, or bottom of the page. You must first select the Relative to Margin Guides command on the menu before the other options become active.

- You can adjust table position even more precisely using the Layout tab in the Format Table dialog box. Specify a horizontal and/or vertical measurement from a specific point on the table, such as its top left corner or center.

- You can also specify wrapping settings for the table. These settings control how any text in a text box will interact with the table if the text box and the table overlap. Text wrapping is covered in Chapter 4.

Try It!   **Changing Table Alignment**

1 In the **PB22Try_xx** file, click on the right border of the *Location* cell (not the table container border) and drag to the left to reduce the width of the cell so it is just wide enough for the entries to fit on one line.

2 Click the right border of the *Class B* column and drag to the left to reduce the column width about one-quarter inch. Repeat this process to reduce the width of the *Class A* column.

3 Click TABLE TOOLS LAYOUT > Align 🔲 > Relative to Margin Guides.

4 Click TABLE TOOLS LAYOUT > Align 🔲 > Align Center.

5 Save the changes to **PB22Try_xx**, and leave it open to use in the next Try It.

Turning Off Automatic Hyphenation

- You may have noticed that Publisher automatically hyphenates text in table cells as well as text boxes. Hyphenation breaks words that will not fit at the end of a line so that part of the word is at the end of one line and the remainder of the word moves to the beginning of the next line.

- Hyphenation is very useful when you are trying to fit the maximum amount of text on a page or when working with columns of text, because it allows a few extra characters to appear on a line than would normally fit and reduces the raggedness of the right edge when text is left aligned.

- When you are working with short lines of text, however, as in a table cell, automatic hyphenation can produce too many undesirable line breaks, interfering with the readability of the text.

- You can turn off automatic hyphenation in a table using the Hyphenation command on the TABLE TOOLS LAYOUT tab.

- Deselect the Automatically hyphenate this story check box to turn off hyphenation. The hyphenation on/off setting applies only to the current story (in this case, the current table).

- You have the same option when working with text in a text box. Use the Hyphenation command on the TEXT BOX TOOLS FORMAT tab to turn off hyphenation for the current text box.

✓ If you never want text hyphenated in new text boxes, you can specify this in the Publisher Options dialog box.

Try It!   Turning Off Automatic Hyphenation

1 In the **PB22Try_xx** file, click anywhere in the table to select it.

2 Click TABLE TOOLS LAYOUT > Hyphenation $_{bc}^{a-}$.

3 Click in the Automatically hyphenate this story check box to remove the check mark. Click OK. Notice that any hyphenated words in the first column move to the next line to eliminate the hyphens.

4 Close the publication, saving changes, and exit Publisher.

Final formatted table

Class	Instructor	Enrollment		Rate		Location
		Class A	Class B	2014 / 2015		
Basic Word Processing Skills with Microsoft Word	Thompson	35	22	$145	$155	Onsite
Advanced Word Processing Skills with Microsoft Word	Jerrod	21	15	$165	$175	HTS
Introduction to Spreadsheets and Microsoft Excel	Tranh	15	10	$145	$155	Onsite
Advanced Spreadsheet Topics with Microsoft Excel	Patel	16	15	$175	$185	HTS

Lesson 22—Practice

Bradley & Cummins Realty has a sales conference coming up to discuss new listings. The listings table has been partially created. In this exercise, you complete the table.

DIRECTIONS

1. Start Publisher, if necessary, and open **PB22Practice** from the data files for this lesson.

2. Save the publication as **PB22Practice_xx** in the location where your teacher instructs you to store the files for this lesson.

3. Click in the first column of the table, and then click **TABLE TOOLS LAYOUT > Insert Left** to insert a new column.

4. With the new column still selected, click **TABLE TOOLS LAYOUT > Merge Cells**.

5. Click in the merged cell, if necessary, and type **New Listings**.

6. Click **TABLE TOOLS LAYOUT > Text Direction**. Then click **TABLE TOOLS LAYOUT > Align Center**.

7. Click on the right gridline of the merged cell and drag to the left until the cell is about three-quarters of an inch wide.

8. Click in the *Address* cell, and then click **TABLE TOOLS LAYOUT > Insert Above**.

9. Select the two blank columns, and then click **TABLE TOOLS LAYOUT > Insert Right** to add two more blank columns.

10. In the blank top row, select the three cells to the right of the *Price* column. (See Figure 22-1.)

11. Click **TABLE TOOLS LAYOUT > Merge Cells**. Then type **Rooms** in the merged cell.

12. In the first cell under the merged *Rooms* cell, type **Total**. Press [TAB] and type **Bed**. Press [TAB] and type **Bath**.

13. Click in the last blank cell at the right end of the top row and type **Contract to**.

14. Select all cells below the *Contract to* heading, and then click **TABLE TOOLS LAYOUT > Diagonals > Divide Up**.

15. Click in the left side of the first diagonal cell and type **Sell**. Click in the right side of the diagonal cell and type **Buy**. Drag the gridline below this cell downward if necessary until you can see the *Buy* text.

16. Type text for the *Total, Bed,* and *Bath* columns as follows.

Total	Bed	Bath
12	3	2
13	4	1.5
10	2	1
12	3	1
15	4	3
14	4	2.5
9	2	2

17. Type text for the *Contract to* column as follows. Adjust row heights as necessary to display the text at the right side of the diagonal.

Sell	Buy
Yes	No
Yes	Yes
Yes	No
Yes	Yes
Yes	Yes
Yes	No
Yes	Yes

18. Select each entry at the right side of the diagonal and click **TABLE TOOLS LAYOUT > Align Bottom Right**.

19. **With your teacher's permission**, print the publication. Your table should look similar to Figure 22-1 on the next page.

20. Close the publication, saving changes, and exit Publisher.

Figure 22-1

New Listings	Address	Agent	Price	Rooms			Contract to	
				Total	Bed	Bath	Sell	Buy
	4456 Whitfield Avenue	Bradley	$455,000	12	3	2	Yes	No
	457 Ludlow Avenue	Cummins	$275,000	13	4	1.5	Yes	Yes
	7845 N. Congress	Johnson	$175,800	10	2	1	Yes	No
	87 Mill Street	Cummins	$258,000	12	3	1	Yes	Yes
	354 E. State Street	Bradley	$425,000	15	4	3	Yes	Yes
	1689 W. Union Street	Klein	$367,500	14	4	2.5	Yes	No
	8484 Fletcher Court	Johnson	$210,400	9	2	2	Yes	Yes

Lesson 22—Apply

You continue to work on the Bradley & Cummins listings table. In this exercise, you format the table to make it more useful and attractive.

DIRECTIONS

1. Start Publisher, if necessary, and open **PB22Apply** from the data files for this lesson.

2. Save the publication as **PB22Apply_xx** in the location where your teacher instructs you to store the files for this lesson.

3. Apply **Table Style 38** to the table and then adjust text in the table as follows:

   a. First, click in the merged cell at the left side of the table. Click **TABLE TOOLS LAYOUT > Split Cells** to unmerge the cells.

   b. Click outside the table to deselect the split cells. Then select the text in the first cell in the first column and drag it down to the second cell.

   c. Select the second cell and all cells below it and merge the cells. Use **Align Center** to align the text in the merged cell.

   d. Apply **22 point bold** to the *New Listings* text.

   e. Apply **13 point bold** to the column headings in the first two rows. Adjust the column width and row height of the *Sell/Buy* cell to display all text.

   f. Apply **12 point** to the remainder of the table.

4. Adjust column widths to remove excess space in the columns. (Do not crowd the text, however.)

5. Adjust alignments as follows:

   a. Select the *Address, Agent,* and *Price* columns and set alignment to **Align Center Left**.

   b. Select the *Rooms, Total, Bed, Bath,* and *Contract to* cells and set alignment to **Align Center**.

   c. Select the room number entries and set alignment to **Align Center**.

   d. Select each of the *Buy* diagonal entries and set alignment to **Align Bottom Right** if necessary.

6. Modify the table fills as follows:

   a. Turn off gridlines.

   b. Select the empty cells in the top row and remove the fill.

c. Apply a fill of **Accent 2 (RGB (45, 162, 191))** to the merged cell at the left side of the table.

d. Select the *Address, Agent,* and *Price* cells and apply the same fill color you just applied to the merged cell. (Click the Fill button to apply the same color.)

e. Select the *Rooms, Total, Bed*, and *Bath* cells and apply a fill of **Hyperlink (RGB (215, 22, 0)), Darker 25%**.

f. Select the three columns that contain room numbers and apply a fill of **Hyperlink (RGB (215, 22, 0)), Lighter 60%**.

g. Select the *Contract to* and *Sell/Buy* cells and apply a fill of **Accent 5 (White), Darker 35%**.

h. Select all the remaining diagonal cells and apply a fill of **Accent 5 (White), Darker 25%**.

7. Apply border options as follows:

a. Select all the cells with diagonals and use the Format Table dialog box to apply **Accent 5 (White) 1.5 pt** formatting to the diagonal lines only.

b. Select all the cells in the second row (starting with *Address* and ending with *Sell/Buy*). Click the Borders drop-down arrow and deselect the Bottom Border option.

c. With the cells still selected, click the Line Weight drop-down arrow and select 3 pt. Click the Line Color drop-down arrow and click Orange from the Standard Colors palette.

d. Click the Borders drop-down arrow and click the Bottom Border option.

8. Choose to align relative to the margin guides, if necessary, and then align the table in the center of the page horizontally and the middle of the page vertically.

9. **With your teacher's permission**, print the publication. Your page should look similar to Figure 22-2.

10. Close the publication, saving changes, and exit Publisher.

Figure 22-2

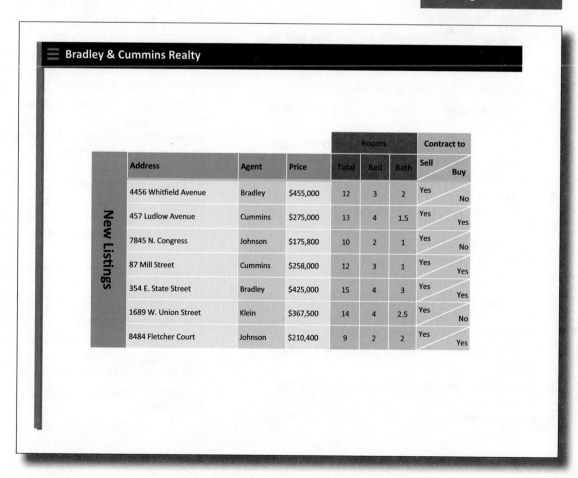

End-of-Chapter Activities

➤ Publisher Chapter 3—Critical Thinking

Create a Resume

One of the most important documents you will create is your resume. A resume can take some time to prepare, but once you have a solid, basic resume, you can use it over and over, updating it as your information changes.

Publisher includes resume templates you can use to create a basic resume, but in this project, you will create your own resume using skills you have learned in this chapter. As you follow the steps below, insert your own information in the resume so that when you have completed this project, you will have a useful job-search document.

DIRECTIONS

1. Start Publisher and select the blank 8.5 × 11" page template. Save the publication as **PBCT03_xx** in the location where your teacher instructs you to store files for this chapter.

2. Change the margins to 1 inch on all sides.

3. Draw a text box the full width of the page and align it with the top margin guide.

4. Type your name, address, city, state, ZIP, phone, and e-mail address in the text box.

   a. Apply a larger font to your name and boldface your name.

   b. Set your contact information on two lines, as shown in Illustration 3A. Adjust the line spacing between the two lines of text.

5. Insert a table that has 3 columns and about 8 rows. Make the center column very narrow to act as a spacer between the first and last column. Adjust column widths so that you have more space in the third column.

6. Turn off hyphenation for the table.

7. **With your teacher's permission**, research on the Web to find out the latest trends in resume preparation. View samples, if possible, and create a list of the types of information you will need to present.

8. Type **Objective** in the first table cell. Apply font formatting of your choice to adjust font, font size, and font style, and then create a style for this side heading.

9. Type an objective for a job you would like. Format the text by adjusting the font and font size, change the alignment if desired, and then create a style for this entry text.

10. In the cell below the *Objective* cell, type **Education**. Apply the correct style, and then list your education in the right column using the correct style. You may want to use tabs to separate data such as the year of graduation, degree conferred, and institution. You can move to a tab stop in a table by pressing CTRL + TAB.

11. Insert headings for your work experience, activities, service projects and community involvement, and any other topics you think important, and then insert the details for each topic. Follow the guidance of your online research for how to present this material. If you have multiple entries for a topic, adjust paragraph spacing between entries to improve readability. You may also want to use bullet formatting for multiple entries.

12. Adjust cell margins for the whole table to Wide, so text will not crowd the table borders.

13. Add borders as you think necessary to improve the appearance and readability of the resume.

14. **With your teacher's permission**, print the publication. Illustration 3A on the next page shows one way the publication could look.

15. Close the publication, saving changes, and exit Publisher.

Marcus MacKay

3400 Wellington Way | Cincinnati, OH 45219
513-555-0090 | marcmackay@onenet.com

Objective	The Sales Manager position [job number 1257] at Jeffry David Clothiers

Education	2011	High school diploma	St. Xavier High School
	2013	Associate Degree	Cincinnati State College
	Currently enrolled in Xavier University College of Business		

Career Achievements

2009–2010   Pier 13

- Worked as a sales clerk for one year.
- Took management training course and worked one year as a manager.

2011–2012   Arlen's Fashions

- Worked in sales and marketing.
- Developed new purchasing strategies and contacts.

2012–2014   Macy's

- Supervised five part-time employees in Ralph Lauren department.
- Implemented hand-held scanner system to make sales anywhere on the sales floor.
- Promoted to Sales Team Leader in 2013.

Professional Affiliations and Service

Member of Business Club, Cincinnati State College.

Member of Pi Kappa Alpha, Xavier University.

LinkedIn Profile: www.linkedin.com/profile/view?id=xxxx_pro

Contributed labor for three houses through Habitat for Humanity, Cincinnati Branch

Leisure activities include running marathons and long-distance

➤ Publisher Chapter 3—Portfolio Builder

Adoption Flyer

Pet Rescue is holding its Autumn Adoption Affair in a few weeks and has asked you to create a flyer to mail to potential volunteers. In this project, you will work with text in a number of ways and create a table for the flyer.

DIRECTIONS

1. Start Publisher, if necessary, and open **PBPB03** from the data files for this chapter.

2. Save the publication as **PBPB03_xx** in the location where your teacher instructs you to store the files for this chapter.

3. Click in the *Autumn Adoption* text box, and then click **TEXT BOX TOOLS FORMAT** > **Margins** [A] > **None**. Then change the line spacing to **1.0** to fit the text in the text box.

4. Change the character spacing of *Pet Rescue* to **Loose**.

5. Select the golden brown shape behind the *Pet Rescue* text and apply formats as follows:

   a. Display the Format AutoShape dialog box and click the **Fill Effects** button.

   b. Click **Gradient fill**, then click the Preset gradients box and select **Medium Gradient - Accent 1**. Click the Direction button and select **Linear Right**. Click **OK**.

   c. In the Line area of the tab, deselect all the border option buttons except for the bottom border.

   d. Select a dark brown border color such as **Followed Hyperlink (RGB (153, 102, 0))**, **Darker 25%** and **3 pt** width. Click **OK**.

6. Format the text in the text box as follows:

   a. Apply **14 point** to all text.

   b. Remove the 6 pt space after for all paragraphs.

   c. Apply **Justify** alignment to the first two paragraphs.

   d. Insert **Drop Cap Style 7** in the first paragraph.

   e. Apply a default first-line indent to the second paragraph.

   f. Create a numbered list with 1, 2, 3 numbering from the last three paragraphs.

   g. Apply the **Diagonal Gradient – Accent 1** shape style to the text box.

7. Use the Insert Table dialog box to create a table with **5** columns and **12** rows. Insert the text shown in Illustration 3B on the next page.

8. Format the text in the table as follows:

   a. Apply **14 point** to all text.

   b. Merge the *Good with* cell with the cell to its right.

   c. Merge the *Name* cell with the cell above it. Merge the *Age* cell with the cell above it. Merge the *Color/Breed* cell with the cell above it.

   d. Merge all cells in the *Cats* row and then merge all cells in the *Dogs* row.

   e. You forgot a column you intended to insert: Click anywhere in the *Age* column and insert a column to the right. Type **Sex** in the first cell of the column, and then fill in the correct genders for each animal, using M or F, according to their names (Ginger is a female).

9. Apply table formats as follows:

   a. Apply **Table Style 7**.

   b. Select the *Children* and *Other Pets* cells and fill with **Accent 1 (RGB (204, 153, 0))**. Then change the font color to **Accent 5 (White)** and apply bold.

   c. Apply **Align Bottom Left** alignment to the *Name* cell. Apply **Align Bottom Center** to the *Age, Sex,* and *Color/Breed* cells. Apply **Align Top Center** to *Good with, Children,* and *Other Pets*.

   d. Apply a white, 1½ pt border below the *Good with* cell.

   e. Insert ¾ pt black borders below each cat and dog name (except below the last dog name).

   f. Click in the *Cats* row and apply a fill of **Accent 1 (RGB (204, 153, 0))**, **Lighter 40%**. Apply the same fill to the *Dogs* row.

   g. Center the age, sex, and Yes/No entries.

10. Adjust the column widths to remove any extra space and display all text on single lines.

11. Ginger has been adopted. Remove her row from the table.

12. Right-align the table horizontally in the area below the text box and adjust the table width to be as wide as the text box.

13. **With your instructor's permission**, print the flyer. Your printout should look similar to Illustration 3C on the next page.

14. Close the publication, saving changes, and exit Publisher.

			Good with	
Name	Age	Color/Breed	Children	Other Pets
Cats				
George	2	White/tabby	Yes	Yes
Max	6 mos	Black	Yes	No
Sadie	1	Black/white	Yes	Yes
Dogs				
Fritz	4	Shepherd	No	No
Molly	9 mos	Cocker	Yes	No
Ginger	1	Beagle mix	Yes	Yes
Princess	3	Standard poodle	No	Yes

Illustration 3B

Autumn Adoption Affair

Pet Rescue

Join us at the Edible Treats pet food store in historic Findlay Market on Saturday and Sunday, September 29 and 30, for our Autumn Adoption Affair. Your help is needed to work with the pets we will be showing and guide prospective adopters to make the right choice. We know we can count on you to give generously of your time.

We will be bringing a total of 30 pets to the Adoption Affair. Some of our favorites are listed below. We ask that you:

1. Call us to verify you will be volunteering.
2. Report on time and sign in.
3. Stay for the full time you have agreed to be present.

Name	Age	Sex	Color/Breed	Good with	
				Children	Other Pets
Cats					
George	2	M	White/tabby	Yes	Yes
Max	6 mos	M	Black	Yes	No
Sadie	1	F	Black/white	Yes	Yes
Dogs					
Fritz	4	M	Shepherd	No	No
Molly	9 mos	F	Cocker	Yes	No
Princess	3	F	Standard poodle	No	Yes

Chapter 4

(Courtesy auremar/Shutterstock)

Working with Graphics

Lesson 23

Working with Online Pictures

> ### ➤ What You Will Learn
>
> Inserting an Online Picture
> Adjusting an Image in a Placeholder
> Formatting Clip Art

WORDS TO KNOW

Clip art
Ready-to-use artwork that may consist of illustrations or photos.

Crop
To remove a portion of an image that is not needed.

Outcropping
Adjusting the cropping handles to increase the size of the crop area.

Pan
To drag an image in a placeholder to position it more attractively.

Software Skills   Clip art can enliven an otherwise boring publication. The Online Pictures command enables you to locate clip art on Office.com or use a search tool to find a clip.

What You Can Do

Inserting an Online Picture

- You have already learned that many Publisher templates include picture placeholders. You can use these placeholders to insert images that will give your publication more visual interest.

- One option for inserting images is to insert clip art. Publisher gives you easy access to thousands of **clip art** images. You can choose from illustrations—line drawings—or photos.

- Use the Online Pictures command in the Illustrations group on the INSERT tab to open the Insert Pictures dialog box, shown in Figure 23-1 on the next page.

- Click in the Office.com Clip Art or Bing Image Search box and type one or more keywords that describe the image you want to find.

  ✓ *A Bing search will identify images anywhere on the Internet. Before you use an image you find with Bing, make sure you have permission from the copyright holder to do so.*

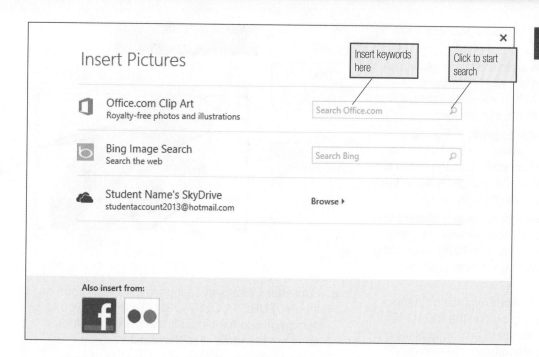

Figure 23-1

- Images that match the keywords display in the Insert Pictures dialog box, as shown in Figure 23-2. Scroll through the images to find one you like and then click it to select it. Click Insert to insert it in the publication.

- It may take a number of searches to find an image you like. Keep trying with different keywords if you don't find what you want on the first try. Click BACK TO SITES if you want to choose a different site to search.

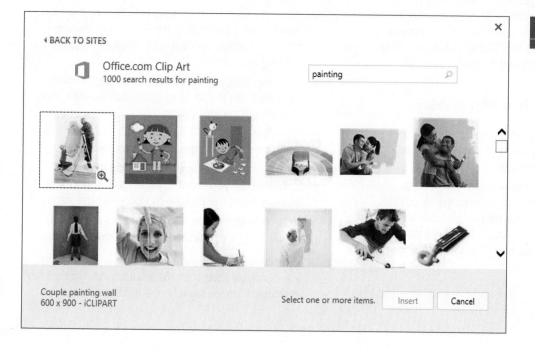

Figure 23-2

- You can insert a clip in a picture placeholder or on the page.
  - To insert the clip in a picture placeholder, select the placeholder before you begin the search for the online picture. When you click Insert, the clip image is inserted in the placeholder.
  - If you want to be able to position the clip anywhere on the page, make sure no placeholders are selected when you insert the clip. It will appear in the middle of the page. You can then move it and resize it as desired.
- Resize a clip art image that is not in a placeholder the same way you have already learned to resize text boxes, by dragging selection handles or using the Object Size information for more precise measuring.
- You can also use the Shape Height and Shape Width boxes in the Size group on the PICTURE TOOLS FORMAT tab to resize an image precisely. Notice when you use these tools that resizing one dimension will automatically resize the other an equivalent amount because the aspect ratio is locked. This prevents unintended distortion while resizing.
- If you have placed a clip art image anywhere on a page, you can delete it by selecting it and pressing DEL . If you want to remove an image from a placeholder, you can select the image, click Change Picture on the PICTURE TOOLS FORMAT tab, and then click Remove Picture.

Adjusting an Image in a Placeholder

- When you insert a clip art image into a picture placeholder, you may need to make a decision about **cropping** the image.
- Photo clips that have the same shape as the picture placeholder (that is, landscape or portrait) will generally fit in the picture placeholder without much overlap. Illustration clips, however, may overlap the placeholder by quite a bit, as shown in Figure 23-3.

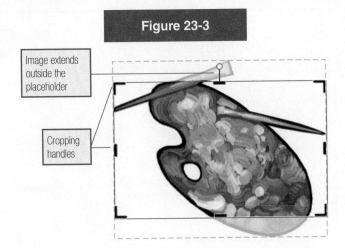

Figure 23-3

Image extends outside the placeholder

Cropping handles

- Publisher's cropping options in the Crop group on the PICTURE TOOLS FORMAT tab allow you to decide how to handle a situation when an image does not fit exactly in a placeholder.
  - You can click the Crop command to trim the graphic to the size defined by the current position of the cropping handles.
  - You can drag the cropping handles to new positions to include more of the image. This is called **outcropping**.
  - You can click on the image to display the Move pointer and then drag the image to position it more attractively in the crop area. This is called **panning**.
  - You can use the Fit option to resize the picture so that it fits in the crop area without distorting the image's aspect ratio.
  - You can use the Fill option to fill the placeholder without distorting the image's aspect ratio.
- When you have an image positioned in the placeholder as you want it, click the Crop tool or click away from the picture to complete the crop.
- You can use the Clear Crop option to remove a previous crop if you want to try a different option.

  ✓ *If you compress images in a publication, as you learn in a later lesson, all areas of an image outside the crop boundary are removed, so you can no longer adjust the crop.*

Try It! Inserting and Adjusting Clip Art

1 Start Publisher and open **PB23Try** from the data files for this lesson.

2 Save the publication as **P23Try_xx** in the location where your teacher instructs you to store files for this lesson.

3 Click INSERT > Online Pictures to display Insert Pictures dialog box.

4 Click in the Office.com Clip Art box and type **paintbrush**.

5 Click the Search icon to begin the search.

6 Scroll down in the clip results to find the clip art shown in the lower-right corner of the illustration at right. Make sure no placeholders are selected on the page and then click the clip image and click the Insert button to insert it.

✓ If you can't find the exact paintbrush shown, insert a similar clip.

7 Click PICTURE TOOLS FORMAT > Shape Width, type **1.6**, and press ENTER. Note that the height measurement adjusts automatically.

8 Drag the image to the lower-right corner of the page and align it with the right and bottom margin guides.

9 Click the picture placeholder on the publication page located above the words *Cruz Art* to select it.

10 Click INSERT > Online Pictures and type **drawing pencils** in the Office.com Clip Art box. Click Search.

11 Click the colored pencils image shown in the illustration at the right, then click Insert.

12 Move the mouse pointer over the image to display the Move pointer and drag the image so the point of the blue-gray pencil at the lower-right side of the image aligns with the bottom crop border. Click PICTURE TOOLS FORMAT > Crop.

13 Save the changes to **P23Try_xx**, and leave it open to use in the next Try It.

Clip art in the publication

Formatting Clip Art

■ The PICTURE TOOLS FORMAT tab becomes active when an image is selected. This tab contains a number of tools you can use to modify the appearance of a clip art image.

✓ Note that these tools are also available for pictures you insert from your own files or from your scanner or camera. You learn about inserting pictures from these sources in the next lesson.

■ The Adjust group offers the following options for changing image appearance.

● Use the Corrections settings to adjust brightness and contrast.

- The Recolor option allows you to change the image to a one-color image using the colors in the current color scheme. The Recolor gallery also gives you the option to make a color in the image transparent. This is often a good way to remove a background color you don't want.

  ✓ *Only certain graphic file types support transparency.*

- Use the Reset Picture command to remove any image adjustments. This command also removes any crop you have applied to the image.

- You can also find the Corrections commands on the Mini toolbar that displays when you right-click an image.

- Some other commands on the PICTURE TOOLS FORMAT tab will look familiar to you from Chapter 3, when you used the DRAWING TOOLS FORMAT tab to format text boxes. You can apply style and border options, for example, as well as picture effects such as shadows, reflections, and glows.

- You will work with the remaining commands on this tab in later lessons.

Try It!   **Formatting Clip Art**

1. In the **P23Try_xx** file, click the paint palette image in the lower-right corner of the page to select it.

2. Click PICTURE TOOLS FORMAT > Recolor 🖼 > More Variations.

3. In the color palette, click the Dark Red standard color.

4. Click the colored pencils image to select it.

5. Click PICTURE TOOLS FORMAT > Corrections ☀ > Brightness: 60%, Contrast: 60%.

6. Click PICTURE TOOLS FORMAT > Picture Border ☑ > Accent 2 (Gold), Lighter 60%. Then click Picture Border ☑ > Weight > 1½ pt.

7. Click PICTURE TOOLS FORMAT > Picture Effects ◘ > Shadow > Offset Diagonal Bottom Right.

8. Click PICTURE TOOLS FORMAT > Picture Effects ◘ > Shadow > Shadow Options.

9. In the Format Shape dialog box, click Color 🎨 ▾ and then click Accent 2 (Gold), Darker 25%. Click OK.

10. Applying the shadow causes the heading to resize. Move the picture up slightly until the *Cruz Art* heading returns to its original size.

11. Save changes, close the publication, and exit Publisher.

Formatted images

Cruz Art

Come to Cruz Art for all your painting and drawing supplies. We also offer art classes for everyone interested in learning more about drawing and painting. Whether you're a beginner or an expert, you'll find what you need at Cruz Art.

Lesson 23—Practice

The Hendricks Inn is co-sponsoring an open house with the Central Kentucky Land Trust, and John Lowery, the owner, would like an advertising flyer to help spread the word. He has started a flyer, and in this exercise you improve it by adding and formatting clip art images.

DIRECTIONS

1. Start Publisher, if necessary, and open **PB23Practice** from the data files for this lesson.

2. Save the publication as **PB23Practice_xx** in the location where your teacher instructs you to store the files for this lesson.

3. Click on the border of a picture placeholder to the left of the *Join the Central Kentucky* text box.

4. Click **INSERT > Online Pictures** 🖼.

5. Type mallard in the Search box. Click the Search icon 🔎

6. Select a clip of a duck swimming in blue water with reeds behind it.

7. Click Insert to insert it in the placeholder.

8. Position the pointer on the duck image in the placeholder to display the Move pointer ✛ and drag the image so the duck is centered in the crop area.

9. Click away from the image to complete the crop.

10. Click **INSERT > Online Pictures** 🖼 to reopen the Insert Pictures dialog box.

11. Type heron in the search box at the top of the page and click the Search icon 🔎 .

12. Click a clip of a blue heron and then click Insert.

13. With the inserted clip selected, click **PICTURE TOOLS FORMAT > Shape Width** 🖾 and type 2.6.

14. Drag the selected clip down to the lower-right corner until you see the right and bottom margin guides highlight.

15. Click the duck clip to select it. Click **PICTURE TOOLS FORMAT > Picture Border** ✎ **> Sample Line Color**. Click the eyedropper anywhere on the blue color of the heron.

16. Click **PICTURE TOOLS FORMAT > Picture Border** ✎ **> Weight > 3 pt.**

17. **With your teacher's permission**, print the document. It should look similar to Figure 23-4 on the next page.

18. Close the publication, saving changes, and exit Publisher.

Figure 23-4

Open House and Wetlands Tour

Join the Central Kentucky Land Trust (CKLT) at The Hendricks Inn for an open house and a rare opportunity to tour **Burr Oak Bend**, the CKLT wetland preservation area just across the street from The Hendricks Inn. This 120-acre stretch of wetland is the home of countless species of wildlife including birds, fish, and small mammals. Come see what CKLT has been doing to help preserve this wildlife habitat, and tour the beautiful Hendricks Inn.

When: September 2, 1:00 p.m. to 5:00 p.m.

Where: The Hendricks Inn
                1478 W. 86th Street
                Hendricks, KY 40291

Who: The public is invited

What: Tours of The Hendricks Inn

                Hiking tours of Burr Oak Bend

                Refreshments

                Raffle drawing

Lesson 23—Apply

John Lowery has asked for another version of the flyer, this one using photos rather than illustrations. He has asked you to search the Web to find appropriate images. (Naturally, you would seek copyright permission before using any of the images you find online in your final publication.) In this exercise, you work with the same text and insert and format different clip art images that you find using a Bing Web search.

DIRECTIONS

1. Start Publisher, if necessary, and open **PB23Apply** from the data files for this lesson.

2. Save the publication as **PB23Apply_xx** in the location where your teacher instructs you to store the files for this lesson.

3. Select the ducks clip, and then click **PICTURE TOOLS FORMAT** > **Change Picture** 🖼 > **Remove Picture**.

4. Delete the heron picture.

5. Select the picture placeholder to the left of the *Open House* heading.

6. Display the Insert Pictures dialog box for online pictures and type the keywords **Portrait of pink flower**.

7. A clip of a pink flower on a dark background appears.

8. Select the picture and then insert the flower clip in the placeholder. Click away from the picture to accept the current crop.

9. Select the flower image again and then click the Set Transparent Color option on the Recolor gallery. Click anywhere on the dark background around the flower to remove it.

10. Recolor the image using the RGB (104, 160, 176), Accent color 1 Light variation. If you see a dark border at the top and bottom of the picture, choose to crop it again and drag the top center crop handle and the bottom center crop handle toward the middle of the image to trim away the borders.

11. Select the empty placeholder to the left of the text and use Bing Image Search to locate and insert a clip art photo of a duck. Look for images that are copyright-free, if possible; you can often determine this from the link at the lower-left corner of the Insert Pictures box.

12. Choose an appropriate crop option for your image to either fill or fit the image in the placeholder.

13. Search for clip art photographs of herons using either Office.com or Bing. Insert the picture and move it toward the lower-right corner. Crop and resize the picture as necessary.

14. Correct both pictures if they need to be improved.

15. Sample a color from either the heron picture or the duck picture to change the picture outline around the duck picture.

16. Apply the Offset Diagonal Bottom Right shadow effect to the heron picture and change the shadow color, if appropriate. In the Format Shape dialog box, also change the shadow distance to **12 pt**.

17. **With your teacher's permission**, print the document. It should look similar to Figure 23-5 on the next page.

18. Close the publication, saving changes, and exit Publisher. Close your browser if necessary.

Open House and Wetlands Tour

Join the Central Kentucky Land Trust (CKLT) at The Hendricks Inn for an open house and a rare opportunity to tour **Burr Oak Bend**, the CKLT wetland preservation area just across the street from The Hendricks Inn. This 120-acre stretch of wetland is the home of countless species of wildlife including birds, fish, and small mammals. Come see what CKLT has been doing to help preserve this wildlife habitat, and tour the beautiful Hendricks Inn.

When: September 2, 1:00 p.m. to 5:00 p.m.

Where: The Hendricks Inn
1478 W. 86th Street
Hendricks, KY 40291

Who: The public is invited

What: Tours of The Hendricks Inn

Hiking tours of Burr Oak Bend

Refreshments

Raffle drawing

Lesson 24

Working with Pictures

❯ **What You Will Learn**

Adding a Picture Placeholder
Inserting a Picture from a File
Changing the Picture
Swapping Pictures
Applying Picture Styles and Formats
Changing Picture Shape
Adding Captions
Applying a Picture As a Page Background

Software Skills   Online clip art can be useful, but it will probably not fill all your illustration needs. You can insert pictures from files that have been created by scanners or digital cameras. Publisher offers a number of formatting and adjustment options you can apply to customize pictures.

What You Can Do

Adding a Picture Placeholder

- As you have learned, most Publisher templates provide at least one placeholder for a **picture** to be inserted; many have more than one so you can insert an illustration as well as a graphic company logo.

- If you are creating a publication from scratch, without using a template, and you want a picture placeholder to make it easy to insert pictures, you can use the Picture Placeholder command in the Illustrations group on the INSERT tab to add a placeholder to the publication.

- This command inserts a placeholder that is 1.25 inches square in the center of the page. You can then resize the placeholder and move it as necessary.

Inserting a Picture from a File

- Clip art images may answer many of your illustration needs, but as you work more extensively with Publisher, you will find that you need pictures that you cannot find in the clip art files. When creating a flyer to advertise the sale of your vintage car, for example, you will want to use a picture of that car, not a generic clip art car.

- You have a number of options for creating or finding picture files. You can create them using a scanner or digital camera, or you can download them from the Internet.

  ✓ *If you use a picture you have acquired from a Web page, make sure it is not copyrighted and that you have permission to use it. Otherwise you might be subject to legal penalties.*

- Publisher accepts a wide variety of graphic formats, including Windows Metafile (.wmf) and Enhanced Metafile (.emf), JPEG (.jpg), Portable Network Graphics (.png), Windows Bitmap (.bmp), Graphics Interchange Format (.gif), Tagged Image File Format (.tif), Computer Graphics Metafile (.cgm), Encapsulated PostScript (.eps), Macintosh PICT (.pct), and WordPerfect Graphics (.wpg).

- You can insert a picture file in a publication using a picture placeholder, or you can insert the picture on the page and then modify its size and location, as you did with clip art images in the last lesson.

- Clicking inside a picture placeholder opens the Insert Pictures dialog box, where you can navigate to the location of the picture file and then insert it. You can then adjust the image in the crop area as you learned in Lesson 23.

- You can place a picture on a page without a placeholder by clicking the Pictures command on the INSERT menu. Publisher places the picture at a default size in the center of the page, and you must move and resize it after insertion.

- When you want to place more than one picture on a page, you can open all pictures at the same time. Publisher stores them in the scratch area.

- You can drag pictures from the scratch area to position them on the page.

- Inserted pictures are **embedded graphics**, which means they are stored inside the Publisher file. You can if desired change an embedded graphic to a linked graphic to reduce the file size of the publication. You learn more about linked and embedded graphics in the next lesson.

Try It!   **Adding a Picture Placeholder and Inserting Pictures**

1. Start Publisher and open **PB24Try** from the data files for this lesson.

2. Save the publication as **PB24Try_xx** in the location where your teacher instructs you to store files for this lesson.

3. Click page 2 in the Page Navigation pane. Then click on the text box in the left column and drag it down to align at the top with the 5 inch ruler guide.

4. Click INSERT > Picture Placeholder. The new picture placeholder displays in the center of the page.

5. Drag the picture placeholder to the top of the left column, at the intersection of the left margin guide and the 1.5 inch ruler guide.

6. Drag the lower-right corner of the picture placeholder down and to the right until it reaches the left column grid guide. Note that the placeholder maintains its original square shape as you drag.

7. Click inside the placeholder on the picture icon to open the Insert Pictures dialog box. Click Browse to the right of From a file, navigate to the location of the data files for this lesson, and click **PB24Try_image1.jpg**. Click Insert, and then click away from the picture to accept the crop.

(continued)

Try It!   **Adding a Picture Placeholder and Inserting Pictures** *(continued)*

(8) Click INSERT > Pictures 🖼, then click **PB24Try_image2.jpg**, hold down `CTRL`, click **PB24Try_image3.jpg** and **PB24Try_image4.png**, and click Insert. The inserted pictures are stored in the publication's scratch area. Click away from the inserted pictures to deselect them.

(9) Position the mouse pointer on the bottom picture in the stack in the scratch area to display the mountain icon, click on it, and drag the picture onto the page.

(10) Align the upper-left corner of the picture with the 5 inch ruler guide and the right column margin guide.

(11) Drag the lower-right corner of the picture to the right margin guide.

(12) Save the changes to **PB24Try_xx**, and leave it open to use in the next Try It.

New pictures inserted

Changing the Picture

- If you find that the picture you have inserted does not work, you can easily replace it with another picture using the Change Picture command in the Adjust group on the PICTURE TOOLS FORMAT tab.

- Clicking the Change Picture option opens the Insert Pictures dialog box so you can locate the replacement picture.

Swapping Pictures

- You have another alternative for changing pictures, and that is to switch the locations of pictures on a page.

- Use the Swap command in the Swap group on the PICTURE TOOLS FORMAT tab to switch the locations of two selected pictures.

- The Swap command also appears on the Mini toolbar that displays if you right-click a picture when more than one picture is selected.

- If you have pictures stored in the scratch area, you can swap them for pictures already placed on the page.

- Click on the mountain icon in the scratch area picture and drag it over the picture you want to swap out until a pink outline appears. The two pictures change places so the original picture moves to the scratch area.

- The swapped pictures are both selected after you make the swap. Click in the scratch area to deselect.

Try It!   Changing and Swapping Pictures

1 In the **PB24Try_xx** file, click in the top picture in the scratch area to display the mountain icon.

2 Drag the scratch area picture over the picture at the upper-left corner of the page until a pink outline appears, and then release the mouse button to replace the picture. Click in the scratch area to deselect both pictures.

3 Click the picture in the upper-left corner of the page, hold down ⇧SHIFT, and click the other picture on the page.

4 Click PICTURE TOOLS FORMAT > Swap 🖼️. The two pictures switch places, maintaining the original sizes of the pictures.

5 Save the changes to **PB24Try_xx**, and leave it open to use in the next Try It.

Applying Picture Styles and Formats

- You can use the tools in the Adjust group on the PICTURE TOOLS FORMAT tab to modify the appearance of pictures, just as you used them to modify clip art images. You can change brightness and contrast, recolor images, apply borders, and add picture effects such as shadows, reflections, and 3-D rotations.

- You can also apply a caption to a picture, as you will learn later in this lesson.

- You can use picture styles from the Picture Styles gallery to apply multiple formats, such as borders, shapes, and shadows, with a single click. Click the More button on the Picture Styles gallery to see all available styles.

- Remove a picture style with the Clear Picture Style command on the Picture Style gallery.

- You can modify picture styles by adjusting the color of the border or shadow effects. This allows you to customize the styles for a particular publication.

Try It!   Applying Picture Styles and Formats

1 In the **PB24Try_xx** file, click page 1 in the Page Navigation pane.

2 Select the picture and then click PICTURE TOOLS FORMAT > Corrections ☀️ > Brightness: 50%, Contrast: 60%.

3 Click PICTURE TOOLS FORMAT > Picture Styles More button ▾ to display the Picture Styles gallery.

4 Click Simple Frame, White on the gallery. Then click PICTURE TOOLS FORMAT > Picture Border 🖊️ > Accent 2 (RGB (173, 194, 153)).

5 Click page 2 in the Page Navigation pane, and then click the picture in the upper-left corner of the page.

6 Click PICTURE TOOLS FORMAT > Corrections ☀️ > Brightness: 50%, Contrast: 60%.

7 Make the same correction to the other picture on the page.

8 Click the upper-left picture again, and then click PICTURE TOOLS FORMAT > Picture Effects 🔲 > Glow > Accent 1, 11 pt glow.

9 Save the changes to **PB24Try_xx**, and leave it open to use in the next Try It.

Changing Picture Shape

- The Crop to Shape cropping option can be used to change the shape of a picture from the standard rectangle or square to an ellipse, rounded rectangle, or the wavy bottomed shape called Flowchart in the Shapes gallery.

  ✓ *You learn more about shapes later in this chapter.*

- You can apply other shapes from the shapes gallery to a picture to give it a more interesting appearance.
- After you choose a shape from the Shapes gallery, cropping handles display so that you can adjust the size and the fill in the new shape.

Try It!   Changing Picture Shape

1. In the **PB24Try_xx** file, click the picture in the right column on page 2 to select it.

2. Click PICTURE TOOLS FORMAT > Crop 🖼 > Crop to Shape to display the Shapes gallery.

3. Click Oval in the top row of the Basic Shapes category. The picture shape changes and cropping handles display.

4. Drag the bottom center cropping handle down about half an inch to make the oval taller than it is wide. Note that the picture does not fill the new shape.

5. Click PICTURE TOOLS FORMAT > Fill 🖼 in the Crop group to fill the new shape with the picture. Click outside the picture to accept the crop.

6. Select the picture again, click PICTURE TOOLS FORMAT > Picture Effects 🔵 > Glow > Accent 1, 11 pt glow.

7. Save the changes to **PB24Try_xx**, and leave it open to use in the next Try It.

Picture style, new shape, and picture effects applied

tumbling over native rocks to a tranquil pool, a shade garden under the high canopy of old oaks and maples, a prairie garden devoted to native species. You can also walk through our vegetable garden, where we grow vegetables for the table, as well as the fruit orchards. Our famous Apple Crumb Cake will taste so much better when you've strolled through the orchard where those apples are harvested.

favorite film. Or, if you're more interested in just getting away from it all, check out the library, where you'll find hundreds of books, comfortable leather chairs for napping or reading, and a sturdy writing desk for catching up on your correspondence.

Outdoors, you'll find a delightful wrap-around porch with comfortable rocking chairs. In summer, the porch is always shady, with a refreshing breeze off the lake to keep you cool. The house is surrounded by specialty gardens: an herb garden (which supplies the zesty herbs you'll taste in many of our foods), a water feature with a stream

Adding Captions

- Use the caption feature to attach a text box to a picture in which you can type information that relates to the picture. The caption is grouped with the picture so that if you need to move the picture, the caption moves as well.

- Use the Caption command in the Picture Styles group on the PICTURE TOOLS FORMAT tab to display a gallery of caption styles. You can choose formatted captions that apply color to the caption box, overlay styles that are positioned partially covering the picture, and simple styles that consist only of plain text.

- You can remove a caption by selecting the No Caption option on the Captions gallery.

Try It!   **Adding Captions**

1 In the **PB24Try_xx** file, click page 1 in the Page Navigation pane.

2 Click the caption text box and drag it into the scratch area. Scroll the window so that the publication page displays at the far left of the window

3 Click the picture to select it, and then click PICTURE TOOLS FORMAT > Caption 🖾. Rest the mouse pointer on some of the caption options to see the Live Preview on the selected picture.

4 Click the Box – Layout 3 caption style.

5 Select the text in the caption and press DEL. Then select the text in the text box in the scratch area and click HOME > Cut ✂.

6 Click in the caption box and click HOME > Paste 🗋. Click the Paste Options button 🗋 (Ctrl)▾ and click Keep Text Only.

7 Click the empty text box in the scratch area and press DEL.

8 Save the changes to **PB24Try_xx** and leave it open to use in the next Try It.

Caption added to picture

Orchard House

Guest Comforts

Being travel enthusiasts ourselves, we know how important it is to have a comfortable bed to sleep in, so all of our rooms have the best in bedding and linens. You'll enjoy luxurious pillow-top mattresses with firm support, 100 percent cotton sheets, and cozy quilts and comforters, as well as thick, absorbent bathrobes and large, fluffy towels.

Each room is furnished with Mission-style furniture typical of the Arts and Crafts movement of the early twentieth century. We have a passion for this style of furnishing, and it shows throughout the house.

Take a stroll under the apple trees at Orchard House Bed & Breakfast.

Applying a Picture As a Page Background

- In Publisher 2013, you can use a picture to create a page background. A picture background can give a page quite a bit of visual interest.
- You can insert a picture as a background by simply right-clicking it and choosing Apply to Background.
- Or, you can use the Format Background dialog box to select a picture for the page background.

- You can choose whether the picture fills the background as a single picture or is tiled to fill the background with multiple images.
- Unless the picture is fairly light, or you don't have much text on the page, you may need to adjust the transparency of the picture in the Format Background dialog box. Increasing transparency prevents the picture from overpowering any text on the page.

Try It!   **Applying a Picture As a Page Background**

① In the **PB24Try_xx** file, click page 3 in the Page Navigation pane.

② Right-click the bottom picture in the scratch area, click Apply to Background, and then click Fill. The picture fills the entire page.

③ Click PAGE DESIGN > Background 🖼 > More Backgrounds to open the Format Background dialog box.

④ Drag the Transparency slider to 60% and click OK. The picture background is now much lighter.

⑤ Save changes, close the publication, and exit Publisher.

Lesson 24—Practice

Parker Conservatory is sponsoring a butterfly show and wants you to start work on a brochure to advertise the show. In this exercise, you begin work on the brochure and the pictures they have provided.

DIRECTIONS

1. Start Publisher, if necessary, and click the **Blank 11 × 8.5"** template to create a new, blank publication. Apply the **Solstice** color scheme.

2. Save the publication as **PB24Practice_xx** in the location where your teacher instructs you to store the files for this lesson.

3. Click **PAGE DESIGN** > **Guides** ⬚ > **Grid and Baseline Guides**. On the Grid Guides tab, click the **Columns** up arrow twice to set **3** columns. Press TAB and type **0.16** in the Spacing box. Click **OK**.

4. Click **INSERT** > **Page** ⬚ > **Insert Duplicate Page**.

5. On page 2, at the top of the left column, click **INSERT** > **Draw Text Box** ⬚ and then draw a text box **0.7** inches high and the full column width. The top of the text box should align with the top margin.

6. Type **Butterflies Galore!**, and then select the text and click **HOME** > **Font** [Times New Roman ▾] > **Times New Roman**. Click **HOME** > **Font Size** [11 ▾] > **26**, and then click **HOME** > **Bold B**.

7. Click **TEXT BOX TOOLS FORMAT** > **Align Center** ☰ and then click **DRAWING TOOLS FORMAT** > **Shape Fill** 🎨 > **More Fill Colors**, and click the orange color on the Standard tab that is third from the left in the row second from the bottom. Click **OK**.

8. Click **INSERT** > **Picture Placeholder** 🖼. Click **PICTURE TOOLS FORMAT** > **Height** ⬚ and type **3.2**. Move the placeholder to the top of the center column.

9. Click in the picture placeholder at the top of the center column. In the Insert Picture dialog box, browse to the data files for this lesson, click **PB24Practice_image1.jpg**, and click **Insert**. Click **PICTURE TOOLS FORMAT > Fit** 🖼 to fit the image in the crop area. Click off the picture to accept the crop.

10. Click **INSERT > Pictures** 🖼, click **PB24Practice_image2.jpg**, hold down [CTRL] and click **PB24Practice_image3.jpg**, and click **Insert**.

11. Deselect the pictures, and then drag the top picture from the scratch area to the left column. Click **PICTURE TOOLS FORMAT > Width** 🖬 and type **3.2**. Position the picture at the bottom of the left column.

12. Drag the bottom picture from the scratch area to the right column. Click **PICTURE TOOLS FORMAT > Width** 🖬 and type **3.2**. Position the picture at the bottom of the right column.

13. Modify the pictures as follows:

    a. Click the picture at the bottom of the left column. Click **PICTURE TOOLS FORMAT > Corrections** ☀ **> Brightness: 50%, Contrast: 70%**.

    b. Click the picture at the top of the center column. Click **PICTURE TOOLS FORMAT > Recolor** 🖼 **> More Variations**. Click the orange color under Recent Colors.

    c. Click the picture at the bottom of the right column. Click **PICTURE TOOLS FORMAT > Corrections** ☀ **> Brightness: 50%, Contrast: 60%**.

14. **With your teacher's permission**, print page 2 of the publication. Your page should look similar to Figure 24-1.

15. Close the publication, saving changes, and exit Publisher.

Figure 24-1

Lesson 24—Apply

In this exercise, you complete the brochure for Parker Conservatory by inserting additional pictures and fine-tuning picture formats and placement.

DIRECTIONS

1. Start Publisher, if necessary, and open **PB24Apply** from the data files for this lesson.

2. Save the publication as **PB24Apply_xx** in the location where your teacher instructs you to store the files for this lesson.

3. Open the three pictures to be used in this project

   PB24Apply_image1.jpg

   PB24Apply_image2.jpg, and

   PB24Apply_image3.jpg

   to make them available in the scratch area.

4. On page 1, apply the orange butterfly picture in the scratch area as a page background. In the Format Background dialog box, change transparency to **75%** and set offsets as follows: **left, 0%**; **right, 50%**; **top, 30%**; **bottom, 30%**.

5. On page 1, create a text box at the top of the right column the full width of the column and 0.7 inches high. Type **PARKER**. Center the text and apply **Times New Roman, 30 point** font.

6. Create another text box the same height and width, and type **CONSERVATORY**. Use the Format Painter to apply the formats from the first text box to the type in the second text box. If text overflows the text box, change text box margins to None. Move the second text box down to about the middle of the column.

7. Drag the top picture from the scratch area and position it below the *PARKER* text box. Modify the image as follows:

   a. Correct the picture to **Brightness: 50%, Contrast: 60%**.

   b. Change width to **3.2** inches.

   c. Crop to the **Oval** shape.

   d. Move the *CONSERVATORY* text box up below the picture so the picture is centered between the two text boxes. (See Figure 24-2 on the next page.)

   e. Apply a 6 pt picture border, and then change the border color to a color you sample from the yellow flower in the picture.

8. On page 2, make the following adjustments to the pictures:

   a. Select the orange butterfly in the center column, click **PICTURE TOOLS FORMAT > Recolor** ![icon], and click **No Recolor**. Then swap this picture with the black butterfly picture in the scratch area.

   b. Swap the pictures in the left column and the right column.

   c. Apply the **Drop Shadow Rectangle** picture style to all three pictures.

9. Insert captions for each picture on this page. Use the **Simple – Layout 2** caption for the pictures in the left and right column, and the **Simple – Layout 1** caption for the picture in the center column. Type the following captions:

   a. For the picture in the left column: **Orange butterfly on yellow marigold flower.**

   b. For the picture in the center column: **Black butterfly on pink hibiscus flower.**

   c. For the picture in the right column: **Orange butterfly on orange marigold flower.**

10. Change the font size for all captions to **12 point**.

11. **With your teacher's permission**, print the document. Page 1 should look similar to Figure 24-2, and page 2 should look similar to Figure 24-3 (both shown on the next page).

12. Close the publication, saving changes, and exit Publisher.

Figure 24-2

PARKER

CONSERVATORY

Figure 24-3

Butterflies Galore!

Black butterfly on pink hibiscus flower.

Orange butterfly on yellow marigold flower.

Orange butterfly on orange marigold flower.

Lesson 25

Combining Text and Pictures

> ## What You Will Learn

Cropping for Effect
Wrapping Text Around Pictures
Editing Wrap Points
Adding a Page Background
Viewing the Graphics Manager
Compressing Pictures
Saving a Publication As a PDF File

Software Skills   Use the Crop tool to control cropping to focus on a specific area of a picture. Apply text wrap settings to flow text around pictures in a publication. You can edit the wrap settings for more control over the wrap. Add a page background for additional visual interest. Display the Graphics Manager task pane to see more information about pictures in a publication. Adjust picture compression settings to control publication file size. You can save any publication as a PDF for distribution online.

What You Can Do

Cropping for Effect

- In the previous two lessons, you worked with crop settings applied automatically to clip art and pictures being imported into placeholders. By default, the crop area is the same size as the placeholder dimensions, which often doesn't give you very much leeway to crop effectively.

- When you insert a picture on the page without placing it in a picture placeholder, you can use the Crop tool to crop more creatively to give your pictures more visual interest.

- Click the Crop command in the Crop group on the PICTURE TOOLS FORMAT tab to display crop handles around the outside edge of the picture. Or, right-click on the picture and click the Crop tool on the Mini toolbar. You can then drag handles as desired to adjust the crop area.

  ✓ *Hold down* CTRL *while dragging a side cropping handle to adjust the opposite side at the same time.*

WORDS TO KNOW

PDF
Stands for Portable Document Format; an Adobe format for distributing documents in electronic format exactly as they would be printed.

Rule of thirds
A rule designers often use to position the focus of an image off center according to a grid that divides the image horizontally and vertically into thirds.

Wrap
To flow text around a picture or other graphic object.

Wrap point
A small black handle on the wrap boundary of an illustration that you can adjust to change wrapping.

- As you work with the cropping handles, consider these guidelines of effective cropping: You should either try to "fill the frame" with the subject or follow the "rule of thirds."

- To fill the frame, crop so that your subject fills your chosen picture size.

- In Figure 25-1, for example, the picture of the mountain goat has the goat in the center of the picture, which gives a somewhat bland effect. If you want to focus only on the goat, you could crop close to the goat to display it at the largest possible size in the publication.

- To use the **rule of thirds**, imagine a grid of lines that divide the picture into thirds horizontally and vertically. Placing the important feature of the picture at one of the intersections of these gridlines can move the focus away from the center to create a more interesting composition.

- The crop shown in Figure 25-2 moves the main focus of the picture to the left side of the crop area so that the goat will be in the leftmost third of the picture.

- As you are planning your crop, remember the Clear Crop command in the Crop group on the PICTURE TOOLS FORMAT tab. Clear Crop removes the most recent crop to restore the picture to its original size.

- You can also use the Reset Picture command in the Adjust group to remove a crop and other formatting changes you have applied to a picture.

Figure 25-1

Figure 25-2

Try It!   **Cropping for Effect**

1 Start Publisher and open **PB25Try** from the data files for this lesson.

2 Save the publication as **PB25TryA_xx** in the location where your teacher instructs you to store the files for this lesson.

3 Click page 2 in the Page Navigation pane.

4 Click INSERT > Pictures 🖼. Navigate to the data files for this lesson, click **PB25Try_image1.jpg**, and click Insert.

5 Crop this picture to "fill the frame":

  a. Click PICTURE TOOLS FORMAT > Crop 🖼.

  b. Drag the bottom center cropping handle up just beneath the trunk of the tree. Drag the left center cropping handle about one-quarter inch to the right. Drag the right center cropping handle just to the right of pink-flowered branches at the right side of the tree.

  c. Click the Crop tool 🖼 to complete the crop.

  d. Click PICTURE TOOLS FORMAT > Shape Width 📐 and type **4**, and then move the picture to the upper-left corner of the page at the intersection of the left and top margin guides. Deselect the picture.

6 Click INSERT > Pictures 🖼. Navigate to the data files for this lesson, click **PB25Try_image2.jpg**, and click Insert.

7 Crop this picture using the "rule of thirds" to focus attention on the rightmost white flowered tree:

  a. Click PICTURE TOOLS FORMAT > Crop 🖼.

  b. Drag the bottom center cropping handle up to just below the trunk of the rightmost white tree. Drag the right center cropping handle to the left, just to the right of the rightmost white-flowered tree. Drag the top center cropping handle downward to just above the three trees. Drag the left center cropping handle to the right, just to the left of the trunk of the leftmost of the three trees.

  c. Click the Crop tool 🖼 to complete the crop.

  d. Click PICTURE TOOLS FORMAT > Shape Width 📐 and type **5**, and then move the picture to the bottom center of the page.

8 Save the changes to **PB25TryA_xx**, and leave it open to use in the next Try It.

Cropped pictures in place

Wrapping Text Around Pictures

- **Wrapping** style controls the way that text in a text box interacts with a graphic when the two objects overlap.

- You make the change to the wrapping style in the graphic's settings, not the text box's settings. If you find you do not have access to wrap settings, the picture may be behind text rather than on top of it.

  ✓ *You learn about adjusting stacking order later in this chapter.*

- Use the Wrap Text command in the Arrange group on the PICTURE TOOLS FORMAT tab to apply one of the following wrapping styles:

  - None: No wrap is applied.

  - Square: Text wraps around the rectangular frame of the graphic object.

  - Tight: Text wraps around the object inside the frame. (This is different from Square only if the object itself is not rectangular.)

  - Top and Bottom: Text stops above the object and continues below it.

  - Through: Text runs through the object frame, but wraps around certain parts of the object. Depending on the object, it can appear the same as either Tight or None.

✓ *You can also find a Wrap Text command on the Mini toolbar that displays when you right-click a picture.*

- For additional wrapping options, click More Layout Options on the Wrap Text menu to open the Format Picture dialog box, shown in Figure 25-3.

- In addition to a wrapping style, you can also choose which sides to wrap on. These settings apply only if you choose a wrapping style that allows wrapping on the sides.

  - Both sides: Wraps text on both sides of the object.

  - Left only: Wraps text only on the left.

  - Right only: Wraps text only on the right.

  - In largest space available: Wraps text only on the side where there is the largest space available (either left or right).

- The Distance from text controls let you specify the amount of white space between the object and the wrapped text. Clear the Automatic checkbox and then enter spacing settings. The distance from text options are available only for Square text wrapping.

Figure 25-3

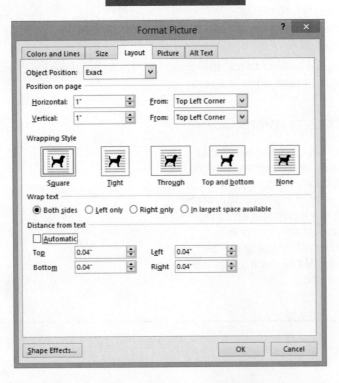

Try It! **Wrapping Text Around Pictures**

1 In the **PB25TryA_xx** file, click the picture in the upper-left corner of page 2.

2 Click PICTURE TOOLS FORMAT > Wrap Text 📄 > More Layout Options.

3 In the Format Picture dialog box, Square wrapping should be selected. In the Distance from text area, click the Automatic check box to deselect it. Click the Right up arrow three times to change the wrapping margin to 0.34 inches. Click OK.

4 Click the picture at the bottom of the page. Click PICTURE TOOLS FORMAT > Wrap Text 📄 > Top and Bottom.

5 Save the changes to **PB25TryA_xx**, and leave it open to use in the next Try It.

Editing Wrap Points

■ When wrapping text around a clip art illustration, you may want to adjust the wrap so the text follows the contour of the illustration for a special effect. You can adjust the wrap by editing wrap points.

■ **Wrap points** are small black handles that define where text wraps around an object. In a rectangular object, there are wrap points at each corner of the object. Irregular-shaped objects such as clip art images may have many more wrap points that follow the contour of the object.

■ You can change the wrap points for an object by setting the wrapping to Tight and then clicking Edit Wrap Points on the Wrap Text menu. This command displays the dotted red wrap boundary line shown in Figure 25-4.

■ You can drag a wrap point to change the position of the wrap boundary. If the object does not have many wrap points, you can add them by CTRL-clicking on the boundary. The more wrap points on the boundary, the more closely you can wrap the boundary around the object.

■ You can remove wrap points you don't need by CTRL-clicking on a wrap point. The pointer takes the shape of black X when you hold down CTRL and move the pointer over a wrap point.

Figure 25-4

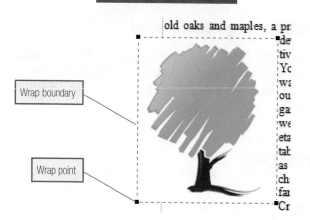

Wrap boundary

Wrap point

Try It!   Editing Wrap Points

1 In the **PB25TryA_xx** file, click page 1 in the Page Navigation pane.

2 Drag the clip art illustration from the scratch area to the right until the left side of the illustration aligns with the left margin guide.

3 Click PICTURE TOOLS FORMAT > Wrap Text 🖼 > Tight. Then click Wrap Text 🖼 > Edit Wrap Points. The wrap boundary and wrap points display.

4 Drag wrap points away from the illustration on the right side to create a margin between the text and the illustration. Delete wrap points if necessary by holding down CTRL and clicking on the wrap point. Your wrap boundary should look similar to the one shown in the illustration.

5 You may need to nudge the illustration with the ↑ or ↓ key to create an attractive wrap. Then click away from the page to accept the wrap.

6 Save the changes to **PB25TryA_xx**, and leave it open to use in the next Try It.

Text wrapped closely around the illustration

Adding a Page Background

■ You can apply a background color or fill effect to the current page using the Background command in the Page Background group on the PAGE DESIGN tab.

■ The Background gallery gives you the choice of solid or gradient backgrounds created from four scheme colors.

■ Click More Backgrounds to open the Format Background dialog box, where you can create a gradient or choose a texture, pattern, or picture fill for the page.

Try It!   Adding a Page Background

1 In the **PB25TryA_xx** file, click PAGE DESIGN > Background 🖺.

2 Hover the mouse pointer over several of the background options on the gallery to see how they look on page 1

3 Click the 10% tint of Accent 2 option.

4 Save the changes to **PB25TryA_xx**, and leave it open to use in the next Try It.

Viewing the Graphics Manager

■ You can see information about pictures in a publication by viewing the Graphics Manager.

■ Select the Graphics Manager check box in the Show group on the VIEW tab to open the Graphics Manager task pane.

■ The Graphics Manager task pane displays a list of the publication's pictures. Click on a picture name to select the picture in the publication and display a drop-down arrow that gives you the following options:

  • Go to this Picture: Takes you to the picture in the publication and selects the picture for editing.

- Save as Linked picture: As you learned in Lesson 24, pictures that you insert in a publication are embedded in the publication. This means they are part of the file. Use the Save as Linked picture command to save the picture as a file that is linked to the publication rather than being a part of the file.
- Replace this Picture: This option is the same as using the Change Picture command to replace the current picture with another from the Insert Pictures dialog box.

- Details: This command opens a dialog box where you can see a preview and information about the picture, such as what type of file it is, what page it is on, the scaling percentage, and the resolution.
- You can change the display of the Graphics Manager task pane to show thumbnails and choose how the pictures are sorted for display.

Try It!   **Viewing the Graphics Manager**

❶ In the **PB25TryA_xx** file, on the VIEW tab, click the Graphics Manager check box.

❷ Click the **PB25Try_blossoms.jpg** picture name in the Graphics Manager task pane.

❸ Click the drop-down arrow and click Save as Linked picture. In the Save As dialog box, navigate to the location where your teacher instructs you to store the files for this lesson. Click the Save as type drop-down arrow and click JPEG File Interchange Format. Click Save.

❹ Click on the PB25Try_image1.jpg file name in the Graphics Manager to display that picture on page 2, and then click the drop-down arrow and click Details.

❺ Review the information about the picture, and then click Close. Click VIEW > Graphics Manager to close the Graphics Manager task pane.

❻ Save the changes to **PB25TryA_xx**, and leave it open to use in the next Try It.

Compressing Pictures

- Publications that have a number of pictures and illustrations can have large file sizes. If you intend to send a publication by e-mail or save it as a Web page, the file size can be an issue.
- You can compress pictures in a publication to reduce the file size of the publication. When you compress images, you throw away some of the picture's data to reduce its file size.
- You may not see a significant difference in the picture's appearance after compressing pictures, but there is a change in quality. If you intend to have a publication professionally printed, you should probably not compress pictures.

- Use the Compress Pictures command in the Adjust group on the PICTURE TOOLS FORMAT tab to open the Compress Pictures dialog box. Here you can see how file sizes will change if compression settings are applied.
- You can choose options for the compression and a target output that will affect how much compression will be applied. You can also choose to apply compression to the currently selected picture or all pictures in the publication.

Try It!   Compressing Pictures

1 In the **PB25TryA_xx** file, click the picture on page 1 to select it.

2 Click PICTURE TOOLS FORMAT > Compress Pictures ⬚.

3 Click the Desktop Printing option in the Target Output area, and then click Compress. Click Yes to confirm.

4 Save the changes to **PB25TryA_xx**, and leave it open to use in the next Try It.

Saving a Publication As a PDF File

■ You can save a publication as a **PDF** file, an electronic format that makes it easy to send a publication via e-mail. Saving to PDF offers the following advantages:

- A viewer does not have to have Publisher to view the publication; PDFs can be read using Adobe Acrobat or Adobe Reader, which can be downloaded free from Adobe.

- A PDF file shows the publication just as it would look if printed, so the viewer sees all your fonts, colors, and pictures just as you formatted them in Publisher.

- Recipients cannot change the file, but they can comment on it (if they have an appropriate PDF reader) to give you feedback.

■ PDF files are not only useful for online distribution but also for printed output. Many commercial printers prefer to print directly from a PDF file. You will learn more about how to prepare a publication for printing using PDF format in Chapter 5.

■ Use the Create PDF/XPS Document option on the Export tab of Backstage view to create a PDF file from the publication.

Try It!   Saving a Publication As a PDF File

1 In the **PB25TryA_xx** file, click FILE > Export.

2 Click Create PDF/XPS Document, and then click Create PDF/XPS 📄.

3 In the Publish as PDF or XPS dialog box, navigate to the location where your teacher instructs you to store the files for this lesson. Click Publish.

4 Change the file name to **PB25TryB_xx**.

5 If you have a PDF reader such as Adobe Acrobat or Adobe Reader, start the application, navigate to the location where you stored the PDF file, and open it.

6 Navigate through the pages of the PDF, and then close the PDF reader.

7 In Publisher, close the publication, saving changes, and exit Publisher.

Lesson 25—Practice

You continue to work on the Parker Conservatory butterfly brochure, which has undergone some changes from the last version you worked on. In this exercise, you insert and crop photos, wrap text around pictures, and add a page background.

DIRECTIONS

1. Start Publisher, if necessary, and open **PB25Practice** from the data files for this lesson.

2. Save the publication as **PB25Practice_xx** in the location where your teacher instructs you to store the files for this lesson.

3. Click page **2** in the Page Navigation pane.

4. Click **INSERT** > **Pictures** . In the Insert Picture dialog box, navigate to the data files for this lesson, click **PB25Practice_image1.jpg**, and click **Insert**.

5. Modify the first picture as follows:

   a. Click **PICTURE TOOLS FORMAT** > **Crop** . Drag the cropping handles to fill the frame with the orange butterfly, as shown in Figure 25-5 on the next page. Click off the page to complete the crop.

   b. With the picture still selected, click the **Object Position** icon to display the Measurement toolbar. Set the X value to **0.5"**, the Y value to **4.4"**, the Width to **2.6"**, and the Height to **1.7"**.

6. With the picture still selected, click **PICTURE TOOLS FORMAT** > **Wrap Text** > **Top and Bottom**.

7. Click **INSERT** > **Pictures** . In the Insert Picture dialog box, navigate to the data files for this lesson, click **PB25Practice_image2.jpg**, and click **Insert**.

8. Modify the second picture as follows:

   a. Click **PICTURE TOOLS FORMAT** > **Crop** . Drag the cropping handles to crop according to the rule of thirds, placing the orange butterfly toward the lower-right of the picture, as shown in Figure 25-5 on the next page. Click off the page to complete the crop.

   b. With the picture still selected, click **PICTURE TOOLS FORMAT** > **Shape Width** and type **4.7**. (The picture should be about 3.65 inches high.) Then position the picture in the upper-right corner of the page, at the intersection of the top and right margin guides.

9. With the second picture still selected, click **PICTURE TOOLS FORMAT** > **Wrap Text** > **More Layout Options**.

10. Click the **Automatic** check box to remove the check mark, and then click the **Left** up arrow twice and the **Bottom** up arrow once. Click **OK**.

11. Click **PAGE DESIGN** > **Background** > **More Backgrounds**. Create a gradient background as follows:

    a. Click **Gradient fill** in the Format Background dialog box.

    b. Click the **Preset gradients** button and click **Top Spotlight - Accent 4**.

    c. Click the **Direction** button and select **Linear Diagonal - Top Left to Bottom Right**.

    d. Click **OK**.

12. **With your teacher's permission**, print page 2 of the publication. It should look similar to Figure 25-5 on the next page.

13. Close the publication, saving changes, and exit Publisher.

Figure 25-5

Butterflies Galore!

Come Fly with Us!

Don't miss the most exciting Butterfly Show in Parker Conservatory's long history. This year, we've rounded up butterflies from all over the world to entertain you during our Spring Show. You'll see butterflies from Asia, Africa, South America, and other exotic locations. Butterflies are incubated here in the Butterfly Nursery at Parker Conservatory (you can watch this fascinating process) and then released into the Special Events area of the Conservatory.

We have made a special effort to find the most colorful species available to give you the most bang for your buck. You'll see bright orange, sulfur yellow, glossy black, luminescent blue, and even green butterflies that you have to look carefully to see among the foliage. Stripes, spots, borders, and splashes of color add to the display.

Photo Contest

Every year, we welcome photographers who want to add to their photo collections images of butterflies they would not ordinarily see around the neighborhood. If you are a keen photographer, join us on Sunday mornings at the Conservatory for special Shutterbug Hours. You're welcome to bring tripods and any other photographic gear you need to capture your images. We promise no one will frown at you while you take all the time you need to set up that once-in-a-lifetime shot. Complementary

coffee will keep you focused!

All photographers, amateur and professional alike, are welcome to enter our Butterfly Photo Contest. Submit your three best shots at any time during the show. When the show is over, our professional photographer judges will review the entries and select the following winners:

- Best Professional Entry
- Best Amateur Entry
- Best Youth Entry (ages 11 to 18)
- Best Child Entry (ages 6 through 10)

All photographs submitted will be returned

Free-range butterflies allow you to get up close for an unimpeded view of these special creatures. If you can bear to sit still while the butterflies flitter around you, you will find that they often land on you to take a break from their journeys from flower to flower.

Lesson 25—Apply

In this exercise, you complete the butterfly brochure. You add another picture and adjust text wrapping around it, link one of the pictures to the brochure, compress pictures, and save the final publication as a PDF.

DIRECTIONS

1. Start Publisher, if necessary, and open **PB25Apply** from the data files for this lesson.

2. Save the publication as **PB25ApplyA_xx** in the location where your teacher instructs you to store the files for this lesson.

3. On page 1, insert the **PB25Apply_image.jpg** file from the data files for this lesson.

4. Resize the picture using the **PICTURE TOOLS FORMAT** > **Shape Width** box to 4 inches wide. Position the image to center it over the space between the left and center columns. (See Figure 25-6 on the next page.)

5. Click **PICTURE TOOLS FORMAT** > **Recolor** > **Set Transparent Color** and click on the white background around the butterfly to remove it.

6. Apply **Tight** text wrapping and then choose to edit the wrap points. Add or remove wrap points and adjust existing wrap points as necessary to create a tight boundary around the butterfly.

7. Adjust the position of the butterfly by nudging it left, right, up, or down with the arrow keys to achieve an attractive wrap. Try to prevent the headings from wrapping.

8. Display the Graphics Manager task pane. Select the flower image on the first page and link it to the publication, saving it with the name **PB25Apply_image2** in the location where your teacher instructs you to store the files for this lesson. Save the file as a JPEG.

9. Compress all pictures in the brochure, leaving the default settings in the Compress Pictures dialog box unchanged.

10. **With your teacher's permission**, print page 1 of the document. Your page should look similar to Figure 25-6.

11. Save the publication as a PDF file with the name **PB25ApplyB_xx**, and then view the PDF if you have a PDF reader. Close the PDF reader.

12. Close the publication, saving changes, and exit Publisher.

Figure 25-6

if you provide a stamped, self-addressed mailer. Parker Conservatory will pay standard rates for winning photographs that can be used for advertising the show next year.

About Parker Conservatory

Parker Conservatory was founded in 1893 by the Parks and Recreation committee of Lexington as an educational facility intended to teach citizens of the town more about horticulture not only of the region but of the world. The structure of the Conservatory, of panels of glass between iron struts, was designed to resemble the Crystal Palace in London. No other structure in the Midwest had every been planned to use so much glass, and the Conservatory was an instant success not only in the city but as a destination attraction throughout the state as well as neighboring states.

From the first, the Conservatory took seriously the mission its founders had envisioned and positioned itself not only as a pleasant environment of tropical foliage, a picturesque stream with a waterfall, and fragrant flowers, but as an educational facility. Ornate signs identified nonnative species and imparted in-

formation on origin and provenance. Lush exterior landscaping provided citizens with ideas for how they could improve their own landscaping with ornamental shrubs, flowers, and trees. The Conservatory also functioned as a repository for seeds, corms, and bulbs of many rare plants, helping to prevent the extinction of plant life that is now being lost every day in tropical rain forest regions.

Visit Us

Parker Conservatory is open seven days a week, every day except Thanksgiving Day, Christmas Day, and New Year's Day. Hours are 10:00 a.m. to 6:00 p.m. Admission is free; a donation is suggested for the continued maintenance of this historic structure. You will find a Gift Shoppe and a Tea Room on the premises for refreshment and shopping.

PARKER

CONSERVATORY

1670 Man O' War Boulevard
Lexington, KY 40513
859.555.9006
www.parkerconservatory.org

Lesson 26

Working with Lines and Shapes

➤ **What You Will Learn**

Drawing Simple Lines and Shapes
Adjusting Complex Shapes
Formatting Lines and Shapes
Grouping and Ungrouping Objects

WORDS TO KNOW

Adjustment handle
The small yellow diamond used to reshape an AutoShape.

AutoShapes
Ready-made shapes that Publisher provides, including lines, basic shapes, flowchart symbols, and callouts.

Group
To link multiple objects together so that they can be selected, moved, and/ or resized as a single entity.

3-D
An object with 3-D effects applied appears to have depth as well as height and width.

Ungroup
To reverse a group operation, so that objects that were formerly separate are once again separate.

Software Skills   You aren't limited to ready-to-use artwork in Publisher; you can also draw your own simple illustrations using Publisher's shape tools. You can easily enliven shapes by formatting with borders, fills, and effects such as Shadow and 3-D. Use the Group command to combine your shapes into a single object.

What You Can Do

Drawing Simple Lines and Shapes

■ The Shapes command in the Illustrations group on the INSERT tab displays a gallery of many shapes that you can easily insert in a publication. The gallery is separated into categories such as Lines, Basic Shapes, and Block Arrows. These shapes are sometimes referred to as **AutoShapes**.

■ All of these shapes are inserted in more or less the same way: Click the desired shape, then drag the crosshair pointer on the page to create a shape of the desired size.

■ Drawn lines can be useful for separating one section of a publication from another, for drawing arrow pointers to call attention to an object, or for connecting objects when creating items such as flow charts.

■ Use the Line shape for straight lines. The Arrow line shape adds an arrowhead at the end of the line. Use the connector lines to create connections between shapes.

■ You can also insert smooth curves, as well as a freeform Scribble line that you draw just as if you were drawing with a pencil.

■ To make a straight or arrow line perfectly vertical, horizontal, or an angle of a multiple of 15 degrees (15, 30, 45, and so on), hold down SHIFT as you draw.

- Simple shapes such as ovals and rectangles can be used to build simple drawings or call attention to other objects on the page.

- You can create not only rectangles with square corners but rectangles with rounded corners.

- To draw a perfect circle or square using the Oval or Rectangle shape, hold down [SHIFT] as you drag. To make a perfect 1 inch by 1 inch square or circle, click on the page rather than dragging.

- You can adjust the position of any shape by dragging it to the desired location, or position it more precisely using the Measurement toolbar.

- Adjust the size of a shape using the Shape Height and Shape Width options on the DRAWING TOOLS FORMAT tab. Unlike when resizing pictures, aspect ratio is not locked for drawing shapes, so you can adjust height or width without automatically adjusting the other dimension.

- You can also adjust shape size by dragging corner or side selection handles.

- If you drag a line from one shape to another, you will see small blue handles to which you can snap the line. This makes it easy to connect objects when creating an illustration.

Try It! Drawing Simple Lines and Shapes

1. Start Publisher and select the Blank 8.5 × 11" template.

2. Save the publication as **PB26Try_xx** in the location where your teacher instructs you to store the files for this lesson.

3. Click INSERT > Shapes > Rounded Rectangle. Drag to create a rectangle about 3.5 inches high by 4 inches wide.

4. Click INSERT > Shapes > Rectangle. Hold down [SHIFT] and drag to create a square about 2 inches by 2 inches.

5. Click INSERT > Shapes > Oval and click on the page to insert a 1 inch circle. Click DRAWING TOOLS FORMAT > Shape Height and click the up arrow to change the height to 1.5 inches. Note that the width measurement does not change.

6. Click on the oval's right side selection handle and drag to the right. Watch the Object Size numbers in the status bar and release the mouse button when the numbers read 1.50 × 1.50 in.

7. Click INSERT > Shapes > Line. Hold down [SHIFT] and drag a line straight down, about 3 inches high.

8. Click INSERT > Shapes > Arrow. Hold down [SHIFT] and drag a line from left to right about 3 inches wide.

9. Drag the arrow line to cross over the straight line.

10. Drag the shapes to create the arrangement shown in the illustration.

11. Save the changes to **PB26Try_xx**, and leave it open to use in the next Try It.

Basic shapes

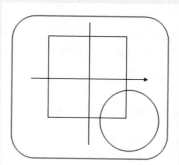

Adjusting Complex Shapes

- Some shapes on the Shapes gallery are more complex than others; these shapes could not be created with basic shapes without combining multiple objects.

- You draw an object using one of these more complex shapes in the same way you draw a basic shape. You often have the option of using one or more **adjustment handles** to reshape a part of the object.

- In Figure 26-1, for example, you can drag the yellow diamond adjustment handle to reshape the cross. Dotted lines show the adjustment you are making. Release the mouse button when the adjustment is to your liking.

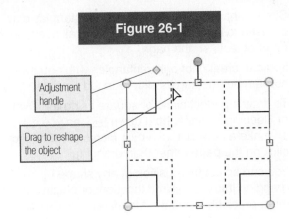

Figure 26-1

Adjustment handle

Drag to reshape the object

Try It!   Adjusting Complex Shapes

1. In the **PB26Try_xx** file, click INSERT > Shapes ✏ > Left Arrow from the Block Arrows category.

2. Drag to create an arrow about 2 inches high by 2.5 inches wide.

3. Click on the adjustment handle and drag to the right about half an inch to reshape the arrowhead.

4. Drag the block arrow up to the right of the other objects.

5. Save the changes to **PB26Try_xx**, and leave it open to use in the next Try It.

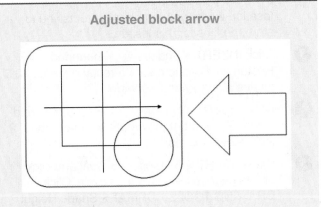

Adjusted block arrow

Formatting Lines and Shapes

- Drawn shapes have outlines just as text boxes do. You can set a shape's outline color and style in the same way as for text boxes using familiar commands on the DRAWING TOOLS FORMAT tab.

- For lines, you can apply an outline color, weight, dash option, or pattern. You can also add arrowheads or other symbols to one or both ends of a line.

- For more control over arrowheads, click the More Arrows option on the Arrows gallery to open the Format AutoShape dialog box. You can choose an arrowhead style to begin and end the line, and you can choose sizes for the beginning and ending arrowheads.

- By default, a shape is filled with the Accent 1 scheme color. Use the Shape Fill command to select a different fill for a shape. You can select one of the scheme colors, a standard color, a color from the Colors dialog box, or a color you sample from anywhere on the screen.

- For shapes, you also have the option of adding a picture, gradient, texture, or pattern as a fill.

- You can also right-click a shape and choose Format AutoShape to open the Format AutoShape dialog box, where you can choose fill and line options for the currently selected shape.

  ✓ *Regardless of the type of object (line, shape, or AutoShape), the dialog box is titled Format AutoShape.*

- You can add shadow, reflection, glow, soft edges, bevel, or **3-D** rotation effects to any shape, including lines, using the Shape Effects command on the DRAWING TOOLS FORMAT tab.

- As you learned in Chapter 3, effect galleries have an Options command, such as 3-D Rotation Options, that opens the Format Shape dialog box, where you can customize and fine-tune the effect.

- The DRAWING TOOLS FORMAT tab offers the Shape Styles gallery for applying combinations of outlines, fills, and shadows.

- Another option for formatting shapes is to add text. Right-click the shape, click Add Text, and type the text at the insertion point in the shape. You can format text using familiar font and alignment commands.

Try It!　Formatting Lines and Shapes

1 In the **PB26Try_xx** file, click the vertical line to select it.

2 Click DRAWING TOOLS FORMAT > Shape Outline ☑ > Weight > 4½ pt. Then click Shape Outline ☑ > Dashes > Dash Dot.

3 Click the horizontal arrow line, and then click DRAWING TOOLS FORMAT > Shape Outline ☑ > Dark Red from the Standard Colors. Click Shape Outline ☑ > Weight > 3 pt.

4 Click the rounded rectangle. Click DRAWING TOOLS FORMAT > Shape Fill ☑ > Picture. Navigate to the data files for this lesson, click **PB26Try_image.gif**, and click Insert. Then right-click the rounded rectangle and click Format AutoShape. Drag the Transparency slider to 20%, and then in the Line area, click the Color drop-down arrow and click No Outline. Click OK.

5 With the rounded rectangle still selected, click DRAWING TOOLS FORMAT > Shape Effects ☑ > Shadow, and click Perspective Diagonal Upper Left in the Perspective category.

6 Click the square and then click DRAWING TOOLS FORMAT > Shape Styles More button ☑. Click the Diagonal Gradient – Accent 1 style.

7 Click the circle, and then click DRAWING TOOLS FORMAT > Shape Fill ☑ > Pattern. Click the Foreground drop-down arrow and click Followed Hyperlink (Plum). Then click the Light vertical pattern that is first on the left in the fourth row of patterns. Click OK.

8 Click the block arrow, and then click DRAWING TOOLS FORMAT > Shape Fill ☑ > Light Green from the Standard Colors palette. Click Shape Outline ☑ > No Outline.

9 With the arrow still selected, click DRAWING TOOLS FORMAT > Shape Effects ☑ > 3-D Rotation > 3-D Rotation Options.

10 In the Format Shape dialog box, click Presets under 3-D ROTATION and click Off Axis 2 Left. Click the Y rotation Down button ☑ three times to change the Y rotation to 11 degrees. Then click the 3-D FORMAT heading to expand options, click in the Size box for the Depth setting, and type **25 pt**. Click OK.

11 Right-click the arrow and click Add Text. Click TEXT BOX TOOLS FORMAT > Align Center ☰. Type **LOOK!**. Select the text, click HOME > Font Size ☑ > 36, and then click HOME > Bold **B** .

12 With the shape still selected, click HOME > Font Color **A** ▾ > Accent 5 (White).

13 Save the changes to **PB26Try_xx**, and leave it open to use in the next Try It.

Formatted shapes

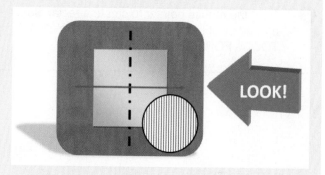

Grouping and Ungrouping Objects

- If you draw an illustration that uses multiple shapes and lines, you may wish to **group** them so you can work with the picture as a single object. This makes it easier to move or resize the illustration.

- You can group any objects, not just drawn lines and shapes. For example, you might group a drawn shape with a piece of clip art or with a text box.

- You use the Group command in the Arrange group on the DRAWING TOOLS FORMAT tab to group objects. Before you click this command, you must select all objects you want to group.

- Select multiple objects by clicking the first, holding down SHIFT, and then clicking additional objects until all are selected. You can also select multiple objects by using the mouse pointer to draw a rectangle around all the objects you want to select.

  ✓ *Remove an object from the selected group by clicking it again while the other objects are selected.*

- After you click the Group command, a selection border surrounds the entire group, with one set of selection handles rather than the selection handles for each object.

- As you learned earlier in the course, you can select any one of the objects in a group to work with by clicking it to display its gray selection handles, each showing an x inside.

- If you need to make more sweeping changes to a grouped illustration, you can **ungroup** it using the Ungroup command in the Arrange group on the DRAWING TOOLS FORMAT tab.

- After you ungroup, all objects display their own selection handles again. Click away from the illustration to deselect all objects before you try to select one object to work with.

Try It!   **Grouping and Ungrouping Objects**

① In the **PB26Try_xx** file, drag the mouse pointer to create a rectangle around all objects on the page. All objects are selected.

② Hold down SHIFT and click the block arrow to remove it from the selection. Then click it again to add it back to the group.

③ Click DRAWING TOOLS FORMAT > Group ⬚.

④ Drag the group to the center of the page.

⑤ Click DRAWING TOOLS FORMAT > Ungroup ⬚. Drag the circle to center it over the square and then click DRAWING TOOLS FORMAT > Shape Fill ◇ > Orange from the Standard Colors palette.

⑥ Drag the mouse pointer to create a rectangle around all objects, and then click DRAWING TOOLS FORMAT > Group ⬚.

⑦ Save changes, close the publication, and exit Publisher.

Grouped shapes

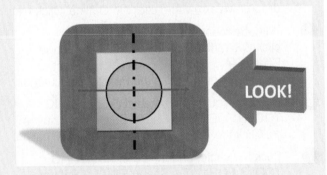

Lesson 26—Practice

Your new client, We Love Toys, has asked you to create a postcard with a map to their new location and a simple illustration to pique interest in the company's old-fashioned toys and games. In this exercise, you draw and format shapes to create the map on the postcard.

DIRECTIONS

1. Start Publisher, if necessary, and click **Postcards** in the BUILT-IN templates. Scroll down to the Blank Sizes category and click **Index Card 6 × 4"**. Select the **Tropics** color scheme and then click **CREATE** to create the publication.

2. Save the publication as **PB26Practice_xx** in the location where your teacher instructs you to store the files for this lesson.

3. Click **PAGE DESIGN** > **Margins** [A] > **Narrow**.

4. Click **INSERT** > **Shapes** > **Rounded Rectangle**.

5. Draw a rectangle **1.2 inches** high by **2.7 inches** wide.

6. Click **DRAWING TOOLS FORMAT** > **Shape Styles More** button [▼], and click **Compound Outline – Accent 1**.

7. Right-click the shape, click **Add Text**, and type **Mailing Label Here**. Then click **TEXT BOX TOOLS FORMAT** > **Align Center** [≡].

8. Drag the shape near the lower-right corner, as shown in Figure 26-2 on the next page.

9. Create the map shown in Figure 26-2 as follows:

   a. Click **INSERT** > **Shapes** > **Oval**, hold down [SHIFT], and drag a circle **0.5 inches** by **0.5 inches**. Click **DRAWING TOOLS FORMAT** > **Shape Fill** > **No Fill**.

   b. Click **INSERT** > **Shapes** > **Line**, hold down [SHIFT] and drag a horizontal line from the right side of the circle about **1 inch** to the right. (The pointer will change shape over the small blue handle at the right side of the circle to let you know you are aligning the line precisely with the circle.)

   c. Click **INSERT** > **Shapes** > **Line**, hold down [SHIFT] and drag a vertical line from the top of the circle about **1 inch** upward.

   d. Click the vertical line, hold down [SHIFT], click the circle, and then click the horizontal line. Click **DRAWING TOOLS FORMAT** > **Group** [⊡], and then click **DRAWING TOOLS FORMAT** > **Shape Outline** [✎] > **Weight** > **2¼ pt**.

   e. Click **INSERT** > **Shapes** > **Rectangle**, and draw a rectangle **0.3 inch** high by **0.5 inch** wide. Click **DRAWING TOOLS FORMAT** > **Shape Fill** [♦] > **Accent 2 (Gold)**. Click **Shape Outline** [✎] > **No Outline**.

   f. With the rectangle still selected, click **Shape Effects** [♦] > **3-D Rotation** > **3-D Rotation Options**. Click the **Presets** button [▦ ▾] and click **Off Axis 2 Left**. Then click **3-D FORMAT**, change Depth to **40 pt**, click **Lighting**, and select **Bright Left**. Click **OK**.

10. Add the street labels as follows:

    a. Click **HOME** > **Draw Text Box** [A▦] and draw a small text box below the horizontal line. Type **Route 32**; adjust the size of the text box if necessary to fit the text, and then move the text box close to the line.

    b. Draw a vertical text box next to the vertical line. Click **TEXT BOX TOOLS FORMAT** > **Text Direction** [▦] and then type **Newtown Road**. Move the text box close to the vertical line.

    c. Draw a text box below the circle and type **Newtown Circle**. Click **HOME** > **Center** [≡].

    d. Select the text in each text box, click **HOME** > **Font Color** [A ▾] > **Accent 3 (Red)**, and then click **HOME** > **Bold** [B].

    e. Click the first label, hold down [SHIFT], and then click the remaining two labels. Click **DRAWING TOOLS FORMAT** > **Group** [⊡].

11. Add the pointers as follows:

    a. Click **INSERT** > **Shapes** > **Arrow**. Draw a line from the top of the *Newtown Circle* text box to the center of the circle. With the arrow still selected, click **DRAWING TOOLS FORMAT** > **Shape Outline** [✎] > **Accent 3 (Red)**. Then click **Shape Outline** [✎] > **Weight** > **1½ pt**.

    b. Click **INSERT** > **Shapes** > **Down Arrow Callout** from the Block Arrows category. Draw the shape **0.8 inches** high by **1.2 inches** wide. Use the adjustment handles to adjust the arrow and the rectangular shape as shown in Figure 26-2.

c. Right-click the shape and click **Add Text**, and then type the following text in the shape. (You can find the heart in the Symbols or Zapf Dingbats font.) Adjust size and paragraph spacing to fit the text, and then select both paragraphs and click **HOME** > **Center** ≡.

We ♥ Toys

576 Newtown Rd

d. Click **DRAWING TOOLS FORMAT** > **Shape Styles More** button ⊡ > **Linear Up Gradient – Accent 1**.

e. Position the label so the arrow points down at the 3-D rectangle, as shown in Figure 26-2.

12. Click the label you just completed, hold down SHIFT, and click the arrow. Click **DRAWING TOOLS FORMAT** > **Group** ⊡. Then, with the group still selected, hold down SHIFT, click on one of the labels to select that group, and then click on one of the lines to select that group. Click **DRAWING TOOLS FORMAT** > **Group** ⊡ to enclose all groups in one group. Move the group into the upper-left corner of the page. Your page should look similar to Figure 26-2.

13. Close the publication, saving changes, and exit Publisher.

Figure 26-2

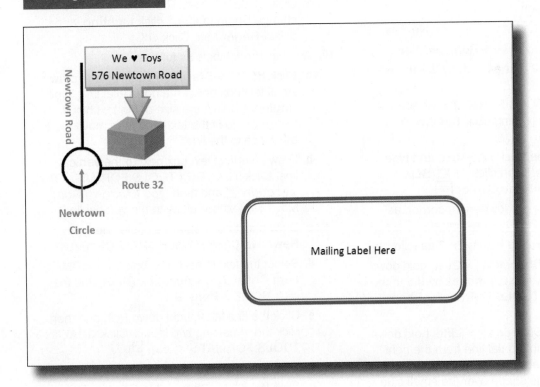

Lesson 26—Apply

In this exercise, you create the illustration for the flip side of the postcard for We Love Toys.

DIRECTIONS

1. Start Publisher, if necessary, and open **PB26Apply** from the data files for this lesson.

2. Save the publication as **PB26Apply_xx** in the location where your teacher instructs you to store the files for this lesson.

3. Create an alphabet block for page 2 of the postcard as follows:

   a. Using the **Rectangle** shape, click on the page to insert a **1 inch** square.

   b. Type the letter **A** in the square; apply the **Castellar** font at a font size of **48 point**. (Use another font if you do not have Castellar.) Use **Align Center** to align the letter.

   c. Fill the square with a bright color of your choice and remove the outline.

   d. Apply the 3-D effect **Off Axis 1 Right** to the block. Using the Format Shape dialog box's 3-D FORMAT options, change the Depth to **75 pt**, and change the Lighting to **Bright Diagonal Bottom Right**.

   e. Click the **Y rotation Up** button ⬆ three times to adjust the rotation of the object.

4. Create two more blocks:

   a. Copy the *A* block. Paste the copy, select the letter *A*, and type **B**.

   b. Change the fill color and adjust rotation options to rotate the block in a different direction. Adjust lighting as desired and experiment with other 3-D settings such as applying a contour color or changing material.

   c. Paste another copy. Select the letter *A* and type **C**.

   d. Change the fill color and adjust the rotation as desired.

5. Arrange the blocks as desired in the top part of the card.

6. Draw a text box about **0.9 inch** high by **1.2 inches** wide and type **We**. Change the font size to **48 point** and apply **Bold**. Draw another text box about **0.9 inch** high by **1.4 inches** wide. Type **Toys**, and format the text the same way as for *We*.

7. Use the **Heart** shape to draw a heart about **0.8 inch** high by **1 inch** wide. Fill the heart with the **Center Gradient – Accent 3** shape style.

8. Position the two text boxes and the heart as shown in Figure 26-3 on the next page. Select all three objects and group them.

   ✓ *Use Publisher's layout guides to help you align the objects.*

9. Draw a horizontal line beneath the group, apply **Accent 3 (Red)** shape outline color, and change the weight to **3 pt**. Click **More Arrows** at the bottom of the Shape Outline > Arrows gallery, and then choose arrow styles and sizes for both ends of the line.

10. Draw a text box below the line and type **Old-Fashioned Toys and Games** in **20 point bold** font.

11. Adjust the positions of the group, the arrow line, and the text box, and then group all objects. Center the group horizontally, with the bottom border of the group on the bottom margin guide.

12. **With your teacher's permission**, print the postcard. (Choose to print one page per sheet on letter-size paper.) Your page 2 should look similar to Figure 26-3 on the next page.

13. Close the publication, saving changes, and exit Publisher.

Figure 26-3

Lesson 27

Arranging Objects

> What You Will Learn

Aligning Objects
Distributing Objects
Rotating and Flipping Objects
Changing Object Stacking

Software Skills   You can fine-tune the position and appearance of objects on a page by aligning, distributing, flipping, and rotating them. Adjust object stacking to control the way objects stack on top of each other on the page.

What You Can Do

Aligning Objects

- For the most professional presentation, you will usually want multiple objects on a page to align in some way. For example, if you have three pictures side by side, aligning them by their tops will give an orderly look to the page. Or, if you have inserted a text box below a picture, you might want the two objects to align at the left, center, or right to provide an appearance of unity between the objects.

- Publisher has a number of alignment options you can employ to line up multiple objects. The Align command in the Arrange group on the DRAWING TOOLS FORMAT tab displays a menu of six alignment options you can use to align objects at the left, center, right, top, middle, or bottom.

  ✓ *The Align command is also available on the PICTURE TOOLS FORMAT tab.*

- Apply an alignment by first selecting the objects you want to align. Then select the desired alignment command from the Align menu.

- The Relative to Margin Guides option on the Align menu is an on/off toggle. It's off by default. When you turn it on, all alignment commands refer to positioning in relation to the margin guides rather than in relation to the other selected objects.

- For example, when Relative to Margin Guides is off, and you choose Align Left for two objects, Publisher determines the leftmost one and then moves the others to match it. When Relative to Margin Guides is on, Publisher moves both items to align with the left margin guide, regardless of their former positions.

- You may want to turn Relative to Margin Guides on to quickly snap a picture to a position on the page. With the command active, you can click Align Center to move a selected object to the horizontal center of the page, for example.

WORDS TO KNOW

Distribute
Space objects evenly, either vertically or horizontally.

Flip
To reverse the orientation of an object from left to right or top to bottom.

Layer
A single level in the stacking order.

Rotate
To revolve an object around a fixed point, usually the center of the object.

■ Publisher gives you another alignment option in the purple object alignment guides that display as you drag objects near other objects. These guides display when the object you are dragging aligns in some way with another object. The purple guides will show you when two or more objects align at the top, middle, bottom, left, center, or right.

■ Using these alignment guides can be a more efficient process than using the Align menu commands, because you do not have to select all objects, just drag the object you want to align.

Try It!   Aligning Objects

1 Start Publisher and click the Blank 8.5 × 11" template to open a new, blank page.

2 Save the publication as **PB27Try_xx** in the location where your teacher instructs you to store the files for this lesson.

3 Click INSERT > Shapes ⬦ > Rectangle and click on the page to insert a 1 inch square. Click DRAWING TOOLS FORMAT > Shape Fill ⬧ > Orange from the Standard Colors palette.

4 Click INSERT > Shapes ⬦ > Oval, hold down [SHIFT], and draw a circle 1.3 inches high and wide to the right of the square. Click DRAWING TOOLS FORMAT > Shape Fill ⬧ > Dark Red from the Standard Colors palette.

5 Click INSERT > Shapes ⬦ > Triangle and click on the page to insert the triangle. Click DRAWING TOOLS FORMAT > Shape Height ⬦, and type **1.2**. Position the triangle to the right of the circle. Click DRAWING TOOLS FORMAT > Shape Fill ⬧ > Blue from the Standard Colors palette.

6 Drag the circle toward the top of the square until you see the purple alignment guide that indicates the tops of the two objects are aligned.

7 Drag the triangle near the circle until you see the purple alignment guide that indicates the bottoms of the two objects are aligned.

8 Click the square, hold down [SHIFT], click the circle, and then click the triangle.

9 Click DRAWING TOOLS FORMAT > Align ⬦ > Align Middle. The objects adjust position to align horizontally at the middle. Click away from the objects to deselect them.

10 Click the circle, hold down [SHIFT], and click the triangle. Then click DRAWING TOOLS FORMAT > Align ⬦ > Align Center. The triangle is centered over the circle.

11 Click on the page to deselect both objects, and then drag the triangle below the square until you see the alignment guide that indicates the two objects align at the left.

12 Save the changes to **PB27Try_xx**, and leave it open to use in the next Try It.

Two objects center aligned

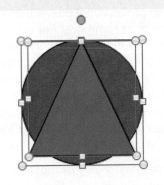

Distributing Objects

- For the most professional appearance when you have multiple objects aligned on a page, you must also consider the gaps between objects. In some situations, you will want multiple items to be spaced evenly to give a neat, organized appearance.

- You can use the Distribute options on the Align menu to **distribute** objects either vertically or horizontally so that there is the same amount of blank space between each object and the others.

- The Distribute options are particularly useful when the objects you are working with are different sizes or shapes. It can be hard to "eyeball" the spaces between objects when they are different shapes.

Try It!   **Distributing Objects**

1 In the **PB27Try_xx** file, move the triangle to the right of the circle and adjust its position until it aligns at the middle with the other two objects. Do not make any attempt to adjust the space between objects. Your arrangement might look similar to the first image in the illustration.

2 Click the square, hold down [SHIFT], click the circle, and then click the triangle.

3 Click DRAWING TOOLS FORMAT > Align [icon] > Distribute Horizontally. The space between the three objects is now the same, as shown in the second image.

✓ *The spaces between objects may not appear to be the same because of the shapes of the circle and triangle. The distribution of space between these two objects is from the right side of the circle and the left point of the triangle base.*

4 Save the changes to **PB27Try_xx**, and leave it open to use in the next Try It.

Space has been distributed horizontally

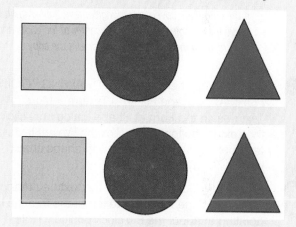

Rotating and Flipping Objects

- When you **rotate** an object, you revolve it around a fixed point, usually the center of the object.

- Most Publisher objects display a white circle rotate handle at the top center of the object that you can drag to rotate the object by any amount.

  ✓ *If you hold down [CTRL] while you drag, the object rotates on its bottom center selection handle rather than the center of the object.*

- The Rotate menu in the Arrange group on the DRAWING TOOLS FORMAT tab gives you additional rotation options.

  ✓ *This command is also available on the PICTURE TOOLS FORMAT tab.*

- Use the Rotate Right 90° or Rotate Left 90° options to rotate an object to the left or right. Or click More Rotation Options to open a Format box where you can specify an exact degree of rotation.

- If the shape you want to rotate is filled with a picture, gradient, or texture, you can choose to have the fill rotate along with the shape. You do not have this option for pattern fills. You can select this rotation option only in a dialog box, not on the Shape Fill menus.

- Note that rotation is not limited to drawing shapes. You can rotate pictures as well as text boxes. A text box rotated to the left or right 90 degrees gives you another option for changing text direction.

- Sometimes an object is not facing the way you want it to. You can use the Flip options on the Rotate menu to change the orientation of an object. You can **flip** an object along its vertical or horizontal axis.

Try It!   Rotating and Flipping Objects

1 In the **PB27Try_xx** file, click INSERT > Pictures, and then navigate to the data files for this lesson.

2 Click **PB27Try_image.jpg** and then click Insert. Click PICTURE TOOLS FORMAT > Shape Height and type **3**.

3 Click PICTURE TOOLS FORMAT > Align > Relative to Margin Guides. Then click Align > Align Center to move the picture to the center of the page.

4 Click the triangle, click HOME > Copy, and then click HOME > Paste.

✓ *If the cat image covers the triangle, move the cat image, move the triangle away from the center of the page, and then re-align the cat image. Then create the copy of the triangle.*

5 With the copy selected, click DRAWING TOOLS FORMAT > Shape Fill > Texture > More Textures. In the Format Shape dialog box, click the Texture button, click the Walnut texture, and then click in the Rotate with shape check box. Click OK.

6 Click on the rotate handle of the textured triangle and drag to the left until the top of the triangle is pointing at about the 8 o'clock position. Note that the wood texture fill rotates along with the shape.

7 To check the rotation, click DRAWING TOOLS FORMAT > Rotate > More Rotation Options. In the Rotation box, type **219**. Position the tip of the rotated triangle over the upper-right corner of the picture.

8 Click the cat picture, and then click PICTURE TOOLS FORMAT > Rotate > Flip Horizontal.

9 Click INSERT > Draw Text Box, and draw a text box below the picture, the same width as the picture and about 0.5 inches high. Type **PERSIAN CAT**. Click TEXT BOX TOOLS FORMAT > Text Fit > Best Fit.

10 Click DRAWING TOOLS FORMAT > Shape Fill > Accent 5 (White), Darker 25%. Then click Shape Fill > Gradient > Linear Up in the Light Variations category.

11 Click DRAWING TOOLS FORMAT > Rotate > Rotate Left 90°. Notice that the gradient did not rotate with the text box.

12 Click Undo. Right-click the text box, click Format Text Box, click Fill Effects on the Colors and Lines tab, and click Rotate fill effect with shape at the bottom of the FILL settings. Click OK twice.

13 Click DRAWING TOOLS FORMAT > Rotate > Rotate Left 90°. Notice that this time, the gradient rotated with the text box. Move the text box to the left of the picture and align it at the bottom using the alignment guides.

14 Save the changes to **PB27Try_xx**, and leave it open to use in the next Try It.

Objects rotated and flipped

PERSIAN CAT

Changing Object Stacking

- Each object you create on a page occupies a single **layer**. Objects stack up in these layers, with the first object you create at the bottom of the stack and the last object at the top.

- This stacking order can sometimes make it a challenge to work with the first objects created, as later objects are on top of them. Some of the graphic shapes on Publisher templates, for example, are at the bottom of the stack of layers, with text boxes and other graphics on top of them.

- You can adjust stacking order using commands in the Arrange group.

  - The Bring Forward command offers options on a drop-down menu to bring a selected object toward the front of the stack (Bring Forward), or all the way to the front of the stack, on top of all other objects (Bring to Front).

  - The Send Backward command offers options to send a selected object toward the back of the stack (Send Backward), or all the way to the back, below all other objects (Send to Back).

- If you have a number of objects on a page, you may need to click Bring Forward or Send Backward several times to position an object where you want it with relation to other objects.

- When you right-click on an object, the Mini toolbar that displays along with the shortcut menu includes the Bring Forward and Send Backward commands to speed the process of changing stacking order.

Try It!   **Changing Object Stacking**

1 In the **PB27Try_xx** file, move the shapes (but not the picture or text box) more or less on top of each other, so that you can see a part of each shape. Your shapes should be in this order from back to front: square, circle, blue triangle, rotated textured triangle.

✓ *If any of your shapes are behind the cat image, move the cat image so you can work with them.*

2 Click the textured triangle to select it, and then click DRAWING TOOLS FORMAT > Send Backward ⬛. Note that the triangle moves back one layer in the stacking order so it is now behind the blue triangle but in front of the circle.

3 Right-click the square and click Bring Forward ⬛ on the Mini toolbar. The square is now in front of the circle.

4 Click the circle, and then click DRAWING TOOLS FORMAT > Bring Forward ⬛ drop-down arrow > Bring to Front. The circle is now in front of all stacked objects.

5 Click the blue triangle, and then click DRAWING TOOLS FORMAT > Send Backward ⬛ drop-down arrow > Send to Back. The blue triangle is now behind all stacked objects.

✓ *You may need to move objects to see that the blue triangle is at the back of the stack.*

6 Close the publication, saving changes, and exit Publisher.

Object stacking has been changed

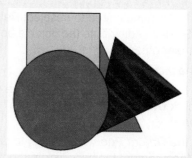

Lesson 27—Practice

The Literacy League is awarding All-Star Volunteer prizes to some of its volunteers, and they need some help with their flyer. Most of the objects you need for the flyer are present in the publication, but you need to do some reorganizing to present the material correctly. In this exercise, you concentrate on displaying all objects in the correct stacking order and aligning objects.

DIRECTIONS

1. Start Publisher, if necessary, and open **PB27Practice** from the data files for this lesson.

2. Save the publication as **PB27Practice_xx** in the location where your teacher instructs you to store the files for this lesson.

3. Click on the text box at the top of the page that is currently behind the aqua banner shape. Click **DRAWING TOOLS FORMAT > Bring Forward** . Drag the text box down until you see the purple alignment guide that indicates the text box has aligned at the middle with the aqua banner shape.

4. Click the text box just below the aqua banner, toward the right side of the page, currently behind the top gray gradient rectangle. Click **DRAWING TOOLS FORMAT > Bring Forward** .

5. Click the gray gradient shape behind the text box you just reordered and drag it to align at the top with the 1.5 inch ruler guide and at the right with the margin guide. Hold down SHIFT and click the other two gray gradient shapes. Click **DRAWING TOOLS FORMAT > Align** > **Align Right**.

6. With the objects still selected, click **DRAWING TOOLS FORMAT > Align** > **Distribute Vertically**. (You may need to deselect Relative to Margin Guides to distribute the objects below the 1.5 inch ruler guide.)

7. Adjust the pictures as follows:

    a. Click the picture nearest the top of the page and click **DRAWING TOOLS FORMAT > Bring Forward** .

    b. Click the **Object Position** icon to display the Measurement toolbar. Click in the x box and type **1.6**. Click in the y box and type **1.6**.

    c. Drag the *Richard Vargas* text box to the right to move it away from the second picture.

    d. Right-click the second picture, and click the **Bring Forward** command twice to bring the picture to the front of the stack.

    e. In the Measurement toolbar, type **1.6** in the x box and **4.55** in the y box.

    f. Drag the third picture straight across until you see the purple alignment guides to tell you the picture aligns at the left and right with the picture above. In the Measurement toolbar, type **7.5** in the y box.

8. Move the *Henry Gonzalez* text box down until the alignment guide shows that it aligns with the top of Henry's picture. Move the text box until the x box in the Measurement toolbar shows **4"**.

9. Select the picture of Richard Vargas and the *Richard Vargas* text box, and then click **DRAWING TOOLS FORMAT > Align** > **Align Top**. Deselect the objects. Then drag the text box to the left (or right) until it you see the alignment guide that indicates it is aligned at the left with the *Henry Gonzalez* text box.

10. Repeat the tasks in step 9 to align the *Cinda Jackson* text box with her picture and the text boxes above.

11. **With your teacher's permission**, print the publication. It should look similar to Figure 27-1 on the next page.

12. Close the publication, saving changes, and exit Publisher.

Figure 27-1

The Literacy League

Henry Gonzalez, Adult Education Tutor

Henry is a carpenter by trade with four years of service to the Literacy League.

"I love helping people learn to read because it opens up their minds to new and exciting ideas and possibilities."

Richard Vargas, Youth Counselor

Richard is the Pastor of Good Shepherd, with three years of service to the Literacy League.

"Children are naturally loving, gentle souls; it's up to us to help them get back to that natural state when their life situations have made them lose touch with that."

Cinda Jackson, Peer Tutor

Cinda is a student who has worked with Literacy League for two years.

"All kids deserve the chance to learn to read, even if they don't always learn it in regular school."

Lesson 27—Apply

The Literacy League flyer needs some additional work before it is complete. In this exercise, you fine-tune the publication by flipping, rotating, and reordering objects.

DIRECTIONS

1. Start Publisher, if necessary, and open **PB27Apply** from the data files for this lesson.
2. Save the publication as **PB27Apply_xx** in the location where your teacher instructs you to store the files for this lesson.
3. Select the *The Literacy League* text box and the aqua banner shape. Middle align the two objects, and then right align them.
4. Flip Cinda's picture horizontally.
5. Add a rotated text box to the publication:
   a. In the scratch area, draw a text box **0.75 inches** high by about **6 inches** wide.
   b. Type the text **All-Star Volunteers!** Change the font to **36 point**.
   c. Click **HOME** > **Character Spacing** ⟷ ▾ > **More Spacing**, and set the scaling for the text to **130%**.
   d. Apply a gradient fill that will rotate with the text box. Use the **Top Spotlight - Accent 1** preset gradient option.
   e. Rotate the text box to the left **90 degrees**, and position the text box along the left margin of the publication.
   f. Increase the height of the rotated text box to extend from the ruler guide at 1.5 inches to the ruler guide at 10 inches. Center the text horizontally and vertically in the text box.
6. Complete the decorative border at the bottom of the publication as follows:
   a. Use the mouse pointer to drag a selection border around the triangles, being careful not to include any other objects in the selection.
   b. Distribute the triangles horizontally, and then group the triangles.
   c. Copy the group, paste a duplicate, and then flip the copy vertically.
   d. Align the top border of the flipped triangle group with the 10 inch ruler guide, and nudge the object to the left or right as necessary so that the tips of the downward-pointing triangles are centered between the tips of the upward-pointing triangles.
   e. Select the original group, remove the outline, and fill with a gradient using a scheme color of your choice.
   f. Select the flipped group, remove the outline, and fill with a gradient using a different scheme color.
   g. Ungroup the flipped group and delete the rightmost triangle.
7. For your final task, add stars to the publication as follows:
   a. Using the **5-Point Star** shape, draw a star in the scratch area about **1.1 inches** high by **1.15 inches** wide. Fill the star with **Orange** from the Standard Colors palette and remove the outline.
   b. Apply the **Offset Diagonal Bottom Right** shadow effect.
   c. Move the star to align with the top of Henry Gonzalez's text box, with the right edge of the shape at the right margin guide.
   d. Use **Send Backward** to move the star behind the text box.
   e. Copy the star, rotate the copy as desired, and align the rotated star with the bottom of Richard Vargas's picture and the left edge of his text box. Send the star backward behind the text.
   f. Paste another copy of the star, rotate it in a different way from the second star, and position it at the right margin, aligning at the bottom of Cinda Jackson's picture.
8. **With your teacher's permission**, print the publication. It should look similar to Figure 27-2 on the next page.
9. Close the publication, saving changes, and exit Publisher.

Figure 27-2

The Literacy League

All-Star Volunteers!

Henry Gonzalez, Adult Education Tutor

Henry is a carpenter by trade with four years of service to the Literacy League.

"I love helping people learn to read because it opens up their minds to new and exciting ideas and possibilities."

Richard Vargas, Youth Counselor

Richard is the Pastor of Good Shepherd, with three years of service to the Literacy League.

"Children are naturally loving, gentle souls; it's up to us to help them get back to that natural state when their life situations have made them lose touch with that."

Cinda Jackson, Peer Tutor

Cinda is a student who has worked with Literacy League for two years.

"All kids deserve the chance to learn to read, even if they don't always learn it in regular school."

Lesson 28

Inserting WordArt

➤ What You Will Learn

Creating WordArt
Editing and Formatting WordArt

WORDS TO KNOW

WordArt
A feature that enables
you to create a graphic
object from text.

Software Skills　WordArt helps you stylize your text with twists, arches, fancy patterns, 3-D effects, and other enhancements. You won't want to set your entire publication in WordArt, of course, but it can make for some stunning headings and attention getters.

What You Can Do

Creating WordArt

■ **WordArt** is a Microsoft Office feature that enables you to enter a few words of text and then manipulate that text in a variety of ways, as if it were a graphic. You can create some very interesting special effects with it.

■ Use the WordArt command in the Text group on the INSERT tab to create WordArt. In the WordArt gallery, you can choose from plain WordArt styles or transform styles that have special shapes. You can then type the text for the WordArt graphic.

■ You can also select text in a text box before issuing the WordArt command; the selected text then displays in the Edit WordArt Text dialog box.

■ By default, WordArt graphics are created using Arial Black as the font, because it is a solid, heavy font that remains readable when transformed into a graphic. You can select any font, however, as well as change font size and font style.

✓ If you don't want to change font formats when creating the WordArt, you can edit the text later to change the formats.

Try It! Creating WordArt

1 Start Publisher and click the Blank 8.5 × 11" template to open a new, blank page.

2 Save the publication as **PB28Try_xx** in the location where your teacher instructs you to store the files for this lesson.

3 Click INSERT > WordArt 𝒜 to display the WordArt Gallery.

4 Click the Fill – Light Orange, Outline – Orange style (the style in the center of the second row from the top).

5 Type **Anderson Farms** to replace *Your Text Here*.

6 Click the Font drop-down arrow, scroll down, and click Corbel. Click the Size drop-down arrow and click 40. Click OK.

7 Save the changes to **PB28Try_xx**, and leave it open to use in the next Try It.

New WordArt

Editing and Formatting WordArt

- You have a number of options for editing and formatting an existing WordArt graphic. You will find tools for editing and formatting on the WORDART TOOLS FORMAT tab.

- Use the Edit Text command to redisplay the Edit WordArt Text dialog box, where you can change wording, font, font size, or font style.

- You have these additional options for formatting the text of the graphic:
  - Use the Spacing command to display a menu of character spacing choices, such as Loose and Tight. These options are the same as those you learned about in Chapter 3 for adjusting the spacing of text.
  - Use the Even Height command to toggle the graphic's letters between normal size and even heights (that is, all letters the same height, including capitals).
  - Use the WordArt Vertical Text command to toggle between normal layout and stacked layout (that is, the letters running vertically but appearing in normal orientation).
  - The Align Text command allows you to select alignment when the WordArt graphic has more than one line. You can choose to align left, center, or right. If one line is longer than another, you can apply word, letter, or stretch justification to make all lines end at the same place.

- Use the WordArt Styles gallery on the WORDART TOOLS FORMAT tab to select a different style for the current WordArt. The styles in this gallery are the same as the ones you chose from when starting the WordArt.

- You have these additional options in the WordArt Styles group:
  - Use the Shape Fill command to select a color or other fill option for the WordArt letters.
  - Use the Shape Outline command to select a color, weight, and style for the letter outlines. You can also turn off outlines for a custom appearance.
  - Use the Change Shape command to display a gallery of different shapes you can apply to the graphic.

- You also have the option of right-clicking a WordArt graphic and selecting Format WordArt on the shortcut menu. The Format WordArt dialog box lets you adjust fill and outline color, size and rotation, position on the page, and wrapping style.

- You will also see a Mini toolbar when you right-click a WordArt graphic that gives you access to commonly used editing options such as Edit Text, Change WordArt Shape, and so on.

- Many WordArt styles have shadow effects applied as part of the style, but you can use the Shadow options on the Shape Effects menu to change the shadow style or adjust its position.

- When the WordArt graphic is selected, you will see an adjustment handle that you can use to change the WordArt appearance. The function of the adjustment handle varies according to the style. You may use it to slant letters, for example, or adjust where text starts and ends in a circular shape.

- You can also adjust the size of a WordArt graphic using the Size options on the WORDART TOOLS FORMAT tab.

- WordArt formatting applies to the entire piece of WordArt; you cannot format one part of it differently from another. Create two separate pieces of WordArt if you need that capability.

Try It!   **Editing and Formatting WordArt**

1 In the **PB28Try_xx** file, click to select the WordArt graphic, if necessary.

2 Click WORDART TOOLS FORMAT > Edit Text. In the Edit WordArt Text dialog box, click just to the right of *Farms*, press [ENTER], and type **Presents**. Click OK.

3 Click WORDART TOOLS FORMAT > Shape Height and type **1.3**.

4 Click WORDART TOOLS FORMAT > Spacing > Tight.

5 Click WORDART TOOLS FORMAT > Even Height. Then click Even Height again to toggle the effect off.

6 Click WORDART TOOLS FORMAT > Align Text > Letter Justify.

7 Click the adjustment handle below the graphic and drag it slightly to the left to slant the letters. Then drag the handle back to its original position to remove the slant.

8 Click WORDART TOOLS FORMAT > Shape Fill > Blue from the Standard Colors palette.

9 Click WORDART TOOLS FORMAT > Shape Outline > Green from the Standard Colors palette. Then click Shape Outline > Weight > 1½ pt.

10 Click WORDART TOOLS FORMAT > Change Shape > Inflate Top.

11 Close the publication, saving changes, and exit Publisher.

Revised WordArt graphic

Lesson 28—Practice

Parker Conservatory has asked you to liven up the brochure you started in Lesson 24. In this exercise, you insert WordArt headings to add visual interest to the brochure.

DIRECTIONS

1. Start Publisher, if necessary, and open **PB28Practice** from the data files for this lesson.

2. Save the publication as **PB28Practice_xx** in the location where your teacher instructs you to store the files for this lesson.

3. On page 1, click **INSERT** > **WordArt** *A* and select the **Gradient Fill – Blue, Outline - Blue** WordArt style. Type **Butterfly Show** on two lines in the Edit WordArt Text dialog box, and then click **OK**.

4. The new WordArt graphic displays in the center of the page. Carefully select it and drag it to the right column. Position it between the *CONSERVATORY* text box and the address text box. Align the left side of the graphic to the column guide at the left side of the column and then drag the right side of the graphic to the right margin guide. Adjust the height of the graphic to **1.65 inches**.

5. Right-click the graphic and click **Format WordArt**. Format the graphic as follows:

   a. Click the **Fill Effects** button to display the Format Shape dialog box with gradient options active.

   b. On the gradient bar, click the leftmost gradient stop. Click the **Color** button and select the **Light Orange** color at the far left of the Recent Colors palette. Click the middle gradient stop, click the **Color** button, and select the second color from the right in the Recent Colors palette (**RGB (248, 233, 104)**). Click the rightmost gradient stop and apply the same color you applied to the left stop.

   c. Click the **Direction** button and click the **Linear Diagonal - Top Left to Bottom Right** option. Click **OK**.

   d. In the Line area of the Format WordArt dialog box, click the **Color** drop-down arrow and click the rightmost color in the Recent Colors palette (**RGB (212, 194, 67)**). Click **OK**.

   e. Click **WORDART TOOLS FORMAT** > **Shape Effects** > **Shadow** > **Shadow Options**. In the Format Shape dialog box, click the **Preset** button and click **Offset Diagonal Bottom Right**; click the **Color** button and click **Followed Hyperlink (RGB (113, 126, 0))**; change the shadow distance to **5 pt**; and click **OK**.

6. Click page 2 in the Page Navigation pane, and select the text in the *Butterflies Galore* text box.

7. Click **INSERT** > **WordArt** *A* > **Fill – None, Outline – Red**. You should see the selected text in the Edit WordArt Text dialog box. Click the **Size** drop-down arrow and click **16**. Click **OK**.

8. Drag the existing *Butterflies Galore* text box into the scratch area, and then move the WordArt into the space that the text box occupied. Drag the right selection handle of the WordArt to the right until the graphic aligns at the right with the text in the center column. The graphic should be 5 inches wide.

9. Format the WordArt as follows:

   a. Click **WORDART TOOLS FORMAT** > **Shape Fill** > **Accent 2 (RGB (254, 184, 10))**, **Lighter 40%**.

   b. Click **WORDART TOOLS FORMAT** > **Shape Outline** > **Accent 1 (RGB (79, 39, 28))**, **Lighter 40%**.

   c. Click **WORDART TOOLS FORMAT** > **Change Shape** *A* > **Wave 1**.

10. Drag the top border of the WordArt up to align with the top margin guide. Drag the bottom border of the WordArt down to align with the 1.5 inch ruler guide.

11. Click on the text box in the scratch area and press [DEL]. Your page should look similar to Figure 28-1 on the next page.

12. Close the publication, saving changes, and exit Publisher.

Figure 28-1

Butterflies Galore!

Come Fly with Us!

Don't miss the most exciting Butterfly Show in Parker Conservatory's long history. This year, we've rounded up butterflies from all over the world to entertain you during our Spring Show. You'll see butterflies from Asia, Africa, South America, and other exotic locations. Butterflies are incubated here in the Butterfly Nursery at Parker Conservatory (you can watch this fascinating process) and then released into the Special Events area of the Conservatory.

Free-range butterflies allow you to get up close for an unimpeded view of these special creatures. If you can bear to sit still while the butterflies flitter around you, you will find that they often land on you to take a break from their journeys from flower to flower.

We have made a special effort to find the most colorful species available to give you the most bang for your buck. You'll see bright orange, sulfur yellow, glossy black, luminescent blue, and even green butterflies that you have to look carefully to see among the foliage. Stripes, spots, borders, and splashes of color add to the display.

Photo Contest

Every year, we welcome photographers who want to add to their photo collections images of butterflies they would not ordinarily see around the neighborhood. If you are a keen photographer, join us on Sunday mornings at the Conservatory for special Shutterbug Hours. You're welcome to bring tripods and any other photographic gear you need to capture your images. We promise no one will frown at you while you take all the time you need to set up that once-in-a-lifetime shot. Complementary coffee will keep you focused!

All photographers, amateur and professional alike, are welcome to enter our Butterfly Photo Contest. Submit your three best shots at any time during the show. When the show is over, our professional photographer judges will review the entries and select the following winners:

- Best Professional Entry
- Best Amateur Entry
- Best Youth Entry (ages 11 to 18)
- Best Child Entry (ages 6 through 10)

Lesson 28—Apply

In this exercise, you create additional WordArt graphics to add pizzazz to the Parker Conservatory brochure.

DIRECTIONS

1. Start Publisher, if necessary, and open **PB28Apply** from the data files for this lesson.

2. Save the publication as **PB28Apply_xx** in the location where your teacher instructs you to store the files for this lesson.

3. On page 1, drag the *PARKER* text box into the scratch area and then select the text in the text box. Insert a new WordArt graphic using the **Fill – White, Outline – Gray** style. Change the font to **Times New Roman** and the size to **32**.

4. Resize the graphic to **0.5** inch high and **2** inches wide.

5. Change the shape to use the Arch Up (Curve) shape, and then move the graphic to center it horizontally in the right column, with the top of the curved graphic at the top margin guide.

6. Change the shape fill to the second color from the right in the Recent Colors palette (**RGB (248, 233, 104)**). Change the shape outline to the second color from the left in the Recent Colors palette (**RGB (202, 195, 80)**). Change the shadow option to **Offset Diagonal Bottom Right**.

7. Move the picture graphic up, if necessary, to sit closer under the curved WordArt graphic.

8. Drag the *CONSERVATORY* text box into the scratch area and then select the text in the text box.

9. Insert a new WordArt that uses the same settings as for the *Parker* WordArt. Resize the graphic to **0.9** inch high and **3.1** inches wide.

10. Apply the same shape fill, shape outline, and shadow settings as for the *Parker* WordArt, and then change the shape to **Arch Down (Curve)**. Center the graphic horizontally in the column and move it up under the picture.

11. Delete the text boxes in the scratch area.

12. Go to page 2. Insert a new WordArt graphic using the **Fill – White, Drop Shadow** style. Type **PHOTOS** and change the font size to **16**.

13. Change the WordArt orientation to vertical, and then adjust the shape width to **1.9**.

14. Position the graphic at the right side of the right column, with the top of the graphic aligned with the top of the paragraph that discusses photographers.

15. Apply **Square** text wrapping, and adjust the wrap to insert **0.14"** on the left side only.

16. Copy the WordArt and then paste it on page 1. Move it to the right side of the center column, beside the *Visit Us* text and aligned with the bottom of the *Visit Us* paragraph.

17. Edit the text to read **VISIT**. Change the shape fill and shape outline to the **Light Orange** color in the Recent Colors palette.

18. **With your teacher's permission**, print the publication. Your first page should look similar to Figure 28-2. Your second page should look similar to Figure 28-3 (both shown on the next page).

19. Close the publication, saving changes, and exit Publisher.

All photographs submitted will be returned if you provide a stamped, self-addressed mailer. Parker Conservatory will pay standard rates for winning photographs that can be used for advertising the show next year.

About Parker Conservatory

Parker Conservatory was founded in 1893 by the Parks and Recreation committee of Lexington as an educational facility intended to teach citizens of the town more about horticulture not only of the region but of the world. The structure of the Conservatory, of panels of glass between iron struts, was designed to resemble the Crystal Palace in London. No other structure in the Midwest had every been planned to use so much glass, and the Conservatory was an instant success not only in the city but as a destination attraction throughout the state as well as neighboring states.

From the first, the Conservatory took seriously the mission its founders had envisioned and positioned itself not only as a pleasant environment of tropical foliage, a picturesque stream with a waterfall, and fragrant flowers, but as an educational facility. Ornate signs identified nonnative species and imparted information on origin and provenance. Lush exterior landscaping provided citizens with ideas for how they could improve their own landscaping with ornamental shrubs, flowers, and trees. The Conservatory also functioned as a repository for seeds, corms, and bulbs of many rare plants, helping to prevent the extinction of plant life that is now being lost every day in tropical rain forest regions.

Visit Us

Parker Conservatory is open seven days a week, every day except Thanksgiving Day, Christmas Day, and New Year's Day. Hours are 10:00 a.m. to 6:00 p.m. Admission is free; a donation is suggested for the continued maintenance of this historic structure. You will find a Gift Shoppe and a Tea Room on the premises for refreshment and shopping.

Parker Conservatory Butterfly Show

VISIT

1670 Man O' War Boulevard
Lexington, KY 40513
859.555.9006
www.parkerconservatory.org

Butterflies Galore!

Come Fly with Us!

Don't miss the most exciting Butterfly Show in Parker Conservatory's long history. This year, we've rounded up butterflies from all over the world to entertain you during our Spring Show. You'll see butterflies from Asia, Africa, South America, and other exotic locations. Butterflies are incubated here in the Butterfly Nursery at Parker Conservatory (you can watch this fascinating process) and then released into the Special Events area of the Conservatory.

Free-range butterflies allow you to get up close for an unimpeded view of these special creatures. If you can bear to sit still while the butterflies flitter around you, you will find that they often land on you to take a break from their journeys from flower to flower.

We have made a special effort to find the most colorful species available to give you the most bang for your buck. You'll see bright orange, sulfur yellow, glossy black, luminescent blue, and even green butterflies that you have to look carefully to see among the foliage. Stripes, spots, borders, and splashes of color add to the display.

Photo Contest

Every year, we welcome photographers who want to add to their photo collections images of butterflies they would not ordinarily see around the neighborhood. If you are a keen photographer, join us on Sunday mornings at the Conservatory for special Shutterbug Hours. You're welcome to bring tripods and any other photographic gear you need to capture your images. We promise no one will frown at you while you take all the time you need to set up that once-in-a-lifetime shot. Complementary

coffee will keep you focused!

All photographers, amateur and professional alike, are welcome to enter our Butterfly Photo Contest. Submit your three best shots at any time during the show. When the show is over, our professional photographer judges will review the entries and select the following winners:

PHOTOS

- Best Professional Entry
- Best Amateur Entry
- Best Youth Entry (ages 11 to 18)
- Best Child Entry (ages 6 through 10)

Lesson 29

Working with Other Applications

➤ What You Will Learn

Inserting Objects from Other Applications
Copying Data from Another Application
Embedding Data from Other Applications
Linking Data and Updating Links
Saving As a Web Page

Software Skills   Sometimes the data you want to include in a publication is in another program's format. You might have a worksheet in Excel, for example, or a flowchart in PowerPoint. There are a number of ways to include such data in your Publisher publication.

What You Can Do

Inserting Objects from Other Applications

- By this point in the course, you should be very familiar with inserting some types of objects, such as pictures and text files.
- Other **object** types, such as data from Excel, PowerPoint, or Access, do not have special import commands, so you must rely on the Object command in the Text group on the INSERT tab to insert these objects.
- You insert objects from different applications if they make it easier to work with a particular kind of data. For example, if you want to be able to manipulate a table of numbers in Publisher, it is simpler to insert a worksheet from an application such as Excel than to calculate formulas yourself and type the numbers in a Publisher table.
- The Object command opens the Insert Object dialog box. Here you can choose to create a new object or place an existing file as an object.
- When you create a new object within Publisher, the new object is **embedded**. You can double-click that object at any time to reopen it for editing in whatever program it was created in. You learn more about embedded objects later in this lesson.

WORDS TO KNOW

Embed
To insert an object so that it maintains a connection between a foreign object in Publisher (that is, an object created using a different program) and the program that created it, so that when you double-click the object, the original program opens to help you edit it.

Link
The connection between a copy of an object and its original source. When the source changes, the copy changes, too.

Object
An object is anything that appears in a publication in its own frame. It can be a picture, a piece of WordArt, a drawn shape, and so on. *Object* can also mean a block of data that comes from another program.

- Create a new object by clicking the Create New button in the Insert Object dialog box. Then choose the object type from the list. The object types on the list come from the installed programs on your system. For example, if you have Adobe Photoshop on your system, you may see an option to insert an Adobe Photoshop Image.

- After you choose an object type, the chosen application opens, and you can create the new object using it. Depending on the application chosen, the commands you need to create the object may be integrated with the Publisher window, or they may be in an entirely separate window.

- Click the Publisher page when you finish creating the object to close the other application and update the object in Publisher. Or, if the application opened in a separate window, use the File, Exit command to return to Publisher.

- You can also use the Insert Object dialog box to navigate to existing files to insert. Clicking the Create from File button in the Insert Object dialog box displays a File text box, in which you can browse to the file you want.

- Inserting an existing file inserts the entire document in that file; you can't choose a specific portion of the document. See the following section if you want only a certain part of the file (such as a few specific cells from a spreadsheet).

- An inserted object is enclosed in a container that you can use to move or resize the object.

Try It!   Inserting Objects from Other Applications

1 Start Publisher and open **PB29TryA** from the data files for this lesson.

2 Save the publication as **PB29TryA_xx** in the location where your teacher instructs you to store the files for this lesson.

3 Click page 2 in the Page Navigation pane. Near the bottom of the page, locate the text box that refers to a sample chart. Select the text box and press DEL.

4 Click INSERT > Object 🔲. In the Insert Object dialog box, make sure the Create New option is selected. Scroll down to locate Microsoft Excel Chart. Click that object type and click OK. A sample chart opens in the publication.

   ✓ This sample chart contains data that does not relate to the current publication, but it shows how an inserted chart object looks in the publication.

5 Click outside the chart to display the light gray container. Drag the container below the *The chart below* text box and align it with the 1 inch vertical ruler guide. Drag the lower-right corner of the container to adjust the container size to about 5.5 inches wide.

6 Click on the Publisher page to see the resized object in place.

7 Save the changes to **PB29TryA_xx**, and leave it open to use in the next Try It.

Sample chart in publication

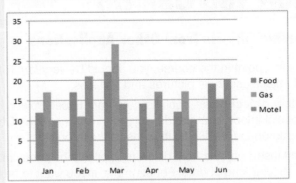

Copying Data from Another Application

- You can use the Clipboard to copy and paste data between applications, just as you learned to do with text blocks in Chapter 1.

- After copying the data in its original application, you have several options for pasting it in Publisher:

  - You can click the Paste command to paste the data in its simplest form. If you copy worksheet cells from Excel, for example, clicking Paste will paste the worksheet data as a Publisher table. You can modify and format the table just as you would any Publisher table.

  - You can click the Paste command's drop-down arrow and select Paste Special to open the Paste Special dialog box, where you have more options for controlling the paste. You will see several options in the As list that create different types of objects, and you also have the option of using Paste or Paste Link as you insert the data.

- The New Table option in the Paste Special dialog box pastes the data in a new Publisher table; this is the same as simply clicking the Paste button.

- The option to paste data as a Microsoft Object (such as a Microsoft Excel Worksheet Object) actually embeds the data. You will learn more about embedding in the next section.

- You will find when simply pasting data that some formats may not copy exactly. Usually, pasting as an object will give you a more exact copy of the data. However, you can usually adjust any formats that need tweaking in Publisher.

Try It!   Copying Data from Another Application

1   Start Word and open **PB29TryB.docx** from the data files for this lesson.

2   Click in the table, and then click TABLE TOOLS LAYOUT > Select ⇘ > Select Table.

3   Click HOME > Copy 📋. Then click the Close button ✖ to close the document and exit Word.

4   Switch to Publisher. In the **PB29TryA_xx** file, with page 1 displayed, click HOME > Paste 📋. The copied table is pasted in the publication.

5   Drag the pasted table by its container to align at the upper-left corner with the 3.88 horizontal ruler guide and the 1 inch vertical ruler guide, below the first text box on page 1.

6   Select the entire table, and then click HOME > Font Size 11 ▾ > 14.

7   Note that the table borders are not exactly like those in the Word document. Click TABLE TOOLS DESIGN > Borders and deselect Inside Vertical Border. Then click TABLE TOOLS LAYOUT > View Gridlines ▦ to turn off gridlines.

8   Click away from the table on the Publisher page to see the final formatted table data.

9   Save the changes to **PB29TryA_xx**, and leave it open to use in the next Try It.

Word table pasted as a table in Publisher

The table below shows staffing assignments for the year. It is obvious that if we continue to offer classes, we will need to recruit more instructors, as all of our current instructors have heavy loads, and Jaime needs time to run the business!

	Qtr 1	Qtr 2	Qtr 3	Qtr 4
Painting with Oils	Cruz	Cruz	Jamison	Parker
Painting with Acrylics	Cruz	Jamison	Cruz	Parker
Watercolor Techniques	Jamison	Jamison	Jamison	Jamison
Basic Drawing	Marquette	Marquette	Cruz	Williams
Drawing with Pen & Ink	Parker	Parker	Cruz	Williams

Embedding Data from Other Applications

- You learned in the last section that you can use the Paste Special dialog box to embed data from another application in Publisher.

- An embedded object maintains a connection to the application in which it was created so that you can use the tools of the original application to edit the embedded object.

- Insert an embedded object by copying it in its original application, clicking the Paste Special command in Publisher, and choosing the option that allows you to paste as an object.

- The embedded object displays in a light gray container that you can use to move or resize it.

- To edit an embedded object, double-click on it. If the object is from another Microsoft Office application, the Ribbon tabs of that application display in place of the Publisher Ribbon, so you can use the original application's tools to modify the object.

- An embedded object is stored in the Publisher file, which can add to the Publisher file size. If file size is an issue, you can consider linking instead. You will learn more about linking in the next section.

Try It!   **Embedding Data from Other Applications**

1 Start Excel and open **PB29TryC.xlsx** from the data files for this lesson.

2 Save the file as **PB29TryC_xx** in the location where your teacher instructs you to store the files for this lesson.

3 Select the cell range A3:F14, the data for the Painting Courses and Drawing Courses. Click HOME > Copy 🖹. Leave the file and Excel open for the next Try It.

4 Switch to Publisher. In the **PB29TryA_xx** file, on page 1, click the Paste drop-down button and click Paste Special.

5 Click Microsoft Excel Worksheet Object, and then click OK.

6 Drag the embedded object to align at the top with the 6.85 horizontal ruler guide below the last text box on page 1.

7 Notice that the totals have not been calculated for the Drawing Courses. Complete this worksheet data as follows:

   a. Double-click on the embedded object to open it for editing. The border changes to a diagonal line border and the Excel Ribbon tabs display.

   b. Scroll down if necessary to see the Drawing Courses data, and click in cell B14, the total cell for Qtr 1.

   c. Click HOME > AutoSum Σ in the Editing group, and then press ENTER. Excel automatically sums the values for the two drawing courses.

   d. Click in the cell you just summed, click HOME > Copy 🖹, drag over cells C14, D14, and E14, and then click HOME > Paste 🖿.

(continued)

Try It!   **Embedding Data from Other Applications** *(continued)*

8 Scroll back up until you see only the Painting Courses and Drawing Courses data, and then click outside the embedded object, twice, to see the corrected embedded data.

9 Save the changes to **PB29TryA_xx**, and leave it open to use in the next Try It.

Embedded data with edits made in Excel

Painting Courses

Class	Qtr 1	Qtr 2	Qtr 3	Qtr 4	Total
Painting with Oils	$ 1,900.00	$ 1,330.00	$ 2,090.00		$ 5,320.00
Painting with Acrylics	1,140.00	760.00	1,520.00		3,420.00
Watercolor Techniques	1,250.00	1,750.00	2,250.00		5,250.00
Total	$ 4,290.00	$ 3,840.00	$ 5,860.00	$ -	$ 13,990.00

Drawing Courses

Class	Qtr 1	Qtr 2	Qtr 3	Qtr 4	Total
Basic Drawing	$ 1,800.00	$ 2,250.00	$ 1,950.00		$ 6,000.00
Drawing with Pen & Ink	514.50	857.50	1,200.50		2,572.50
Total	$ 2,314.50	$ 3,107.50	$ 3,150.50	$ -	$ 8,572.50

Linking Data and Updating Links

- The process of **linking** data from one application to another is similar to embedding. Instead of storing the data from the other application in Publisher, however, the data remains in its original file and only a link is placed in Publisher.

- The link between the two applications means that when data is changed in the original application, it will also be changed in the linked object that resides in Publisher.

- You can edit a linked object by double-clicking it in Publisher to open the original file. You do your editing in the original file, not in Publisher.

- Use the Paste Special dialog box to insert a linked object. Select the Paste Link option to create the link.

- You can paste a link only if the copied data is from a saved file.

- If you make changes to the original data, the linked object in Publisher will not immediately update. The next time the Publisher file is opened, you will be asked if you want to update links.

- You can also add the Edit Links to Files command to a Ribbon tab or the Quick Access Toolbar and use it to update links at any time, open the original (source) file, or change the source file.

| **Try It!** | **Linking Data and Updating Links** |

1 In the **PB29TryC_xx** file in Excel, select the cell range A16:F24, the cells that show the data for All Courses, as well as the Total for Year row.

2 Click HOME > Copy 🗐 .

3 Switch to Publisher. In the **PB29TryA_xx** file, on page 2, click the Paste drop-down button and click Paste Special.

4 Select Paste Link in the Paste Special dialog box, and then click OK.

5 Drag the container to the intersection of the 1 inch vertical ruler guide and the 2 inch horizontal ruler guide.

6 Save the changes to **PB29TryA_xx**, and click FILE > Close.

7 Switch to Excel and complete the worksheet as follows:

  a. Click in cell E18 and type **1520**. Press ⏎ and type **950**. Press ⏎ and type **2500**. Press ⏎ and type **1350**. Press ⏎ and type **686**. Press ⏎ .

  b. Click Save 🖫 on the Quick Access Toolbar, and then click the Close button to close the workbook and exit Excel.

8 Start Publisher. Open **PB29TryA_xx** from the list of recent publications. Click Yes when asked to update links.

9 Click page 2 to see the updated data in the linked object.

10 Save the changes to **PB29TryA_xx**, and leave it open to use in the next Try It.

Linked object shows update

All Courses					
Class	Qtr 1	Qtr 2	Qtr 3	Qtr 4	Total
Painting with Oils	$ 1,900.00	$ 1,330.00	$ 2,090.00	$ 1,520.00	$ 6,840.00
Painting with Acrylics	1,140.00	760.00	1,520.00	950.00	4,370.00
Watercolor Techniques	1,250.00	1,750.00	2,250.00	2,500.00	7,750.00
Basic Drawing	1,800.00	2,250.00	1,950.00	1,350.00	7,350.00
Drawing with Pen & Ink	514.50	857.50	1,200.50	686.00	3,258.50
Total	$ 6,604.50	$ 6,947.50	$ 9,010.50	$ 7,006.00	
				Total for Year	$ 29,568.50

Saving As a Web Page

■ You can save a publication in HTML format for use as a Web page.

■ You can locate a Web site template on Office.com if you use the Search for templates search box in the New tab in Backstage view. If you choose to download this template and open it, Publisher displays a WEB tab that provides a number of commands for working with the Web pages.

  ✓ *You will work with some of these options in Chapter 5 when you work with e-mail templates.*

■ You can save any publication as a Web page so it can be displayed in a browser or added to another Web site.

■ Use the Export tab in Backstage view and the Publish HTML command to save a publication as a Web page. You can choose from the following options:

  ● Web Page (HTML) saves the publication with the suggested name index.htm and a folder that contains supporting materials such as the pictures and shapes on the publication page.

  ● Single File Web Page (MHTML) saves the publication with the .mht extension in a single file that includes all supporting images.

■ As you learned in Chapter 1, you cannot view a Web page in Publisher without Publisher's converting it to a publication. Use your browser to view a publication you have saved in HTML format.

■ Note that if your publication has more than one page, saving it as HTML will convert only the first page of the publication to a Web page.

Try It!   **Saving As a Web Page**

1 In the **PB29TryA_xx** file, click FILE > Export.

2 Click Publish HTML, and then click the drop-down arrow beside Web Page (HTML) in the right pane and click Single File Web Page (MHTML). Click Publish HTML 🖳.

3 In the Save As dialog box, navigate to the location where your teacher instructs you to store the files for this lesson. Change the file name to **PB29TryD_xx** and click Save.

4 Save changes to the **PB29TryA_xx** file, close it, and exit Publisher.

5 Start your browser, and then click File > Open and click the button that allows you to browse for files. Navigate to your solution folder, click **PB29TryD_xx.mht**, and click Open. Click OK to display the file.

6 View the Web page, then click File > Exit to close the page and exit your browser.

Lesson 29—Practice

In this lesson, you work on Flora's Strategic Plan. You insert an object, copy information, and embed worksheet data.

DIRECTIONS

1. Start Publisher, if necessary, and open **PB29PracticeA** from the data files for this lesson.

2. Save the publication as **PB29PracticeA_xx** in the location where your teacher instructs you to store the files for this lesson.

3. Start Excel and open **PB29PracticeB.xlsx** from the data files for this lesson. Click the **Seasonal Data** tab at the bottom of the worksheet if necessary to display the Seasonal Data information.

4. Select the cell range **A5:F11** (the cells that show the yearly data for spring, summer, fall, and winter, and the Totals row and Average column). Click **HOME > Copy** 🖹.

5. Save the Excel worksheet as **PB29ApplyC_xx** in the location where your teacher instructs you to store the files for this lesson. (You are saving this file with the Apply name because you will use it for linking in the Apply exercise.) Then close the file and exit Excel.

6. Switch to Publisher, and then click **HOME > Paste** drop-down arrow > **Paste Special**.

7. Click **Microsoft Excel Worksheet Object**, and then click **OK**.

8. Drag the embedded worksheet up below the first paragraph in the text box, and drag left or right until the alignment guide indicates it is centered horizontally on the page. Click **HOME > Wrap Text** 🖹 **> Top and Bottom**.

9. Edit the embedded worksheet as follows:

   a. Double-click the embedded object to open it for editing.

   b. Scroll down to display the *Totals* row. Click in cell **B11**, and then click **HOME > AutoSum Σ**. Press [ENTER] to accept the calculation.

   c. Click in cell B11 again, click **HOME > Copy** 🖹, drag to select cells **C11:E11**, and click **HOME > Paste** 📋. (Don't worry if some of your worksheet cells display #### signs.)

   d. Scroll up and click in cell **F6**, the first cell under the *Average* heading. Type the following formula: **=average(b6:e6)**. Press [ENTER].

   e. Click in cell **F6** again, click **HOME > Copy** 🖹, drag to select cells **F7:F10**, and click **HOME > Paste** 📋.

   ✓ *If you see a formula warning box to the left of cell F6, you can click it and then click Ignore error.*

10. Scroll up to display the column headings (*Spring, Summer,* etc.). Then click on the small black selection handle in the center of the bottom diagonal-striped border (your pointer will become a double-pointed arrow) and drag down to display the *Totals* row if that row is not already displayed.

11. Click outside the embedded object to see the object in place on the page. Your page should look similar to Figure 29-1.

12. Click page **2** in the Page Navigation pane.

13. Start Word and open **PB29PracticeC.docx** from the data files for this lesson.

14. Click the SmartArt organization chart to select it, and then click **HOME > Copy** 📋. Click the **Close** button ✗ to close the file and exit Word.

15. In the **PB29PracticeA_xx** file, click **HOME > Paste** 📋.

16. Click **PICTURE TOOLS FORMAT > Shape Height** ↕️ and type **3**. Drag the chart object beneath the first text box on the page, and move it from side to side until you see the center alignment guide. Your page should look similar to Figure 29-2, shown on the next page.

17. Close the publication, saving changes, and exit Publisher.

Figure 29-1

Flora Strategic Plan—2015

At this strategic planning meeting, we will address one of the most important issues facing us, and that is how to increase revenue during the winter months. We regularly experience good sales figures during the spring, summer, and fall, but winter is traditionally a slow time, with revenues far below those of the other seasons.

	Spring	Summer	Fall	Winter	Average
2010	$45,270	$51,630	$34,700	$11,310	$35,728
2011	$47,100	$65,900	$43,850	$12,740	$42,398
2012	$51,940	$68,730	$55,150	$13,950	$47,443
2013	$43,650	$56,840	$33,790	$10,620	$36,225
2014	$48,400	$59,780	$41,880	$11,230	$40,323
Totals	$236,360	$302,880	$209,370	$59,850	

We have several ideas for increasing sales. We have been asked many times, for example, why we don't sell greens and trees during the holiday season, and clients have also expressed an interest in high-end garden accessories such as teak benches, tables, and chairs, as well as other decorative items such as statuary and fountains.

We will be following the flow chart shown at the right to investigate each option. We have good communication with our customers, who always seem willing to stop and talk about what items they wish we would stock, so we hope the market research will be an enjoyable process.

As we investigate each of the ideas we have already identified by brainstorming, we will assign it either to the pile of possibles or the pile of rejected ideas. When we have analyzed the possibles for one idea with sufficient interest, we will create a plan of action. We do not plan on being hasty with this process; it would be a shame to short-change our existing customers doing what we do best—supplying high-quality plants—while chasing the next money-making scheme.

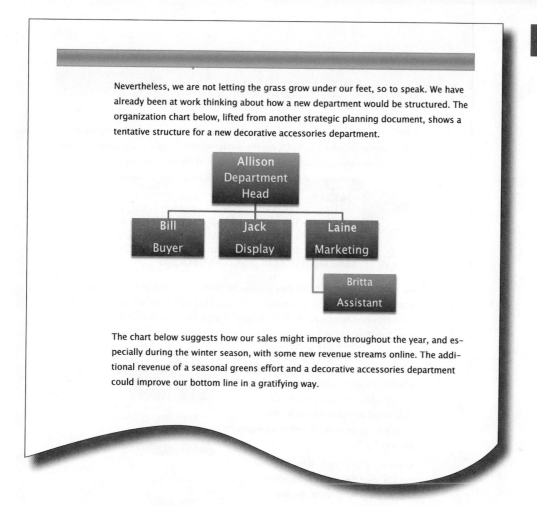

Figure 29-2

Nevertheless, we are not letting the grass grow under our feet, so to speak. We have already been at work thinking about how a new department would be structured. The organization chart below, lifted from another strategic planning document, shows a tentative structure for a new decorative accessories department.

The chart below suggests how our sales might improve throughout the year, and especially during the winter season, with some new revenue streams online. The additional revenue of a seasonal greens effort and a decorative accessories department could improve our bottom line in a gratifying way.

Lesson 29—Apply

You continue to work on the Flora strategic planning publication. In this exercise, you insert another object in the publication, link data from an Excel workbook, and then update the link in the publication.

DIRECTIONS

1. Start Publisher, if necessary, and open **PB29ApplyA** from the data files for this lesson.

2. Save the publication as **PB29ApplyA_xx** in the location where your teacher instructs you to store the files for this lesson.

3. Choose to insert an object on page 1. Select the **Create from File** option, browse to the data files for this lesson, and select **PB29ApplyB.pptx**. Modify the inserted object as follows:

a. Position the top of the container about even with the top of the second paragraph below the embedded worksheet object. Move the container so that the rightmost flow chart object is at the right margin.

b. Apply **Tight** text wrapping (**HOME > Wrap Text**) and set the wrap option to wrap to the left side only.

c. Choose to edit the wrap points. Adjust wrap points as necessary to create a wrap boundary fairly close to the left side of the flow chart, but not too tight (see Figure 29-3 on the next page).

Figure 29-3

Flora Strategic Plan—2015

At this strategic planning meeting, we will address one of the most important issues facing us, and that is how to increase revenue during the winter months. We regularly experience good sales figures during the spring, summer, and fall, but winter is traditionally a slow time, with revenues far below those of the other seasons.

	Spring	Summer	Fall	Winter	Average
2010	$45,270	$51,630	$34,700	$11,310	$35,728
2011	$47,100	$65,900	$43,850	$12,740	$42,398
2012	$51,940	$68,730	$55,150	$13,950	$47,443
2013	$43,650	$56,840	$33,790	$10,620	$36,225
2014	$48,400	$59,780	$41,880	$11,230	$40,323
Totals	$236,360	$302,880	$209,370	$59,850	

We have several ideas for increasing sales. We have been asked many times, for example, why we don't sell greens and trees during the holiday season, and clients have also expressed an interest in high-end garden accessories such as teak benches, tables, and chairs, as well as other decorative items such as statuary and fountains.

We will be following the flow chart shown at the right to investigate each option. We have good communication with our customers, who always seem willing to stop and talk about what items they wish we would stock, so we hope the market research will be an enjoyable process.

As we investigate each of the ideas we have already identified by brainstorming, we will assign it either to the pile of possibles or the pile of rejected ideas. When we have analyzed the possibles for one idea with sufficient interest, we will create a plan of action. We do not plan on being hasty with this process; it would be a shame to short-change our existing customers doing what we do best—supplying high-quality plants—while chasing the next money-making scheme.

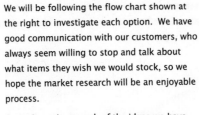

4. Start Excel and open **PB29ApplyC_xx.xlsx** from the location where you stored it.

5. Click the **Projected Income** tab at the bottom of the worksheet window, and then click on the chart to select it. Click **HOME > Copy**.

6. Switch back to Publisher and display page 2. Use the **Paste Link** option to paste the chart. Move the chart to align it at the left with the 1.5 inch vertical ruler guide and at the bottom with the bottom margin guide. Then save and close the publication.

7. Switch back to the Excel workbook and insert the following data in the Projected Income worksheet.

  a. In the Seasonal greens row, click in cell **D9** and type **2000**, press TAB and type **8000**, and press TAB.

  b. In the Garden accessories row, click in cell **B11** and type **10000**, press TAB and type **14000**, press TAB and type **15000**, press TAB and type **10000**, and press TAB.

8. Save the changes to the Excel workbook, close the file, and exit Excel.

9. Open the **PB29ApplyA_xx** publication from the Recent list. Click **Yes** when asked to update links.

10. **With your teacher's permission**, print the publication. Page 1 should look similar to Figure 29-3, and page 2 should look similar to Figure 29-4.

11. Close the publication, saving changes, and exit Publisher.

Figure 29-4

Nevertheless, we are not letting the grass grow under our feet, so to speak. We have already been at work thinking about how a new department would be structured. The organization chart below, lifted from another strategic planning document, shows a tentative structure for a new decorative accessories department.

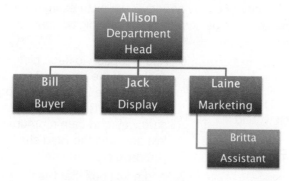

The chart below suggests how our sales might improve throughout the year, and especially during the winter season, with some new revenue streams online. The additional revenue of a seasonal greens effort and a decorative accessories department could improve our bottom line in a gratifying way.

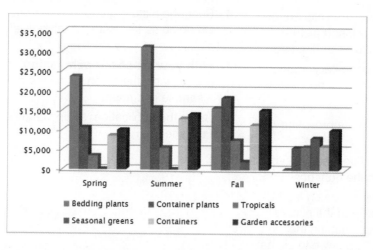

End-of-Chapter Activities

➤ Publisher Chapter 4—Critical Thinking

Traveling Abroad

In this project, you will create a one-page document that displays some of the sights of a city you hope to visit or have visited. Before you begin this project, use the Internet to gather information on sights to see and things to do in the city you want to visit. Remember to provide proper citations for any information you take directly from the Internet. Search clip art files for pictures or illustrations of the city. If you have already visited the city, you may already have pictures in digital format that you can use, or pictures that can be scanned to create digital images.

DIRECTIONS

1. Start Publisher and select the blank 8.5 × 11" page template. Save the publication as **PBCT04_xx** in the location where your teacher instructs you to store the files for this chapter.

2. Apply a color scheme and a font scheme of your choice.

3. Use WordArt to insert the name of your destination city at the top of the page. Adjust formats such as fill, outline, shadow, and text effects as desired.

4. Add illustrations to your page:

   a. Insert at least three illustrations from clip art, or use other picture files. You may insert picture placeholders, or insert the pictures on the page.

   b. Use one of the pictures as a page background, adjusting transparency and offset as necessary.

   c. Crop the pictures attractively.

   d. Align or distribute the pictures to improve the layout of the page.

   e. Swap or change the pictures if desired until you have the pictures you want in the right positions.

5. Use the Rectangle tool to draw a shape on top of one of the pictures. Sample a color in the picture for the fill. Then send the rectangle behind the picture and nudge it to the right and down to act as a shadow. You may apply the same kind of shadow to your other pictures, or use other picture styles or effects.

6. Add a caption to each picture to identify the subject of the picture. If you find that the captions seem to take up too much room, ungroup the caption and the picture, resize the caption to be narrower, and then regroup the picture, the caption text box, and the filled shape behind the picture if you have created one.

7. Add a text box that fills the page. Type in the text box the information you have gathered about the sights in your pictures. Adjust text formats as desired, and adjust picture sizes and positions if necessary to fit the text.

8. Bring the picture groups to the front and set text wrapping so text will wrap attractively around the pictures.

9. **With your teacher's permission**, print the publication. Illustration 4A on the next page shows a sample document.

10. Close the publication, saving changes, and exit Publisher.

Paris: City of Lights

Arc de Triomphe

Among the most popular sites to visit in Paris are the Arc de Triomphe, the Eiffel Tower, and Notre Dame Cathedral.

The Arc de Triomphe (Arch of Triumph) was commissioned in 1806 by Napoleon Bonaparte to commemorate his many victories, but in fact, he did not live to see the completion of the arch. It was not completed until 1836.

The arch was designed by Jean Chalgrin and based on a Roman arch. Reliefs on the arch depict some of Napoleon's most famous battles, including the Battle of Aboukir and the Battle of Austerlitz. The arch also includes the Grave of the Unknown Soldiers, dedicated to the unknown dead of World War I.

You can see the top of the Eiffel tower from anywhere in Paris, as it rises over 980 feet tall. A visit to Paris would not be complete without a visit to this iconic landmark. At the time it was completed, it was the tallest structure in the world by quite a large margin.

The Eiffel Tower was built for the World Exposition of 1889, and was initially intended as a temporary structure. It was designed by Gustave Eiffel, and took two years to build. Each of the 12,000 iron pieces that make up the tower was designed individually to have exactly the right shape. Over 7 million nails were required to build the tower.

Although many disliked the tower when it was built, because its proportions were so magnificent in comparison with other structures, Parisians quickly adopted the tower as a symbol of the City of Lights.

Notre-Dame Cathedral, though not the largest or most ornate, may be the most famous church in Europe. Construction began in 1163 and was not completed until 1345. The spire was added in the 19th century. It was the first large cathedral in France and became a pattern for the later cathedrals at Chartres and Amiens.

Notre-Dame is known for its rose windows; the north, completed in the 13th century, has a diameter of almost 43 feet.

The cathedral was extensively damaged during the French Revolution and not restored until the 19th century.

Notre-Dame de Paris

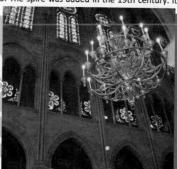

➤ Publisher Chapter 4—Portfolio Builder

Pet Rescue

Pet Rescue has asked you to create another flyer to hand out at a holiday open house. The text for the flyer has already been written. In this project, you will use features you have learned about in this chapter to add graphical content to the flyer.

DIRECTIONS

1. Start Publisher, if necessary, and open **PBPB04A** from the data files for this chapter.

2. Save the publication as **PBPB04A_xx** in the location where your teacher instructs you to store the files for this chapter.

Complete the Title Column

1. With page 1 selected, click **INSERT** > **Pictures** 🖼 and navigate to the data files for this project. Click **PBPB04_image1.jpg** and then click **Insert**.

2. Click **PICTURE TOOLS FORMAT** > **Crop** 🖼 > **Crop to Shape**. Select **Oval** from the Shapes gallery. Drag the cropping handles to create a tight crop around the front dog's head.

3. Adjust the shape of the oval using the cropping handles so the picture is as wide as the column and includes the dog's ears but as little of the background dog as possible.

4. Click **PICTURE TOOLS FORMAT** > **Corrections** ☀ > **Brightness: 50%, Contrast: 60%**.

5. Click **PICTURE TOOLS FORMAT** > **Picture Border** 🖉 > **Accent 1 (RGB (119, 95, 85))**. Click **Picture Border** 🖉 > **Weight** > **4½ pt**.

6. Position the picture with the top of the border at the 1 inch ruler guide. Adjust width if necessary to fit within the column guides.

7. Click **INSERT** > **WordArt** 𝒜 > **Gradient Fill – Purple, Outline – White**.

8. Type **Pet Rescue** in the Edit WordArt Text dialog box and then click **OK** to insert the graphic. Move it below the dog image in the right column of page 1, and adjust the width to stretch the graphic from the left column border to the right margin guide.

9. With the graphic still selected, click **WORDART TOOLS FORMAT** > **Shape Fill** 🎨 > **Accent 1 (RGB (119, 95, 85))**.

10. Click **INSERT** > **Shapes** ⬡ > **Rectangle** and draw a rectangle as tall as the page (**8.5 inches**) and **3.8 inches** wide. Align the top, right, and bottom edges of the shape with the page edges so the shape covers the right column on page 1. The left edge of the shape should extend into the gutter space between the center and right columns.

11. Right-click the shape, click **Format AutoShape**, and click the **Fill Effects** button. Create a gradient as follows:

    a. Click the **Top Spotlight - Accent 4** Preset gradient.

    b. Click the rightmost gradient stop (Stop 3 of 3), click the **Color** button, and click **Accent 1 (RGB (119, 95, 85)), Lighter 60%**.

    c. Click the **Linear Right** direction. Click **OK**.

    d. In the Line area, click the **Color** drop-down arrow and click **No Outline**. Click **OK**.

12. Click **DRAWING TOOLS FORMAT** > **Send Backward** ⬚ > **Send to Back**.

13. Click the address text box, click **DRAWING TOOLS FORMAT** > **Shape Styles More** button ▾ > **Diagonal Gradient – Accent 4**.

Complete Page 1

1. Click **INSERT** > **Online Pictures** 🖼, and type the keyword **cat**. In the search results choose a close-up of a cat looking at the camera, similar to the one shown in Illustration 4B on the next page.

   ✓ *If you do not find this picture, look for a similar one.*

2. Crop the picture to an oval, as shown in Illustration 4B. Apply the **5 Point Soft Edges** picture effect.

3. Resize the picture to be **2.3 inches** wide and position it in the upper-left corner of the page, at the intersection of the 1 inch ruler guide and the left margin guide.

4. Click **PICTURE TOOLS FORMAT** > **Wrap Text** 🖹 > **Tight**. Then choose to wrap to the right side only.

of unwanted kittens that may have a very hard life, if they can manage to survive at all in harsh conditions. Male cats also become more tractable, resulting in fewer injuries from fighting. If you are interested in participating in the TNR process, contact us for more information about renting traps and how to get trapped cats to us for surgery.

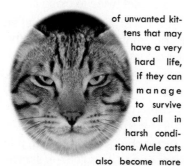

What Is the Adoption Process?

Potential permanent owners must undergo an in-home interview and for dog adoption must show proof of a fenced yard. If you are adopting a cat or kitten that has previously lived outside, you must promise to keep the cat indoors. There is an adoption fee to cover the cost of veterinary services, vaccina-

tions, and boarding until the pet is adopted.

What Support Is Available?

Pet Rescue offers pet ownership classes for new dog and cat owners once a month in several cites throughout the Midwest. Classes are free to the public, including Pet Rescue adoptive families, but a $25 donation is requested if possible.

How Can You Help?

Even if you are not able to adopt a pet at this time, you can help us at Pet Rescue with your donations of time, funds, or goods. We are always in need of:

- Dog and cat food
- Heavy duty trash bags
- Cat litter
- Unscented bleach
- Laundry soap and dishwashing liquid
- Latex gloves
- Newspaper and paper towels
- Hand sanitizer

Pet Rescue

Local Office:

2077 W. 166th Street
Indianapolis, IN 46240

Phone: 212-555-9191
Fax: 212-555-9089
E-mail: rjames@petrescueindy.org

Complete Page 2

1. Click **INSERT** > **Pictures** and navigate to the data files for this project. Click **PBPB04_image2.jpg** and then click **Insert**.

2. Click **PICTURE TOOLS FORMAT** > **Crop** and then crop the picture attractively using the "rule of thirds" or "fill the frame" focus. Then adjust the picture to be **3.2 inches** wide and position it at the bottom of the left column on page 2.

3. Click **PICTURE TOOLS FORMAT** > **Corrections** > Brightness: 50%, Contrast: 60%.

4. With the picture still selected, click **PICTURE TOOLS FORMAT** > **Caption** > **Reversed – Layout 2**. Type the caption **Jane was a feral cat who was successfully trapped, spayed, and adopted.**

✓ *If adding the caption does not cause the first line of the Some of the services paragraph to move to the center column, click Caption > No caption, and then adjust the cropping to increase the height of the picture.*

5. Click **INSERT** > **Picture Placeholder**. By dragging the right side and bottom center selection handles, resize the placeholder to **2.7 inches** high by **3.2 inches** wide. Position the placeholder at the top of the right column, with the top border at the 1 inch ruler guide.

6. Click the picture symbol in the placeholder to open the Insert Pictures dialog box. Type **cat** in the Office.com Clip Art Search box.

7. In the search results, scroll down through several panes of results to find a picture of a cat rubbing its head against a dog's nose. (See Illustration 4C on the next page.) Adjust the position of the two animals in the placeholder, and then click off the picture to accept the crop.

   ✓ *If you do not find this picture, look for a similar one.*

8. Start Excel and open **PBPB04B.xlsx** from the data files for this project.

9. Select the range **A4:D12**, and click **HOME >** **Copy** .

10. Switch to Publisher, and click **HOME > Paste** drop-down arrow > **Paste Special**. Click **Microsoft Excel Worksheet Object** to embed the worksheet, and then click **OK**.

11. Position the embedded object at the top of the center column on page 2, within the column guides.

12. Double-click the object to open it for editing, and click in cell **D5**. Type the formula **=B5-C5** and press ENTER .

13. Click in cell **D5** again, click **HOME > Copy** , drag over cells **D6:D12**, and click **HOME >** **Paste** .

14. Adjust the position of the data to display at the top of the diagonal-line border, and then drag the diagonal line border down to display all data. Click outside the object twice to close it.

15. Click **INSERT > Shapes** > **Line**, and then draw a straight horizontal line just above the text box in the center column.

16. Click **DRAWING TOOLS FORMAT > Shape Outline** > **Followed Hyperlink (RGB (153, 102, 0)), Lighter 40%**. Then click **Shape Outline** > **Weight > 4½ pt**.

17. **With your teacher's permission**, print the publication. Page 1 should look similar to Illustration 4B on the previous page, and page 2 should look similar to Illustration 4C on the next page.

18. Close the publication, saving changes, and exit Publisher. Exit Excel.

What Is Pet Rescue?

Pet Rescue is a non-profit corporation that exists for the betterment of homeless companion animals. We are based in Decatur, Illinois, but our operations extend all over the Midwest. Our ultimate goal is to place homeless animals in permanent homes, but we also maintain a system of foster homes where animals await permanent placement. While in the Pet Rescue system, animals receive any necessary veterinary care through our network of veterinarians, practicing at reduced rates for the good of our pets.

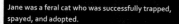

Jane was a feral cat who was successfully trapped, spayed, and adopted.

	Non-member Fees	Member Discount	Member Fees
Adoption	$65.00	$16.25	$48.75
Spay	$45.00	$11.25	$33.75
Neuter	$40.00	$4.00	$36.00
Rabies	$15.00	$3.00	$12.00
Distemper	$15.00	$3.00	$12.00
Nail trim	$10.00	$2.00	$8.00
Fleas	$10.00	$2.00	$8.00
FIV test	$10.00	$2.00	$8.00

Some of the services we offer to homeless cats and dogs are shown in the chart at the top of the center column. As you can see, you can save money on many services if you become a member of Pet Rescue. Your member discount is valid not only for any feral animals you are taking care of but your own pets and those you might adopt from Pet Rescue.

What Is the Rescue Process?

When we receive an animal, it goes through an evaluation with one of our staff members, and is checked by a veterinarian. If it is immediately ready for

placement, volunteers try to find it a permanent home while it lives with a foster family. If some training or rehabilitation is required, the animal goes to a special foster home specializing in that type of treatment.

We also support the TNR system for feral cats. TNR—trap, neuter, return—is a tested and proven method for managing colonies of homeless cats. After you trap the cat, we spay or neuter the animal and give it supportive care overnight, then return the cat to you in the trap. You can then return the cat to its outdoor home. This process has been very successful in reducing the number

Chapter 5

(Courtesy Monkey Business Images/Shutterstock)

Exploring Publication Types

Lesson 30
Working with Flyers

- Creating a Flyer with Tear-Offs
- Changing the Template Design
- Manually Inserting a Coupon Tear-Off
- Customizing a Contact Information Tear-Off

Lesson 31
Creating Greeting Cards

- Creating a Greeting Card
- Customizing a Greeting Card Message
- Changing Card Template Options
- Creating an Envelope
- Customizing an Envelope for a Greeting Card

Lesson 32
Creating Publications to Distribute via E-mail

- Creating an E-mail Publication
- Adjusting the Page Size of an E-mail Publication
- Inserting a Hyperlink
- Using E-mail Preview and Testing Hyperlinks
- Sending a Publication via E-mail

Lesson 33
Working with Newsletters

- Creating a Newsletter
- Changing the Newsletter Page Content
- Working with Text in a Newsletter
- Inserting a "Continued" Notation

Lesson 34
Creating Mailing Labels

- Creating a Sheet of Return Address Labels
- Creating Mailing Labels and Starting the Mail Merge Wizard
- Creating a Recipient List
- Preparing the Publication for a Merge
- Creating a Merged Publication

Lesson 35
Creating Postcards

- Creating a Postcard
- Sorting and Filtering the Recipient List for a Merge
- Personalizing a Publication with Mail Merge
- Previewing and Printing the Personalized Publications

Lesson 36
Creating a Brochure

- Creating a Brochure
- Using Find and Replace
- Using Custom Colors
- Using the Design Checker
- Embedding Fonts
- Exporting for Commercial Printing

End-of-Chapter Activities

Lesson 30

Working with Flyers

> ## **What You Will Learn**

Creating a Flyer with Tear-Offs
Changing the Template Design
Manually Inserting a Coupon Tear-Off
Customizing a Contact Information Tear-Off

WORDS TO KNOW

Flyer
A single-page sheet designed for mass distribution.

Tear-off
A feature designed to be torn or removed from a flyer, such as a coupon or a response form.

Software Skills   Publisher includes a variety of sophisticated templates you can use to create a flyer that is interesting, eye-catching, and functional. For example, you can insert a tear-off such as a coupon or response form.

What You Can Do

Creating a Flyer with Tear-Offs

- Publisher comes with a set of **flyer** templates that offer a range of designs.
- You can select from generic designs, plus many special-purpose designs for uses such as events, marketing, sales, and announcements.
- You customize a flyer using the same options you use to customize any template, including color scheme, font scheme, and business information.
- In addition, once you select a template, you can select a **tear-off** from the Tear-offs drop-down menu in the right pane of the New tab in Backstage view.
- Available tear-offs include contact information, coupons, order forms, response forms, and sign-up forms.

Try It!   Creating a Flyer with Tear-Offs

1 Start Publisher, if necessary.

2 On the New tab in Backstage view, click BUILT-IN and then click Flyers.

3 Under Marketing, click Bounce.

4 In the right pane, click the Tear-offs drop-down arrow and then click Coupon.

5 Under Options, remove the check from Include graphic.

6 Click the CREATE button.

7 Save the publication as **PB30Try_xx** in the location where your teacher instructs you to store the files for this lesson, and leave it open to use in the next Try It.

Add a tear-off to a flyer in Backstage view

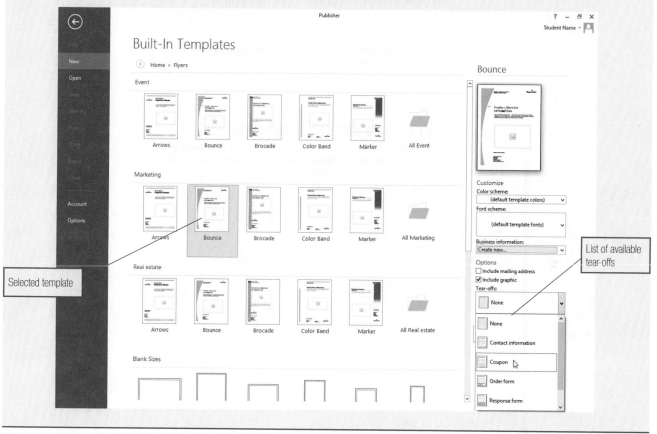

Changing the Template Design

- You can change the template design—including the tear-off—at any time using the options in the Change Template dialog box, as you learned to do in Chapter 2. Changing the template design replaces the design elements in the current publication.

- To open the Change Template dialog box, click the Change Template button on the PAGE DESIGN tab of the Ribbon.

- You can select a different template, or customize the color scheme, font scheme, tear-offs, or other options of the existing template.

- Before applying the changes, Publisher prompts you to select whether you want to apply the template to the current publication or create a new publication.

Try It!   **Changing the Template Design**

1 In the **PB30Try_xx** file, click the PAGE DESIGN tab and then, in the Template group, click the Change Template button 📄.

2 Under Marketing, click Color Band.

3 In the right pane, click the Color scheme drop-down arrow and click Parrot.

4 In the right pane, click the Tear-offs drop-down arrow, and click Contact information.

5 Click OK.

6 Click to select the Apply template to the current publication option button, and then click OK.

7 Save the changes to **PB30Try_xx**, and leave it open to use in the next Try It.

Flyer with contact information tear-offs

ROBBINS IMAGING

Business Tagline or Motto

Product/Service Information

Place text here that introduces your organization and describes your specific products or services. This text should be brief and should entice the reader to want to know more about the goods or services you offer.

Tel: 555 555 5555

Name 555 555 5555
Name 555 555 5555
Name 555 555 5555
Name 555 555 5555
Name 555 555 5555
Name 555 555 5555
Name 555 555 5555
Name 555 555 5555
Name 555 555 5555
Name 555 555 5555
Name 555 555 5555

Manually Inserting a Coupon Tear-Off

- Coupon tear-offs are building blocks.
- You can manually insert a coupon tear-off the way you would insert any building block.
- The available coupon building blocks display in the Advertisements gallery which you access from the Building Blocks group on the INSERT tab.
- Customize the content of the building block the way you would customize any object. For example, you can edit the text or change the formatting.
- When you manually insert a coupon, it displays in addition to existing tear-offs rather than replacing them.

Try It! **Manually Inserting a Coupon Tear-Off**

1 In the **PB30Try_xx** file, click INSERT > Advertisements 🖼 to display the Advertisements gallery.

2 Scroll down to see the Coupons category, and then click the Open Background building block. The coupon displays on the flyer page.

3 In the coupon, click Name of Item or Service to select it, and type **First Visit**.

4 Click 00% OFF to select it, and type **$10 OFF**.

5 Save the changes to **PB30Try_xx**, and leave it open to use in the next Try It.

Flyer with added coupon tear-off

Customizing a Contact Information Tear-Off

■ The Contact Information tear-off includes a series of ten grouped text boxes.

■ By default, each text box includes contact name and phone number. The text direction flows from the top of the box to the bottom.

■ When you customize the information in one of the text boxes, the content in the other text boxes is synchronized to match.

■ Before distributing the flyer, you can cut between the boxes so anyone who is interested in the information can easily tear it off and take it.

Try It!   **Customizing a Contact Information Tear-Off**

---

1 In the **PB30Try_xx** file, increase the zoom to 110% if necessary.

2 Click in the text box on the far left of the Contact information tear-off.

3 Select the existing text and then type **Hair Clips Salon** and press ENTER .

4 Type **555-7670**.

5 Click anywhere outside the tear-off to synchronize the contact information. All tear-offs change to show the information entered on the far-left tear-off.

6 Close the publication, saving changes, and exit Publisher.

Customize contact information tear-offs

Lesson 30—Practice

In this exercise, you create a flyer advertising a dog grooming service. The flyer is designed for posting in local businesses and includes a tear-off with the contact information of the groomer.

DIRECTIONS

1. Start Publisher, if necessary.
2. On the New tab in Backstage view, under BUILT-IN, click **Flyers**.
3. Under Marketing, click **All Marketing**.
4. Scroll down, and under More Installed Templates click **Blends**.
5. In the right pane under Customize, click the **Color scheme** drop-down arrow and click **Plum**.
6. Click the **Font scheme** drop-down arrow and click **Online**.
7. Under Options, click to clear the **Include mailing address** and **Include graphic** check boxes, if necessary.
8. Click the **Tear-offs** drop-down arrow and click **Contact information**.
9. Click the **CREATE** button.
10. Save the publication as **PB30Practice_xx** in the location where your teacher instructs you to store the files for this lesson.
11. In the text box at the top of the page, replace the sample company name with **Paw Washer**. Increase the font size to **28 points** and resize the text box to display all text.
12. Replace the sample text *Product/Service Information* with **Dog Grooming**.
13. Replace the sample informational text with the following:

    With today's busy schedules, it's easy to overlook your dog's grooming. Whether your pet needs a bath, a manicure, or just a good brushing, let me take care of it for you!

    I am a dog lover with three of my own, and I will treat your pet with care. Your dog will come home smelling sweet and looking neat.

    Paw Washer is a mobile service, so I come to you! No need to drop off or pick up your pet.

14. Align the text box at the left margin, and vertically so the top is even with the 4 inch mark on the vertical ruler.
15. Insert a new text box sized **2.75 inches** high by **2.5 inches** wide. Align it with the right margin, and vertically so the top is even with the 4 inch mark on the vertical ruler.
16. In the new text box, increase the font size to **12 points** and type the following:

    Available services
    • **Baths**
    • **Nail clipping**
    • **Haircuts**
    • **Dead hair removal**
    • **Show grooming**
    • **Teeth cleaning**

17. Delete the *Business Tag Line* text box and the *Organization logo* information if it is displayed on your flyer.
18. Edit the telephone information to **Tel: 387-555-5585**.
19. Customize the tear off contact information by replacing the sample text *Name* with your own name, and the sample phone number with **387-555-5585**.
20. Check and correct the spelling in the publication, and then save the changes.
21. **With your teacher's permission**, print the publication. It should look similar to Figure 30-1 on the next page.
22. Close the publication, saving changes, and exit Publisher.

Figure 30-1

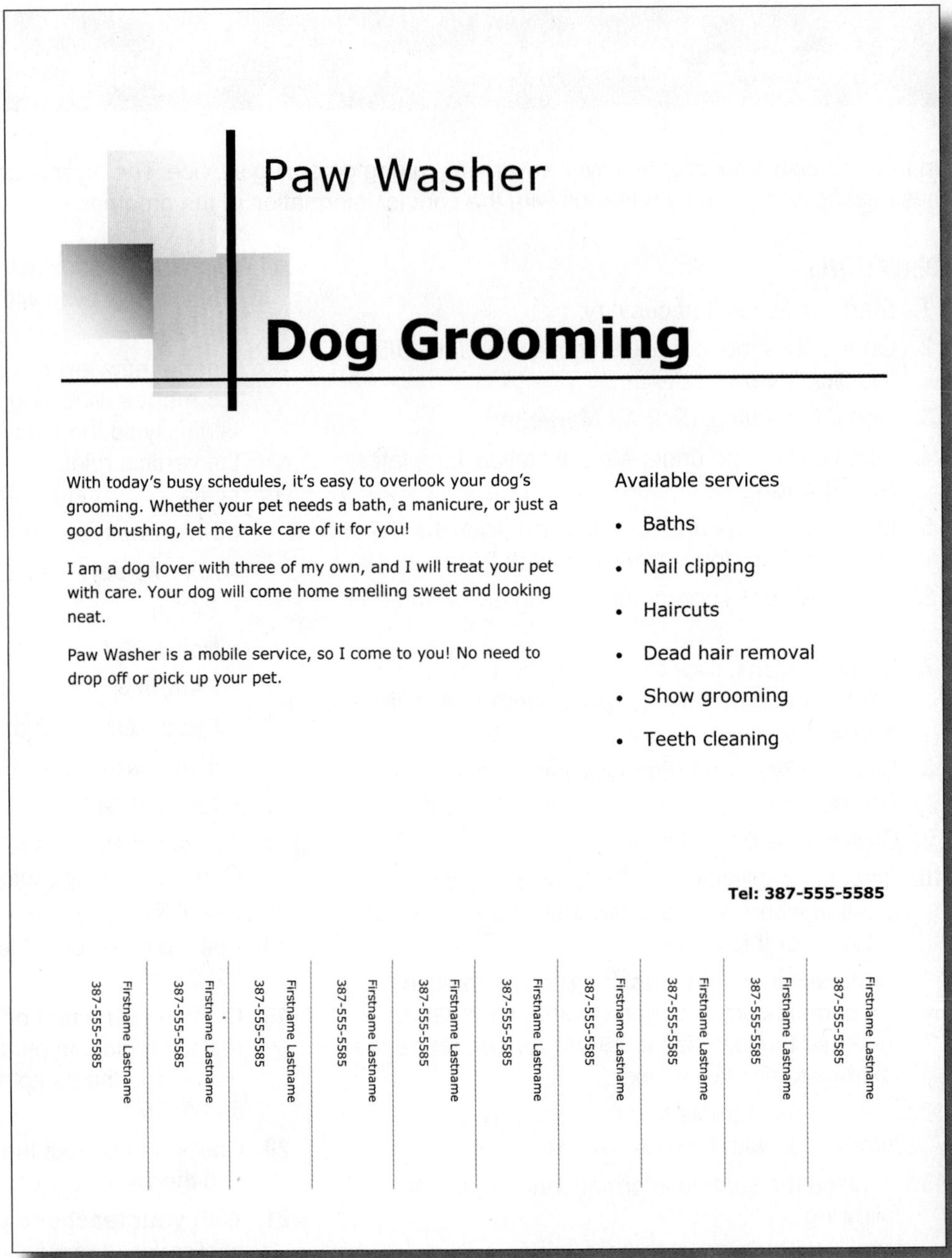

Paw Washer

Dog Grooming

With today's busy schedules, it's easy to overlook your dog's grooming. Whether your pet needs a bath, a manicure, or just a good brushing, let me take care of it for you!

I am a dog lover with three of my own, and I will treat your pet with care. Your dog will come home smelling sweet and looking neat.

Paw Washer is a mobile service, so I come to you! No need to drop off or pick up your pet.

Available services

- Baths
- Nail clipping
- Haircuts
- Dead hair removal
- Show grooming
- Teeth cleaning

Tel: 387-555-5585

Firstname Lastname
387-555-5585

Firstname Lastname
387-555-5585

Firstname Lastname
387-555-5585

Firstname Lastname
387-555-5585

Firstname Lastname
387-555-5585

Firstname Lastname
387-555-5585

Firstname Lastname
387-555-5585

Firstname Lastname
387-555-5585

Firstname Lastname
387-555-5585

Firstname Lastname
387-555-5585

Firstname Lastname
387-555-5585

Firstname Lastname
387-555-5585

Lesson 30—Apply

You continue to work for the Paw Washer dog grooming service. In this exercise, you create another flyer with a coupon, designed to be delivered directly to potential customers.

DIRECTIONS

1. Start Publisher, if necessary, and open **PB30Apply** from the data files for this lesson.

2. Save the publication as **PB30Apply_xx** in the location where your teacher instructs you to store the files for this lesson.

3. Change the template to **Marketing Color Band**.

4. Change the Color scheme to **Aspect**.

5. Change the Font scheme to **Basis**.

6. Change the Tear-offs to **Coupon**.

7. Apply the changes to the current publication.

8. In the Extra Content task pane, click the **With today's busy** drop-down arrow and click **Insert**, then close the Extra Content task pane.

9. Position the two text boxes as shown in Figure 30-2 on the next page. Decrease the font size of the *Available services* text to **11 point**.

10. Delete the *Business Tagline or Motto* text box.

11. Increase the font size of the company name *Paw Washer* at the top of the page to **36 points** and increase the size of the text box to display all text.

12. In the lower-left of the page, delete the *Organization Logo*, and delete all other company information.

13. In the coupon tear-off object, replace the sample text *Name of Item or Service* with **Nail Clipping**.

14. Replace the sample text *00% Off* with **Free with Any Service**.

15. Replace the sample text *Organization Name* with **Paw Washer**.

16. Replace the sample text *Describe your location by landmark or area of town* with **New Customers Only**.

17. Replace the sample telephone number with **387-555-5585**.

18. Replace the sample *Expiration date* with today's date.

19. Change the picture to **PB30Apply_image.gif** from the data files for this lesson. Then delete the previous picture from the scratch area.

20. Save the changes to the publication.

21. Insert the **2 for 1 coupon** building block and use the Align drop-down list to position it in the middle of the page relative to margin guides. Align the left side of the coupon with the left edge of the text above the coupon.

22. Replace the sample text *Name of Item or Service* with **Buy One Bath and Get the Second Bath Free!**

23. Replace the sample text *Organization Name* with **Paw Washer**.

24. Replace the sample text *Describe your location by landmark or area of town* with **New Customers Only**.

25. Replace the sample telephone number with **387-555-5585**.

26. Delete the expiration date.

27. Check and correct the spelling in the publication, and then save the changes.

28. **With your teacher's permission**, print the publication. It should look similar to Figure 30-2 on the next page.

29. Close the publication, saving changes, and exit Publisher. If necessary, click **OK** to delete the items in the Extra Content task pane.

Figure 30-2

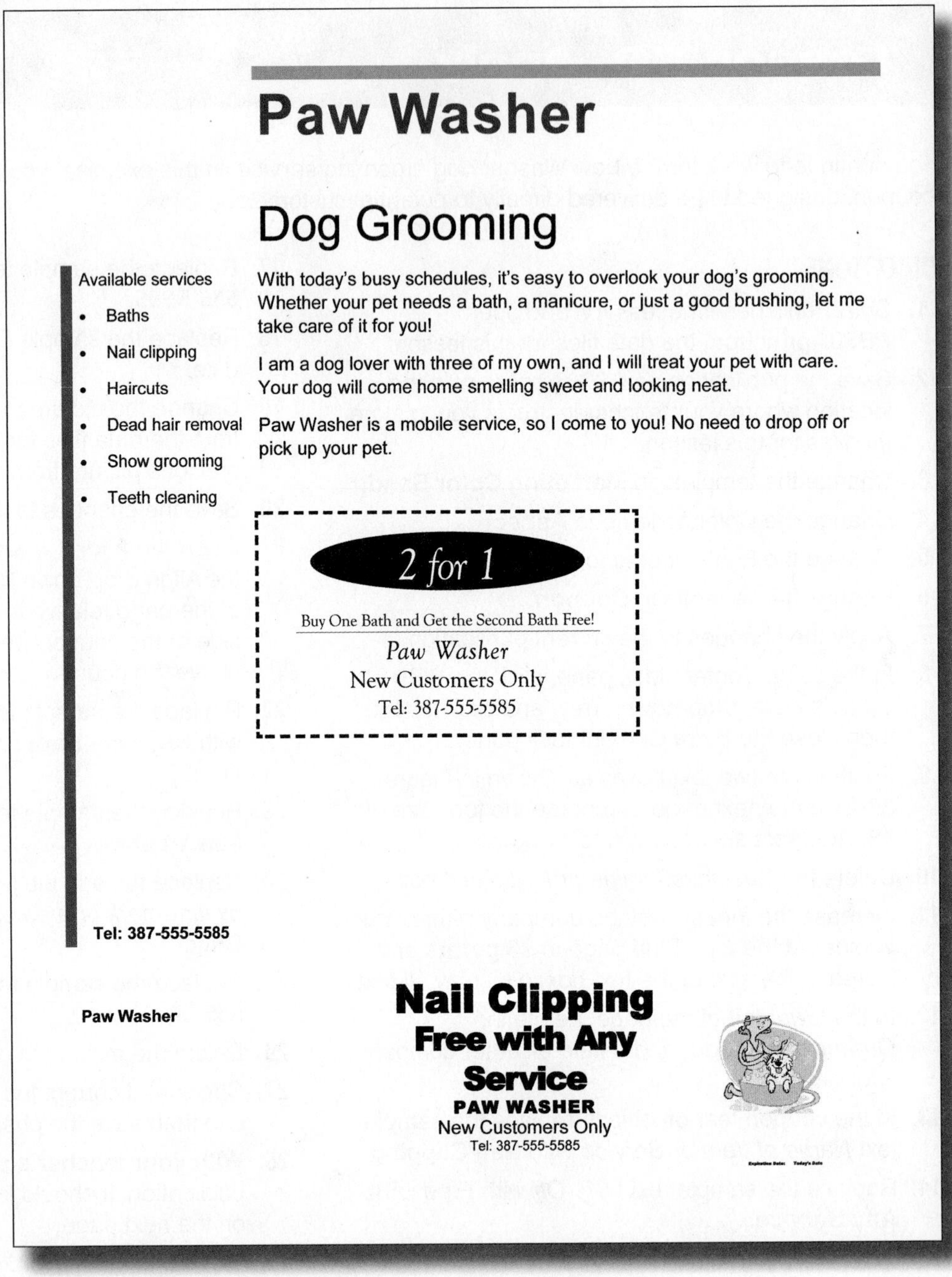

Paw Washer

Dog Grooming

Available services

- Baths
- Nail clipping
- Haircuts
- Dead hair removal
- Show grooming
- Teeth cleaning

With today's busy schedules, it's easy to overlook your dog's grooming. Whether your pet needs a bath, a manicure, or just a good brushing, let me take care of it for you!

I am a dog lover with three of my own, and I will treat your pet with care. Your dog will come home smelling sweet and looking neat.

Paw Washer is a mobile service, so I come to you! No need to drop off or pick up your pet.

2 for 1

Buy One Bath and Get the Second Bath Free!

Paw Washer
New Customers Only
Tel: 387-555-5585

Tel: 387-555-5585

Paw Washer

Nail Clipping
Free with Any
Service
PAW WASHER
New Customers Only
Tel: 387-555-5585

Expiration Date: Today's Date

Lesson 31

Creating Greeting Cards

➤ **What You Will Learn**

Creating a Greeting Card
Customizing a Greeting Card Message
Changing Card Template Options
Creating an Envelope
Customizing an Envelope for a Greeting Card

Software Skills   Use Publisher to create greeting cards and invitations. You can print the publications on plain paper, or on special cardstock. You can even print the recipient's name and address directly on a matching envelope.

What You Can Do

Creating a Greeting Card

- Publisher includes templates for many types of greeting cards, including thank-you notes and birthday cards.

- When you select Greeting Cards on the New tab in Backstage view, the card templates are sorted into categories, such as Birthday, Holidays, and Occasions and Events.

- You can customize the cards using standard customization options such as Color scheme and Font scheme.

- Most cards are designed to have four pages—front, inside left, inside right, and back.

- For most card templates, you can select a **half-fold** or **quarter-fold** page size:
  - A quarter-sheet side fold uses an 8.5" × 11" sheet, which you fold in half, and then in half again after printing. The resulting card is 4.25" × 5.5" and opens right to left.
  - A quarter-sheet top fold uses an 8.5" × 11" sheet, which you fold in half, and then in half again after printing. The resulting card is 4.25" × 5.5" and opens bottom to top.
  - A half-sheet side fold uses an 8.5" × 11" sheet, which you fold in half after printing. The resulting card is 8.5" × 5.5".

- Some card templates also offer layout options that you use to determine the arrangement of objects on the page.

Try It!   **Creating a Greeting Card**

1 Start Publisher, if necessary.

2 On the New tab in Backstage view, under BUILT-IN, click Greeting Cards.

3 Under Birthday, click Birthday 3.

4 In the right pane, under Customize, click the Color scheme drop-down arrow and click Flow.

Select and customize a Greeting Card template

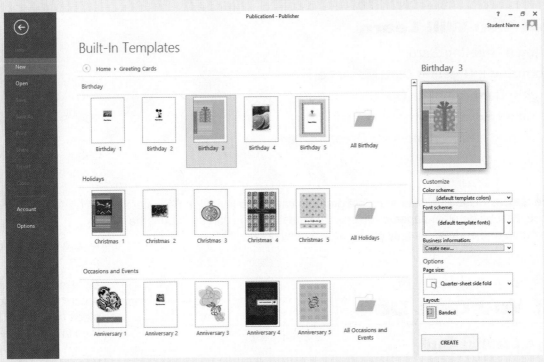

5 Click the Font scheme drop-down arrow and click Capital.

6 Under Options, click the Page size drop-down arrow and click Half-sheet side fold.

7 Click the Layout drop-down arrow and click Greetings Bar.

8 Click CREATE.

9 Save the publication as **PB31TryA_xx** in the location where your teacher instructs you to store the files for this lesson. Leave it open to use in the next Try It.

Page 1 of a birthday card

Customizing a Greeting Card Message

- Each greeting card template includes a verse or message.
- You can change the verse to customize the card.

- You can select from a list of Available messages in the Suggested Verse dialog box, which you open by clicking the Options button on the PAGE DESIGN tab.
- Alternatively, you can simply edit the text displayed in the publication the way you would edit any text.

Try It! Customizing a Greeting Card Message

1. In the **PB31TryA_xx** file, click pages 2 and 3 in the Page Navigation pane.

2. Click PAGE DESIGN > Options ✎ to display the Suggested Verse dialog box.

3. In the list of Available messages, click Hip, hip, hooray.

4. Click OK.

5. Click page 4 in the Page Navigation pane.

6. Increase the zoom, if necessary, then replace the sample user name with your own name. Press [ENTER] and type today's date.

7. Save the changes to **PB31TryA_xx**, and leave it open to use in the next Try It.

Select and preview a card message

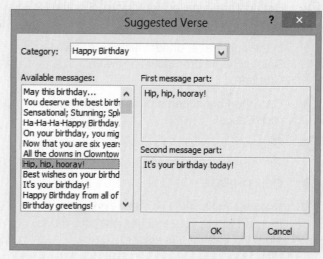

Changing Card Template Options

- You can change the template or template options using the same commands you use to change to a different type of template (refer to Lesson 30).

- For example, when you change the options, you may need to select whether to apply the changes to the current publication or to create a new publication.

Try It! Changing Card Template Options

1. In the **PB31TryA_xx** file, click PAGE DESIGN > Change Template 📄.

2. Under Birthday, click All Birthday, and then click Birthday 6.

3. In the right pane, under Customize, click the Color scheme drop-down arrow and click Cranberry.

4. Click the Font scheme drop-down arrow and click Casual.

5. Under Options, click the Page size drop-down arrow and click Quarter-sheet side fold.

6. Click the Layout drop-down arrow and click Retro Orbits.

7. Click OK.

8. Close the publication, saving changes. Leave Publisher open to use in the next Try It.

Creating an Envelope

- Use the New tab in Backstage view to select an Envelope template to create an envelope publication.

- Envelope templates include options similar to other types of templates, so you can customize your envelope to match your greeting card.

- In addition, they include placeholder text boxes for entering the mailing and return addresses.

Try It!   Creating an Envelope

1 In Publisher, on the New tab in Backstage view, under BUILT-IN, click Envelopes.

2 Under More Installed Templates, click the Retro template.

3 In the right pane, under Customize, click the Color scheme drop-down arrow and click Cranberry.

4 Click the Font scheme drop-down arrow and click Casual.

5 Under Options, click to clear the Include logo check box.

6 Click CREATE.

7 Save the publication as **PB31TryB_xx** in the location where your teacher instructs you to store the files for this lesson.

8 Replace the sample business name with your own name, and the sample return address with your school address. Delete unnecessary lines of sample text.

9 Click the text in the mailing address placeholder text box and type the following:

Mr. George McSweeney
1111 Main Street
Anytown, NY 11111

10 Save the changes to **PB31TryB_xx**, and leave it open to use in the next Try It.

Customizing an Envelope for a Greeting Card

- Most envelope templates are available in two page sizes suitable for business letters: #6¾, which is 6.5 inches by 3.625 inches, and #10, which is 9.5 inches by 4.125 inches. Blank envelope templates are available in a variety of sizes.

- However, a greeting card envelope must be in a size that matches your card and the envelope you have available for use. Usually, that means creating a custom page size. (Refer to Lesson 8 for information on customizing page sizes.)

- For example, for a half-sheet fold card, you will need an envelope approximately 6.75 by 8.75 inches. For a quarter-sheet fold, you will need an envelope approximately 4.5 by 5.75 inches.

  ✓ *Alternatively, you may be able to download an envelope template that matches your greeting card size.*

- When you customize the envelope page size, you may have to adjust the position of the address and return address text boxes.

- Custom page sizes display in the page size gallery so you can use them again in the future or delete them.

Try It! Customizing an Envelope for a Greeting Card

1 In the **PB31TryB_xx** file, click PAGE DESIGN > Size ⬚ > Create New Page Size.

2 In the Name box, type **Quarter Side Fold Card**.

3 In the Width box, type **5.75**.

4 In the Height box, type **4.5**.

5 Click OK.

Create a custom envelope size

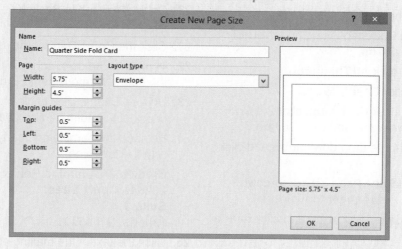

6 Select all objects that comprise the return address. Align them left relative to the margin, and nudge them up to the top margin. Select the text box with the dotted line border and adjust it to 1.2 inch high. Reposition the light tan graphic object at the lower-right corner of the dotted line box.

7 Select the mailing address text box and align it at the right with the right margin and at the top at 2.3 inches on the vertical ruler.

8 Click PAGE DESIGN > Size ⬚ to display the gallery of page sizes.

9 Right-click the Quarter Side Fold Card custom page size, click Delete, and then click Yes in the confirmation dialog box.

10 Close the publication, saving changes, and exit Publisher.

The greeting card envelope

Lesson 31—Practice

Bradley & Cummins Realty wants you to prepare a thank-you card to a client who recently closed on a new home. In this exercise, you create both the card and the envelope.

DIRECTIONS

1. Start Publisher, if necessary.
2. On the New tab in Backstage view, under BUILT-IN, click **Greeting Cards**.
3. Under Thank You, click **All Thank You**.
4. Scroll down and click **Thank You 1**.
5. In the right pane under Customize, click the **Color scheme** drop-down arrow and click **Cavern**.
6. Click the **Font scheme** drop-down arrow and click **Etched**.
7. Under Options, click the **Page size** drop-down arrow and click **Quarter-sheet top fold**.
8. Click the **Layout** drop-down arrow and click **Image Classic**.
9. Click the **CREATE** button.
10. Save the publication as **PB31PracticeA_xx** in the location where your teacher instructs you to store the files for this lesson.
11. In the Page Navigation pane, click to display pages 2 and 3.
12. Click **PAGE DESIGN** > **Options** ✎.
13. In the list of Available messages, click **Thanks for your business**, and then click **OK**.
14. On page 3, select the second sentence and replace it by typing **All of us at Bradley & Cummins Realty wish you great happiness in your new home.**
15. Press [ENTER] and type **Sincerely,** press [ENTER] and type your name.
16. Display page 4 and replace the sample user name with **Bradley & Cummins**. Type a comma and then type today's date.
17. Check and correct the spelling in the publication, and then save the changes.
18. **With your teacher's permission**, print the publication. It should look similar to Figure 31-1 on the next page. Fold it to create the card.

19. Close the publication, saving changes.
20. On the New tab in Backstage view, under BUILT-IN, click **Envelopes**.
21. Click the **Color Band** template.
22. Verify that the color scheme is set to **Cavern** and the Font scheme is set to **Etched**.
23. Under Options, click to clear the **Include logo** check box, and then click **Create**.
24. Replace the sample company name and address with the following:

    Bradley & Cummins Realty
    2828 N. Court Street
    Suite 3
    Athens, OH 45701

25. Click the text in the mailing address placeholder and type the following:

    Mr. and Mrs. Snow
    559 Blueberry Lane
    Athens, OH 45701

26. Save the publication as **PB31PracticeB_xx** in the location where your teacher instructs you to store the files for this lesson.
27. Click **PAGE DESIGN** > **Size** 🗋 > **Create New Page Size**.
28. In the Name box, type **Quarter Top Fold Card**.
29. In the Width box, enter **5.75**.
30. In the Height box, enter **4.5**.
31. Click **OK**.
32. Select all objects that comprise the return address, group them, and align them in the top left, relative to the margin.
33. Select the mailing address text box and align it in the center, right relative to the margin.
34. Check and correct the spelling in the publication, and then save the changes.

Figure 31-1

Firstname Lastname

Sincerely,

home.
wish you great happiness in your new
All of us at Bradley & Cummins Realty

Thanks for your business.

Made especially for you by:
Bradley & Cummins, Today's Date

THANK YOU

---

35. **With your teacher's permission**, print the envelope. It should look similar to Figure 31-2 on the next page.

✓ *You may print on plain paper.*

36. Close the publication, saving changes, and exit Publisher.

Figure 31-2

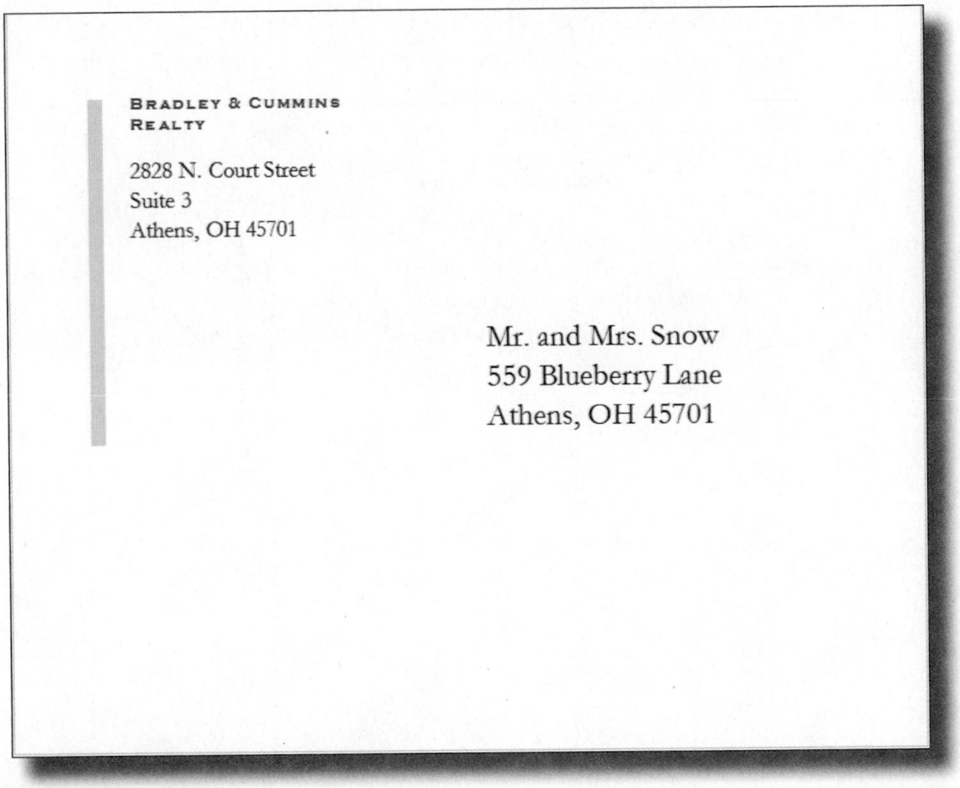

BRADLEY & CUMMINS
REALTY

2828 N. Court Street
Suite 3
Athens, OH 45701

Mr. and Mrs. Snow
559 Blueberry Lane
Athens, OH 45701

Lesson 31—Apply

You continue to work on greeting cards for Bradley & Cummins Realty. In this exercise, you create an anniversary card for clients who bought a new home one year ago.

DIRECTIONS

1. Start Publisher, if necessary, and open **PB31Apply** from the data files for this lesson.

2. Save the publication as **PB31ApplyA_xx** in the location where your teacher instructs you to store the files for this lesson.

3. Change the template to **Congratulations 1**.

   ✓ *You will find the template in the Greeting Cards > All Occasions and Events folder.*

4. Change the color scheme to **Ocean** and the Font scheme to **Binary**.

5. Verify that the Page size is set to **Quarter-sheet top fold**.

6. Change the Layout to **Art Bit**.

7. Apply the changes to the current publication.

8. Display pages 2 and 3, open the Suggested Verse dialog box, click the **Category** drop-down arrow, and click **Anniversary**.

9. In the list of Available messages, click **Anniversaries come around once a year...**, and then click **OK**.

10. On page 3, edit the second sentence to **We made a note of it!**

11. Press [ENTER] and type **Congratulations on one year in your home.**

12. Press [ENTER] and type **From** and then type your name followed by **and all your friends at Bradley & Cummins Realty**.

13. On page 4, edit the sample text *Today's Date* to the actual date.

14. Check and correct the spelling in the publication and then save the changes.

15. **With your teacher's permission**, print the publication. It should look similar to Figure 31-3. Fold it to create the card.

16. Close the publication, saving all changes.

17. Create a new envelope publication using the **Accessory Bar** template.

18. Apply the **Ocean** Color scheme and the **Binary** Font scheme and do not include a logo.

19. Replace the sample company name and address with the following:

    Bradley & Cummins Realty
    2828 N. Court Street
    Suite 3
    Athens, OH 45701

20. Click the text in the mailing address placeholder and type the following:

    The Peale Family
    68 Sunset Drive
    Athens, OH 45701

21. Save the publication as **PB31ApplyB_xx** in the location where your teacher instructs you to store the files for this lesson.

22. Apply the **Quarter Top Fold Card** custom page size you created in the previous project.

23. Adjust the size and position of all objects to fit the new page size.

Figure 31-3

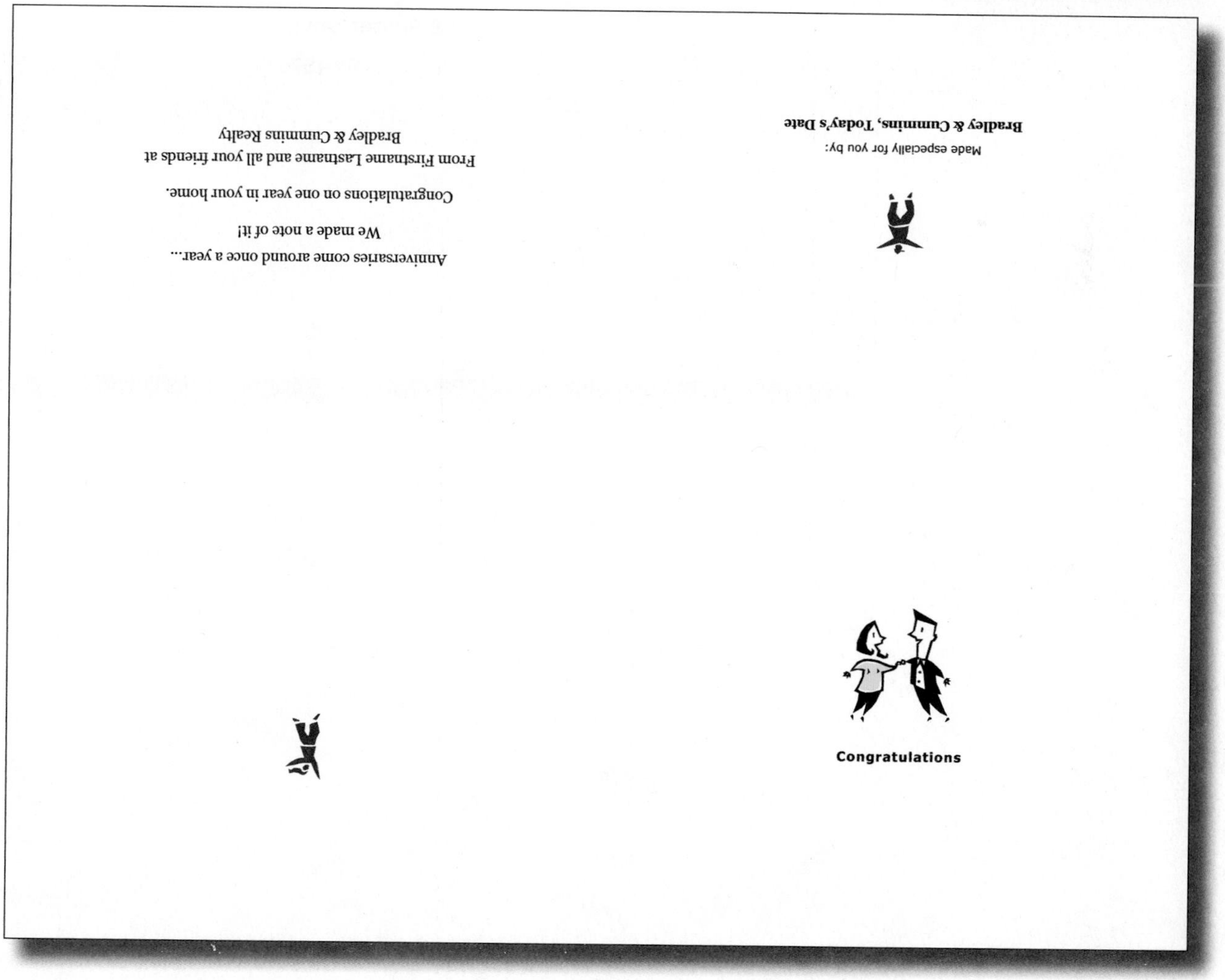

Bradley & Cummins Realty

From Firstname Lastname and all your friends at

Congratulations on one year in your home.

We made a note of it!

Anniversaries come around once a year...

Bradley & Cummins, Today's Date

Made especially for you by:

Congratulations

24. Check and correct the spelling in the publication, and then save the changes.

25. **With your teacher's permission**, print the envelope. It should look similar to Figure 31-4.

   ✓ *You may print on plain paper.*

26. Delete the **Quarter Top Fold Card** custom page size.

27. Close the publication, saving changes, and exit Publisher.

Figure 31-4

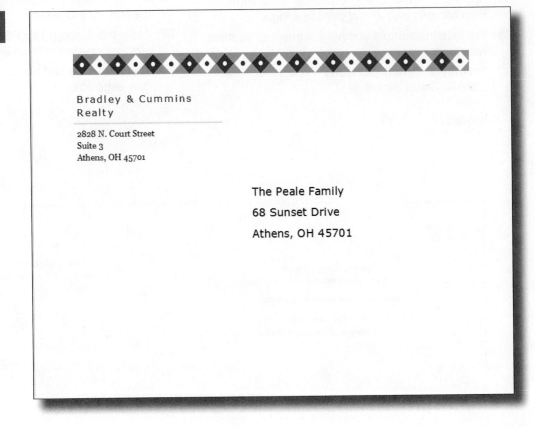

Bradley & Cummins
Realty

2828 N. Court Street
Suite 3
Athens, OH 45701

The Peale Family

68 Sunset Drive

Athens, OH 45701

Lesson 32

Creating Publications to Distribute via E-mail

› What You Will Learn

Creating an E-mail Publication
Adjusting the Page Size of an E-mail Publication
Inserting a Hyperlink
Using E-mail Preview and Testing Hyperlinks
Sending a Publication via E-mail

Software Skills   Publisher provides many options for sending publications via e-mail, including as an attachment to a message or as the message body itself. In any case, the result is a professional-looking message that will be noticed.

What You Can Do

Creating an E-mail Publication

- You can send any publication as an e-mail message using the FILE > Share > Email commands.

- However, if you use one of Publisher's E-mail templates, the publication is ideally sized and formatted to display correctly when opened in an e-mail program.

- To create a new e-mail publication, select E-mail as the template type on the New tab in Backstage view, choose one of the available e-mail templates, select customization options, and click CREATE.

- You can preview a publication in your browser program before sending it to see how it will look when the recipient opens it.

WORDS TO KNOW

Destination location
A file, Web page, or new e-mail message that is displayed by clicking a hyperlink.

Hyperlink
Text or a graphic linked to a destination file or location. Click the link to display the destination.

URL
Uniform Resource Locator. The path or address to a file on the Internet.

Try It!   **Creating an E-mail Publication**

1   Start Publisher, if necessary.

2   On the New tab in Backstage view, under BUILT-IN, click E-mail.

3   In the Event/Activity category, click Marker.

4   In the right pane, under Customize, click the Color scheme drop-down arrow and click Alpine.

5   Click the Font scheme drop-down arrow and click Basis.

6   Click CREATE.

7   Save the publication as **PB32Try_xx** in the location where your teacher instructs you to store the files for this lesson, and leave it open to use in the next Try It.

Adjusting the Page Size of an E-mail Publication

- By default, the page size of a publication based on an e-mail template is Large, which is 5.818 inches wide by 66 inches high.

- If your publication is not going to fill the entire 66 inches, you can change the page size to Short, which is 5.818 inches wide by 11 inches high.

- The page size options are available in the Size gallery that displays when you click PAGE DESIGN > Size.

  ✓ Note that the margins for e-mail pages are set to 0" on all sides because the publication is designed to be viewed on-screen, not printed.

Try It!   **Adjusting the Page Size of an E-mail Publication**

1   In the **PB32Try_xx** file, click PAGE DESIGN > Size 🗅.

2   Under Built-In, click Short.

3   Save the changes to **PB32Try_xx**, and leave it open to use in the next Try It.

Inserting a Hyperlink

- A **hyperlink** is text or a graphic object that is set to display a **destination location** when it is clicked.

- The destination might be a Web page, a new e-mail message, a different page in the current document, or any document stored on your system or network.

- To create a hyperlink, select the text or graphic, click INSERT > Hyperlink, then specify the destination location in the Insert Hyperlink dialog box.

  - You can type the destination **URL** or path in the Address box.

  - If you have recently viewed the destination, you may be able to select it from a list displayed in the dialog box.

  - Alternatively, you can browse your system folders or the Web to locate and select the destination.

- When you create a hyperlink to an e-mail address, you may also enter the text you want to display in the Subject box in the message header. When the recipient clicks the hyperlink, the e-mail program opens with a new message displayed; the To and Subject boxes are already filled in.

- By default, hyperlink text is formatted in a color dependent on the current template with an underline.

- You can edit and format hyperlink text the same way you edit and format regular text.

- When you right-click a hyperlink, you can select the Edit Hyperlink command to open the Edit Hyperlink dialog box so you can change the hyperlink destination.

- You can select Remove Hyperlink to remove the hyperlink from the text or graphic.

Try It!   **Inserting a Hyperlink**

① In the **PB32Try_xx** file, select the text *Learn More* in the text box below the image of the clock. (Increase the zoom, as necessary.)

② Click INSERT > Hyperlink 🌐 to open the Insert Hyperlink dialog box.

③ If necessary, under Link to, click Existing File or Web Page.

④ Click in the Address box and type **http://www.pearsoned.com**, the destination location that will display when someone clicks the hyperlink, and then click OK.

Insert a hyperlink to a Web page

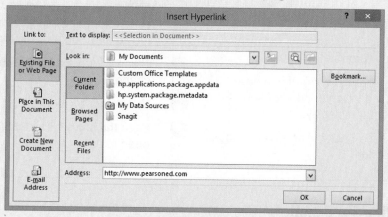

⑤ In the publication, select the sample text *Contact person e-mail:someone@example.com*, and replace it by typing your name. Press [ENTER] and type the e-mail address that your teacher tells you to use, such as your own or your teacher's.

⑥ Select the e-mail address you just typed, and click INSERT > Hyperlink 🌐.

⑦ Under Link to, click E-mail Address.

⑧ In the E-mail address box, type the e-mail address you entered in step 6.

✓ *If the address displays in the Recently used e-mail addresses list, click it to insert it into the E-mail address box.*

⑨ In the Subject box, type **Event Info Request**, and then click OK.

⑩ Save the changes to **PB32Try_xx**, and leave it open to use in the next Try It.

Insert a hyperlink to an e-mail address

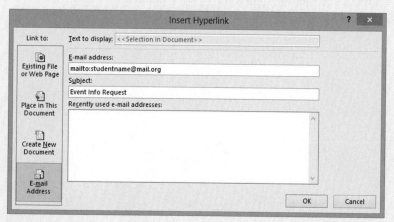

Using E-mail Preview and Testing Hyperlinks

- You can preview a publication in your browser program before sending it to see how it will look when the recipient opens it.

- While previewing the publication, you can test the hyperlinks to make sure they work correctly.

Try It! Using E-mail Preview and Testing Hyperlinks

1. In the **PB32Try_xx** file, click FILE > Share.

2. Under Share, click E-mail Preview.

3. Click the E-mail Preview button 🔍 to display the publication in your browser.

4. Click the Learn More hyperlink. If you have a connection to the Internet, the Pearson Education home page displays.

5. Click your browser's Back button to return to your Web publication.

6. Click the link to the e-mail address. If a security dialog box displays, click Allow or OK to continue. Your e-mail program should open, with the To and Subject boxes already filled in.

7. Close your e-mail program without saving any changes.

8. Close your browser.

9. Save the changes to **PB32Try_xx**, and leave it open to use in the next Try It.

Sending a Publication via E-mail

- When you are ready to send a publication via e-mail, use the FILE > Share command.

- You can create an e-mail message from the current page or from all pages of a multipage document, or you can send the entire publication as an attachment to a message.

- You can also choose to convert a publication to PDF or XPS format and then attach it to a message.

- When you choose to send a publication as an attachment, your e-mail program opens with a new message displayed; the publication is already attached. You fill in the message header, type a message, and click Send.

✓ If you choose to send as PDF or XPSs, Publisher saves a copy of the publication in the selected format and attaches it to the message.

- When you choose to create a message from the publication, the message displays within Publisher. You can access tools for managing the message as you would in your e-mail program, and you can use Publisher commands to work in the publication.

✓ Not all Publisher commands are available.

- In addition, Publisher runs the Design Checker to identify potential problems, such as overlapping text and graphics. You can fix problems and make other changes or improvements before sending the message.

Try It!   **Sending a Publication via E-mail**

1 In the **PB32Try_xx** file, click FILE > Share.

2 Click Send as Attachment.

3 In the To box, enter your teacher's e-mail address.

4 In the Cc box, enter your own e-mail address.

5 In the Subject box, type **32 Send as Attachment**.

6 In the message body, type **I am sending this publication as a message attachment**. Press ⟨ENTER⟩ and type your name.

7 Click the Send button ⌷══▪.

8 In the **PB32Try_xx** file, click FILE > Share.

9 Click Send Current Page.

Send Using E-mail options in Backstage view

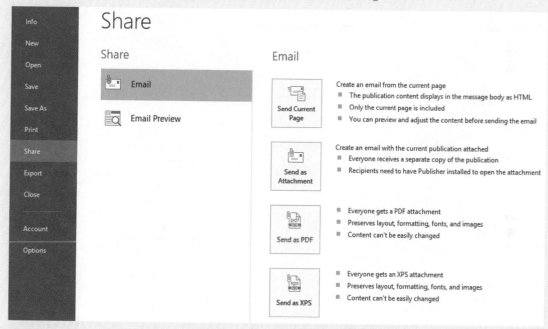

10 In the To box, enter your teacher's e-mail address.

11 In the Cc box, enter your own e-mail address.

12 In the Subject box, type **32 Send as Message**, and then type your name.

13 Click the Send button ⌷══▪.

14 Start or switch to your e-mail program, and send all messages.

15 When the messages arrive in your inbox, open them, and compare the way the publication was sent.

16 Close your e-mail program.

17 Close the publication, saving changes, and exit Publisher.

(continued)

Try It!   **Sending a Publication via E-mail** *(continued)*

Send a publication as an e-mail message

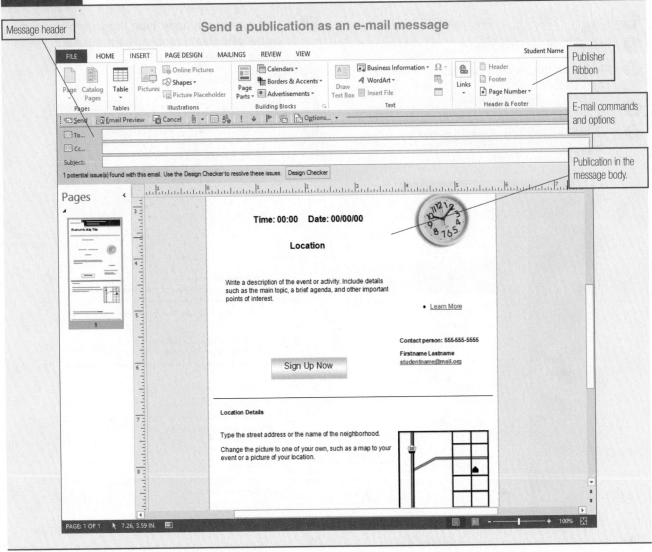

Lesson 32—Practice

You have been asked to prepare a publication to distribute via e-mail for the Geology Club at Cutler College. The publication is an invitation to the club's open house, which you will attach to an e-mail message.

DIRECTIONS

1. Start Publisher, if necessary.
2. On the New tab in Backstage view, under BUILT-IN, click **E-mail**.
3. Under Event/Activity, click **Marker**.
4. In the right pane under Customize, click the **Color scheme** drop-down arrow and click **Concourse**.
5. Click the **Font scheme** drop-down arrow and click **Apex**.
6. Click the **CREATE** button.
7. Save the publication as **PB32Practice_xx** in the location where your teacher instructs you to store the files for this lesson.
8. Click **PAGE DESIGN** > Size 🗋 > **Short**.
9. Increase the zoom as necessary, and then replace the sample text as follows:

Sample Text	Replace With
Business Name	**The Geology Club of Cutler College**
Event or Activity Title	**Meet, Greet, and Eat!**
Event Heading	**Geology Club Open House**
Time	**5:00 p.m.**
Date	**Today's Date**
Location	**212 Stevenson Hall**
Description paragraph	**Stop by to learn more about the Geology Club of Cutler College. Talk to current members, prospective members, and faculty. Enjoy free food while you get to know why you should join.**
Contact person	**Contact: Your name**
Contact person e-mail	**The e-mail your teacher instructs you to use.**

10. Delete the *Business Tagline or Motto* placeholder, the Organization logo, and all placeholders below the horizontal line below the Sign Up Now button.
11. Select the text *Learn More* in the text box below the image of the clock.

12. Click **INSERT** > **Hyperlink** 🌐.
13. If necessary, under Link to click **Existing File or Web Page**.
14. Click in the Address box and type **http://education.usgs.gov**, and then click **OK**.
15. Select the e-mail address you entered for the contact person, and click **INSERT** > **Hyperlink** 🌐.
16. Under Link to, click **E-mail Address**.
17. In the E-mail address box, type the e-mail address you entered for the contact person.

    ✓ *If the address displays in the Recently used e-mail addresses list, click it to insert it into the E-mail address box.*

18. In the Subject box, type **Open House**, and then click **OK**.
19. Check and correct the spelling in the publication, and then save the changes.
20. Click **FILE** > **Share**.
21. Under Share, click **E-mail Preview**, and then click the **E-mail Preview** button 🔍.
22. Click the **Learn More** hyperlink. If you have a connection to the Internet, the USGS Education home page displays.
23. Click your browser's **Back** button to return to your Web publication.
24. Click the link to the e-mail address. If a security dialog box displays, click **Allow** or **OK** to continue. Your e-mail program should open, with the To and Subject boxes already filled in.
25. Close your e-mail program and your browser without saving any changes.
26. Click **FILE** > **Share**.
27. Click **Send as Attachment**. If necessary, click **OK** to save the publication.
28. In the To box, enter your teacher's e-mail address.
29. In the Cc box, enter your own e-mail address.
30. In the Subject box, enter **Open House Invitation**.

31. In the message body, type **For information about free food, check out the attached invitation!** Press ENTER and type your name.

32. Click the **Send** button 📧.

33. Start or switch to your e-mail program, and send all messages.

34. When the message arrives in your inbox, open the attachment.

35. **With your teacher's permission**, print the publication. It should look similar to Figure 32-1.

36. Close your e-mail program, then close the publication, saving changes, and exit Publisher.

Figure 32-1

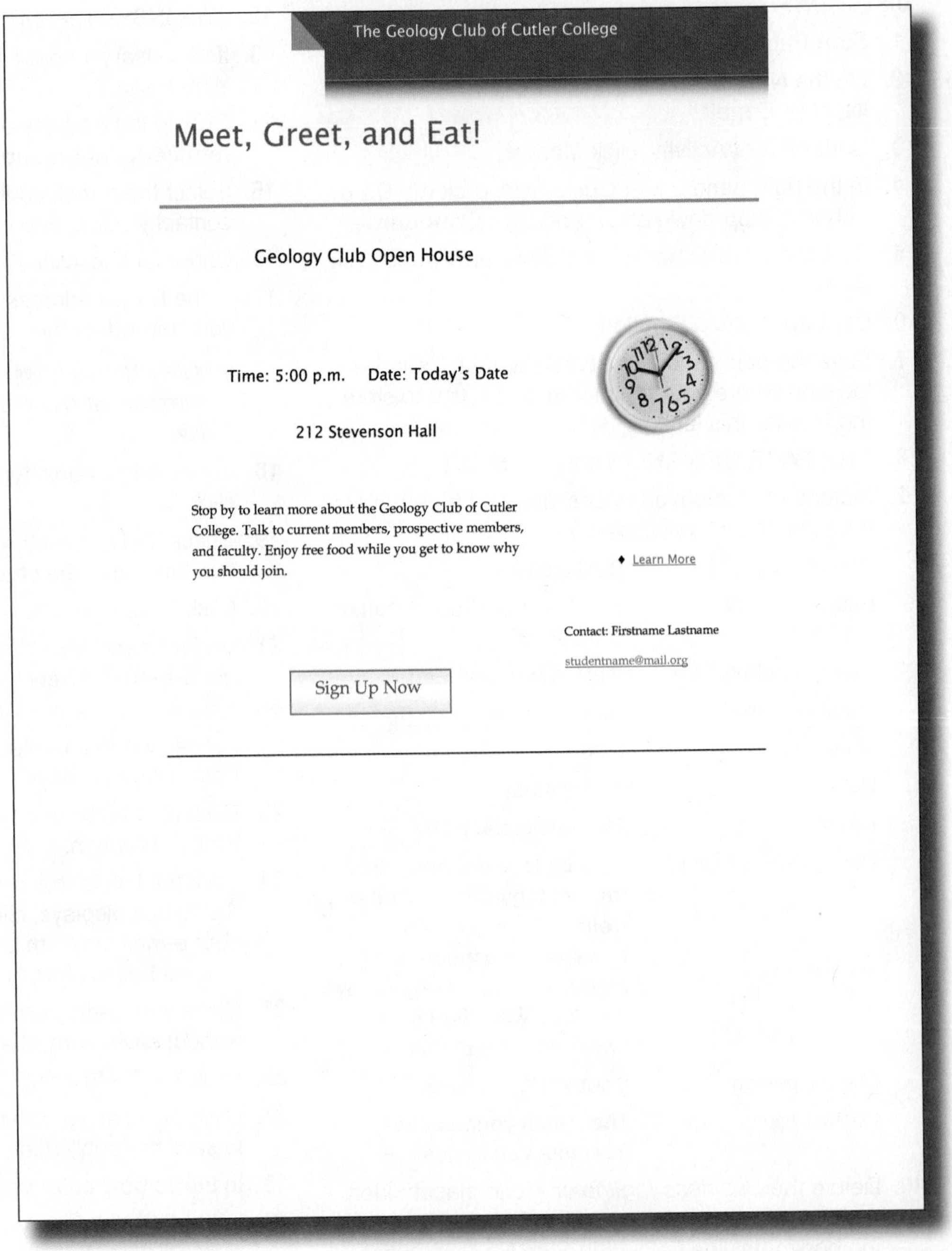

The Geology Club of Cutler College

Meet, Greet, and Eat!

Geology Club Open House

Time: 5:00 p.m.   Date: Today's Date

212 Stevenson Hall

Stop by to learn more about the Geology Club of Cutler College. Talk to current members, prospective members, and faculty. Enjoy free food while you get to know why you should join.

♦ Learn More

Contact: Firstname Lastname

studentname@mail.org

Sign Up Now

Lesson 32—Apply

The Geology Club needs another e-mail publication. In this exercise, you create a letter announcing the club's new faculty advisor, which you will send as an e-mail message.

DIRECTIONS

1. Start Publisher, if necessary, and open **PB32Apply** from the data files for this lesson.

2. Save the publication as **PB32Apply_xx** in the location where your teacher instructs you to store the files for this lesson.

3. Change the template to **Marker** in the Letter category.

4. Change the color scheme to **Concourse** and the Font scheme to the default template font.

5. Change the page size to **Short**.

6. Delete the *Organization logo* placeholder, the *Business Tagline or Motto* placeholder, and the placeholder displaying the text *Your Signature*. Also delete the sample graphic.

7. Replace the sample text *Letter* with the text **Geology Club Announces New Advisor**.

8. Replace the sample text *Student's Name* with your own name and *Today's Date* with the current date.

9. Close up the extra space between the body of the letter, the closing, and your name. Move the last two paragraphs and the horizontal line closer to the text box with your name and the date.

10. Select the text **click here** on the second to last line of the document, and insert a hyperlink to your school's Web site home page, or to the page your teacher instructs you to use.

11. Change the sample e-mail address on the last line of the document to the address that your teacher instructs you to use, then select it and insert a hyperlink to that e-mail address, using the Subject text **More Information**.

12. Check and correct the spelling in the publication, and then save the changes.

13. Preview the publication as it will look as e-mail, and test the hyperlinks.

14. Send the current publication page as an e-mail message.

15. In the To box, enter your teacher's e-mail address.

16. In the Cc box, enter your own e-mail address.

17. In the Subject box, type **New Geology Club Advisor**.

18. Click the **Send** button ⃞.

19. Start or switch to your e-mail program, and send all messages.

20. When the message arrives in your inbox, open it.

21. **With your teacher's permission**, print the publication. It should look similar to Figure 32-2 on the next page.

22. Close your e-mail program, and then close the publication, saving changes, and exit Publisher.

Figure 32-2

Geology Club of Cutler College

Geology Club Announces New Advisor

Dear Club Member,

As most of you know, our long-time faculty advisor, Professor Rebecca Knight, recently announced her retirement. As a result, the club has been actively seeking a new advisor.

We are pleased to announce that Professor Samuel Lang has agreed to the position. Professor Lang has been with the department for seven years. He has participated in many club activities over the years, and has often filled in for Professor Knight at functions and events.

Although we will miss Professor Knight very much, we are excited to have Professor Lang officially on board. We know he will bring a lot of enthusiasm and knowledge to the club.

You will have the opportunity to greet Professor Lang at the club's up-coming open house.

On behalf of the club's officers,

Firstname Lastname

Today's Date

To remove your name from our mailing list, please click here.

Questions or comments? E-mail us at studentname@mail.org or call 555-555-5555

Lesson 33

Working with Newsletters

➤ What You Will Learn

Creating a Newsletter
Changing the Newsletter Page Content
Working with Text in a Newsletter
Inserting a "Continued" Notation

Software Skills   Publisher includes a variety of templates that you can use to quickly design a newsletter publication. The template sets up the publication in columns, and includes placeholders for typical newsletter elements such as a title, headings, graphics, a table of contents, and text.

What You Can Do

Creating a Newsletter

- Create a **newsletter** to provide information on a regular basis.

- The Newsletters templates are similar to other types of templates; select a design on the New tab in Backstage view and then customize it using the options in the right pane.

- The Newsletter templates all include four pages, by default. You can add or delete pages after creating the publication, as necessary.

- In addition to selecting color scheme and font scheme, you can select from two page sizes: one-page spread or two-page spread.

- If you choose the two-page spread, Publisher assumes double-sided printing and adjusts the page number positions appropriately.

- Entering, editing, and formatting newsletter content is similar to entering, editing, and formatting content in any publication. Simply select the placeholder and type text or insert a graphic. Apply formatting as necessary, such as changing the font size. You can delete placeholders you don't need, resize them, or rearrange them.

- To help you develop an effective newsletter, the sample text in the template placeholders includes information such as the number of words that can fit in each story, as well as suggestions for the type of content to include.

Try It!   Creating a Newsletter

1 Start Publisher, if necessary.

2 On the New tab in Backstage view, under BUILT-IN, click Newsletters.

3 Under Installed Templates, click Color Band.

4 In the right pane, under Customize, click the Color scheme drop-down arrow and click Urban.

5 Click the Font scheme drop-down arrow and click Basis.

6 Under Options, click the Page size drop-down arrow and click Two-page spread.

7 Click CREATE.

8 Take a moment to examine the layout and design on each page, and read the suggestions included in the sample story text.

9 Save the publication as **PB33Try_xx** in the location where your teacher instructs you to store the files for this lesson, and leave it open to use in the next Try It.

Changing the Newsletter Page Content

- Use the Options command in the Template group on the PAGE DESIGN tab to change the layout and content of the pages in a newsletter.

- For the first and last page, you can change the number of columns.

- For inside pages, you can change the number of columns and also select content placeholders and building blocks to include, such as the number of stories, a calendar, or an order form.

- You can also insert building blocks from the Building Blocks Library.

- Note that each page can have a different number of columns.

- Also, the number of columns refers to the layout of the main body of the newsletter, where you enter the article text. There are fixed columns on the left, right, or both sides of pages in most templates for inserting elements such as pictures, highlight text, or a table of contents.

- Note that as with other types of templates, when you modify the template or the page content design, Publisher may overwrite changes you have already made. For that reason, it is best to set up the content and design before you begin removing or adding placeholders or entering text or graphics.

Try It!   Changing the Newsletter Page Content

1 In the **PB33Try_xx** file, click page 1 in the Page Navigation pane and then click PAGE DESIGN > Options ✎ to display the Page Content dialog box.

2 Click the Columns drop-down arrow, click 2, and then click OK.

3 Click pages 2 and 3 in the Page Navigation pane and then click PAGE DESIGN > Options ✎. Note that the Page Content dialog box displays different options than were available for page 1.

4 Verify that *Left inside page* appears in the Select a page to modify box.

5 Click the Columns drop-down arrow and click 2.

6 In the Content for page list, click Calendar, and then click OK.

7 Click PAGE DESIGN > Options ✎, click the Select a page to modify drop-down arrow, and click Right inside page.

8 Click the Columns drop-down arrow and click 1.

9 In the Content for page list, click Order form, and then click OK.

10 Save the changes to **PB33Try_xx**, and leave it open to use in the next Try It.

(continued)

Changing the Newsletter Page Content *(continued)*

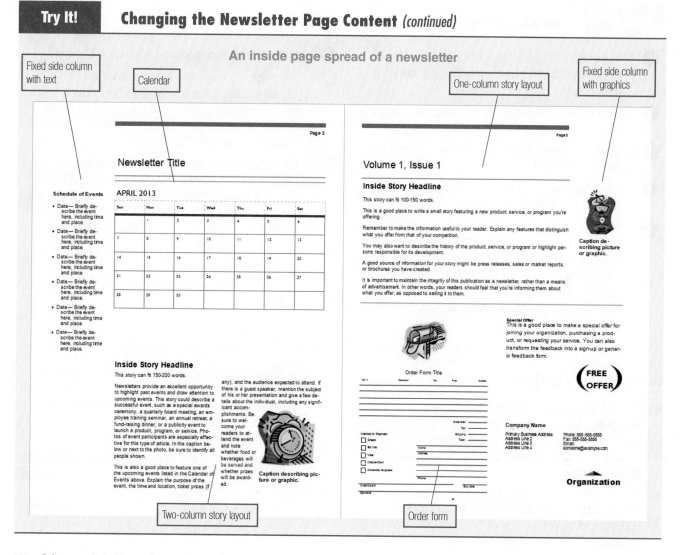

An inside page spread of a newsletter

Fixed side column with text

Calendar

One-column story layout

Fixed side column with graphics

Two-column story layout

Order form

Working with Text in a Newsletter

- When a newsletter page is divided into multiple columns, each story is composed of a series of linked text boxes. (Refer to Lesson 10 for more on linking text boxes.)

- For example, in a three-column layout, the beginning of the story will be in the text box in the first (left) column, which is linked to the text box in the middle column, which is linked to the text box in the last (right) column.

- Recall from Lesson 10 that when you select a linked text box, an arrow appears that you can click to move to the next or previous linked text box.

- To accommodate more text, you can manually link the last text box to another text box on the same page or a different page.

- You can also resize the text boxes or the text.

- Because typing a lengthy article in a small text box can be challenging, you may decide to insert text from other files, such as a Word document. (Refer to Lesson 6 for more on inserting text from other files.)

- If the selected text box is not large enough to fit all of the inserted text, Publisher will prompt you to use the Autoflow feature to link the current text box with the next available text box. You can choose to flow the text or to skip the text box.

- Alternatively, you can cancel the Autoflow process and manually link the text boxes.

Try It!   Working with Text in a Newsletter

1. In the **PB33Try_xx** file, click page 1 in the Page Navigation pane. Increase the zoom, if necessary.

2. Under the *Secondary Story Headline*, click the text box placeholder in the left column.

3. Click the arrow to move to the next linked text box (in the right column).

4. Click CTRL + A to select the sample placeholder text and click INSERT > Insert File 📄.

5. Navigate to the data files for this lesson, select the Word document **PB33Try_import.docx**, and then click OK. Publisher converts the text and fills the two linked text boxes on page 1. It then moves to the first available text box on page 2 and displays an Autoflow confirmation dialog box.

6. In the confirmation dialog box, click Cancel.

7. On page 1, under the *Secondary Story Headline*, click the Text in Overflow button ••• for the text box in the right column. The mouse pointer changes to a pitcher so you can link the overflow to another text box.

8. Click page 4 in the Page Navigation pane. Under the *Back Page Story Headline*, click the text box placeholder in the left column. Publisher links the story and inserts the overflow text from page 1.

9. Save the changes to **PB33Try_xx**, and leave it open to use in the next Try It.

Inserting a "Continued" Notation

- To help readers locate information when a newsletter story is linked from one page to another, you can set Text Box options to automatically display a "Continued on page" or "Continued from page" notation.

- For example, if a story on page 1 is linked to a text box on page 3, the notation on page 1 displays, (Continued on page 3) and the notation on page 3 displays, (Continued from page 1).

- The page number is inserted in a page number reference field so if the content moves to a different page, Publisher automatically updates the page number reference.

- The notation takes up space; you may have to adjust the text flow, the text size, or the placeholder size to fit the content once the notation is displayed.

Try It!   Inserting a "Continued" Notation

1. In the **PB33Try_xx** file, on page 4, right-click the text box in the left column under the *Back Page Story Headline* and click Format Text Box on the shortcut menu.

2. In the Format Text Box dialog box, click the Text Box tab.

3. Under Text autofitting, click to select the Include "Continued on page..." and the Include "Continued from page..." check boxes, and then click OK.

4. Click page 1 in the Page Navigation pane, right-click the text box in the right column under the *Secondary Story Headline*, and click Format Text Box on the shortcut menu.

5. In the Format Text Box dialog box, click the Text Box tab.

6. Under Text autofitting, click to select the Include "Continued on page..." and the Include "Continued from page..." check boxes, and then click OK.

7. Close the publication, saving changes, and exit Publisher.

(continued)

Try It!   **Inserting a "Continued" Notation** *(continued)*

"Continued" notations help readers locate text

Continued from notation on page 4

Secondary Story Headline

Zebras travel in large herds, and often mingle with other wildlife, such as wildebeest. The most distinguishing feature of a zebra is, of course, the black and white stripes.

The stripes help protect the animals by providing camouflage; when they

stand close to one another, it is difficult for predators to see where one zebra begins and another ends.

We will see many zebras while we are on Safari. Herds made up of tens

(Continued on page 4)

Back Page Story Headline

(Continued from page 1)

of thousands of zebra have been known to migrate across the Serengeti plains.

One of the most thrilling moments of a Voyager Travel Adventures African Safari is when you encounter a pride of lions. Lions are called the King of Beasts for a reason. They are majestic,

huge, and dangerous. They are found in savannas, grasslands, dense bush, and woodlands.

Lions generally sleep during the day and hunt at night. We often find them lounging on rocks in the sun

They live in groups called prides, so when we come across one lion there are likely to

be others nearby. Usually, there is one male with multiple females. Viewing a pride with cubs is a particularly exciting event.

Continued on notation on page 1

Lesson 33—Practice

Jaime Cruz, the owner of the Cruz Art Supplies store, would like you to create a newsletter to advertise new products. In this exercise, you create the newsletter, arrange the content and layout., and replace some sample placeholders with Jaime's content.

DIRECTIONS

1. Start Publisher, if necessary.
2. On the New tab in Backstage *view,* under BUILT-IN, click **Newsletters**.
3. Under More Installed Templates, click **Accessory Bar**.
4. In the right pane, click the **Color scheme** drop-down arrow and click **Trek**.
5. Click the **Font scheme** drop-down arrow and click **(default template fonts)**.
6. Under *Options*, click the **Page size** drop-down arrow and click **One-page spread**.
7. Click the **CREATE** button.
8. Save the publication as **PB33Practice_xx** in the location where your teacher instructs you to store the files for this lesson.

9. Click **INSERT > Footer** and type your name in the footer area. Click **Close Master Page** ☒.
10. Select page 1, and click **PAGE DESIGN > Options** ✐.
11. Click the **Columns** drop-down arrow, click **2**, and then click **OK**.
12. Select page 2, and click **PAGE DESIGN > Options** ✐.
13. Click the **Columns** drop-down arrow and click **2**.
14. In the Content for page list, click **Calendar**, and then click **OK**.
15. Select page 3, and click **PAGE DESIGN > Options** ✐.
16. Click the **Columns** drop-down arrow and click **1**.
17. In the Content for page list, click **Order form**, and then click **OK**.

18. Select page 4, and click **PAGE DESIGN >
Options** ✎.

19. Click the **Columns** drop-down arrow, click **1**, and
then click **OK**.

20. Increase the zoom as necessary, and then replace
the sample text on page 1 as follows:

Sample Text	Replace With
Newsletter Title	What's New at Cruz
Business Name	Cruz Art Supplies
Newsletter Date	Today's Date
Lead Story Headline	New Gifts and Supplies Are In!

21. On page 1, delete the following placeholder
objects:

- Special points of interest
- Inside this issue
- Secondary Story Headline
- Two text boxes under Secondary Story Headline

Page 1 should look similar to Figure 33-1.

Figure 33-1

What's New at Cruz

Cruz Art Supplies

New Gifts and Supplies Are In!

This story can fit 175-225 words.

The purpose of a newsletter is to provide specialized
information to a targeted audience. Newsletters can
be a great way to market your product or service,
and also create credibility and build your organization's identity among peers, members, employees,
or vendors.

First, determine the audience of the newsletter. This
could be anyone who might benefit from the information it contains, for example, employees or people interested in purchasing a product or requesting
your service.

You can compile a mailing list from business reply
cards, customer information sheets, business cards
collected at trade shows, or membership lists. You
might consider purchasing a mailing list from a
company.

If you explore the Publisher catalog, you will find
many publications that match the style of your
newsletter.

Next, establish how much time and money you can
spend on your newsletter. These factors will help

Caption describing picture or graphic.

determine how frequently you publish the newsletter and its length. It's recommended that you publish your newsletter at least quarterly so that it's
considered a consistent source of information. Your
customers or employees will look forward to its
arrival.

Volume 1, Issue 1

Today's Date

Firstname Lastname

23. On page 2, replace the sample *Schedule of Events* text as follows, deleting sample text that you do not replace:

    2nd—Watercolor demonstration

    10th—Show opening

    22nd—Framing class

    24th–29th—Sale

24. On page 3, delete the *Organization logo* placeholder, if necessary.

25. Edit the coupon as follows:

    a. Replace *00%* with **15%**.

    b. Replace the sample text under the heading *Special Offer* with the following:

       Bring this newsletter in to receive 15% off any one item. Offer valid this month only. Cannot be combined with other discounts.

    c. Delete the graphic in the coupon.

26. Replace the sample *Order Form Title* with **Order Form**.

27. Replace the sample business contact information with the following, deleting sample text you do not replace:

    326 Ludlow Avenue
    Cincinnati, OH 45220
    Phone: 513-555-5555
    E-mail jaimec@cruzart.net

    Pages 2 and 3 should look similar to Figure 33-2.

Figure 33-2

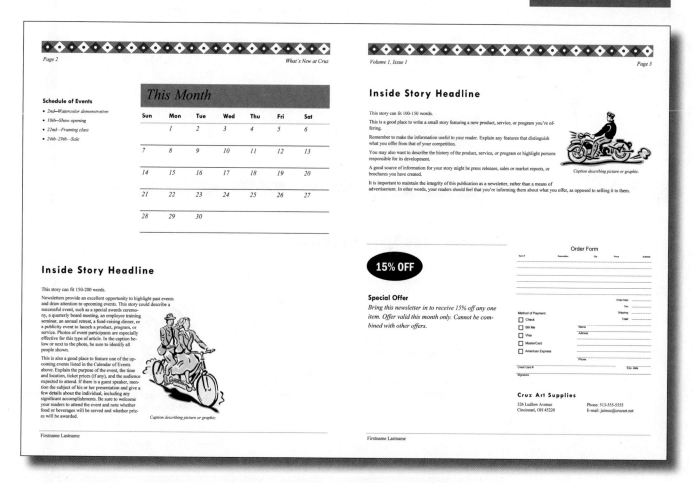

28. On page 4, delete the *Organization logo* placeholder and the *Business Tagline or Motto* placeholder.

29. Replace the sample text *We're on the Web!* and the sample URL with **Visit us on the Web! www.cruzart.net**

30. Replace the sample text to the right of the company contact info with the following:

    Cruz Art is an independently owned and operated art supply store. We are proud to say that we have been in business at the same location for more than 25 years.

    We specialize in hard-to-find products for the serious artist, craft supplies, and unique gifts. We also sponsor exhibitions, shows, and contests, and offer classes on a regular basis.

    Stop by to learn more!

31. Page 4 should look similar to Figure 33-3.

32. Check the spelling in the publication, correct errors, and then save the changes.

33. **With your teacher's permission**, print the publication.

34. Close the publication, saving changes, and exit Publisher.

Figure 33-3

Cruz Art Supplies

326 Ludlow Avenue
Cincinnati, OH 45220

Phone: 513-555-5555
E-mail: jaimec@cruzart.net

Cruz Art is an independently owned and operated art supply store. We are proud to say that we have been in business at the same location for more then 25 years.

We specialize in hard-to-find products for the serious artist, craft supplies, and unique gifts. We also sponsor exhibitions, shows, and contests, and offer classes on a regular basis.

Stop by to learn more!

Visit us on the Web! www.cruzart.net

Back Page Story Headline

This story can fit 175-225 words.

If your newsletter is folded and mailed, this story will appear on the back. So, it's a good idea to make it easy to read at a glance.

A question and answer session is a good way to quickly capture the attention of readers. You can either compile questions that you've received since the last edition or you can summarize some generic questions that are frequently asked about your organization.

A listing of names and titles of managers in your organization is a good way to give your newsletter a personal touch. If your organization is small, you may want to list the names of all employees.

If you have any prices of standard products or services, you can include a listing of those here. You may want to refer your readers to any other forms of communication that you've created for your organization.

You can also use this space to remind readers to mark their calendars for a regular event, such as a breakfast meeting for vendors every third Tuesday of the month, or a biannual charity auction.

If space is available, this is a good place to insert a clip art image or some other graphic.

Caption describing picture or graphic.

Firstname Lastname

Lesson 33—Apply

You continue to work on the Cruz Art newsletter. In this exercise, you replace images and import text to finalize the newsletter.

DIRECTIONS

1. Start Publisher, if necessary, and open **PB33Apply** from the data files for this lesson.
2. Save the publication as **PB33Apply_xx** in the location where your teacher instructs you to store the files for this lesson.
3. Insert your name in the footer on all pages.
4. On page 1, replace the sample text *Newsletter Date* with today's date.
5. Also on page 1, replace the sample picture with **PB33Apply_image1.gif**. Then delete the caption.

   ✓ *Click twice on the picture to select the group and then the picture inside the group. Use the PICTURE TOOLS FORMAT > Change Picture > Change Picture command to replace the picture.*

6. Replace the sample picture on page 2 with **PB33Apply_image2.gif**, and choose the Fit option in the Crop group. (Deselect the new picture and the swapped picture, then reselect the new picture to make Crop settings available.) Then delete the caption.
7. Replace the sample picture on page 3 with **PB33Apply_image3.gif**, and then delete the caption.
8. Replace the sample picture on page 4 with **PB33Apply_image4.gif**, and choose the Fit option in the Crop group. Then delete the caption. Delete all images from the scratch area.
9. On page 1, select the sample content in the left text box under the headline and insert the Word file **PB33Apply_import1.docx** from the data files for this lesson. Click **Yes** once to autoflow the text into the text box on page 2. Use the Format Painter to apply the text format from the second paragraph of body text (the paragraph that begins *Celebrate 50 years*) to the first paragraph in the text box (the one that begins *There's always something new*).

   ✓ *If the right column ends with the Riso Print Gocco heading, adjust the depth of the first column until the heading moves to page 2.*

10. Select to display the "Continued on page" notation at the end of the right text box on page 1, and the "Continued from page" notation at the top of the right text box on page 2.
11. On page 2, replace the sample text *Inside Story Headline* with **Get Crafty!**
12. On page 3, replace the sample text *Inside Story Headline* with **Get Gifts!**
13. Select the text in the text box under the headline and insert the Word file **PB33Apply_import2.docx**.
14. On page 4, replace the sample text *Back Page Story Headline* with **New Custom Frames**.
15. Select the text in the text box under the headline and insert the Word file **PB33Apply_import3.docx**.
16. Check and correct the spelling in the publication, and then save the changes.
17. **With your teacher's permission**, print the publication. Page 1 should look similar to Figure 33-4, pages 2 and 3 should look similar to Figure 33-5, and page 4 should look similar to Figure 33-6.
18. Close the publication, saving changes, and exit Publisher.

Figure 33-4

What's New at Cruz

Cruz Art Supplies

New Gifts and Supplies Are In!

There's always something new and interesting in stock at Cruz Art! Whether you are shopping for yourself or for others, you'll find it here. Check out these great, new arrivals!

Derwent Watercolor Pencils

Special Edition Set

Celebrate 50 years of pure, consistent color from Derwent's Watercolor Pencils. This limited edition collection of 36 pencils in the original livery box design celebrates Derwent's continuing commitment to produce the highest quality pencils. $21.88. Other sizes and options are available.

Winsor & Newton

Soft Pastel Sets

Drawing on over 160 years of color-making experience, Winsor & Newton has developed a range of artists' soft pastels formulated to the very highest standards. They use only the purest, highest-grade pigments in high concentration to provide brighter, stronger, and cleaner colors. They have a supple, creamy consistency that minimizes dust and provides even texture throughout the pigment range, perfect for blending and layering. Each color is available in a range of five tints.

Each full stick is labeled with information about color, tint, and light fastness. We carry the complete range of full sticks in open stock, so it's easy to maintain the value and completeness of your sets. Winsor & Newton Artists' Soft Pastels are non-toxic and permanent. Regular sticks measure 64 mm × 10 mm (2.5" × .375" in diameter), and are paper-wrapped. Half sticks measure 32 mm × 10 mm (1.25" × .375"), and are unwrapped.

- Set of 12, $18
- Set of 24, $36
- Set of 36, $55
- Set of 72, $109
- Set of 12 half-sticks, $9
- Set of 24 half-sticks, $18

Winsor & Newton's quality and reputation make Artists' Soft Pastels an outstanding choice for gifts. Sets are attractively packaged, and pastels are protectively encased in foam inserts to prevent damage or breakage.

(Continued on page 2)

Volume 1, Issue 1

Today's Date

Firstname Lastname

Figure 33-5

This Month

Sun	Mon	Tue	Wed	Thu	Fri	Sat
						6*
	1	2	3	4	5	6*
7	8	9	10	11	12	13
14	15	16	17	18	19	20
21	22	23	24	25	26	27
28	29	30				

Schedule of Events
- 2nd—Watercolor demonstration
- 10th—Show opening
- 22nd—Framing class
- 24th - 29th—Sale

Get Crafty!

(Continued from page 1)

Riso Print Gocco B6 Hi Mesh Stamp Kit

Print Gocco is a small, household screen printing kit that is extremely popular in Japan. It's an outstanding, low-cost way to set up and learn screen printing technology. Use it to create cards, invitations, posters, or even T-shirts. The greeting card kit contains everything you need to make five screen printing originals, and as many prints as you wish. Print size is 3½" × 5½" (9 cm × 14 cm), the perfect size for greeting cards, place cards, invitations, or announcements. The following materials are included:

- 5 screens
- flash lamp and 10 bulbs
- 7 colors of ink
- a fine-tip pen
- printing paper
- a 20 minute video "How to Use Print Gocco"
- batteries
- An 18-page, full-color booklet with ideas and complete instructions

A selection of accessories is also available, so you can use your imagination to expand the creative possibilities. Overall, the kit measures 6¾" × 6" × 15" (17 cm × 15 cm × 38 cm). $139.

Get Gifts!

Spectra Treasure Chest of Paper Bag Puppets

Kids will love this on a rainy afternoon! Created to encourage young imaginations, this kit is truly a treasure chest. It contains the basic ingredients to create up to 175 paper bag puppets. Kids will have fun inventing characters, animals, monsters, or more as they develop skills with a variety of media. Adults can guide classes or groups of kids with the easy to follow project sheet and use the sturdy box to organize materials when not in use. $32.

Leclerc Dorothy Table Loom

Ever wanted to create your own woven artwork but been held back by the large amount of space required for a loom? This loom weaves up to 15¾" (40 cm), a practical size for schools, hobbyists, and occupational therapy. The four harness levers may be set on either the right or left side of the loom. The Leclerc Dorothy Table Loom is collapsible for storage. It includes 12-dent reed, 400 wire heddles, a shuttle, a reed hook, lease sticks, two beam slicks with cords, and instructions. The Dorothy is made of red birch with a colonial finish. $395.

15% OFF

Special Offer

Bring this newsletter in to receive 15% off any one item. Offer valid this month only. Cannot be combined with other offers.

Order Form

Item #	Description	Qty	Price	Subtotal

Order total: _____
Tax: _____
Shipping: _____
Total: _____

Method of Payment
- ☐ Check
- ☐ Bill Me
- ☐ Visa
- ☐ MasterCard
- ☐ American Express

Name _____
Address _____
Phone _____
Credit Card # _____ Exp. date _____
Signature _____

Cruz Art Supplies

326 Ludlow Avenue
Cincinnati, OH 45220

Phone: 513-555-5555
E-mail: jaimec@cruzart.net

Figure 33-6

Cruz Art Supplies

326 Ludlow Avenue
Cincinnati, OH 45220

Phone: 513-555-5555
E-mail: jaimec@cruzart.net

Cruz Art is an independently owned and operated art supply store. We are proud to say that we have been in business at the same location for more then 25 years.

We specialize in hard-to-find products for the serious artist, craft supplies, and unique gifts. We also sponsor exhibitions, shows, and contests, and offer classes on a regular basis.

Stop by to learn more!

Visit us on the Web!
www.cruzart.net

New Custom Frames

Cruz Art has a large selection of ready-made and custom picture frames as well as a large variety of picture framing tools, picture frame mats and boards, and picture framing hardware and supplies. We recently started carrying a line of deep canvas custom frames. These elegant wood frames come in natural or black and feature a cap stem design. They are ideal for canvas, photos, or prints, matted or mounted.

- Rabbet depth is 2-5/8"

- Overall depth is 3"

- Face is 1-1/4"

- Simple assembly required

- Instructions included

Firstname Lastname

Lesson 34

Creating Mailing Labels

➤ What You Will Learn

Creating a Sheet of Return Address Labels
Creating Mailing Labels and Starting the Mail Merge Wizard
Creating a Recipient List
Preparing the Publication for a Merge
Creating a Merged Publication

Software Skills   Use Publisher to create and print mailing labels that you can use to mail publications such as newsletters and advertising flyers. You can use a Labels template to quickly create a sheet of labels with the same address suitable for using as a return address label, and you can use Mail Merge to easily create labels for names and addresses stored in a database. You can select from a long list of standard mailing label sizes so you can be certain the labels will print correctly.

What You Can Do

Creating a Sheet of Return Address Labels

- Publisher comes with a selection of Labels templates that you can use to print information on standard-sized business labels.
- You select the template that matches the actual label sheets you have on which to print, and Publisher uses a table to set up the publication to match the size and position of the individual labels.
- Some templates create a blank publication; you must insert the objects you need, including text boxes and/or graphics. Some templates include objects.
- You can create address labels as well as labels for DVDs, cards, bookplates, identification, and other uses.
- By default, Publisher designs the label publication to print one sheet of the same label.
- For mailing labels, this is useful for creating return address labels.
- Use the Mail Merge feature as described in the next section to create mailing labels with different information in each label to use for a mass mailing.

WORDS TO KNOW

Address list
A simple data source file which includes the information needed for an address list, such as first name, last name, street, city, state, and so on.

Data source
A file containing the variable data that will be inserted during the merge.

Mail merge
A process that inserts variable information into a standardized document to produce a personalized or customized document.

Merge block
A set of merge fields stored as one unit. For example, the Address block contains all the name and address information.

Merge field
A placeholder in the main document that marks where an item of variable data such as a first name, a last name, or a ZIP code will be inserted from the data source document.

Recipient
The entity—a person or organization—who receives a mailing. The recipient's contact information is stored in the data source.

Try It!　　**Creating a Sheet of Return Address Labels**

1 Start Publisher, if necessary.

2 On the New tab in Backstage view, under BUILT-IN, click Labels.

3 Under Manufacturers, click Avery US Letter, or click the name of the manufacturer of the actual labels on which you plan to print.

4 Click 5660 Easy Peel Address Labels, or click the label number of the actual labels on which you plan to print.

5 In the right pane, under Customize, click the Color scheme drop-down arrow and click Alpine.

6 Click CREATE.

7 Save the publication as **PB34TryA_xx** in the location where your teacher instructs you to store the files for this lesson.

8 On the HOME tab, click the Draw Text Box button 🄰 and draw a text box the same size as the margin guides on the publication.

9 Set the font size to 9 and the paragraph spacing to None. If you are using different labels, you may have to adjust the font size and spacing so the text fits.

10 Type the following address:
Bradley & Cummins Realty
2828 N. Court Street
Suite 3
Athens, OH 45701

11 Click FILE > Print. Note that Publisher sets up the publication to print a complete sheet of labels.

12 **With your teacher's permission**, print the labels. If you do not have a sheet of labels, you may print on plain paper.

13 Close the publication, saving changes. Leave Publisher open to use in the next Try It.

A sheet of return address labels ready to print

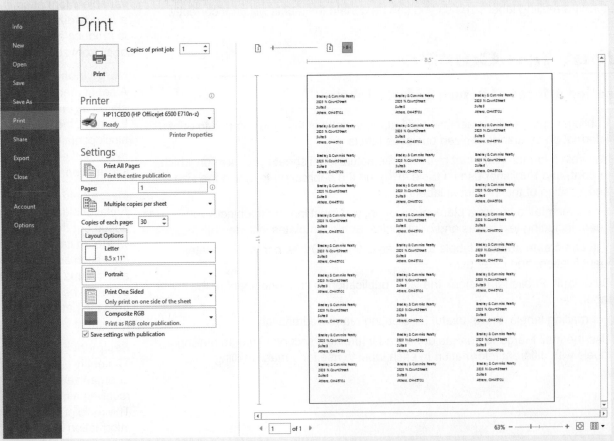

Creating Mailing Labels and Starting the Mail Merge Wizard

- Once you select a Labels template, you can use Publisher's **Mail Merge** Wizard to create customized mailing labels.

- The Mail Merge Wizard displays in a task pane and prompts you through the necessary steps.

- Instead of using the Mail Merge Wizard, you can use the commands on the MAILINGS tab of the Ribbon. The steps and features are the same.

- In addition, you can use a mail merge to create customized documents other than mailing labels. For example, you could customize an advertising flyer with individual names.

  ✓ *Use the E-Mail Merge Wizard to create customized e-mail messages.*

Try It!   **Creating Mailing Labels and Starting the Mail Merge Wizard**

① With Publisher open and displaying Backstage view, click Labels under BUILT-IN templates.

② Under Manufacturers, click Avery US Letter, or click the name of the manufacturer of the actual labels on which you plan to print.

③ Click 5660 Easy Peel Address Labels, or click the label number of the actual labels on which you plan to print.

④ In the right pane, under Customize, click the Color scheme drop-down arrow and click Aspect.

⑤ Click CREATE.

⑥ Save the publication as **PB34TryB_xx** in the location where your teacher instructs you to store the files for this lesson.

⑦ Click the MAILINGS tab.

⑧ Click the Mail Merge button drop-down arrow 🖹 and then click Step-by-Step Mail Merge Wizard. The Mail Merge Wizard task pane displays.

⑨ Save the changes to **PB34TryB_xx**, and leave it open to use in the next Try It.

Mail Merge task pane

Creating a Recipient List

- A mail merge requires a **data source** where the **recipient** addresses and other variable information are stored.

- The data source must be set up in columns and rows, with the column headers in the first row.

- If you have a data source in a compatible file format—such as Excel, Access, or a Microsoft Office **Address List**—you may select it as an existing data source.

- The content in the columns in the existing data source must match the Publisher merge fields. For example, in an address list, you must have a column containing first names and one containing last names if you want to use those fields in the merge.

- Once you create and save an address list data source file, you can use it again for other merges.

- Alternatively, you can create a new data source by typing the recipient information into columns in the New Address List dialog box and saving the information as a Microsoft Office Address List.

- A data source remains associated with the publication until you change the data source or remove it.

- When you open a publication that has a data source, a Microsoft Publisher confirmation dialog box displays so you can select to open the publication and access the data source or open the publication without the data.

Try It!   Creating a Recipient List

1 In the **PB34TryB_xx** file, in the Mail Merge task pane, under Create recipient list, click the Type a new list option button, and then click Next: Create or connect to a recipient list. The New Address List dialog box displays.

   ✓ If you have an existing Address List in a compatible format, click the Use an existing list option button, click Next: Create or connect to a recipient list, and then navigate to and open the file.

2 Type **Mr.**, press TAB, type **John**, press TAB, and type **Smith**.

3 Press TAB twice, type **111 Main Street**, and press TAB twice.

4 Type **Athens**, press TAB, type **OH**, press TAB, and type **45701**.

5 Click New Entry. Publisher completes the first entry and moves to a new row so you can type the information for another entry.

6 Repeat steps 2 through 5 to enter the following information for two more recipients:

9 Click OK. The options for preparing your publication display in the Mail Merge task pane. Keep the publication open to use in the next Try It.

Add names to a new address list

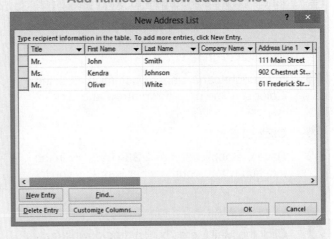

Title	First Name	Last Name	Address Line 1	Address Line 2	City	State	ZIP Code
Ms.	Kendra	Johnson	902 Chestnut Street	Apt. 5	Athens	OH	45701
Mr.	Oliver	White	61 Frederick Street		Athens	OH	45701

7 Click OK. The Save Address List dialog box displays.

8 Save the address list as **PB34TryC_xx** in the location where your teacher instructs you to store the files for this lesson. The Mail Merge Recipients dialog box displays, with all entries selected.

Preparing the Publication for a Merge

- Prepare the publication by inserting the **merge block** or **merge fields**.
- For labels, it is easiest to use the Address merge block, which includes all fields for a standard mailing address.
- If you insert individual fields, such as First Name, Last Name, and ZIP Code, you must type the required punctuation, such as the comma between the city and state.

- Publisher inserts the merge block or merge fields in a text box object. You can resize the text box to fit the labels, and adjust font and paragraph formatting as necessary.
- You can also customize the publication to include content you want to display on all labels. For example, you might insert a company logo.

Try It! Preparing the Publication for a Merge

1. In the **PB34TryB_xx** file, in the Mail Merge task pane, under More items, click Address block. The Insert Address Block dialog box opens. The default options are correct for mailing labels.

2. Click OK. Publisher inserts the <<AddressBlock>> merge block in a text box in the publication.

3. Select the text box and resize it to fit within the margin guides of the publication.

4. Select the text in the text box. Change the font size to 10 point, if necessary, and the paragraph spacing to None. Change line spacing to 1.0.

5. In the Mail Merge task pane, click Next: Create merged publications.

6. Save the changes to **PB34TryB_xx**, and leave it open to use in the next Try It.

AddressBlock in the publication

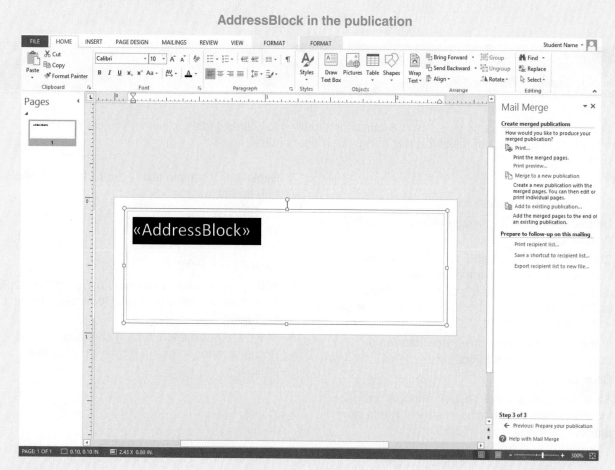

Creating a Merged Publication

- You have the option of previewing, printing, or saving the publication as a new file to edit or print later. You can also add the publication to the end of an existing publication.

- Publisher sets up a merged publication so that each recipient's information is on a separate page. In order to print one label for each recipient, you must set the Records option to print multiple pages per sheet on the Print tab in Backstage view.

- Publisher also provides options you can use to follow up the mailing. For example, if the mailing is for marketing, you may want to keep a record of the recipients so you know who received the mailing and when.

- Follow-up options include printing the recipient list, saving a shortcut to the recipient list, or exporting the recipient list to a new file.

Try It!   Creating a Merged Publication

1   In the **PB34TryB_xx** file, in the Mail Merge task pane, click Print preview to display the Print tab in Backstage view.

    ✓ *The Print tab displays if you click Print, also.*

2   Under Settings, click the drop-down arrow on the Multiple copies per sheet button.

3   Click Multiple pages per sheet.

4   **With your teacher's permission**, click Print. You may print the labels on a label sheet, or on plain paper.

5   Close the publication, saving changes, and exit Publisher.

Lesson 34—Practice

The Orchard House Inn wants you to create labels for a mailing to clients. In this exercise, you create return address labels and customer mailing labels using a new data source.

DIRECTIONS

1. Start Publisher, if necessary.
2. On the New tab in Backstage view, under BUILT-IN, click **Labels**.
3. Click **All Mailing and shipping**, and then click **Garden (Avery 5160)** in the Installed Templates category, or click the name of the manufacturer and then the label number of the actual labels on which you plan to print.
4. In the right pane, click the **Color scheme** drop-down arrow and click **Lilac**.
5. Click **CREATE**.
6. Save the publication as **PB34PracticeA_xx** in the location where your teacher instructs you to store the files for this lesson.

7. Replace the sample text in the textbox placeholder with the following:

   Orchard House Inn
   29 Bumblebee Lane
   Ormond Beach, FL 32174

8. Click **FILE > Print**.

9. **With your teacher's permission**, print the labels. The sheet should look similar to Figure 34-1 on the next page.

10. Close the publication, saving changes. Leave Publisher open to use in the next part of this project.

Figure 34-1

11. On the New tab in Backstage view, under BUILT-IN, click **Labels**.

12. Click **All Mailing and shipping**, and then click **Garden (Avery 5160)** in the Installed Templates category, or click the name of the manufacturer and then the label number of the actual labels on which you plan to print.

13. Click **CREATE**.

14. Save the publication as **PB34PracticeB_xx** in the location where your teacher instructs you to store the files for this lesson.

15. Click the **MAILINGS** tab, click the **Mail Merge** button drop-down arrow 📄, and then click **Step-by-Step Mail Merge Wizard**.

16. In the Mail Merge task pane, under Create recipient list, click the **Type a new list** option button, and then click **Next: Create or connect to a recipient list**. The New Address List dialog box displays.

17. In the New Address List dialog box, enter the following information for five recipients:

Title	First Name	Last Name	Address Line 1	Address Line 2	City	State	ZIP Code
Ms.	Elizabeth	Brown	64A State Road		Tampa	FL	33601
Ms.	Maria	Valero	8990 Ocean Way	Apt. 2B	Tampa	FL	33601
Mr.	Seth	McGraw	433 Manatee Avenue		Citrus Park	FL	33624
Mr.	John	Arbedian	1123 East Sunset Highway		Tampa	FL	33601
Mr.	Patrick	Costello	9 Plantation Boulevard		Tampa	FL	33601

18. Click **OK**. Save the address list as **PB34PracticeC_xx** in the location where your teacher instructs you to store the files for this lesson

19. Click **OK** in the Mail Merge Recipients dialog box.

20. In the publication, select the sample text.

21. In the Mail Merge task pane, under More items, click **Address block**, and then click **OK** in the Insert Address Block dialog box.

22. In the Mail Merge task pane, click **Next: Create merged publications**.

23. In the Mail Merge task pane, click **Print Preview**.

24. Under Settings, click the drop-down arrow on the Multiple copies per sheet button.

25. Click **Multiple pages per sheet**.

26. **With your teacher's permission**, click **Print**. You may print the labels on a label sheet, or on plain paper. They should look similar to Figure 34-2.

27. Close the publication, saving changes, and exit Publisher.

Figure 34-2

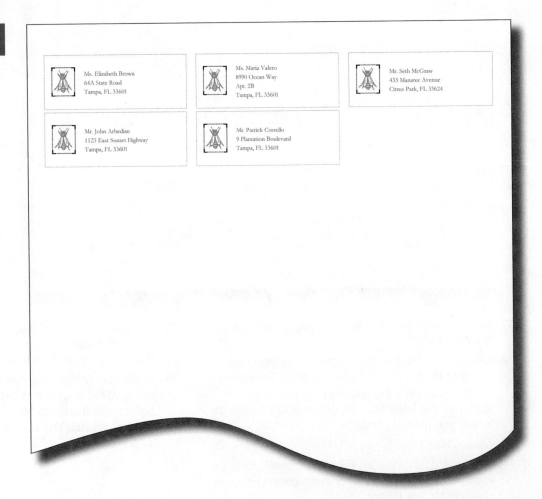

Lesson 34—Apply

Orchard House Inn needs some additional mailing labels. In this exercise, you create customer mailing labels using an existing data source.

DIRECTIONS

1. Start Publisher, if necessary, and select the template for the labels on which you will print, or select the **Retro (Avery 5160)** template. (Click **Labels** > **All Mailing and shipping** to locate the template.)

2. Set the color scheme to **Sagebrush** and use the default template font.

3. Create the publication and save it as **PB34Apply_xx** in the location where your teacher instructs you to store the files for this lesson.

4. Start the Mail Merge Wizard and select to use an existing list, and then click **Next: Create or connect to a recipient list**.

5. In the Select Data Source dialog box, navigate to the location where the data files for this lesson are stored, select the **PB34Apply_data.accdb** database file, and then click **Open**.

6. Click **OK** in the Mail Merge Recipients dialog box.

7. Replace the sample text in the publication with the **Address block** merge block.

8. Preview the labels and set Publisher to print multiple pages per sheet.

9. **With your teacher's permission**, print the labels. You may print the labels on a label sheet, or on plain paper. They should look similar to Figure 34-3.

10. Close the publication, saving changes, and exit Publisher.

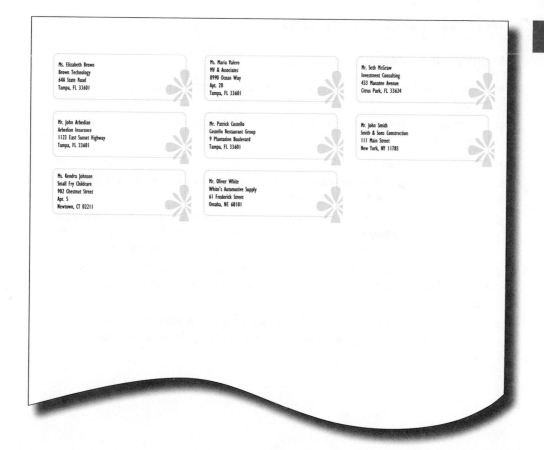

Figure 34-3

Lesson 35

Creating Postcards

❯ **What You Will Learn**

Creating a Postcard
Sorting and Filtering the Recipient List for a Merge
Personalizing a Publication with Mail Merge
Previewing and Printing the Personalized Publications

WORDS TO KNOW

Filter
To exclude certain information on criteria you specify.

Sort
To arrange in alphabetical or numerical order.

Software Skills   Use a Publisher Postcard template to quickly create a two-sided postcard for mailing. Use mail merge to set up the cards so addresses print in the correct spot. You can also use mail merge to personalize the message to each recipient. Before merging, you can sort and filter the address list to include only certain recipients and to print in alphabetical or numerical order.

What You Can Do

Creating a Postcard

- Select from Publisher's variety of Postcard templates to create a postcard publication.
- Postcard template customization options include color and font schemes, page size, and side 2 information.
- Select from two page sizes: Quarter-sheet (5.5 × 4.25") and Half-sheet (8 × 5.5").
- By default, all postcard templates include space on side 2 for organization information and the mailing address.
- Use the Side 2 information option to add other content placeholders such as a map, speaker notes, promotional text, or appointment text. You can also select to display only the mailing address, or only the organization information.
- Of course, you can customize the publication using standard editing and formatting commands, including moving, inserting, formatting, or deleting content.
- You can print postcards on regular cardstock and cut them out by hand, or you can buy blank postcard paper and feed it into your printer as a custom paper size.

Try It!   **Creating a Postcard**

① Start Publisher, if necessary.

② On the New tab in Backstage view, under BUILT-IN, click Postcards.

③ Under Marketing, click Brocade.

④ In the right pane, under Customize, click the Color scheme drop-down arrow and click Redwood.

⑤ Click the Font scheme drop-down arrow and click Aspect.

⑥ Under Options, click the Page size drop-down arrow and click Quarter-sheet if necessary.

⑦ Click the Side 2 information drop-down arrow and click Map.

⑧ Click CREATE.

⑨ Save the publication as **PB35Try_xx** in the location where your teacher instructs you to store the files for this lesson, and leave it open to use in the next Try It.

Sorting and Filtering the Recipient List for a Merge

- Use the Mail Merge Wizard or the buttons on the MAILINGS tab to create a mass mailing with postcards the same way you created mailing labels in Lesson 34.

- Once you select or create a recipient list data source for a merge, you can use commands in the Mail Merge Recipients dialog box to **sort** and/or **filter** the list.

- For example, you can sort the list so the publications print in alphabetical order by last name, or in ascending order by ZIP code.

- You can filter the list to exclude recipients who do not match certain criteria. For example, you can include only those recipients who live in a certain city, or whose last appointment was after a certain date. Excluded recipients will not be included in the merge.

- To sort, you select the column by which you want to sort, and then select to sort in ascending or descending order. You can sort based on content in up to three columns.

- To set up a filter, you select the column (field), select a comparison such as equal to or less than, and then enter the value to compare, such as a specific city name or a date.

Try It!   **Sorting and Filtering the Recipient List for a Merge**

① In the **PB35Try_xx** file, click MAILINGS > Select Recipients 🗔 > Use an Existing List.

② Navigate to the location where the data files for this lesson are stored, select the Access database file **PB35Try_data.accdb**, and then click Open.

③ In the Mail Merge Recipients dialog box, under Refine recipient list, click Sort.

④ In the Filter and Sort dialog box, click the Sort by drop-down arrow, and then click Last Name.

Set options for sorting recipients

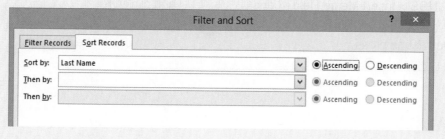

(continued)

Try It!   **Sorting and Filtering the Recipient List for a Merge** *(continued)*

5 Click OK.

6 Under Refine recipient list, click Filter.

7 Click the Field drop-down arrow and click City. The Comparison box should display Equal to, which is what you want.

8 Click the Compare to box and type **Ormond Beach**, and click OK. Publisher displays only recipients who live in Ormond Beach.

9 Click OK to close the Mail Merge Recipients dialog box. Then save the publication and leave it open to use in the next Try It.

Set options for filtering recipients

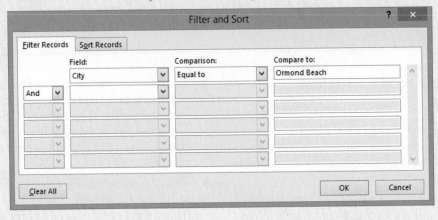

Personalizing a Publication with Mail Merge

- Use Mail Merge to personalize a publication such as a postcard. For example, you might insert the First Name field to personalize the salutation or greeting.

- To personalize a publication, you insert merge fields at the location where you want the data for that field to display.

Try It!   **Personalizing a Publication with Mail Merge**

1 In the **PB35Try_xx** file, click page 1 in the Page Navigation pane if necessary, and select the text in the text box below the headline *Product/ Service Information*.

2 Type **Dear** and press the spacebar.

3 Click MAILINGS > Insert Merge Field ▦ and click First Name.

4 Type a comma, and press ENTER.

5 Type **Bring in this postcard to receive 10% off your next purchase!**

6 Click page 2 in the Page Navigation pane.

7 Select the text in the mailing address placeholder, click MAILINGS > Address Block ▤, and click OK.

8 Save the changes to **PB35Try_xx**, and leave it open to use in the next Try It.

Previewing and Printing the Personalized Publications

- You can use the Preview Results button on the MAILINGS tab to see how each individual publication will look when printed.

- The button is a toggle; click it to toggle back and forth between viewing the field codes and viewing the recipient data.

- Use the Finish & Merge button to print the publications, save them in a new file, or add them to an existing file.

Try It! | Previewing and Printing the Personalized Publications

1 In the **PB35Try_xx** file, click MAILINGS > Preview Results . The publication displays the data for the first recipient.

  ✓ *If the field codes display, click the Preview Results button again.*

2 Click page 1 to view the personalized information, then click the Next Record ▶ button on the Ribbon to see the personalized information for the second, and last, recipient.

3 Save the publication, and then click MAILINGS > Finish & Merge > Merge to Printer to display the Print tab in Backstage view.

4 Under Settings, click the drop-down arrow on the Multiple copies per sheet button, and click One page per sheet.

5 If necessary, select the size of the paper on which you plan to print.

6 If you are using a printer that can print on both sides of a page, click the Print One Sided drop-down arrow and click the Print on Both Sides setting that matches your printer.

7 **With your teacher's permission**, print the postcards, reinserting the paper to print side 2, if necessary.

8 Close the publication, saving changes, and exit Publisher.

Personalized data on side 1   Personalized data on side 2

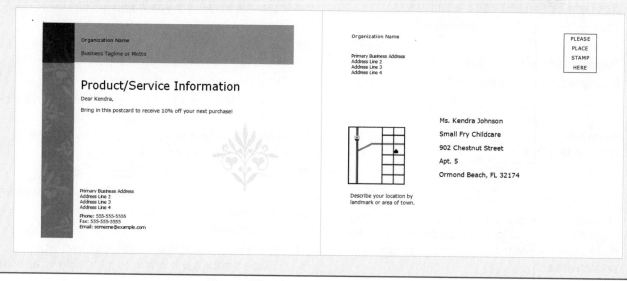

Lesson 35—Practice

Primary Physicians, LLC has asked you to create personalized postcards to send to patients. In this exercise, you create appointment reminders.

DIRECTIONS

1. Start Publisher, if necessary.
2. On the New tab in Backstage view, under BUILT-IN, click **Postcards**.
3. Under Marketing, click **Bounce**.
4. In the right pane, under Customize, click the **Color scheme** drop-down arrow and click **Navy**.
5. Click the **Font scheme** drop-down arrow and click **Basis**.
6. Under Options, click the **Page size** drop-down arrow and click **Half-sheet**.
7. Click the **Side 2 information** drop-down arrow and click **Address only**.
8. Click **CREATE**.
9. Save the publication as **PB35Practice_xx** in the location where your teacher instructs you to store the files for this lesson.
10. On side 1, delete the *Organization logo* and *Business Tagline or Motto* placeholders.
11. Change *Product/Service Information* to **Appointment Notice**.
12. Replace sample text as follows:

    Business Name   **Primary Physicians, LLC**

    Business address and contact info
    485 Union Avenue
    Suite 1A
    Amesville, OH 45711
    Phone: 740-555-5555
    Fax: 740-555-5556
    E-mail:doctor@priphy.net
13. Replace the sample picture with **PB35Practice_image.jpg** from the data files for this lesson. Delete the replaced image from the scratch area.
14. Save the changes.
15. Click **MAILINGS** > **Select Recipients** 🖳 > **Use an Existing List**.
16. Navigate to the location where the data files for this lesson are stored, select the Access database file **PB35Practice_data.accdb**, and then click **Open**.

17. In the Mail Merge Recipients dialog box, under Refine recipient list, click **Sort**.
18. In the Filter and Sort dialog box, click the **Sort by** drop-down arrow and click **Last Name**.
19. Click the **Then by** drop-down arrow and click **Last Appointment**.
20. Click to select the **Descending** option button to the right of Last Appointment, and then click **OK**. Publisher sorts the recipients. (Scroll the Mail Merge Recipients to the right to see the Last Appointment field.)
21. Under Refine recipient list, click **Filter**.
22. Click the **Field** drop-down arrow and click **Last Appointment**.
23. Click the **Comparison** drop-down arrow and click **Less than**.
24. Click the **Compare to** box and type **6/1/14**, and click **OK**. Publisher displays only recipients whose last appointment was before June 1, 2014.
25. Click **OK** to close the Mail Merge Recipients dialog box.
26. On page 1 of the postcard, click to select the text in the text box to the right of the picture.
27. Type **Dear** and press the spacebar.
28. Click **MAILINGS** > **Insert Merge Field** 🖾 and click **Title**.
29. Press the spacebar, click **Insert Merge Field** 🖾, and click **Last Name**.
30. Type a comma, and press ⏎ENTER.
31. Type **We last saw you on** and press the spacebar.
32. Click **Insert Merge Field** 🖾 and click **Last Appointment**.
33. Type a period, press the spacebar, and type **Please contact the office to schedule your next appointment**.
34. Click page 2. Select the text in the mailing address placeholder, click **MAILINGS** > **Address Block** 🖹, and click **OK**.
35. Click **Preview Results** 🔍 to display the data for the first recipient.

36. Click page 1 to view the personalized information, then click the **Next Record** button ▶ on the Ribbon to see the personalized information for the second recipient.

37. Click the **Next Record** button ▶ again to see the personalized information for the third recipient, and then again to view the last recipient.

38. Save the publication, and then click **MAILINGS** > **Finish & Merge** 📑▸ > **Merge to Printer** to display the Print tab in Backstage view.

39. Under Settings, click the Multiple copies per sheet drop-down arrow, and click **One page per sheet**.

40. If you are using a printer that can print on both sides of a page, click the next down arrow and click the **Print on Both Sides** setting that matches your printer.

41. **With your teacher's permission**, print the postcards, reinserting the paper to print side 2, if necessary. The postcard for the first recipient should look similar to Figure 35-1.

42. Close the publication, saving changes, and exit Publisher.

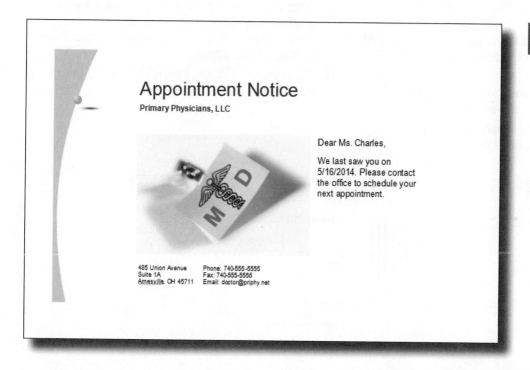

Figure 35-1

Appointment Notice
Primary Physicians, LLC

Dear Ms. Charles,

We last saw you on 5/16/2014. Please contact the office to schedule your next appointment.

485 Union Avenue   Phone: 740-555-5555
Suite 1A   Fax: 740-555-5556
Amesville, OH 45711 Email: doctor@priphy.net

Lesson 35—Apply

You continue to work for Primary Physicians, LLC. In this exercise, you create a postcard to give patients information on the practice's new offices.

DIRECTIONS

1. Start Publisher, if necessary, and create a new publication using the following options:
   - Cascade Postcard template (under All Marketing > More Installed Templates)
   - Waterfall color scheme
   - Civic font scheme
   - Quarter-sheet page size
   - Address only Side 2 information

2. Save the publication as **PB35Apply_xx** in the location where your teacher instructs you to store the files for this lesson.

3. Delete the *Business Tagline or Motto* and *Organization logo* placeholders.

4. Replace sample content as follows:

Business Name   **Primary Physicians, LLC**

Business address and contact info
**485 Union Avenue
Suite 1A
Amesville, OH 45711
Phone: 740-555-5555
Fax: 740-555-5556
E-mail:doctor@priphy.net**

Product/Service Information   **New Office Location**

Description text
We are pleased to announce the opening of our new office location at 9002 E. State Street in Athens.

Please let us know if it will be more convenient for you to see your physician at the new location.

Note that the telephone, fax, and phone numbers will remain the same.

5. Select to use the **PB35Apply_data.accdb** database file as a recipient list.

6. Sort the recipient list in descending order alphabetically by last name.

7. Filter the list to include only the recipients who live in **Athens, OH**.

8. Draw a new text box below the text *New Office Location* on side 1, type **Dear**, and personalize each postcard using the recipient's title and last name. Include all necessary spacing and punctuation.

9. On side 2, replace the text in the mailing address placeholder with the **Address Block** merge block.

10. Preview the postcards.

11. **With your teacher's permission**, print the postcards, one per sheet. (Use double-sided printing if possible.) The first postcard should look similar to Figure 35-2.

12. Close the publication, saving changes, and exit Publisher.

Figure 35-2

Primary Physicians, LLC

485 Union Avenue
Suite 1A
Amesville, OH 45711

Phone: 740-555-5555
Fax: 740-555-5556
Email: doctor@priphy.net

New Office Location

Dear Mr. White,

We are pleased to announce the opening of our new office location at 9002 E. State Street in Athens.

Please let us know if it will be more convenient for you to see your physician at the new location.

Note that the telephone, fax, and phone numbers will remain the same.

Lesson 36

Creating a Brochure

❯ What You Will Learn

Creating a Brochure
Using Find and Replace
Using Custom Colors
Using the Design Checker
Embedding Fonts
Exporting for Commercial Printing

Software Skills Use Publisher's Brochures templates to create brochures you can print on both sides of a single sheet of paper, and then fold into thirds or fourths. You can print the brochure yourself, or create a master and send it to a commercial or photo printing service. Use Find and Replace to locate a word or phrase in a publication, and then replace it with other wording.

What You Can Do

Creating a Brochure

- Publisher comes with many templates for creating brochures.
- The templates are organized into categories including Informational, Event, Price List, and Fundraiser.
- You can customize the font scheme and color scheme just as you can with other types of templates.
- For some brochure templates, you can select a page size option for using three or four panels. If you choose a four-panel page size, you will need to print on legal-size paper rather than letter size.
- Publisher sets up the publication with two pages that are divided into columns matching the number of panels you selected.
- In addition, you can choose to include a customer address for mailing or a form building block, such as an order form, response form, or sign-up form.

WORDS TO KNOW

CMYK
A color model that creates colors by combining percentages of cyan, magenta, yellow, and black.

Color model
A system used to define standard colors for printing or displaying onscreen.

HSL
A color model that defines colors based on their hue, saturation, and lightness.

PANTONE®
A color model that defines specific spot colors using color numbers.

RGB
A color model that creates colors by combining different values of red, green, and blue.

Spot color
A color used for accent areas, rather than for blending into complex colors.

Try It!　Creating a Brochure

1 Start Publisher, if necessary.

2 On the New tab in Backstage view, under BUILT-IN, click Brochures.

3 Under Informational, click Tabs.

4 In the right pane, under Customize, click the Color scheme drop-down arrow and click Civic.

5 Click the Font scheme drop-down arrow and click Civic.

6 Under Options, click the Page size drop-down arrow and click 3-panel, if it is not already selected.

7 Click to select the Include customer address check box.

8 Click the Form drop-down arrow and click Response form.

9 Click CREATE.

10 Save the publication as **PB36Try_xx** in the location where your teacher instructs you to store the files for this lesson, and leave it open to use in the next Try It.

Select customization options to create a brochure

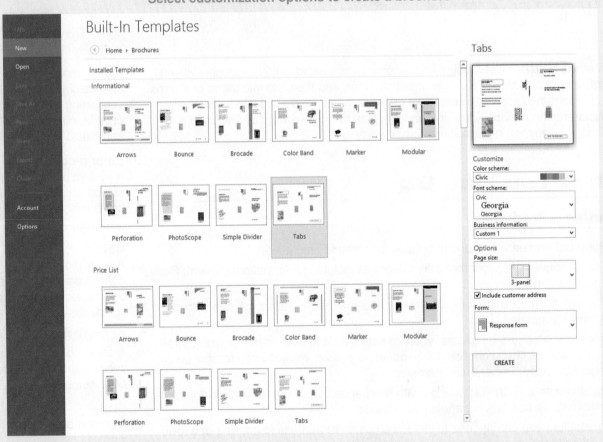

Using Find and Replace

- Use the options in the Find and Replace task pane to find and/or replace one or more occurrences of a word or phrase within a publication.
- For example, if you misspell a name, you can find it and replace it with the correct spelling.
- You type the text to find in the Find what box, and the replacement text in the Replace with box.
- Publisher moves through the document selecting text that matches the text entered in the Find what box.
- You can replace the current selection only, or replace all occurrences at once.

- You can set options to find whole words only and to match the case of the find what text.
- For example, by finding whole words only, you would find the word *product*, but not the word *products*.
- By matching the case, you would find *product*, but not *Product*.
- You can also select to search the entire publication, or to search from the insertion point up to the beginning of the publication or down to the end of the publication.

Try It!   Using Find and Replace

① In the **PB36Try_xx** file, click HOME > Find 🔍 to display the Find and Replace task pane with only the Find options displayed.

② In the Search for box, type **555-555-5555**, and then click Find Next. Publisher selects the first occurrence of the Find what text.

③ Click Find Next again to select the next occurrence of the Find what text.

Find and Replace task pane

Find and Replace ▾ ✕

Find or Replace
- ○ Find
- ⦿ Replace

Search for

Search for:
`555-555-5555` ▼

Replace with:
`617-555-5555` ▼

[Find Next]

[Replace]

[Replace All]

Find options
- ☐ Match whole word only
- ☐ Match case

Search: `All` ▼

④ Click Find Next again. Publisher displays a message indicating it has completed searching the publication.

⑤ Click OK, then click HOME > Replace ᵃᵇ/ₐc.

   ✓ *You can also simply click the Replace option button in the task pane.*

⑥ In the Replace with box, type **617-555-5555**, and then click Find Next to select the search text.

⑦ Click Replace to replace the selected text with the Replace with text, and select the next occurrence of the search text.

⑧ Click Replace All to replace all remaining occurrences of the Find what text. Publisher completes the replacement process, and displays a message indicating there are no more occurrences of the matching text.

⑨ Click OK, then close the Find and Replace task pane.

⑩ Save the changes to **PB36Try_xx**, and leave it open to use in the next Try It.

Using Custom Colors

- Colors for printing and viewing onscreen can be defined using numeric values. That means instead of just clicking Blue on a palette, you can enter the value for a very specific blue.

- This is useful for matching a color on a company logo, letterhead, or other branded object.

- The values differ depending on the **color model** or system you are using; the colors, however, may be the same.

- Publisher supports the four most common color models:

  - **RGB** (Red, Green, Blue)
  - **HSL** (Hue, Saturation, Lightness)
  - **CMYK** (Cyan, Magenta, Yellow, Black)
  - **PANTONE®**

- You can find the values for colors using these models online or on printed color cards.

- To apply a custom color, use the options on the Custom or PANTONE tab of the Colors dialog box as you have done previously in this course when defining exact RGB colors.

- Defining a custom color using a system such as PANTONE places a **spot color** in your publication.

Try It! **Using Custom Colors**

1 In the **PB36Try_xx** file, on page 1, select the sample text *Back Panel Heading*.

2 Click the HOME > Font Color drop-down arrow ⒜⁃ and click More Colors to display the Colors dialog box.

3 Click the Custom tab, if necessary.

4 Click the Color model drop-down arrow and click HSL.

5 Set the Hue value to 150, the Sat value to 220, and the Lum value to 140, and then click OK.

6 Deselect the text box in which the text is located (now you can see the custom color applied to the text).

7 Reselect the text box. Click DRAWING TOOLS FORMAT > Shape Outline drop-down arrow ✎. Notice the custom color displays under Recent Colors.

8 Click More Outline Colors to open the Colors dialog box, with the Custom tab displayed.

9 Click the Color model drop-down arrow and click CMYK.

10 Set the Cyan value to 45, the Magenta value to 80, the Yellow value to 40, and the Black value to 15, and then click OK.

11 Click the Shape Outline drop-down arrow again, click Weight, and click 3 pt. If necessary, click TEXT BOX TOOLS FORMAT > Text Fit 🔲 > Shrink Text On Overflow.

12 With the text box still selected, click DRAWING TOOLS FORMAT > Shape Fill 🖌 > More Fill Colors.

13 In the Colors dialog box, click the PANTONE tab.

14 Click the 413C swatch (the top swatch in the vertical array of color swatches) and click OK.

15 Save the changes to **PB36Try_xx**, and leave it open to use in the next Try It.

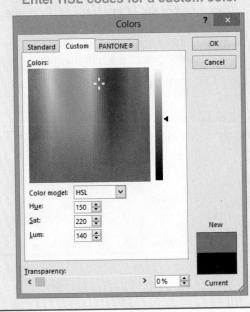

Enter HSL codes for a custom color

Using the Design Checker

- As you are preparing a publication for final output, you should use Publisher's Design Checker to identify potential problems in the publication.

- The Design Checker searches a publication for a number of issues such as missing or hidden graphics, text in the overflow area that has not yet been placed, objects that are partially off the page, and so on.

- You find the Design Checker on the Info tab in Backstage view.

- Problems are listed in the Design Checker task pane. As you fix each problem, the listing is removed from the task pane.

- You can choose to run general design checks, final publishing checks, web site checks, and e-mail checks.

- You can remove checks from the Design Checker list if you don't want the Design Checker to identify those types of problems in future.

Try It! Using the Design Checker

1. In the **PB36Try_xx** file, click on the picture at the bottom of the left column, and then click again to select only the picture in the grouped object.

2. Right-click the picture, click Change Picture, and then click Remove Picture.

3. Click FILE > Run Design Checker. The Design Checker task pane opens and displays four issues.

   ✓ Make sure that only the Run general design checks check box is selected at the top of the pane.

4. The first issue, Page has space below top margin, indicates that the Design Checker has detected empty space below the top margin of the page. This is usually an intentional part of the design and will not affect print quality.

   ✓ If you do not see this issue, click Design Checker Options at the bottom of the task pane, click the Checks tab, and make sure all check boxes are selected. Then click OK.

5. Point to the Page has space below top margin item to display the down arrow, and then click the arrow.

6. Click Never Run this Check Again. This removes the item for both page 1 and page 2.

7. Click the *Picture is missing* item to select the group in the left column where you deleted the picture.

8. Delete the empty picture placeholder and the caption to remove the item from the Design Checker task pane.

9. Click the *Story with text in overflow area* item to go to page 2. The text box in the center column is highlighted.

10. In a real publication, you would edit the text or add a text box to place the overflow text. For this publication, delete the second Secondary heading and the text below it in the center column to address the issue.

11. Click the Close Design Checker button.

12. Save the changes to **PB36Try_xx** and leave it open to use in the next Try It.

Embedding Fonts

- In order for a printing service to print your publication the way you want, it must have all of the fonts that you use.

- If not, it may substitute different fonts, and the result will not be what you expect.

- To make sure the fonts are available, you can embed them in the publication file.

- The option for embedding fonts is in the Fonts dialog box, which you access from the Manage Embedded Fonts button on the Info tab in Backstage view.

- The Fonts dialog box lists the font name, type, source, and whether there are any license restrictions that prohibit you from embedding the font in your publication.

- Embedding fonts increases the file size, so you should only embed the fonts that the printing service does not have.

- Common system fonts such as Times New Roman and Arial do not have to be embedded because they are available on most systems.

- Use the Don't Embed button to mark a font that does not have to be embedded.

- When you open a publication in which fonts are embedded, the Load Fonts dialog box displays. Click OK to load the embedded fonts.

Try It!   **Embedding Fonts**

❶ In the **PB36Try_xx** file, click FILE to display the Info tab in Backstage view.

❷ Click Manage Embedded Fonts 🖺 to display the Fonts dialog box.

❸ Click to select the Embed TrueType fonts when saving publication check box.

❹ Click OK.

❺ Save the changes to **PB36Try_xx**, and leave it open to use in the next Try It.

Exporting for Commercial Printing

- Earlier versions of Publisher enabled users to select settings for commercial printing. A user could choose to output using the CMYK color model, for example, for materials that would be printed on a four-color commercial press, or using the RGB model for a publication that would be printed on a desktop printer.

- Publisher 2013 has been designed to simplify the output process so that you do not have to decide which color model is best for your publication. All publications use the RGB color model by default.

- If you intend to have your publication printed professionally, you have several options for exporting your file.

- You can save your publication as a PDF, as you learned to do in Chapter 4. Most commercial printers can print directly from a PDF because of the amount of information that is exported with the file when you convert to this format.

- Publisher will add to the PDF during the export process information about other color models you have used in the publication, such as CMYK or PANTONE spot colors. The commercial printer can retrieve this information from the PDF to ensure that your colors are printed correctly.

- If you click the Options button in the Publish as PDF or XPS dialog box, the Publish Options dialog box shown in Figure 36-1 opens to give you options for controlling the quality of the PDF file.

Figure 36-1

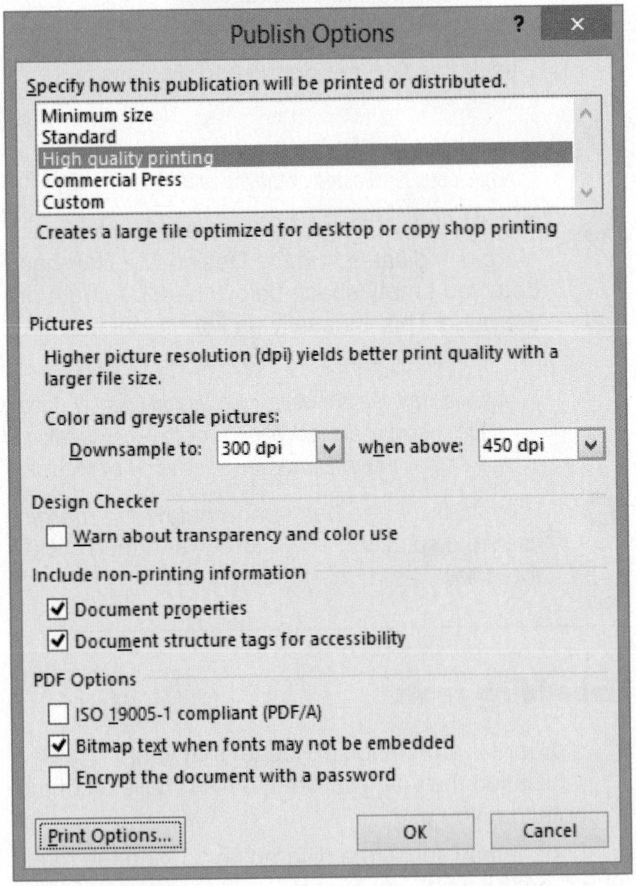

- Click the Print Options button to open the Print Options dialog box, where you can choose how to lay out the pages you are printing; adjust paper size; and select all pages, the current page, or a page range to print.

- The Export tab in Backstage view has several other important options for outputting your publication. The Pack and Go area of the tab offers three options that help you organize your publication's materials for transport to a photo printing center, a commercial printer, or another computer.

- Use the Save for Photo Printing option to create a separate picture file of each page of the publication.

- These picture files can be printed at any photo printing center, just as you would print any file from a digital camera.

- You can choose to save the publication as JPEG or TIFF images. JPEG images generally have smaller file sizes; TIFF images are generally higher quality.

- Use the Save for a Commercial Printer option to export your publication for a professional print service.

- Pack and Go creates a Compressed (zipped) file containing all the required files, including graphics and fonts. You, or the printing service, can simply extract the files when you need them.

- The Save for a Commercial Printer option enables you to select the file quality and file type that your printing service requests.

- There are four quality levels:
  - Commercial Press
  - High quality printing
  - Standard
  - Minimum size

- There are three file type options:
  - Both PDF and Publisher .pub files
  - PDF file
  - Publisher .pub file

- On the final page of the Pack and Go Wizard for commercial printing, the Print a composite proof check box is selected by default so you can print a proof of your publication.

- Use Save for Another Computer to start the Pack and Go Wizard using default quality and file type options.

Try It!   **Saving for a Commercial Printer**

1. In the **PB36Try_xx** file, click FILE > Export to display the Export tab in Backstage view.

2. Under Pack and Go, click Save for a Commercial Printer.

3. Click the Commercial Press drop-down arrow and click Standard.

4. Click the file type drop-down arrow and click Publisher .pub file.

5. Click the Pack and Go Wizard button.

6. Click the Browse button and navigate to the location where your teacher instructs you to store the files for this lesson.

7. In the Choose Location dialog box, click New folder and name the folder **PB36Try_xx**.

8. Click Select folder, and then click Next in the Pack and Go Wizard dialog box.

9. On the final page of the Pack and Go Wizard, click to deselect the Print a composite proof check box, and then click OK.

10. Close the publication, saving changes, and exit Publisher.

Lesson 36—Practice

The Greene Dental Practice has asked you to create a pediatric dental brochure for their patients. In this exercise, you prepare the brochure to be printed by a photo printing center.

DIRECTIONS

1. Start Publisher, if necessary.
2. On the New tab in Backstage view, under BUILT-IN, click **Brochures**.
3. Under Informational, click **Color Band**.
4. In the right pane, under Customize, click the **Color scheme** drop-down arrow and click **Wildflower**.
5. Click the **Font scheme** drop-down arrow and click **Punch**.
6. Under Options, verify that the Page size is set to **3-panel**, that the **Include customer address** check box is clear, and **Form** is set to **None**.
7. Click **CREATE**.
8. Save the publication as **PB36Practice_xx** in the location where your teacher instructs you to store the files for this lesson.

Complete Page 1

1. On page 1, in the left panel, replace the sample text *Back Panel Heading* and the paragraphs under it with the following:

   Pediatric Clinic

   Every child deserves access to high-quality dental care. Green Dental Practice offers low-cost cleaning and checkup services on the third Tuesday of every month for children and teens up to 18 years of age.

   Our professional staff offers confidential care on a sliding cost scale based on income. No one is denied care because of an inability to pay. Please contact the office to learn more.

2. Replace the sample picture with **PB36Practice_image1.png** from the data files for this lesson.
3. Ungroup the picture and the caption and delete the caption and its text box.

4. Resize the picture to **2 inches** high by **2 inches** wide and position so that the Object Position information indicates the upper-left corner is at **1.25, 5.45**.
5. Save the changes.
6. In the middle panel, delete the *Organization logo*, if necessary, and replace the business name and contact information with the following, deleting any sample text you do not replace:

   Green Dental Practice, LLC
   100 N. Highway 47
   Suite 101
   Indianapolis, IN 46240
   Phone: 317-555-0938
   E-mail: dentist@cleanteeth.net

7. In the right panel, replace the sample text *Business Tagline or Motto* with **Dr. Tim Green, DDS** and the sample text *Product/Service Information* with **Healthy Teeth! Happy Smiles!**
8. Select the text **Healthy Teeth! Happy Smiles!**
9. Click **HOME > Font Color** drop-down arrow ▲▾ and click **More Colors** to display the Colors dialog box.
10. Click the **Custom** tab if necessary, and then click the **Color model** drop-down arrow and click **CMYK**.
11. Set the **Cyan** value to **80**, the **Magenta** value to **5**, the **Yellow** value to **90**, and the **Black** value to **10**, and then click **OK**.
12. Replace the sample picture with **PB36Practice_image2.png**. Outcrop the picture by dragging the top and bottom crop handles outward to display the picture completely.
13. At the bottom of the right panel, delete the sample telephone number.
14. Save the changes to the publication.

Complete Page 2

1. On page 2, replace the sample *Main Inside Heading* with **Quality Pediatric Dental Care You Can Afford**.

2. In the left panel, replace the text with the following:

   At Green Dental Practice, your child's smile is important to us. We take great pride in making our young patients feel comfortable and helping them to understand the importance of healthy teeth.

   Our state-of-the-art dental care facility offers the latest and best treatments for every need. Bring your family in for:

   - **Routine checkups**
   - **Cleaning**
   - **Fillings**
   - **Sealants**
   - **Braces**
   - **Injury and emergency care**

3. Replace the sample picture with **PB36Practice_image3.png** from the data files for this lesson.

4. Ungroup the picture and the caption and delete the caption and its text box.

5. Outcrop the picture to display it completely, and resize it to **1.5 inches** high by **1.2 inches** wide.

6. Position the picture so the Object Position information reads **1.75, 6**.

7. In the middle panel, at the top, replace the sample picture with **PB36Practice_image4.png** from the data files for this lesson.

8. Ungroup the picture and the caption and delete the caption and its text box.

9. Replace the sample text *Secondary Heading* and the text below it with the following:

   Our Dental Staff

   Dr. Tim Green, DDS, is our senior dentist. He has over 20 years of experience working with both children and adults.

   Dr. Green is assisted by two dental hygienists: Sheila S. Abernathy and Paul Brown. Both Sheila and Paul are licensed and certified and have many years of experience working with children.

   Our receptionist is Linda McGill. Mrs. McGill cheerfully takes your calls and e-mails, schedules your appointments, and answers your questions.

10. Replace the second sample *Secondary Heading* and the text below with the following:

    Our Location

    Green Dental Practice is conveniently located on Highway 47 just off I-465. Visit our Website at www.cleanteeth.net or call the office for directions.

    Our Facility

    Our current facility was constructed in 2001. It includes four patient examination rooms and the most current technology, including digital x-ray systems.

    Our waiting area is child-friendly, including games, books, and an extraordinary fish tank. Mrs. McGill will be happy to help you identify the many different fish in the tank.

    Our Community Partners

    Green Dental Practice is an active participant in many community organizations and events. We partner with the Toothmobile, a mobile dental care service that visits communities throughout central Indiana. We sponsor youth sports teams for both girls and boys. We are also a member of the chamber of commerce, and provide dental hygiene education in many local schools.

11. Copy the formatting from the secondary heading *Our Location* to *Our Facility* and *Our Community Partners*.

12. Decrease the height of the text box in the middle panel to force the text starting with *Our Facility* to the right panel.

13. Click **HOME** > **Replace** ᵃᵇ⁄ₐꞓ to display the Find and Replace task pane.

14. In the Search for box, type **Green**.

15. In the Replace with box, type **Greene**.

16. Under Find options, click to select the **Match whole words only** and **Match case** check boxes.

17. Click **Find Next** to select the first occurrence of the text *Green*, then click **Replace**.

18. Click **Replace All**, and then click **OK**. Close the Find and Replace task pane.

Prepare the Publication for Printing

1. Delete all the replaced pictures from the scratch area.
2. Click **FILE** > **Run Design Checker** . If necessary, click in the **Run general design checks** and **Run final publishing checks** check boxes.
3. Resolve the Design Checker issues as follows:
   a. Click the *Object is not visible* item to display an empty text box in the center column of page 1. Delete the object.
   b. Click *Picture is not scaled proportionally* to select the picture in the left column of page 2.
   c. Use the Measurement toolbar to change the picture's width to **1.3 inches**.
4. Close the Design Checker.
5. Click **FILE** > **Manage Embedded Fonts** .
6. Click to select the **Embed TrueType fonts when saving publication** check box, and then click **OK**.
7. Check the spelling in the publication, correct errors, and then save the changes.
8. **With your teacher's permission**, print the publication, reinserting the paper to print side 2, if necessary. Page 1 should look similar to Figure 36-2, and page 2 should look similar to Figure 36-3, shown on the next page. Fold the printed page in thirds to create the brochure.
9. Click **FILE** > **Export**. Under Pack and Go, click **Save for Photo Printing**.
10. Accept the file type setting of **JPEG Images for Photo Printing**.
11. Click the **Save Image Set** button .
12. Navigate to the location where your teacher instructs you to store the files for this lesson. Create a new folder named **PB36Practice_xx**.
13. Click **Select folder**. The images are stored in the new folder.
14. Close the publication, saving changes, and exit Publisher.

Figure 36-2

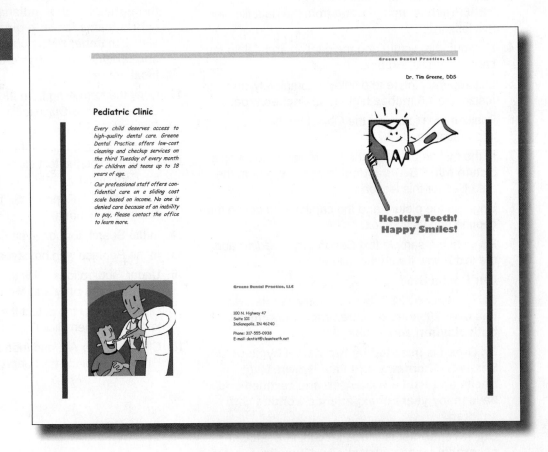

Figure 36-3

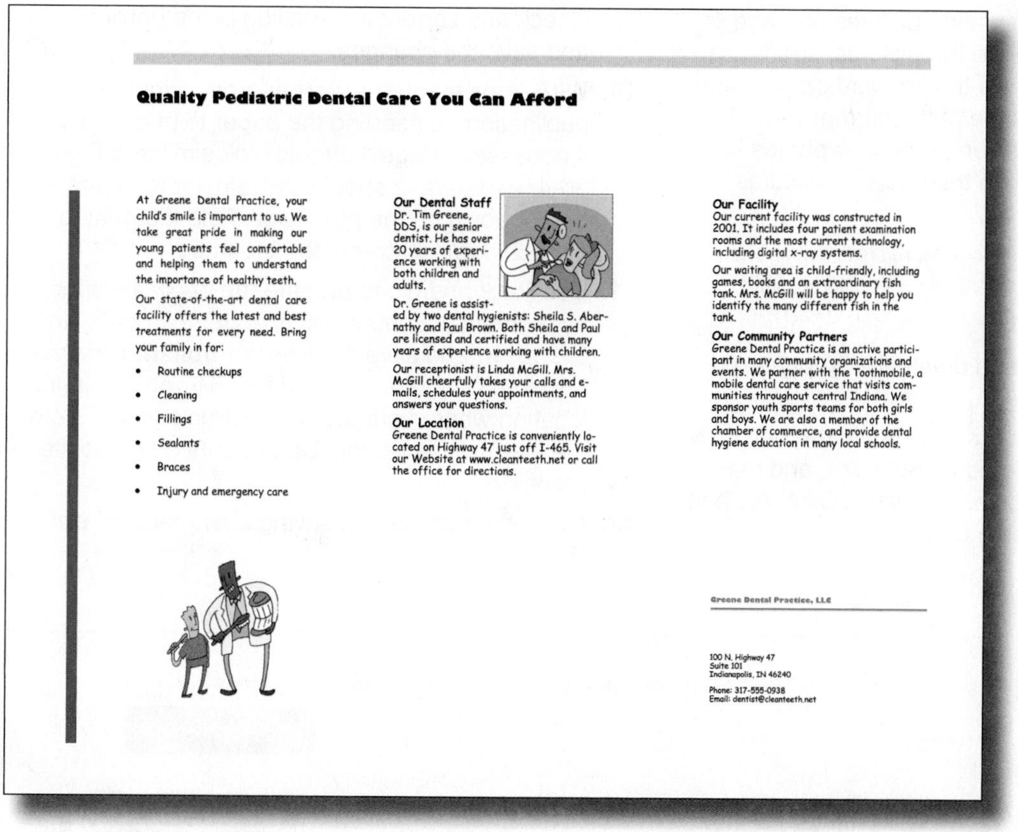

Figure 36-3

Lesson 36—Apply

The Greene Dental Practice has been bought by Janine Browne. In this exercise, you edit the brochure to reflect the change in ownership and to give the brochure a more professional appearance. Then you prepare it for printing at a commercial printer.

DIRECTIONS

1. Start Publisher, if necessary, and open **PB36Apply** from the data files for this lesson. Click OK in the Load Fonts dialog box.

2. Save the publication as **PB36Apply_xx** in the location where your teacher instructs you to store the files for this lesson.

3. Use Find and Replace to replace all occurrences of the text *Tim* with the text **Janine**, matching case.

4. Use Find and Replace to replace all occurrences of the text *Greene* with the text **Browne**, matching case and finding whole words only.

5. In the right panel on page 1, change the color of the text **Healthy Teeth! Happy Smiles**! to a custom **RGB** color with the values: **Red: 135, Green: 70**, and **Blue: 115**.

6. Set Publisher to embed TrueType fonts.

7. Run the Design Checker, making sure the Run general design checks and Run final publishing checks check boxes are selected.

8. Address issues as follows:

    a. You don't have to worry about the object partially off the page on page 1; this object is designed to bleed off the page.

b. Replace the low resolution pictures on page 1 by choosing to change the pictures, searching for clip art photos with the keyword *dentist*, and inserting them in place of the current clip art. Adjust size and position of the new photos as necessary, and delete the replaced pictures from the scratch area.

    ✓ *If the keyword* dentist *does not return enough photos, use other related keywords such as* children, smile, *or* dental *to locate photos.*

c. On page 2, select and delete the empty text box.

d. Click **Design Checker Options** at the bottom of the task pane, click the **Checks** tab, and make sure all check boxes are selected. Click **OK** and then close the Design Checker.

9. Check and correct the spelling in the publication and save the changes.

10. **With your teacher's permission**, print the publication, reinserting the paper to print side 2, if necessary. Page 1 should look similar to Figure 36-4, and page 2 should look similar to Figure 36-5, shown on the next page. Fold the printed page in thirds to create the brochure.

11. Use Pack and Go to prepare the publication for a commercial printing service. Set the quality to **Standard** and save the files in **Publisher format** only in a new folder named **PB36Apply_xx** in the location where your teacher instructs you to store the files for this lesson. Do not print a composite proof.

12. Close the publication, saving changes, and exit Publisher.

Figure 36-4

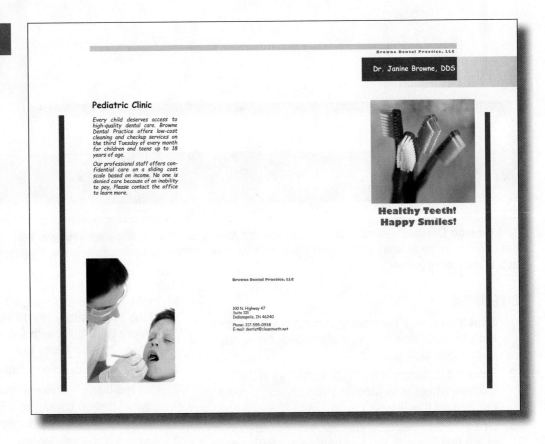

Browne Dental Practice, LLC

Dr. Janine Browne, DDS

Pediatric Clinic

Every child deserves access to high-quality dental care. Browne Dental Practice offers low-cost cleaning and checkup services on the third Tuesday of every month for children and teens up to 18 years of age.

Our professional staff offers confidential care on a sliding cost scale based on income. No one is denied care because of an inability to pay. Please contact the office to learn more.

Healthy Teeth! Happy Smiles!

Browne Dental Practice, LLC

100 N. Highway 47
Suite 101
Indianapolis, IN 46240

Phone: 317-555-0938
E-mail: dentist@cleanteeth.net

Figure 36-5

Quality Pediatric Dental Care You Can Afford

At Browne Dental Practice, your child's smile is important to us. We take great pride in making our young patients feel comfortable and helping them to understand the importance of healthy teeth.

Our state-of-the-art dental care facility offers the latest and best treatments for every need. Bring your family in for:

- Routine checkups
- Cleaning
- Fillings
- Sealants
- Braces
- Injury and emergency care

Our Dental Staff

Dr. Janine Browne, DDS, is our senior dentist. She has over 20 years of experience working with both children and adults.

Dr. Browne is assisted by two dental hygienists: Sheila S. Abernathy and Paul Green. Both Sheila and Paul are licensed and certified and have many years of experience working with children.

Our receptionist is Linda McGill. Mrs. McGill cheerfully takes your calls and e-mails, schedules your appointments, and answers your questions.

Our Location

Browne Dental Practice is conveniently located on Highway 47 just off 1-465. Visit our Website at www.cleanteeth.net or call the office for directions.

Our Facility

Our current facility was constructed in 2001. It includes four patient examination rooms and the most current technology, including digital x-ray systems.

Our waiting area is child-friendly, including games, books, and an extraordinary fish tank. Mrs. McGill will be happy to help you identify the many different fish in the tank.

Our Community Partners

Browne Dental Practice is an active participant in many community organizations and events. We partner with the Toothmobile, a mobile dental care service that visits communities throughout central Indiana. We sponsor youth sports teams for both girls and boys. We are also a member of the chamber of commerce, and provide dental hygiene education in many local schools.

Browne Dental Practice, LLC

100 N. Highway 47
Suite 101
Indianapolis, IN 46240

Phone: 317-555-0938
E-mail: dentist@cleanteeth.net

End-of-Chapter Activities

➤ Publisher Chapter 5—Critical Thinking

Flyer with Coupon

In this project, create a flyer for a club, organization, or business announcing an event. Include a coupon for a special purchase, such as a discount or 2-for-1 offer. Contact a printing service to find out what requirements it would have if you hired it to print the flyers from a PDF file, and then prepare the flyer accordingly. You may work individually or in small teams.

DIRECTIONS

1. Start Publisher and use a flyer template to create a publication using the color scheme and font scheme of your choice. Do not include a mailing address or a graphic, but do include a coupon.

2. Save the publication as **PBCT05A_xx** in the location where your teacher instructs you to store the files for this project.

3. Replace the sample text with the text appropriate for your flyer. For example, replace the sample business information with the information for your club, organization, or business.

4. Replace sample pictures with pictures appropriate for your flyer. Remove the pictures you replaced from the scratch area.

5. Insert additional text and graphics and change colors and other formatting to make the flyer eye-catching and appealing. Use at least one custom color in the flyer.

6. Run the Design Checker to locate any problems and then fix them.

7. Check and correct the spelling and save the publication.

8. **With your teacher's permission,** print a copy of the flyer.

9. Contact a printing service company by e-mail, telephone, or in person and discuss the requirements and costs of printing the flyer. Explain that this is for a school project, and that you will not actually be printing the publication.

10. Adjust PDF settings to match the printer's requirements. For example, choose the quality setting recommended by the printer.

11. Export the file as a PDF with the name **PBCT05B_xx** using the PDF settings you adjusted.

12. Close the publication, saving changes, and exit Publisher.

➤ Publisher Chapter 5—Portfolio Builder

Newsletter Customized with Mail Merge

In this project, you will create a two-page newsletter for the local chapter of a fan club and address each copy to the members whose names you have in a database file.

DIRECTIONS

1. Start Publisher, if necessary, and create a publication based on the **Blends** Newsletter template using the **Two-page spread** page size. Use the default template color and font schemes and include the customer address.

2. Save the publication as **PBPB05_xx** in the location where your teacher instructs you to store the files for this project.

3. Delete pages 2 and 3.

4. Apply a **2-column** layout to both remaining pages.

5. On page 1, replace the business name with **Benjamin Price Fan Club**, the sample newsletter title with **The Price Report**, and *Newsletter Date* with the actual date.

6. Delete the **Inside this issue** placeholder.

7. Replace the *Lead Story Headline* text with **Benjamin Comes to Town!**

8. Replace the lead story text by inserting the text from the Word document **PBPB05_import1.docx** from the data files for this project. Cancel Autoflow.

9. Manually link the lead story text to the left text box on page 2 under the *Back Page Story Headline*, deleting the remaining sample text in the right text box if necessary.

10. Turn off automatic hyphenation for the story and insert **Continued to** and **Continued from** indicators.

11. On page 1, ungroup the sample picture and the caption and delete the caption.

12. Replace the sample picture with **PBPB05_image.jpg** from the data files for this project. Outcrop the picture as necessary to display the entire picture, and position it between the two columns of text, below the headline (refer to Illustration 5A on the next page). Change text wrap distance from text to **0.14 inches** at the left and right sides of the picture.

13. Replace the sample text *Secondary Story Headline* with **Price Merchandise Swap Meet**.

14. Replace the secondary story text by inserting the text from the Word document **PBPB05_import2.docx** from the data files for this project.

15. Replace the sample text *Special points of interest* and the bullet items with the following:

    Dates to Remember:

    May 30: Fan club trip to opening night of "Happiness" at the Phoenix Theater

    October 2: Benjamin Price merchandise swap meet at the home of Nicole Bennett

16. On page 2, replace the sample business address information with

    544 Washington Way
    Washington, IL 62582

17. Delete the sample phone and fax information and replace the sample e-mail address with **mail@pricefanclub.org**.

18. Delete the *Business Tagline or Motto*, *Organization logo*, and *We're on the Web* placeholders.

19. Replace the sample *Back Page Story Headline* with **Benjamin Comes to Town**.

20. Delete the sample picture and caption and insert a clip art picture of a tuba. Size and position the picture to fill the space where the second column of text would be (refer to Illustration 5B).

21. Use Find and Replace to replace all occurrences of the text **clarinet** with the text **tuba**.

22. Check the spelling in the publication, correct errors, and save the changes.

23. Run the Design Checker and correct any issues.

24. **With your teacher's permission**, print the publication, using double-sided printing if possible. Page 1 should look similar to Illustration 5A and page 2 should look similar to Illustration 5B.

25. Create a mail merge to address the newsletter using the **PBPB05_data.accdb** database file from the data files for this project as the data source, and inserting the **Address Block** merge block to replace the sample customer address.

26. Preview the results for each record.

27. Close the publication, saving changes, and exit Publisher.

Illustration 5A

BENJAMIN PRICE FAN CLUB

THE PRICE REPORT

Volume 1, Issue 1

Today's Date

BENJAMIN COMES TO TOWN

Exciting news, Price fans! Benjamin Price has just announced that he will be appearing in the play "Happiness" at the Phoenix Theatre in Indianapolis from May 30 through June 15 of this year. Tickets are available now by calling 317-555-0971.

"Happiness" is a comedy about growing up unpopular in a Midwestern high school in the 1970s. Benjamin will be playing the lead, Norman Neiderman, a much beleaguered

"nice guy" who struggles for acceptance from the popular kids.

I spoke with Benjamin on the phone the other day, and he had this to say: "I am really looking forward to having fun with the role of Norman. Because I grew up in a small Midwestern town myself, many of the characters and situations are

(Continued on page 2)

Dates to Remember:

- May 30: Fan club trip to opening night of "Happiness" at the Phoenix Theater

- October 2: Benjamin Price merchandise swap meet at the home of Nicole Bennett

PRICE MERCHANDISE SWAP MEET

Do you have any Benjamin Price merchandise to buy or sell? Lunchboxes? Posters? Autographed items?

In October, the fan club will be hosting a swap meet where you can buy and sell your merchandise, and maybe pick up that special item you have

always wanted for your collection. It will be held at the home of Nicole Bennett, 123 S. Main St. in Indianapolis, starting at 7:00 p.m. and running until 10:00 p.m. So dig through that closet and find some Benjamin souvenirs to turn into cold hard cash!

BENJAMIN PRICE FAN CLUB

544 Washington Way
Washington, IL 62582

Email: mail@pricefanclub.org

Type address here or use Mail Merge
to automatically address this
publication to multiple recipients.

BENJAMIN COMES TO TOWN

(Continued from page 1)

familiar to me. I even played in the band myself, just like Norman, although I played the drums instead of the tuba." When asked whether he was planning to take tuba lessons to prepare for the part, Benjamin laughed. "No," he said, "I think that Norman is probably not a very good tuba player either, so in that sense my portrayal will be very true to the character."

The fan club is organizing a shuttle bus to go to the opening night performance on May 30. The doors open at 7:30 p.m. with open seating, so we plan to arrive at the theatre no later than 6:30 p.m. to stand in line. If you are interested in riding the shuttle, please call Gretchen at 317-555-0375.

Index